LOUIS XIV

LOUIS XIV

Anthony Levi

CONSTABLE • LONDON

Constable & Robinson Ltd
3 The Lanchesters
162 Fulham Palace Road
London W6 9ER
www.constablerobinson.com

First published in the UK by Constable,
an imprint of Constable & Robinson Ltd 2004

A copy of the British Library Cataloguing in
Publication Data is available from the British Library

ISBN 1-84119-425-5

Printed and bound in the EU

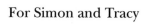

For Simon and Tracy

Contents

Illustrations

Between pages 138 and 139

Louis XIV on horseback in front of a besieged city, painting by René Antoine Houasse (1645–1710). Photo: akg-images.

Cardinal Mazarin, painting by Philippe de Champaigne (1602–74). © Photo Réunion des Musées Nationaux – Harry Bréjat.

Portrait of King Louis XIV's mother, Anne of Austria, and his wife, Queen Maria-Teresa, Aunt and Niece, painting by Simon Renard de Saint-André (1613–77). © Photo RMN – Gérard Blot.

A view of Versailles in 1668, painting by Pierre Patel (1605–76). © Photo RMN – Arnaudet.

Marly, painting by Denis Piere Martin (1663–1742). © Photo RMN.

Colbert presenting the members of the Royal Academy of Sciences to Louis XIV, circa 1667, Henri Testelin (1616–95). © Photo RMN – Gérard Blot.

Françoise Athénaïs de Rochechouart (Marquise de Montespan), from an engraving after a painting by an unknown artist, *Madame de Montespan*, H. Noel Williams, 1903.

Louis XIV in costume as the 'Sun King' for the ballet *La Nuit, Le Grand Siècle*, Emile Bourgeois, 1896.

The Palais-Royal in 1679, *Louise de la Vallière et la Jeunesse de Louis XIV*, Jules Lair, 1907.

Versailles. Detail of painting above by Patel (1605–76), *Histoire du Château de Versailles, Versailles Sous Louis XIV*, vol. 1, Pierre de Nolhac, 1911.

The Louvre and the Tuileries, *Histoire de France*, vol. 4, F.P.G. Guizot, 1875.

Preface

This biography is born of an interest in seventeenth-century French literature which dates back to schooldays. It began when I first started to wonder what made French literature so different from literature written in English, and why its interest was thought to lie in historical periods different from those from which our English texts were taken. In the course of an academic career, my interest both narrowed in focus, to the sixteenth and seventeenth centuries in France, and broadened in scope, reaching widely beyond France, especially to Germany, and extending from literary history to its background in general culture, the visual arts and architecture, political and social history, theology and philosophy.

Behind it all loomed the towering figure of Louis XIV. It did not matter that he was not born until 1638. As little as thirty years ago I recall the dismissive remark of an Oxford colleague that seventeenth-century French literature, at that date still called 'classical', did not start until the major pieces of the elder of the two Corneille brothers, Pierre, dating from the late 1630s. The unsustainability of that view subsequently provided me with a rich vein of investigation, but the fact remained that behind a great constellation of literary and other masterpieces of French culture in the seventeenth century brooded the awe-inspring presence of the king. That, too, turned out not to be true, at least not in the sense in which I first believed it. But what does remain true, even after writing this biography, is that behind the literature and the visual arts of seventeenth-century France lies an exceedingly rich, diverse and powerful culture, and behind that culture, at least for most of the second half of the century, lies the king.

This biography attempts a portrait of Louis XIV, exploring what it felt like to preside in the way he did, with the upbringing, power, wealth and prestige he was either given or achieved, over the creation of the culture of seventeenth-century France.

Acknowledgements

The greatest debt I have, which it also gives me great pleasure to acknowledge, is that to my students, among whom were always those who unerringly, if disconcertingly, asked the important direct questions and were annoyingly often discerning enough to spot the sloppy thinking or intellectual laziness in my answers. Looking subsequently for more satisfactory replies often led to richly rewarding conclusions. It used to be argued that university teaching could be undertaken only if actively supported by the teacher's private research. I have come to think that private research often requires the stimulus of direct student questioning to provide it with motive power and to keep it from getting lost in side tracks.

I do, however, also have great pleasure in acknowledging with gratitude grants awarded by the Leverhulme and Carnegie Trusts, as well as fellowships awarded by Harvard, Fordham and Georgetown Universities, the Humanities Research Council of the Australian National University, the Huntington Library in Pasadena and the British Council. I am also grateful to the British Academy and the Universities of Oxford, Warwick and Saint Andrews for grants towards research travel.

It would be invidious to single out individuals to whom to express my gratitude, whether they have taught me or I have taught them, and whether I have drawn on their works, in which case they are mentioned in the notes, or whether, having known them personally, I have drawn on conversations often held long ago. None the less, I

[xiii]

Acknowledgements

should like to acknowledge the lasting encouragement of Mollie
Gerard Davis, who sharpened and focused my interest in seventeenth-
century French studies when I was a student in 1956, who subsequently supervised my doctoral thesis, and who remained a constant
and ever-welcoming guide and friend throughout my professional
career, right up to her death in 2001. In the field of seventeenth-
century studies it is to her, and to Robert Shackleton, who not only
taught me but also subsequently examined my doctoral dissertation,
that I owe most. More recently I have profited from information,
expertise and invaluable advice always generously available to me
from Professor Richard Parish.

A.L.
2003

Chronology

1638 5 September. Birth of
dauphin Louis to Anne of
Austria
1639 Revolt of Nu-Pieds
1640 Birth of second child,
Philippe, to Anne of
Austria
1642 Death of Richelieu
1643 Louis's solemn baptism
Death of Louis XIII, and
accession of Louis XIV
Regency of Anne of
Austria whose lover,
Mazarin, assumes power
Defeat of anti-Mazarin
cabal, 'Les Importants'
Victory of Condé's son,
later 'le grand Condé',
over Spaniards at Rocroi
Publication of Antoine
Arnauld's Jansenist *De la
fréquente communion*
1647 Louis catches smallpox
1648 Treaties of Westphalia

France remains at war
with Spain
1648 Opening of Fronde
Le grand Condé, having
succeeded to the Condé
title, blockades rebel-held
Paris
1650 Condé, having joined
rebels, arrested with
Conti and Longueville
1651 Release of princes and
exile of Mazarin
Louis XIV's majority
declared
1652 Return of Mazarin and
his voluntary second exile
1653 Fronde ends with return of
France to royal allegiance
1654 Louis's *Sacre*
(Coronation)
1655 Contracts gonorrhoea
1658 Contracts typhoid
Emotional obsession with
Marie Mancini

1659 Treaty of Pyrenees ends
Spanish war
Reinstatement of Condé
1660 Marriage of Louis and
Maria-Teresa, Infanta of
Spain
Death of Gaston
d'Orléans, brother of
Louis XIII
Solemn entry of Louis
into Paris
1661 Death of Mazarin
Marriage of king's
brother to Henriette
d'Angleterre and Louis's
own liaison with her
Beginning of Louis's
interest in Louise de la
Vallière
Fall of Fouquet and
transfer of power to
Colbert
Birth of Grand Dauphin
1662 Carrousel to celebrate
birth of dauphin
Bossuet preaches at court
against adultery
1663 Colbert begins drive for
central control of cultural
activities
1664 Inaugural fête at
Versailles, *Les Plaisirs de
l'Ile enchantée*
Fouquet's sentence
pronounced and
increased by Louis to life
imprisonment
Foundation of East India
Company

1665 Arrival of Bernini in Paris
1666 Death of Anne of Austria
1667 Appointment of La Reynie
as *lieutenant de police*
Mme de Montespan
replaces Louise de la
Vallière as royal mistress
1667–78 'War of Devolution'
against Spanish
Netherlands
1668 Treaty of Aix-la-Chapelle
Divertissement at Versailles,
where major buiding
begins
1670 Treaty of Dover between
France and England
1671 Second marriage of
Louis's brother, Philippe
d'Orléans
1672–78 Dutch war against
United Provinces.
Passage of Rhine at
Tolhuis
1673 Reform of *Académie
française* by Colbert
1675 Death of Turenne
Louis shows increased
interest in Mme de
Maintenon
1678–79 Treaty of Nijmegen
ends war
1679 Institution of 'Chambre
ardente' to try cases of
poisoning
1680 Marriage of dauphin
Paris confers on Louis
title of 'le grand'
1681 Inauguration of Canal
des Deux Mers

1682 Court moves to Versailles
Birth of duc de Bourgogne,
heir of dauphin
Declaration of Gallican
articles by Assembly of
Clergy

1683 Deaths of queen and of
Colbert
Power of Louvois,
secretary of state for war
now unchallenged
Main building at Marly
completed
Probable date of Louis's
marriage to Mme de
Maintenon

1685 Mansart instructed to erect
buildings for Saint-Cyr
Revocation of Edict of
Nantes

1686 Louis's operation for anal
fistula

1688 War of League of
Augsburg begins

1688 Excommunication of
Louis

1689 Devastation by France of
Palatinate

1690 Battle of the Boyne

1691 Death of Louvois

1693/4 Fénelon's
Rémonstrances

1697 Peace of Ryswick

1701 Death of Louis's brother,
Philippe

1701–14 War of the Spanish
Succession against
Austria, England and
United Provinces

1703 Battle of Blenheim, first
of Marlborough's series
of victories

1708–9 Disastrously severe
winter

1711 Death of Grand Dauphin,
leaving his son, the duc
de Bourgogne, Louis's
grandson, heir to the
throne

1712 Deaths of duc de
Bourgogne and of his
elder surviving son, the
duc de Bretagne, leaving
Bourgogne's youngest
son, the infant duc
d'Anjou, as Louis's heir.
Anjou will become Louis
XV
French victory at Denain

1713 Treaties of Utrecht end
war of the Spanish
Succession

1713 Issue by Rome of anti-
Jansenist *Unigenitus*

1715 Death of Louis XIV

This heavily-pruned genealogy is primarily designed to show the proximity to the throne of the princes of the blood, of particular importance when Louis XIV's descendants in the direct line predeceased the king himself. Only legitimate and legitimized children are shown, and children who did not reach adulthood are omitted unless they are of special importance. The inter-marriage of cousins means that some names occur more than once in the table. The table reflects the conventional belief that Louis XIII was the father of Louis XIV.

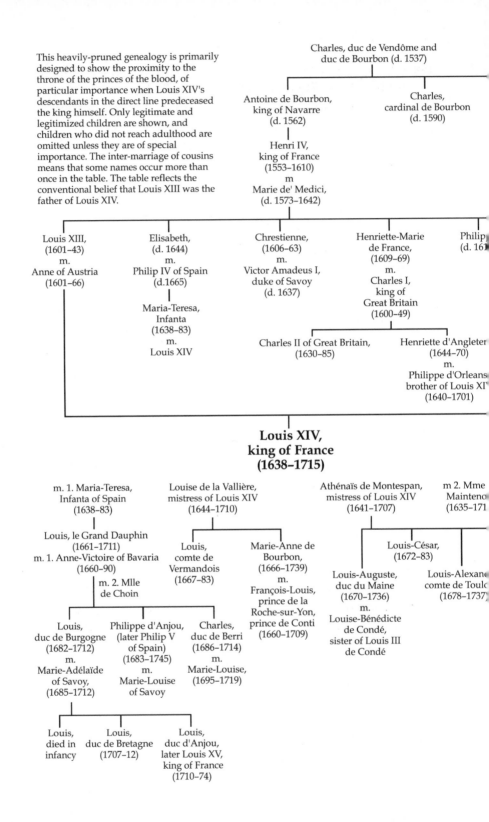

Charles, duc de Vendôme and duc de Bourbon (d. 1537)

Antoine de Bourbon, king of Navarre (d. 1562)

Charles, cardinal de Bourbon (d. 1590)

Henri IV, king of France (1553–1610)
m
Marie de' Medici, (d. 1573–1642)

Louis XIII, (1601–43) m. Anne of Austria (1601–66)

Elisabeth, (d. 1644) m. Philip IV of Spain (d.1665)

Maria-Teresa, Infanta (1638–83) m. Louis XIV

Chrestienne, (1606–63) m. Victor Amadeus I, duke of Savoy (d. 1637)

Henriette-Marie de France, (1609–69) m. Charles I, king of Great Britain (1600–49)

Philip (d. 16

Charles II of Great Britain, (1630–85)

Henriette d'Angleter (1644–70) m. Philippe d'Orleans brother of Louis XI (1640–1701)

Louis XIV, king of France (1638–1715)

m. 1. Maria-Teresa, Infanta of Spain (1638–83)

Louise de la Vallière, mistress of Louis XIV (1644–1710)

Athénaïs de Montespan, mistress of Louis XIV (1641–1707)

m 2. Mme Mainteno (1635–171

Louis, le Grand Dauphin (1661–1711) m. 1. Anne-Victoire of Bavaria (1660–90)
m. 2. Mlle de Choin

Louis, comte de Vermandois (1667–83)

Marie-Anne de Bourbon, (1666–1739) m. François-Louis, prince de la Roche-sur-Yon, prince de Conti (1660–1709)

Louis-César, (1672–83)

Louis-Auguste, duc du Maine (1670–1736) m. Louise-Bénédicte de Condé, sister of Louis III de Condé

Louis-Alexand comte de Toulc (1678–1737)

Louis, duc de Burgogne (1682–1712) m. Marie-Adélaïde of Savoy, (1685–1712)

Philippe d'Anjou, (later Philip V of Spain) (1683–1745) m. Marie-Louise of Savoy

Charles, duc de Berri (1686–1714) m. Marie-Louise, (1695–1719)

Louis, died in infancy

Louis, duc de Bretagne (1707–12)

Louis, duc d'Anjou, later Louis XV, king of France (1710–74)

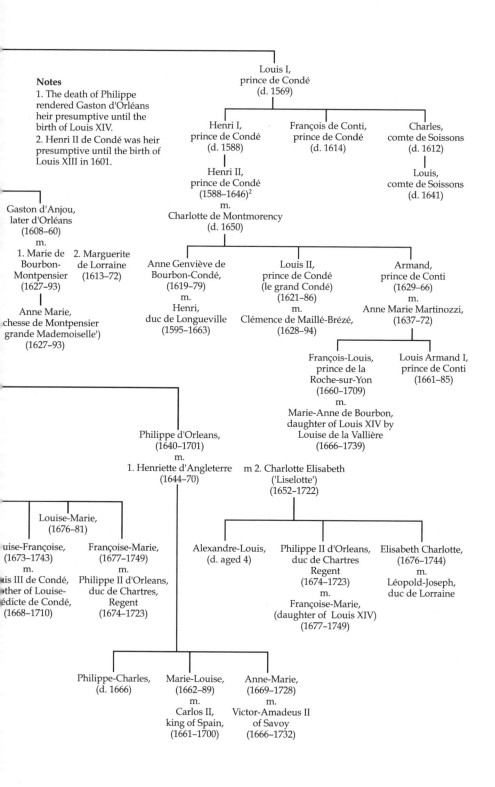

Notes
1. The death of Philippe rendered Gaston d'Orléans heir presumptive until the birth of Louis XIV.
2. Henri II de Condé was heir presumptive until the birth of Louis XIII in 1601.

Louis I,
prince de Condé
(d. 1569)

Henri I,
prince de Condé
(d. 1588)

François de Conti,
prince de Condé
(d. 1614)

Charles,
comte de Soissons
(d. 1612)

Henri II,
prince de Condé
(1588–1646)[2]
m.
Charlotte de Montmorency
(d. 1650)

Louis,
comte de Soissons
(d. 1641)

Gaston d'Anjou,
later d'Orléans
(1608–60)
m.
1. Marie de
Bourbon-
Montpensier
(1627–93)

2. Marguerite
de Lorraine
(1613–72)

Anne Genviève de
Bourbon-Condé,
(1619–79)
m.
Henri,
duc de Longueville
(1595–1663)

Louis II,
prince de Condé
(le grand Condé)
(1621–86)
m.
Clémence de Maillé-Brézé,
(1628–94)

Armand,
prince de Conti
(1629–66)
m.
Anne Marie Martinozzi,
(1637–72)

Anne Marie,
chesse de Montpensier
grande Mademoiselle')
(1627–93)

François-Louis,
prince de la
Roche-sur-Yon
(1660–1709)
m.
Marie-Anne de Bourbon,
daughter of Louis XIV by
Louise de la Vallière
(1666–1739)

Louis Armand I,
prince de Conti
(1661–85)

Philippe d'Orleans,
(1640–1701)
m.
1. Henriette d'Angleterre
(1644–70)

m 2. Charlotte Elisabeth
('Liselotte')
(1652–1722)

Louise-Marie,
(1676–81)

uise-Françoise,
(1673–1743)
m.
uis III de Condé,
ther of Louise-
édicte de Condé,
(1668–1710)

Françoise-Marie,
(1677–1749)
m.
Philippe II d'Orleans,
duc de Chartres,
Regent
(1674–1723)

Alexandre-Louis,
(d. aged 4)

Philippe II d'Orleans,
duc de Chartres
Regent
(1674–1723)
m.
Françoise-Marie,
(daughter of Louis XIV)
(1677–1749)

Elisabeth Charlotte,
(1676–1744)
m.
Léopold-Joseph,
duc de Lorraine

Philippe-Charles,
(d. 1666)

Marie-Louise,
(1662–89)
m.
Carlos II,
king of Spain,
(1661–1700)

Anne-Marie,
(1669–1728)
m.
Victor-Amadeus II
of Savoy
(1666–1732)

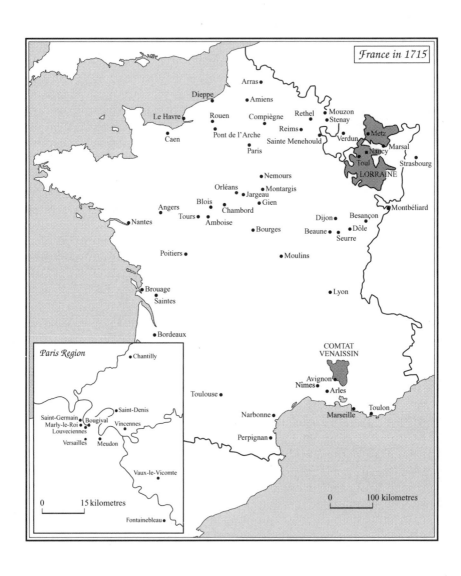

France in 1715

Arras
Amiens
Dieppe
Le Havre
Rouen
Compiègne
Rethel
Mouzon
Stenay
Pont de l'Arche
Reims
Verdun
Metz
Caen
Sainte Menehould
Marsal
Paris
Nancy
Toul
Strasbourg
LORRAINE
Nemours
Montbéliard
Orléans
Montargis
Jargeau
Blois
Gien
Angers
Chambord
Dijon
Besançon
Tours
Amboise
Beaune
Dôle
Nantes
Bourges
Seurre
Poitiers
Moulins
Lyon
Brouage
Saintes
Bordeaux

COMTAT
VENAISSIN

Paris Region

Chantilly

Avignon
Nîmes
Arles
Toulouse
Saint-Denis
Narbonne
Toulon
Saint-Germain
Bougival
Marseille
Marly-le-Roi
Vincennes
Louveciennes
Perpignan
Versailles
Meudon

Vaux-le-Vicomte

0   15 kilometres

0   100 kilometres

Fontainebleau

North-east France

IJSSELMEER

Amsterdam

Ryswick

Nijmegan

Ijssel

Bruges

Ghent

Scheldt

Dunkirk

Ypres

Courtrai

Oudenaarde

Brussels

Maastricht

Brühl

Aachen

Armentières

Lille

Tournai

Ath

Ramillies

Liège

Lens

Lens

Mons

Fleurus

Namur

Hesdin

Arras

Douai

Valenciennes

Denain

Charleroi

Cambrai

Landrecies

Avesnes

Rocroi

Charleville

Bouillon

Sedan

Thionville

Verdun

Metz

0   50 kilometres

Toul

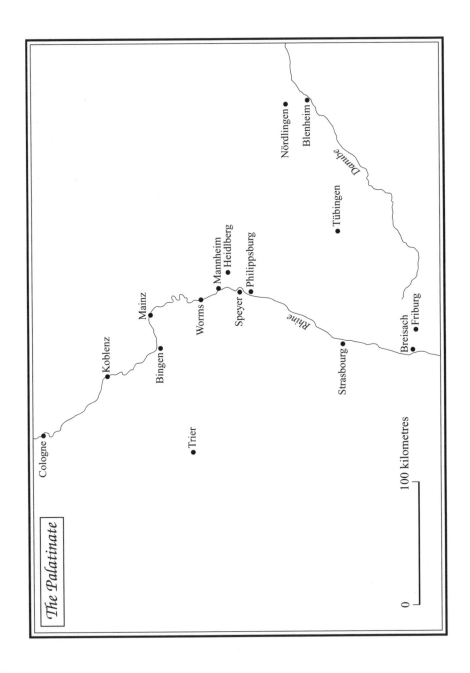

The Palatinate

Cologne

Koblenz

Trier

Bingen

Mainz

Worms

Mannheim
Heidlberg

Speyer
Philippsburg

Rhine

Strasbourg

Breisach
Friburg

Nördlingen
Blenheim

Danube

Tübingen

0   100 kilometres

1

Louis's Inheritance

Louis XIV was in his day monarch of Europe's grandest nation. Despite the price of peasant starvation, financial bankruptcy and military defeat which he ended up having to pay, for antagonizing the rest of Europe, Louis XIV was arguably one of the most politically effective European monarchs ever to reign. Iconographically depicted as a god of ancient mythology, as Apollo and as the sun, he was treated accordingly, given the appropriate accoutrements and trained to act those parts.

But that he was invested from infancy to old age with privilege and power unprecedented in medieval or early modern Europe does not alone explain the fascination of his biography. At its core is the story of the abnormal experience generated by the clash between being *le Roi soleil,* custodian of the grandeur of France, and the guilt felt by an ordinarily sensitive human being whose day-to-day decisions affected the welfare, lives and deaths of tens of thousands at a time. What compulsively engages the attention is rather the attempt to reconcile his own inevitable half-belief in the extravagant quasi-divine *persona* created for him with endurance of the failures, guilt, agonies of conscience and the consequences of erroneous choices, which are the ordinary destiny he shared with other mortals. It was an attempt that failed.

In spite of the systematic burning of sensitive papers, which he supervised even from his deathbed, and the dispersal of much archival material, most of the essential external facts and circumstances of Louis's life are widely known. It is chiefly his internal conflicts which have visibly left historians floundering in their efforts to understand him. A general concentration of attention on Louis's military activity and on the court life he created at Versailles has monopolized interest, while Louis's interior insecurities and intimate devotional life have been relatively neglected by his biographers, whether his more or less contemporary memorialists all with axes to grind, or subsequent chroniclers of his reign, seeing in it an idealization of France's past. Neither memorialists nor historians have left us a sustained psychological portrait of Louis XIV.[1]

What sort of person was he? There is general agreement that he was seriously, even superstitiously devout, personally courageous, athletic when young and physically strong when ageing. Many contemporaries remark on an apparent imperturbability, which the evidence does not altogether bear out, and on the fastidious courtesy of the manner he cultivated, for which testimony is strong. There can be no doubt at all about his womanizing and his gluttony. A huge self-importance was scarcely to be avoided.

By the late fifteenth century the three massive power blocs of Spain, France and the Holy Roman empire had gradually agglomerated on the central landmass of western Europe, from which the Italian peninsula was cut off by the Alps and the British Isles by the Channel. In addition, between France and imperial territory, the duchy of Burgundy stretched from the Low Countries in the north to the Mediterranean and Savoy, whose capital was then Turin. When in 1477 the Burgundian ruler died defending Lorraine, the duchy itself dissolved into a score of component independent provinces, allowing two great dynasties to emerge in western Europe, each with aspirations to become pan-European powers.

Louis XIV inherited the leadership of the Bourbons in the long confrontation with the Austro-Spanish Habsburgs for hegemony in Europe. Conflict between them stretched back to the defeat in 1519 of François I, France's young Valois king, by Charles I, king of Spain and earliest of the Habsburgs, in the election as Holy Roman emperor. In that year Charles I of Spain became the emperor Charles V. Catholic France and its mainly Protestant north European allies were the political rivals of the Catholic powers united under the emperor, which included Spain, the Low

Countries, Naples, Milan and, more loosely, Bavaria and what is now Austria.

The strong dynastic links forged in vain throughout the seventeenth century to keep the peace between France and Spain did not achieve their purpose. Military hostilities between the two countries continued to be frequent and bitter, although Louis XIV's mother was the Habsburg Anne of Austria, and his aunt Elizabeth, eldest daughter of Henri IV of France, had married Philip IV of Spain. Louis himself was to marry the Spanish infanta, daughter of Philip IV.

Confrontation arose originally in the early sixteenth century, when François I attempted to vindicate his claim to the Milanese succession, which he wanted for his dauphin. In the second quarter of the seventeenth century, Louis XIII, following the plans of Richelieu, his first minister, to win a cultural identity for a politically fragmented France, continued to fight the Spaniards. Richelieu died in 1642, only months before Louis XIII, the king he served, when Louis XIV was still four. Louis's mother, Anne of Austria, became regent, and real power passed to Giulio Mazarini, an Italian and originally a papal diplomat, whom Richelieu had groomed for it.

Louis XIV was himself more anxious to strengthen France's northern and eastern frontiers than to establish a foothold on the Italian peninsula. His wars were directed towards appropriating parts of the old Burgundian empire in the Low Countries and to encroaching on territory beyond France's eastern borders in an effort to make the Rhine France's frontier, and to control a buffer zone beyond it to the east. The tardy creation of France as a nation with a unitary cultural identity had not taken place until the internal religious wars of the late sixteenth century had died out, and was the work of Richelieu, the originator of the vision for France which Louis XIV was to inherit.

Politically aggressive, Louis was also touchy about anything which affected his dignity. Although a few occasional instances of genuine kindness can be alleged on his behalf, he more often than not showed himself lacking in consideration for other people's feelings, took some satisfaction in humiliating them, behaved with extravagant prodigality and was quite often downright brutal. Although he was the repository of supreme political, jurisdictional and executive power in the period of astonishing French cultural brilliance which took place in late seventeenth-century France, historians have achieved little real understanding about what unified his personality.

To solve the enigma with which the personality of Louis presents the historian, recourse must be had to the turbulent cultural background of the seventy-two years between 1643, when Louis XIV acceded to the throne, and 1715, when he died four days short of his seventy-seventh birthday. During that period, the personal, social and religious culture of France was dramatically changing, and in ways not often understood. It moved from a euphoric optimism not yet fully deflated when Louis was born, through a phase of hesitant uncertainty, towards the bleakly austere decades at the end of the reign. But new and different forms of optimism were bring gestated beneath the officially promoted culture, often in popular rather than high cultural circles, although they did not finally emerge victorious until the partisans of the *modernes* gained the ascendancy in the wake of the literary *Querelle des anciens et des modernes,* which had turned on the cultural superiority of modern over antique cultural values.[2]

Between the onset of the widespread use of printing in the sixteenth century and the technological advances of the nineteenth which led to modern media like photography, cinema, radio and television, the written word was the principal imaginative forum at the disposal of a literate society to identify, assess and modify its personal and social values. To understand the changing values informing seventeenth-century French society, one must keep in mind changes in the focus of imaginative interest of its key literary figures, novelists and playwrights as well moralists and preachers.

During the first third of the seventeenth century, French writers, whether sacred or profane, did not generally explore the human condition for its tragic potential. The imaginative needs of later periods have led to the relative neglect or misinterpretation of the whole generation of writers which informed the values of the society into which Louis was born. It was a generation which included François de Sales, Descartes, the elder and more famous of the Corneille brothers, Pierre and such novelists as Honoré d'Urfé and Gomberville, all of whom were chiefly interested in teaching or exploring the great heights of moral heroism of which human beings were capable, and left no doubt of their belief in the high potential of human nature.

It was in the years just preceding and following Louis's birth in 1638 that the confident cult of the heroic began to be questioned

[4]

in spiritual teaching and imaginative literature alike. Louis could never quite understand the hostility to him elsewhere in Europe which his own attempt to emulate the warrior ideals of Henri IV was to inflame. Under his leadership the adulation of military heroism helped to sustain a value system which much of the rest of Europe had outgrown, and in France criticisms were to be loudly and clearly articulated in literary terms by authors like Fénelon and La Bruyère well before the end of the reign, as France moved towards the social values which it would embrace in the eighteenth century. There is a connection between the neoclassical forms and themes of French literature, architecture and the visual arts which emerged in the mid century and the new severity in spiritual norms being promoted by one of the two major traditions which developed from the mystical theology of Pierre de Bérulle.[3] Any new account of the rise and fall of Louis's popularity with his people and of his confidence in himself must take more than usually into account the changes in the ambient culture indicated by the work of its major imaginative artists, its religious and secular writers and thinkers and the way in which they all interacted with political pressure.

As the north-eastern frontiers of France with the Spanish Low Countries and the unstable eastern frontiers altered during Louis's reign, the size of France's population varied. It changed, too, with the quality of harvests, the prevalence of war and the incidence of disease. Normally, however, it is assessed at a relatively stable figure of around 20 million within the boundaries of modern France, and is not generally supposed to have varied by much more than 5 per cent or so from that figure.[4]

This gave France an unsustainable population density of some four times that of England, and therefore an overall structural need for emigration. In view of the wars with Spain, surprisingly much of that need was satisfied by the establishment of French colonies in the cities of the Iberian peninsula. The overpopulation nevertheless left France short of trained craftsmen. The task of enticing the learned and the skilled to enhance the glories of Louis's court fell to Jean-Baptiste Colbert, the *intendant* whom Mazarin – Richelieu's successor who had become a cardinal and French national, dropping the final 'i' from his Italian name – had bequeathed to Louis XIV. After Mazarin's death in 1661, when Louis was twenty-two, Colbert was to become Louis's principal and all-powerful adviser for a score of years and to continue to follow Richelieu's blue-print for strengthening the culture, the economy and the political power of France.

The over-population relative to other countries and to France's natural resources also made it easier for Louis even in times of peace to maintain a standing army of some 150,000, much to the dismay of the rest of Europe. At least until Colbert set about building up an industrial base, the large population also made it possible for France, with few mineral resources and no precious metals, to depend on a largely rural economy, low yielding and manpower-intensive. One consequence was that, at the date of Louis's accession, France had a relatively low literacy rate.

At least 80 per cent and probably more of the total seventeenth-century adult population of France must have been illiterate, either peasants, working on the land, or, if male, jobbing workers who undertook equivalent forms of work in the towns. They were often driven there by semi-starvation or its imminent prospect in the countryside. There can at best have been only a comparatively small number of hundreds of thousands of adult males, little more than a million in all France, if indeed as many, with even a rudimentary reading knowledge. It was they, too, who most easily emigrated.

The church, all secular administration, fiscal, military, judicial, scientific and much mercantile activity, like the introduction of double-entry accounting being imported from Italy, depended on the literate and numerate sections of the population. It was their views, attitudes, debates, values and concerns, rather than those of the ancient military aristocracy or the artisan class, the military or the peasantry, which acted directly on the more highly developed, artistic forms of French culture, setting ideals and values under the leadership of Colbert, and generally in advance of the court and the monarch.

The educationally cultivated section of the population was over-whelmingly concentrated in Paris, Normandy and the north-east, although it was obviously not confined to those areas. The one notable respect in which Colbert failed to persuade Louis concerned the status of Paris, which Colbert wanted to make the real capital of France and the seat of its administration. During the sixteenth century the old forts of the Loire valley had been adapted as residential palaces, with the kings of France spending more time at

Amboise, Blois or Chambord near the seats of France's grander families than in Paris. The relative importance of Paris increased under Richelieu, but declined again after his death, when the court moved mostly between Saint-Germain and Fontainebleau until Louis finally erected his new château at Versailles for himself, his large family, his court and his government.

The importance of Lyon, based on the independence with which its location on the road to Italy and the absence of such repressive institutions as a university or a *parlement* endowed it, had declined since the sixteenth century. Its book fair explains an earlier concentration of literacy in the south-east, drawing on a supply of readers of French sufficient to make profitable as much as a century before Louis's accession the printing and pirating of every kind of material, from ephemera of all sorts to the lengthy books of such writers as Rabelais or Montaigne.

Literacy was clearly a huge career advantage, and education therefore at a premium.[5] It was the literary elite which administered church and state, provided pastoral and medical care together with what education there was, ran France's regions, cities and commercial enterprises. It both produced and consumed its celebrated architecture, its brilliant feats of engineering and its renowned literature, from crude political pamphlets to sometimes elegant, delicate and subtle works of poetry and fiction. It produced verse that was sometimes witty and sometimes aspired to be epic, and a society which, at its educated peak, was both cultivated and refined, and of which a strong wave of feminism was a by-product. It was this elite which finally determined the value system to which even the Sun King was constrained to conform or with which he would be forced to clash.[6]

Louis XIV and the great figures of the realm, bourgeois tax farmers as well as aristocrats, displayed their standing with a magnificence that, while visual, did not depend on literacy. They built sumptuous mansions full of magnificent sculptures, elegantly gilt decorated, exquisitely wrought furniture with exotic inlays, and paintings by the Italian and Dutch masters, but also by Poussin, Claude Lorraine, Philippe de Champaigne, Mansart and Le Brun, La Tour and the Le Nain brothers. They patronized theatrical troupes and invited them to perform in their houses and gardens.

The buildings were set in enormous parks full of promenades, fountains, pools, canals, trees planted in carefully calculated geometrical patterns and gardens artfully laid out to achieve their maximum effects, which included fountains which could be turned on to soak their unsuspecting admirers at the twist of a handle. Musical entertainment vied or combined with ballets, often using spectacular mechanical devices to propel chariots and putti across the sky, to stage mock naval battles, to produce the comedy-ballet which was to grow into opera, or to accompany the enormous and artistically elaborate firework displays which showed off the great gardens.

It has not often been noticed that it was the relatively small pool of available educated talent which explains not only the patronage of an army of distinguished foreigners, many of whom came to work in France, but also the strongly visual nature of seventeenth-century French culture generally, as well as some of the store set on music. The church could get its message over to a wide public only through visual media, pulpit instruction which tended to be reduced to moral exhortation, what could be sung in church and primitive forms of drama. It relied extensively on paintings, statues, buildings and arte-facts to stimulate the devotion of the faithful, exploiting music in courts, cathedrals and abbeys to make its services attractive. Classical myths, taken from a relatively small corpus of sources, chiefly Homer, Virgil and Ovid, were frequently invested with allegorical Christian religious significance.

In literature there is heavy emphasis on drama, which did not require a literate audience. It was Richelieu during the 1630s who brought it in off the streets and saw to the examination of its poten-tial as high art, presiding over the emergence of acting as a pro-fession. Except in the colleges, where drama was a form of rhetorical training, acting at the beginning of the century had been the monopoly of itinerant vagabond companies, mostly working the fairs. Molière ran away to join one such troupe as late as 1643.

It helps towards an appreciation of the nature of Louis XIV's kingdom to know that the general public, although restricted to the 'decently dressed', were admitted to admire the stupefying grandeur of the royal palaces and gardens, and to gain entry to entertainments devised for the court, but subsequently played for the Parisian public.[7] Colbert was opposed to admitting the public to the gardens of the royal palaces where the court chiefly resided, Fontainebleau, Saint-Germain, the Tuileries, the Louvre and then Versailles, but when he was overruled, charged for the franchise to provide seats in the gardens. In a strange and minor way, that arrangement reflects the clash within Louis himself between the populist attitude he affected and the elitist tyranny he exercised.

2

The *Dieudonné*

At the end of 1637, France appeared to be heading for disintegration. Richelieu was working to forge the French nation into a cultural unity, but had not yet succeeded. Its sickly king, the tubercular Louis XIII, born in 1601, had already once nearly died. On 30 September 1630 the doctors had not expected him to live through the day. Although on that occasion he recovered, his health had by 1637 begun its slow terminal decline. There was no issue in the direct line and the heir presumptive was his ambitious and hostile younger brother, Gaston d'Orléans, born in 1608, and the favourite child of his mother, Marie de' Medici, herself openly hostile to her elder son, the king, and in exile since 1631.

Gaston's first wife had died in childbirth, and he had subsequently married the sister of the duke of Lorraine, Marguerite de Vaudémont, in the first days of 1632. Debauched and frequently disgraced, Gaston had long been the irresponsible rallying point of a disaffected nobility being progressively stripped of its authority. He had been involved in multiple conspiracies to dethrone his elder brother, to take his place and to murder Richelieu, his brother's mentor as well as his chief minister.

His succession would inevitably have entailed in France the victory of the political Catholicism, entailing subjection to Spain, advocated against Richelieu by Pierre de Bérulle, like Richelieu a cardinal, and a leading figure in the early seventeenth-century 'Catholic revival'.[1] Gaston's succession would necessarily also have led to France's renewed political fragmentation, to the destruction of the sense of cultural identity which Richelieu was fostering, and to the restoration of power to the remnants of the old feudal nobility. It might well have provoked with equally disastrous results a Bourbon coup led by Condé, whose father was the senior first cousin of Henri IV, father of Louis XIII, and who was the prince of the blood next in line for the throne after Gaston.

Richelieu's fears were largely shared by the expanding educated bourgeoisie, from among whom the office-holders in the *parlements* were drawn, and who, like Richelieu, were mostly heirs to a tradition which, in the light of the experience of the religious wars of the preceding century, preferred to keep religious considerations out of politics. They were aware of the catastrophe for France which would follow the apparently inevitable inheritance of power by Gaston, or its not improbable seizure by Condé. Only if Louis XIII produced a male heir who survived long enough to become king might it be possible to salvage all that Louis XIII, Richelieu and the suffering people of France had agonizingly, if not always willingly, achieved in bringing about the country's political and cultural unification, and developing the maritime potential for the creation of its future wealth.

Louis XIII's queen was a Spanish Habsburg, Doña Ana Maria Mauricia (Anne of Austria), daughter of Philip III of Spain and Margaret of Austria and great grand-daughter of the emperor Charles V. Born on 21 September 1601, six days before her future husband, she was brought up markedly repressed and intensely pious in the heavy formality of the Spanish court. Her marriage to Louis XIII took place at the same time as the marriage of her brother, the future Philip IV of Spain, to her husband's sister, Elizabeth, daughter of Henri IV, as part of an effort to forge a strong Franco-Spanish alliance.

When she married in 1615, she and her husband were only fourteen. She indisputably had two miscarriages, in 1622 and 1626, and there were rumours of more. According to a letter to the doge, Louis XIII himself spoke to Angelo Carrario, the Venetian ambassador, of a total of four before 1638.[2] When, at 11.22 on the morning of Sunday, 5 September 1638, Anne of Austria gave birth after five hours of labour to a male child, 'a little later than the doctors had expected' at the smaller of the two châteaux of Saint-Germain-en-

Laye, rejoicing at the birth of a dauphin was genuine, intense and universal. Only those, like Gaston, whose closeness to the succession it diminished, had reason for displeasure.[3]

The queen had been assisted by a lady-in-waiting and the midwife. The king, who had just sat down to dinner, went to her, and, on learning that it was a boy, fell to his knees to thank God. Messengers were immediately despatched with the news, throwing their hats in the air in a pre-arranged signal to pass the news across the Seine that it was a boy, since the pont de Neuilly was at the time unusable. Prisoners were released, and free wine was dispensed in Paris until supplies ran out on the Wednesday. Meanwhile the king went to the bigger and grander vieux château at Saint-Germain, his preferred residence, for a *Te Deum,* after which the infant was *ondoyé* (sacramentally baptized) by the bishop of Meaux , and handed over to his wet nurse.[4]

Richelieu returned to Paris from the front, where he had been supervising the recapture from the Spaniards of Le Catelet, arriving on 2 October, and had a piece included in the *Gazette* expressing his delight and reporting on the happiness of king and queen.[5] Prompted by Richelieu, but thinking more of the war against Spain than of the succession, Louis XIII had put France under the special protection of the Virgin Mary in a proclamation of 11 December 1637, begging her to bring peace to France and promising in return to celebrate the feast of her assumption into heaven on 15 August with particular magnificence. When Louis signed the letters patent and registered the dedication on 10 February 1638, after public announcement of the pregnancy in Théophraste Renaudot's recently founded *Gazette*, he added prayers for the successful birth of a male child.

Anne was scarcely a fortnight off her thirty-seventh birthday, but it was not only on account of her age that her pregnancy had been greeted by astonished if gratified joy. True, it was surprising that at her age she should bring a child to term for the first time after at least two earlier miscarriages, but the amazement was greater because she had been alienated from her husband certainly for twelve years, and probably for more.[6]

That Anne should not only have become pregnant again, but should have come to term and given birth to a healthy male child, was regarded by much of the population as a miraculous consequence of the dedication, a belief boosted by a number of the prophecies which were not at all unusual in the exuberantly baroque devotional life of early seventeenth-century France. The letters patent of 11 December placing the country under the Virgin's protection had been signed on 10 February 1638, and the child was soon commonly known as God's gift, the *Dieudonné*[7] and his birth often referred to as miraculous in a way that implied a divine intervention beyond the merely metaphorical. There even appears to be a correlation between the birth of the dauphin and the growth in France of the cult of the infant Jesus.[8]

The three-day public rejoicing in Paris covered the spectrum from religious acts of thanksgiving to public carousing, with processions, bell-peals, fireworks and bonfires. Anne herself had a commemorative chapel built in thanksgiving at the convent of Val-de-Grâce, religious headquarters of the Spanish community. In another characteristically baroque manifestation of devotion, the Blessed Sacrament was widely exposed for adoration, and the traditional thanksgiving hymn, the *Te Deum,* was everywhere solemnly sung.

In spite of the widespread euphoria, doubts were nevertheless raised about the infant's paternity. In the circumstances it was inevitable that there should be some cynicism about the way in which the political crisis of the succession had been resolved. Louis XIII's pattern of obsessional homosexual relationships, often with older men, but also with adolescents, had long been the subject of common gossip.[9] It is quite likely that his marriage had never been consummated at all, although documentation purporting to show that it had been, first in 1615 when the couple were fourteen, and then in 1619, had been assiduously compiled and fed to the Spanish court. In 1626, one of the several serious plots to put Gaston on the throne had envisaged the queen's remarriage to Gaston after the annulment of her marriage to Louis XIII on grounds of non-consummation.[10]

Even if Louis was responsible for the pregnancies which resulted in the two provable miscarriages, those historians confident of his paternity of the future Louis XIV and of his brother Philippe agree with the report in Montglat's sporadically reliable *Mémoires* that Louis early developed a repugnance at physical contact with his wife.[11] Any marital relations between them were certainly over from 1626, when Louis's public attitude to Anne changed suddenly and markedly for the worse, perhaps as a result of the miscarriage that year of what was a potential heir. Anne was no longer made regent for northern France when the king was absent, or placed in his private hierarchy above his mother, with whom the king remained on seriously bad terms. His customary but purely formal late evening visits to Anne were in 1626 abruptly curtailed, and court gossip about the state of his marriage intensified.

Anne was lively, flirtatious and fun-loving but, deprived in France of her Spanish entourage, was lonely and desperate for the male admiration which she easily and copiously attracted. She liked to game, slept a good deal and was inclined to be lazy, but also, like Louis XIV later, combined an active extra-marital sex life with serious religious devotion. Exactly how her confessor squared her intense piety with prolonged adultery is a matter for speculation better left until the same problem is met as it confronted the confessors of Louis XIV.

It is commonly assumed that Montmorency, brother of Condé's wife, was Anne's lover. Among other possible liaisons, there may conceivably have been a brief affair in 1625 with the duke of Buckingham, lightly veiled in the memoirs of Anne's loyal lady-in-waiting, Françoise de Motteville. The whole court knew that Anne and Buckingham were strongly attracted to one another, and Anne's attendants were later to be dismissed because they once in 1625 discreetly absented themselves to leave the couple alone. In 1646, long after Buckingham had been assassinated in 1628, Anne was to give his son 30,000 livres.

Homosexual relationships of the type in which Louis XIII was involved, although rife at court and the subject there of open comment, were considered not only mortally sinful, but also criminal enough to warrant the death sentence, which was in fact from time to time imposed on miscreants lower down the social scale.[12] Given her husband's proclivities as well as his incentive to project the picture of a normal marriage, the question of the paternities involved in Anne's miscarriages of 1622 and 1626 needs reopening.

The conception of Anne's first child, born on 5 September 1638, has traditionally been dated 5 December 1637, the date on which Louis XIII, who had intended to stay the night at Saint-Maur-des-Fossés, is said to have been driven by a storm to take shelter in his wife's quarters in the Louvre, which was undergoing perpetual reconstruction, and where his own quarters were at that date without a roof. Most modern historians are at best non-committal about the 1756 narrative of this story in the Jesuit Père Henri Griffet's three-volume *Histoire du règne de Louis XIII*. Griffet, writing more than a century after the event, relies on Montglat and Mme de Motteville,[13] who herself reports it only as hearsay. For a host of reasons Griffet's narrative simply provokes incredulity. The medically unexpected length of the pregnancy invites the suspicion that someone was concealing the date of conception.

What was not widely known even at court was that, while France had been formally at war with Spain since 1635, Anne had been treasonably corresponding in Spanish with the enemies of the country of which she was queen, and against which her husband, the king, was from time to time personally leading his troops. The new cardinal governor of the Spanish Netherlands and Philip IV, the king of Spain, were her brothers. Anne was helping to thwart a Franco-English alliance which would have been seriously detrimental to Spanish interests.

Some correspondence, which included treasonable letters from Anne to her closest friend, Mme de Chevreuse, was intercepted and handed to Richelieu. Anne's courrier was immediately sent to the Bastille and she herself was immediately assigned new living quarters at Chantilly. On 17 August she signed a confession. However bad her relations with her husband had previously been, the treachery of the summer of 1637 can only have made them worse. When, at the end of the year, the estranged and politically disloyal Anne became pregnant, Louis was chronically ill with tuberculosis. It is unlikely that any casual meeting between them, whether or not the result of a storm, ever took place, and extremely dubious that, if it did, it would have led to the resumption of marital intercourse between the spouses.

If Louis XIII was not the father of the dauphin who became Louis XIV, it becomes a near certainty that Mazarin was.[14] In the context of a history of France, and *a fortiori* a biography of Louis XIV, the matter is important enough to demand serious consideration of the evidence. Were Mazarin to have been his father, and were Louis XIV to have known it, which is another near certainty, the need for the unremitting dissimulation which permeated the whole of his life would go very far towards explaining the tensions perceptible in the personality of the adult Louis XIV. He would have lived out his long reign aware that the universal assumption of his subjects that his absolute monarchical authority had been divinely bestowed on him by right of birth at the moment of Louis XIII's death was without foundation.

It is beyond any possible dispute that Mazarin and Anne were already very strongly attracted to one another in the mid 1630s, and that by the early 1640s they had become lovers. The question to be resolved is when that happened. The twenty-seven-year-old Mazarin, a doctor of law and a military captain before becoming a papal diplomat, had first met and impressed Richelieu in January 1630, later that year successfully negotiating on Richelieu's behalf with the Spaniards in northern Italy and Savoy.[15]

Mazarin is known to have duelled as a young man and to have proved attractive to high-born ladies before Anne of Austria. He set out to please, and mimicked Richelieu in his obsessive concern for detail, specifying the colour and size of a new dog he wanted Lionne, the later foreign minister, to have sent from Parma to give to Louis XIII, asking Maurice de Savoie to send a troupe of Italian players who had been performing at Nice, but to make sure that they had improved their act, reinforcing his request with a letter to their leader, Leandro.

He first met Anne in 1632, before returning to Rome, where, although he was still a layman, Urban VIII made him a canon of Saint John Lateran and a protonotary, also bestowing on him an abbacy and a priory. Already on that 1632 visit to Paris, before Mazarin had any clerical status at all, tongues started wagging at court. Tallemant tells us that Richelieu, presenting Mazarin to Anne, had said to her 'Madame, you will like him. He looks like Buckingham.' Richelieu was right. The prince de Marcillac, later to become La Rochefoucauld, author of the *Réflexions ou Sentences et Maximes morales,* noticed the queen's obsession, and a letter of Richelieu dated 27 January 1632, almost openly alludes to her passion. In November 1634 Mazarin was back on a mission to Paris as nuncio and, although he failed to prevent the open declaration of war between France and Spain, he became very close to Richelieu, and naturally met Anne again.

Early in 1636 he took up the post of Cardinal Antonio Barberini's vice-legate at Avignon accorded to him in 1632, and when he returned to Rome in October 1636, he did not forget Anne. Anne spoke her native Castilian with him, was forward with him in speaking about her desire for a child, and accepted a series of gifts from him when he returned to Rome: gloves, perfumes, fans and other 'bagatelles'. He was in the habit of ordering for Anne the choicest hams and cheeses from Italy, and from Portugal the first oranges of the season. Once, gambling in her presence, Mazarin had gently insisted, *soavi accenti,* on giving Anne the 15,000 livres he won.

He quickly also grew close to Richelieu in spite of his greater inclination to conclude peace with Spain. The friendship he formed with Anne of Austria in the intimacy of their shared Castilian came as a bonus through which the problem of the succession to the childless Louis XIII came to look to Richelieu as if it might possibly be resolved in a manner consistent with his vision for France.

Even before Richelieu's death, Mazarin had lived in style. He was famed as much for his meticulous personal grooming as for keeping the best table in Paris. It is a tribute to his skill, and no doubt also to Richelieu's, that Mazarin, who discussed affairs daily with Richelieu, had retained the favour of both Richelieu and Anne for over three years, in spite of their mutual hostility. He appears even to have brought about some sort of *rapprochement* between them. It suited Richelieu to use Mazarin to keep open communications with the queen, and Mazarin became virtually essential to Richelieu, long accustomed to look beyond his own death, when Anne became mother of the dauphin. Mazarin's ambitions, abilities and relationship with the queen made him the ideal person for Richelieu to groom to succeed him as the director of French domestic and foreign policy, and the daily training to which Richelieu subjected him was both assiduous and rigorous.

Mazarin's skill in ensuring that his true relationship with Anne had remained sufficiently concealed for his appontment as her chief minister and intimate adviser to have caused surprise in May 1643 was considerable. That Mazarin was deliberately deploying care to reveal nothing during the final conspiracy to assassinate Richelieu in 1642, when he was never far from either Anne or Richelieu, is confirmed in his surviving notebooks, where there is astonishingly no mention at all of Anne, although she was wrongly suspected at the time of conniving at the project to assassinate Richelieu.

Quite apart from any natural reluctance to face the disconcerting possibility that Mazarin may well have been the father of Louis XIV, and in spite of how much that hyopthesis would explain about what was to happen later, historians and biographers have fallen back on two reasons to reject it. Mazarin was not in Paris[16] and, even if he had been, Anne was being too closely watched for the conception to have been contrived.[17]

Disconcertingly, Georges Dethan in his *Mazarin et ses amis* has printed a hitherto unpublished letter of Mazarin to the English diplomat, Lord Walter Montagu,[18] which is dated 'Paris, 16 September 1637'. The letter is a copy in the French foreign affairs archives of an original known to have been destroyed in a house fire in England. Professor Dethan assumes that the place-name is simply a copyist's error, presumably because anything which brings nearer the possibility that Louis XIV was the illegitmate offspring of Mazarin is hostile to loyal French historical opinion, and because Mazarin is not otherwise known to have been absent from Rome at that date. But it nevertheless constitutes at least *prima facie* evidence that he was indeed in Paris late in 1637. 'Copyists' mistakes', especially when they remove such inconvenient evidence as Mazarin's presence in Paris late in 1637, need to be regarded with suspicion.

The contention that the surveillance of the queen following the discovery of the treasonable letters was too close to permit of adultery is simply untrue. It may well have meant a close watch on her correspondence, and on the access to her of possible messengers, but it is unlikely to have extended to so close a protégé of Richelieu as Mazarin. The necessary occasion could quite easily have been arranged by Richelieu, never adverse to employing a bribe or a threat for the sake of France, and it required the further connivance only of Anne, Mazarin and of the king.

Louis XIII, already at times seriously ill with the tuberculosis which was to kill him, Richelieu and Mazarin all had compellingly strong grounds for avoiding at any cost the apparently imminent succession of Gaston to the throne, and Anne was not only already in love with Mazarin, but she urgently needed a male heir if she was not to be relegated to nothing should her husband, as seemed ever more likely, pre-decease her.[19] The king had not only been repeatedly betrayed by his brother, whom he disliked, but was also concerned to vindicate himself against the gossip that he was and always had been incapable of consummating his marriage. Richelieu quite simply wanted to avoid the destruction by Gaston of all that he had achieved for France with and through Louis XIII.

In the higher echelons of this society, secrecy was not difficult to arrange. No direct evidence survives for instance for the undisputed facts that Louis XIV married Mme de Maintenon, and that his son secretly married Mlle de Choin, although it is certain that both marriages took place, and for validity required a clergyman with jurisdiction and witnesses. This was a society in which discretion was essential for self-preservation, in which spying was endemic, and dissimulation a necessity for those in power or in a position to covet it. One of the characteristics of Louis XIV's reign was to be the well-founded fear that sensitive information would fall into unwelcome hands. Richelieu openly advocated and practised the immediate burning of sensitive letters. Louis XIV had papers burnt in front of him less than a week before his death.[20]

Correspondence was regularly opened, read and resealed, but recipients rarely knew that letters addressed to them or written by them had been read until the moment when action was taken against them. The first letter to Anne from Mirabel, the Spanish ambassador in Brussels in 1637, discovered quite by chance, was obviously a reply to something she had sent, and led to a successful dissimulation of several weeks on the part of both the king and Richelieu while the entrapment leading to her confession was woven round her. The culture of dissimulation was highly developed. Louis XIV was notoriously to dissimulate for weeks in 1661 while manoeuvring the *surintendant des finances,* Nicolas Fouquet, into the situation in both time and place most propitious for his arrest. Anne's ostentatious devotional life and her prodigality in charitable works, while not devoid of virtuous motivation, none the less helped to shield the reputation which her relationship with Mazarin certainly endangered.

Louis XIII's own known attitudes and actions are finally quite consistent with Mazarin's paternity of Anne's child. The king returned from the front in Picardy for the birth of Anne's child on 18 August 1638. The following day he grumbled in a letter to Richelieu at the delayed delivery of the child when he announced his intention of going to Versailles for two or three days.[21] Later he would make Mazarin the godfather, allow him to become the dauphin's surrogate father, publicly enabling him to act as if indeed he were the real father. But, after the dauphin's birth, he treated his wife atrociously. While her life had seemed in danger the king had told Marie de

Hautefort, one of Anne's ladies-in-waiting who was in attendance with court members outside the delivery chamber, that she should not worry, 'I shall be happy if the child can be saved. You Madame will be consoled for the mother'.[22] Immediately after the dauphin's birth, the king spent as much time as he could away from Saint-Germain, staying at Chantilly, Versailles, Saint-Maur, Grosbois and with Richelieu at Rueil. When he was at Saint-Germain, he stayed at the vieux château, and not with his wife and Louis at the subsequently destroyed château neuf.

He had not forgotten the treason of the summer of the year before, and now systematically humiliated Anne whenever possible. He also imposed on her as governess for the dauphin Mme de Lansac, whom she detested, and dismissed her lady-in-waiting, Mme de Senecey, to whom she was attached. Most importantly, he sought to frustrate the established custom that the mother of a king who was a minor should be regent. He arranged that, in the event of his own death before the dauphin Louis reached his majority, Anne should be bound by a council, in which he went so far as to include Gaston, to give it constitutional weight.[23]

If Louis's behaviour is at least consistent with Mazarin's paternity of Anne's infant son, the physical appearance of the grown Louis XIV, which has been described as 'oriental',[24] appears neither to confirm nor to cast doubt on it. It may merely be noted that Saint-Simon's low opinion of Louis XIV's intelligence certainly underestimated it. Louis XIV possessed spiritual and mental capabilities nearer to those of Mazarin than to those of Louis XIII. More important are the very passionate love affair into which Anne's relationship with Mazarin is known to have developed, the paternal role towards the young monarch which Mazarin was allowed to play, and the immediacy with which Mazarin took over the government of France on the death of Louis XIII in 1643. From 1643 the openness of the relationship between Anne and Mazarin, their domestic arrangements in Paris and Anne's support of Mazarin during his later public disgrace, make it clear that they formed with the young king a close family intimacy. It seems virtually certain that he was the father of the infant who became Louis XIV.

Mazarin had been able to help France with the munitions held in the papacy's enclave near Avignon, the comtat Venaissin, in February 1636, allowing Richelieu to demonstrate his familiarity with the young diplomat, now in French pay, with an atrocious pun on the change from the scented powders ('poudres odoriférantes'), which he supplied to Anne in times of peace, to the explosive ('fulminantes') sort required in war. On his return to Rome, where he held the comfortable position of head of household to Antonio Barberini, one of the pope's cardinal nephews and the titular legate for whom Mazarin had acted as vice-legate in Avignon, Mazarin sought to favour French interests. He amassed for Richelieu the collection of statuary destined for his great château in Poitou, although he did not succeed in obtaining for himself the nunciature in Paris to which he aspired.

The council of Trent had laid down the convention by which there should be national representatives in the college of cardinals, alongside the most senior curial officials and those ex-nuncios whose candidature was supported by the sovereigns to whose courts they had been affected. Richelieu had long been urging the appointment to the college of cardinals of Père Joseph, his close adviser on foreign affairs, and Urban VIII actually consented to raise him to the purple on the day he died, 18 December 1638. Richelieu immediately substituted Mazarin's name, himself writing to Mazarin to inform him.

It was partly to render himself capable of receiving ecclesiastical benefices in the gift of the French king, but principally in order to enable himself legitimately to be regarded as the French candidate for a red hat, that Mazarin had acquired French nationality in June 1639. By October 1639 relations between France and the papal curia had become tense enough for Richelieu to think it time for Mazarin to move from Rome to France. Mazarin left from Civitavecchia on 14 December 1639, and was finally elevated to the purple on 15 December 1641.

A letter to Queen Christina of Sweden from the Dutch Huig de Groot (Grotius), who was acting as Swedish ambassador to France, informed her that Louis had been born with two teeth already emerging, which was exceptionally hard on his wet nurses, whose nipples so bled from his voracity. By January 1639, the dauphin was already on his ninth nurse. Mme de Lansac, wholly trusted by Louis XIII, was in total charge of the dauphin's regime, chose and changed the wet nurses, but is said by Henri Arnauld in his memoirs to have been responsible, due to the way she held him, for a deformity which began to develop in one of Louis's legs.

Generally he was a well-formed, robust infant, the object, according to Mme de Motteville, of all the repressed affection which his mother might have bestowed on a more receptive husband than Louis XIII.[25] Anne, the object of a new respect as mother of the dauphin, very unusually refused to leave her infant son to the care of the usual platoon of female attendants, and insisted on playing with him herself, wheeling him in his carriage, making of him 'her principal pleasure',[26] and no doubt dangerously prolonging and intensifying his emotional dependence on her.

As a result, Louis XIII was not only aroused the more easily to jealousy, as there were occasions when it was particularly important to him to have his already suspect paternity publicly respected, but his hostility to Anne nurtured in the infant a dislike and fear of him. Louis XIII would have removed the child from his mother's care if Richelieu had not succeeded in dissuading him. In January 1640, when Louis was sixteen months old, Louis XIII nearly did send him to Amboise, and he continued to bully Anne with the threat of removing first the sole son and then both Louis and his brother Philippe, born in 1640.

Louis XIII was both surprised and hurt when the young Louis failed to show real warmth towards him on the rare occasions when he was at home. There are a number of anecdotes confirming Louis XIII's spiteful dislike of his wife, like his harsh reproach to her that her close friend, Mme de Chevreuse, had slept with her brother, Philip IV of Spain, or his less than gentle announcement to her of the death of her brother, the Cardinal-Infante governor of the Low Countries, 'Votre frère est mort', after concealing the fact from her for twenty-four hours.

On Louis XIII's return from the siege of Arras in September 1640, he was welcomed by the two-year-old dauphin who had not seen the king for four months, but resented being dragged by the child to his mother, and the child's tears when left alone with him and his male companions. He publicly reproached the queen, 'The dauphin cannot stand the sight of me,' and wrote to Richelieu, 'I am very ill-satisfied with my son . . . he must be removed from the queen as soon as possible.' The child was frightened again a few days later by his father, whom he saw in night-shirt and bonnet and whom, thus accoutred, he refused to go near. The child was made to ask on his knees for pardon for crying in the presence of Louis. The mediation of the bishop of Lisieux appeased the king's anger, although he continued in his private letters to Richelieu to issue threats of separating the dauphin, and later both her children, from the queen.

Richelieu's closeness to Louis XIII and his determination to oppose the political Catholicism of Anne's entourage had led inevitably to Anne's bitter hostility to him, but, at least after the dauphin had been born, he patently needed to be able to re-open friendly relations with her. Mazarin, whose daily discussion of affairs with Richelieu had already begun, was the obvious channel. By sometime in 1641 it had become clear to Richelieu that Mazarin alone could take over from him. If Louis XIII or Richelieu were to die, it seemed to Richelieu, only Mazarin could hope to create a prosperous France at peace with Spain, and only Mazarin could successfully promote Richelieu's ambitions for a strong, independent France with a Spanish alliance, probably to be achieved by the marriage of the dauphin with the infanta, both born in 1638.

For some months from early in the year of Louis's birth France was beginning to gain the upper hand as the Thirty Years War slowly resolved itself from hostilities between Catholic and Protestant powers into a struggle chiefly pitting France against Spain. In May France had won a naval victory in the Atlantic, and late in December, France's ally, Bernard of Saxe-Weimar, took Breisach on the Rhine, about fifty kilometres north of Basle, cutting all imperial communications between the Low Countries and the Alps, the emperor's two principal concentrations of military power. A large Spanish fleet had been destroyed by France's Dutch allies in the English Channel, and the French would take Hesdin in June 1639. The war had begun to go well for France.

Spain, where in 1638 inflation was running at 80 per cent, had lost northern Brazil to the Dutch, much diminishing its supply of precious metals, down to 60 per cent by weight of what it had been a decade before, while the proportion of lower priced silver to more valuable gold had doubled. The loss of Brazil also cost Spain control of the main source of Europe's sugar supply, while imperial finances were still being damaged by the low prices of rye and wheat, scarcely off their 1630 low points, and by the price of cloth in Milan, depressed since 1636.

But France, too, was unable to pay for the war. Even Lopez, Richelieu's hitherto reliable financier in Amsterdam, could find no money. Both France and Spain wanted peace, but each was holding out to get the best possible terms, and imperial forces began making up for their losses against France in the north by some important victories on the Italian peninsula. Then came the French victory over Savoy at Turin in September 1640. Mazarin negotiated the subsequent Turin settlement on Richelieu's behalf, but for all its forty-one ships and six armies, France was failing to take full advantage of its military victories. Just two days after Louis's birth the duc de la Valette had failed to order his troops into the breached walls of Fuenterrabia, just to the west of the present Franco-Spanish border on the Bay of Biscay, with the result that they were routed with heavy casualties.[27]

A few days later Louis XIII's sister, Elisabeth, married to Philip IV of Spain, gave birth to a daughter. It did not take more than an instant for Richelieu and his French counterpart Gaspar de Guzmán, count-duke of Olivares, whose career almost exactly matched that of Richelieu date for date, to realize that the marriage of the new French dauphin to the new Spanish infanta might one day solve Europe's major political problems. Unfortunately, it did not.

In 1638, the year of Louis's birth, Madrid was making overtures for peace with the Dutch, independently of its continuing war with France. The Portugese uprising against Spain, probably stirred up with help from Richelieu's agents, roughly coincided with the rising against Madrid in Catalonia, Spain's eastern province, where disease and Condé's forces had combined to wreak horrific destruction. Spain was imploding under pressures from both east and west. The repression of the Catalonian uprising by Madrid was fierce, and Richelieu, himself sounding out the possibilities of peace, was forced to take Catalonia into French suzerainty. When Anne's brother, the Cardinal Infante, died in December 1641, France was being conciliatory towards Spain, and Louis XIII ordered mourning at the French court.

Anne herself acknowledged that it was only Richelieu's firm guidance which prevented the king from separating her from her children. Anne's hostility to Richelieu seems to have diminished, probably on account of his mildness with her after the treason of 1637, and Richelieu had been astute enough to defuse Anne's potential as a focus for further subversion. Her other ally was Montigny, captain of the guards in charge of the security of the princes, who obtained the trust of Mme de Lansac and was able to assist in preventing the separation of Anne from her children by declaring that the air was better at Saint-Germain than at Amboise, or wherever else might be mentioned. The position of Saint-Germain on a hill overlooking the Seine valley was indeed spectacular.

Anne's second child, Philippe, was born on 21 September 1640, two years to within a fortnight after Louis. Anne's attitude to him was very different,[28] and the paternity of Philippe, conceived probably at the very end of 1639, must be regarded as substantially less assured than that of Louis. His interests were in every way subordinated to those of his elder brother, to whom he was always expected to defer. Whereas Louis had been at risk of being smothered by maternal affection, Philippe came nearer to being subjected to emotional deprivation. The queen did not visit him even when he was sick. It seems likely that, in some blinkered attempt, abetted or initiated by Mazarin, to avoid any danger that Philippe would come to challenge his elder brother's position as dauphin, and later as king, as Gaston d'Orléans had never ceased to challenge the position of Louis XIII, she started to treat Philippe as if he had been a girl.

In 1641, the year after Philippe's birth, Richelieu, having wrung more money out of the clergy, had risked humiliating the *parlements* by depriving them of any residual political role. Louis XIII held a *lit de justice* expressly forbidding the sovereign courts to take cognizance of state affairs, or administrative or financial matters, and of anything pertaining to government. That spring, an intercepted letter from the duc de la Valette to his father, d'Epernon, showed that Soissons, a prince of the blood and Condé's cousin, was conspiring with two other dukes to advance with Spanish backing into France.[29]

Richelieu thought he had enough evidence to deprive Soissons of the governorship of Champagne and to have Bouillon deprived of his French estates. Soissons and Bouillon had to submit or move to open rebellion. They decided on rebellion. The rebellion failed after its forces had been successful at La Marfée. Soissons was killed, or may, as is often alleged, have shot himself by mistake, having formed the ill-advised habit of using his pistol to push open his visor. Bouillon asked for pardon and that evening dined with Richelieu.

The treaty with the rebels which Olivares had signed for Spain specified that the rights of the king, queen and Louis would be respected, but that Gaston would be lieutenant-general, and there would be peace with Spain. He offered troops and finance. Olivares hoped for little, but felt it worthwhile to throw the dice one more time on the slim chance of an honourable peace. There followed in 1642 the final journey of Louis XIII to take Perpignan, capital of Roussillon. At the king's insistence Richelieu followed two or three days behind. Both men knew that each was terminally ill.

The king, suspecting the loyalty of Gaston and the queen, wanted both to accompany the expedition, leaving Louis and Philippe at Vincennes, of which Chavigny, the minister on whom Richelieu had come chiefly to rely, was governor. In the end, the king left on 27 January 1642, and at Richelieu's intercession Anne received permission to stay until April with Louis and Philippe at Saint-Germain. On 30 April she received notification from Chavigny to set out for Fontainebleau, the first stop on the journey south, leaving behind her children. Gaston also was allowed to remain behind.

It is quite possible that, even at three and a half, Louis realized, however intuitively or obscurely, that he was a pawn in some form of hostility between his mother and the figure he took to be his father, who held from a distance a daunting power over what happened to his mother and himself. Louis's later distaste for mentioning Louis XIII may well ante-date any realization that he was not his son, and it may well have been Louis XIII's antagonism towards his mother which kept her elder son unusually close to her emotionally.

Richelieu and his entourage had met up with the king at Fontainebleau, Lyon, Moulins and Narbonne, where Richelieu's illness overcame him at the beginning of May. Anne meanwhile managed to find medical reasons to delay her departure, in the hope that Richelieu would persuade the king to cancel the instruction. A great deal of play-acting and diplomatic activity was deployed but, after a visit by Chavigny, whom the king had come to dislike, the king finally relented on 26 May. The queen was informed on 13 June that she was allowed to remain with her children, although supervision of all her commerce was intensified.

At Valence Mazarin had received the cardinal's hat from the king on 26 February, and he stayed at Narbonne with Richelieu's entourage. Mazarin and Chavigny accompanied Richelieu when he left, carried on a stretcher, for Arles, where Richelieu hoped to find relief from the Roman baths. Early in June Richelieu received at Arles a leaked or stolen copy of the treasonable treaty between the French rebels and Spain. Louis XIII, himself too ill to stay on at Perpignan, had gone to take the waters at Montfrin, north-east of Nîmes, stopping on the way at Narbonne, where Chavigny brought him from Richelieu a copy of the treaty on the evening of 12 June. Louis XIII was appalled, and called for Mazarin to be with him. Anne was still at Saint-Germain, where in an obviously treasonable act she had signed a set of blank letters intended for use as orders after the rebellion.

Richelieu, knowing he was close to death, returned to Paris, and the king, whose confidence in him may have faltered during the rebellion, promised to retain the secretaries of state after Richelieu's death, and to appoint Mazarin as Richelieu's successor. Richelieu had failed to have the education of the queen's children confided to himself, although he did succeed in having La Mothe le Vayer appointed as Louis's future tutor.[30] During his last weeks, his relations with the queen may again have grown cooler,[31] but he had extracted from the king promises to reject any peace which did not leave France in possession of her conquests and guarantee her Lorraine, Pinerolo, Roussillon, Breisach and the Alsatian towns nearest to Lorraine. Richelieu's health swiftly began to fail again. Pleurisy set in on 28 November, and Richelieu died peacefully on the afternoon of 4 December 1642.

Mazarin, smoothly succeeding Richelieu, declared the king's principal preoccupation to be the continuance of the war, but in March 1643 Louis XIII's illness became life-threatening again, for the third time in a year. His final arrangements for making his queen, Anne of Austria, regent after his death had included making Gaston d'Orléans her lieutenant-general and subjecting her to the majority vote of a council composed of Gaston, Mazarin, Condé as senior prince of the blood, Séguier the chancellor, Bouthillier the financial *surintendant* and Chavigny, minister for foreign affairs. The resignation as minister for war of Sublet des Noyers, closely linked to Richelieu and inevitable after Richelieu's death, had been brought about by Mazarin and accepted on 10 April. Michel le Tellier was to be appointed in his place.[32]

Drawn up on 20 April, Louis's declaration had been registered by the Paris *parlement* on 21 April, a matter of days before he died on 14 May. Louis XIII had attempted to make his testamentary dispositions irreversible, but Mazarin had at the time made it clear to Anne that he could and would safeguard her interests, although he had also helped Louis draw up the declaration which, if implemented, would have prevented Anne from becoming regent with full delegated monarchical powers. He must have known how easy it would be to have that declaration annulled when the time came, but thought it strategically safer to gain the speedy acquiescence of the Paris *parlement*, glad to be released at last from the stranglehold of Richelieu, largely maintained by Louis XIII since Richelieu's death the preceding December.

The dauphin Louis was by now four and a half, and the king arranged for his formal baptism in the Sainte-Chapelle of the vieux château at Saint-Germain on 21 April, inviting Mazarin to be godfather, no reply having been received to an invitation to the pope to fill that role which, given the low point of Franco-curial relations, surprised no one. The godmother was the princesse de Condé and the officiant the *grand aumônier*, the bishop of Meaux. The child was formally named Louis.

On 14 May 1643 Louis XIII died in the château neuf at Saint-Germain,[33] apparently of peritonitis and a perforated colon, probably tubercular in origin, and of a tubercular infection of the lungs. Anne had cared for him during his last days, and the young princes had several times been brought to the bedside of the dying king. At about a quarter to three on Thursday 14 May, Ascension Day, the four-and-a-half-year-old dauphin became the fourteenth king of France to be called Louis.

3

The Boy King

From the moment of Louis XIII's death, Louis XIV was the legitimate king of France. He was immediately surrounded by guards on the orders of his mother, anxious to forestall any possible *coup,* such as may have been feared from the entourages of Gaston d'Orléans and Condé. From the very beginning Louis was encouraged to be conscious of what he would later call his job of being king, his *métier du roi,* repository of all royal jurisdiction in France by virtue of an authority directly conferred on him by God, the source of all sovereignty, both sacerdotal and secular.[1] At the same time he was still a small boy in need of an education, and of an upbringing suitable to his future state and the role in government which those currently in control of the kingdom, essentially Mazarin and his mother, intended him to play.

On the day after the death of Louis XIII, Friday 15 May, the royal household drove with all its furniture and a small army of soldiery in a long cavalcade to the Louvre. It was the custom of the royal family to vacate a residence immediately after a royal death within it and, like the major nobility, they emptied their houses as they vacated them, taking with them quite elaborate furnishings, like wall-hung tapestries. The journey that day took seven hours and was apparently much slowed by enthusiastic crowds and speeches from the governor of Paris and from the head of the municipal government, *prévôt* of the merchants, on entry into the city.

Saturday and Sunday were filled with the reception of officials and ambassadors, and by Monday negotiations behind the scenes had been completed for what would happen at the meeting that day of the *parlement,* called together for the *lit de justice* needed for the four-year-old king to confer the necessary powers on his mother as regent, and to have them registered to render them valid.[2] Negotiation was necessary because the proceedings on 18 May need not have been a mere formality. With only an infant king, no person or body had legitimate jurisdiction to impose, or even strictly to approve any new constitutional settlement. No one person or body of persons could claim the regency as of right. Anne's first chaplain, the bishop of Beauvais had put himself forward as a possible first minister. Condé had refused the request of Beaufort, son of Vendôme, the legitimized son of Henri IV, to leave Anne alone with the body of her husband, since that would have signified allowing her a primacy at least of dignity, and a possible tacit acknowledgement that she was his legitimate successor as sole regent for Louis XIV.

The first of France's fundamental laws, the Salic law, most recently promulgated on 28 June 1593, ensured that the monarchy was bestowed not by simple heredity, as in common law, but by right of succession in order of male primogeniture.[3] Louis XIV was therefore immediately king and had even at the age of four to mediate whatever arrangements were made for the regency. The Paris *parlement* was called together for a *lit de justice* on Monday 18 May technically not to ratify, which it had no constitutional authority to do, but to register.[4]

At the *lit de justice* Mme de Lansac lifted the young king on to his throne. Louis stumbled over his memorized sentence of greeting to the assembly and told it that he assented to what the chancellor, Pierre Séguier, was going to say. Séguier then announced the deal that had been brokered by Mazarin. This entailed the bestowal on Anne of an untrammelled regency, with the council, composed as she should wish, to be merely consultative. In return, Anne conceded to the *parlement* the promise of a larger political role in the nation's affairs, and promised its members automatic elevation from the *noblesse de robe* to the *noblesse de race* within eighteen months.[5] Given Anne's new powers, her total ignorance of the mechanisms of government and war, her foreign origins and her now publicly manifest reliance on Mazarin, that meant in effect that the recently naturalized Mazarin had made himself, pending Louis's majority, the *de facto* ruler of France. The court was openly astonished when Anne made Mazarin her principal minister immediately after her husband's death.[6] It had not been clear to the unperceptive court quite how obviously Mazarin had prepared as well as entitled himself to Richelieu's succession.

Mazarin had been named chief minister by 21 May 1643, that is within three days of Anne's formal appointment to the regency and two days after news reached Paris that Condé's son, the duc d'Enghien, had won the battle of Rocroi. He was twenty-two, and had been appointed by Richelieu to lead the Picardy army over Henri de la Tour d'Auvergne, later the vicomte de Turenne.[7] After Richelieu's death, discipline had become lax and morale low.[8] The foreign soldiers were deserting, feeling no longer obliged by their oath of allegiance to a dying king, and French officers were going absent. Enghien wrote to his father that he had few horses, little fodder and could not move his artillery.

Rocroi had been merely a village just inside the French border, roughly halfway between Brussels to the north and Reims to the south. François I had recognized the military importance of the site a century earlier, and it had been surrounded by a wall with five bastions and a moat, but contained a garrison of only 400. Enghien had about 23,000 troops, of which a third were cavalry. The Spaniards, under Don Francisco Melo with a bigger army and more artillery, intended to attack it after crossing the Meuse and then advance on Reims before moving along the Marne valley towards Paris, where they boasted they would have their winter quarters.

Enghien's generalship when, with the battle half lost, he contrived to take the Spaniards from the rear, quickly became the subject of legend. Enghien lost 2,000 men, with another 2,000 captured, but left 8,000 Spaniards dead, taking 6,000 prisoners and capturing 200 flags and 60 standards. The battle on 19 May began at three a.m. and was over by ten-thirty. The Spanish Anne of Austria was tempted to use the victory as the basis of a peace treaty from which she could negotiate from a position of strength. Mazarin, however, realized the importance for Anne, to say nothing of himself, of establishing her identification with French nationalist ambitions by continuing the French struggle with the house of Austria.

Now that the king of France was no longer an alienated husband but a much loved son, and urged by Mazarin, Anne did not long hesitate before sending the necessary orders to the young general on 27 May. She was prepared in the name of France to continue the war against her brother, the king of Spain, and her cousin, the emperor Ferdinand III, son of Ferdinand II and emperor since 1637. Enghien went on to capture Thionville, twenty-five kilometres north of Metz, strategically important because it protected Alsace, provided a base from which to cut the imperial forces off from the Spanish Netherlands, and opened the way for a French attack on Flanders.[9]

Anne wrote to Enghien telling him with what pleasure the young Louis XIV had followed a plan of the defences and siege operations. Other sources, like the memoirs of the king's rather older boyhood companion Louis-Henri Loménie de Brienne, confirm that Louis was being trained to derive boyish pleasure from military behaviour, and was very soon to take an interest in guns. He was being trained to exult in military victory at a date and in a court at which military ceremonial and courage in the face of danger, such as that shown personally by Enghien at Rocroi and Thionville, must in a four-year-old have precluded the possibility of any perception of warfare's other moral dimensions. The *Gazette* congratulated the king on the letter he wrote to Enghien after Rocroi 'the encouragements . . . more like what might be expected from one much older than he,' as if the four-year-old boy had himself composed the letter.[10]

Mazarin's relationship with the young king was complex. It is overwhelmingly likely that he was the physical father, certain that he was the godfather, and clear that he acted in an ordinary domestic capacity as surrogate father. Already before the death of Louis XIII, Mazarin had made arrangements to leave his residence, the hôtel de Clèves, near the Louvre, buying the hôtel Tubeuf, at the corner of the rue Vivienne and the rue des Petits-Champs, just across the road from the Palais-Royal, formerly the Palais Richelieu, which Richelieu had had built to be left to the king.[11] Mazarin brought his elder sister, Mme Martinozzi, with her son and daughters from Italy[12] to live there, and appointed Mme de Senecey to be the children's governess. The daughters became very close to Anne and were among the close childhood companions of Louis and Anne's second son, Philippe.

As soon as the guards' building was finished October 1643, Anne moved over the road into the Palais-Royal. Its garden was, she explained, so much more suitable than the Louvre for her children to play in. A month later, she explained that she needed to move into the Palais Royal to get away from the construction work perpetually in progress at the Louvre. She saw Mazarin every evening, was closeted with him for hours at a time and refused to act except on his advice, if necessary feigning ill-health until it became available.

Mazarin had already planned Anne's move before Louis XIII's death, and his notebooks make it clear that he had at the same date planned to take up residence as soon as seemed discreet within the Palais-Royal itself. Richelieu had kept his gardens private, where necessary by erecting high walls. An opening was made in the wall so that Mazarin had only to cross the road from his new hôtel to be in the garden of the Palais-Royal. He moved in to avoid, Anne explained to her council, the need to walk through the extensive garden perhaps several times on the same day. His rooms were separated from hers by a 'petite galerie'. Olivier Lefèvre d'Ormesson, the revered and famously upright magistrate and diarist, hoped he would not use them, but from 23 November 1644, he did. The hypothesis that Mazarin and Anne had not become lovers certainly before the death of Louis XIII appears indeed difficult to sustain.

He officially became the *surintendant* of the regent's household in 1645, and early enrichment only indirectly related to offices conferring power began with his appointment to the lucrative superintendance of the maritime Compagnie du Nord in 1645, primarily a fishing enterprise. In addition to direct *gratifications* he was also appointed *surintendant des bâtiments,* giving him authority over the cultural matters in which Richelieu had hoped to organize a European preeminence for France, together with the governorship of Toulon and the captaincy of the royal residence of Fontainebleau where, as at the Palais-Royal, he had apartments adjoining those of Anne herself.

A 1643 despatch from the Venetian envoy, Angelo Contarini, written on the king's fifth birthday tells us that Louis was sturdy and serious, rather solemn and insistent on being shown respect, even by his younger brother. By the spring of 1644 the five-year-old was deriving great pleasure from reviewing the Swiss guards in the Bois de Boulogne, and had even been given his own imitation military company of children. When he was nine Mazarin would have a large model fortification made in the garden of the Palais-Royal for the king to play in with his companions. Louis held a *lit de justice* on

7 September 1645 to celebrate his seventh birthday, and in the summer of 1647 Mazarin accompanied the now eight-year-old king and his mother to the northern frontier, where the French were facing defeat at Armentières, to stimulate enthusiasm among the troops and to help by their presence to persuade the nobility to mobilize themselves. He held another *lit de justice* on 15 January 1648 at which Omer Talon, the *avocat général,* spoke of the indigent state of France, but at which the king none the less duly promulgated Mazarin's plans for further taxation.

Mazarin's style may have differed from that of Richelieu, than which it was more feline and duplicitous, but his policies remained similar, if clearly less principled and more pragmatic, more orientated towards peace abroad and leniency at home. Louis, aged nine, heard further woefully accurate accounts of the condition of the populace at his fourth *lit de justice* on 31 July, but was then delighted to hear of Condé's victory at Lens.

Enghien had succeeded to the Condé title on his father's death in December 1646, becoming the new first prince of the blood. A national hero after Rocroi, his demands for the promotion of his Huguenot second-in-command were none the less refused. A furious letter to Anne had had to be suppressed before despatch by Enghien's father and never reached her, but Enghien's constant demands for money for the army and rewards for its officers irritated Mazarin and opened up a rift with unforeseen and alarming consequences later in Louis's reign.[13]

From the age of seven, when he was emancipated from female tutelage, Louis's studies were directed by Hardouin de Péréfixe, a minor if enthusiastically patriotic historian, to be rewarded with the see of Rodez and eventually to become archbishop of Paris. Péréfixe, in charge of a squad of half a dozen tutors for various subjects, taught Louis history and the liberal arts and wrote a series of textbooks which extolled the virtues of peace.[14] None the less Louis's whole upbringing did little to discourage him from regarding military conquest as a commendable aim.

He was not, as far as we know, energetically flogged as Louis XIII had been. The penalty for transgressions, like using language picked up in the stables, was normally confinement to his room. Marie Dubois, seigneur de Lestoumière, who had bought himself first one half, then the other half of the post of *valet de chambre,* does however relate a frequently repeated anecdote in his *Souvenirs*.[15] On one occasion when Louis, aged nine, was taken to Amiens on a journey to encourage the troops, Anne apparently felt it necessary to remind him that she retained authority over him and threatened to have him beaten to show him that 'they could beat at Amiens as well as they could in Paris'. It follows that he must have been at least occasionally physically beaten, which can have done nothing to diminish his sense of insecurity, later to be disguised by his use of the minutiae of court ritual and monarchical authority. On this occasion Louis apparently cried with rage before going to the queen and asking forgiveness on his knees, promising obedience to his mother's wishes in future. He had tested his royal authority against that which his mother still held over him, and found the limitations imposed by age and dependency. He was duly forgiven.

Naturally enough, the young king did not always easily find the proper balance between the attitudes appropriate to his two different roles. On the one hand he was king, with authority to rule bestowed by God and commonly believed to be endowed with the gift of curing by laying his hands on the sick, manifesting his status as a conduit of divine power. On the other, he was successively small boy, adolescent, young man and finally husband, father and administrator of France's government, a role which, by the date of Mazarin's death, he had been persuaded it was his divine duty to play, however well or ill it conformed to his temperamental inclinations. Whatever they did with their time, French kings could not abdicate their divine appointment.

In March 1646 Mazarin was entrusted with the 'superintendence of the government and the conduct' of the king and his brother. Charles de Sainte-Maure, duc de Montauzier, later to be succeeded by Nicolas de Neufville, marquis de Villeroy, was appointed Louis XIV's governor, responsible to Mazarin. Voltaire was to take the clearly mistaken view in his *Le Siècle de Louis XIV* that Mazarin deliberately prolonged the childhood of Louis XIV for as long as he could.[16]

Among those other than Mazarin who had charge of him as a child, Louis himself was probably closest to La Porte, imprisoned at the Bastille by Richelieu for his role as go-between in forwarding the treasonable correspondence of the queen in 1642. Released, like so many others, after Richelieu's death, he was ennobled by 1643, and his post of *premier valet de chambre* to the young king allowed him to replace the regular tutor in the nightly readings from Mézeray's *Histoire de France*, selecting for preference those passages in which Mézeray stressed the failures of Louis's weaker royal predecessors.[17] Fiercely loyal to Anne, La Porte was also hostile to Mazarin, and is credibly said to have tried to implant an early distrust of the cardinal in the young king's mind.[18] There is, however, no evidence that he succeeded.

After his nomination as chief minister, Mazarin succeeded in changing the membership of the king's executive council, now known as the *conseil d'en-haut*.[19] He managed to keep the elderly chancellor, Pierre Séguier, the brother of the Carmelite prioress of Pontoise with whom Anne remained on intimate terms, but who was unpopular with the *parlement* over which he presided. Anne disliked Séguier on account of his treatment of her when her correspondence with the Spanish court had been discovered in 1637,[20] and the Paris *parlement* was hostile because he had presided over the court at Lyon which had condemned to death François de Thou, one of their own, for conniving at the 1643 rebellion against Louis XIII. When Séguier had had to compliment the new Regent on behalf of the *parlement* at the *lit de justice* of 18 May 1643, his text was gracious enough, but the assembly tittered at the embarrassed stammers occasioned by his public *volte-face*.

The regent on the other hand succeeded in having two secretaries of state who had been particularly close to Richelieu, Claude de Bouthillier and his son Léon le Bouthillier, comte de Chavigny, removed from the council. Mazarin gave Claude de Bouthillier's responsibility for finance at first jointly to Nicolas Bailleul, a senior judge, and Claude de Mesmes, comte d'Avaux. Avaux was a diplomat, who was replaced as early as October 1643, by Michel Particelli d'Emery, an *intendant* well known to Mazarin who in 1647 became the sole *surintendant des finances*.

Chavigny was brought back in September, although Mazarin kept for himself the secretariat for foreign affairs, relying for help on the brilliant and experienced diplomacy of Hugues de Lionne, whom he was to introduce into the regent's household as *sécretaire des commandements de la reine*, a post which involved drawing up the most important documents for her signature. Lionne also gradually took over the distribution of benefices which was notionally the responsibility of a *conseil de conscience* whose meetings Mazarin contrived to make increasingly infrequent.

The regent herself, having called back Marie de Hautefort, dismissed Mme de Lansac, finally permitting her mischievous high-spirited, but cunning old friend of the 1620s, Mme de Chevreuse, to return from exile. Since Mme de Chevreuse was identified with a policy of immediate peace with Spain contrary to the policy being pursued by Mazarin, and since Louis XIII had specifically desired her exile to be maintained, Anne must be seen as already asserting her new authority.

Mazarin, seeking to remain firm while appeasing the most potentially resentful members of the nobility, gave Languedoc back to Gaston d'Orléans, whose lands and charges had been confiscated in 1642, paid his gambling debts and allowed him to inherit the French lands confiscated from his mother, Marie de' Medici, the Luxembourg palace, the district of Mont-Parnasse in Paris, the duchy of Alençon and the viscountcies of Carentan and Saint-Lô. The governorship of Champagne was bestowed on Enghien, and Condé recovered Chantilly, confiscated on the execution of Montmorency after his rebellion in 1632.

None the less, in spite of a general beneficence, and a willingness to offer charges, rewards, offices and bribes, Anne, encouraged by Mazarin, also knew how to remain firm. Government of Brittany and the admiralty were not returned from Richelieu's family to the seditious Vendômes, illegitimate offspring of Henri IV, nor Sedan to the rebellious Bouillons. Mazarin urged Anne not to diminish her power, which she was not disposed to do, regarding it as held in trust for Louis XIV. Not surprisingly, and in spite of the rehabilitations, attempts were made to force Anne to dismiss Mazarin. Perhaps she would yield to another cardinal who, once raised to the purple, might replace him? Mazarin sweetly pointed out to each of two possible candidates, the bishop of Beauvais and Sublet de Noyers, that the other had legitimate aspirations. Condé was played off against Beaufort, the Vendôme candidate for chief minister. All of this political manoeuvring suggests that, whatever private gossip might be hinting at, Anne's liaison with Mazarin was either not yet certain knowledge at court or, more probably, made little difference to the political manoeuvring among those close to government.

The scandal of Mazarin's closenes to Anne was, however, becoming more widely seen as a useful weapon, and pressure was being exercised through whispers and mutters, bishops and abbesses. La Porte listed the rumours for her, warned her that she was looking towards the fate of Marie de' Medici, who died in poverty and exile after the murder of Concini, whom she had appointed, and that others would take it in their hands to get rid of Mazarin if she did not.

There were others, too, in Anne's entourage, like Marie de Hautefort, who were loyal to her. She let it be known to Anne that the regent needed to be careful of the gossip she was generating about her relationship with Mazarin. Anne replied, alluding to the common reference to homosexuality as 'the Italian vice', that, being Italian, Mazarin's sexual inclinations would also be 'Italian'. It is known that they were not, but it is also known from his notebooks that he succeeded in making Mme de Chevreuse, one of the century's great seductresses, and her step-sister Mme de Guémené, suppose that he was not attracted to women.[21] His mastery of the art of dissimulation was superb, but it is appparent that Mazarin and Anne were within months of the death of Louis XIII conscious of the need to put up a smokescreen to disguise the nature of their relationship.[22]

Meanwhile, however, a clique of power-hungry nobles hoped that the government would be recruited from the patrician châteaux and would be formed through the skilful scheming of Mme de Chevreuse, who hoped to wrest back for the Vendômes the lands which had been given to Richelieu's family. Unhappily for Mme de Chevreuse, Condé, whose son, Enghien, had married Richelieu's niece, wanted them for himself. The young king himself was made the target of intrigue by those opposed to Mazarin and was urged to remove Richelieu's portraits from his quarters.

Mazarin was trying hard to be gentle and had foresightedly tried to buy off Mme de Chevreuse with considerable bribes, but behind the opposition forming within months of the regent's accession, there was soon to be a squabbling coalition of great families. In the context of aristocratic rivalries in France at this time, it is necessary to understand the part exact social propriety could still be made to play in the control of a generally ambitious if sporadically fractious court, which the potentially troublesome could always be invited to join, where they might be tamed with time-consuming ritual, and which was actually ruled in the name of a five-year-old. It is also note-worthy that Louis XIV was already being trained in the usefulness of merely social forms of compulsion for the task to be imposed on him by his kingship. He was to become an expert in the manipu-lation of minutely graduated social displays of approval and displeasure.

The situation was complex. Bitter jealousy broke out among the women. Beaufort had aspired to Enghien's sister, Anne-Geneviève de Bourbon-Condé, but the Condés gave her to Longueville, who therefore broke off with Mme de Montbazon, not as young, or as pretty, or as well born. She was obliged to make do with Beaufort. Enghien's sister had become in June 1642 the Mme de Longueville who was later to play a considerable role in defending and promoting the dying fortunes of the Condé family. Still living out the final gasps of the early seventeenth-century ethic of chivalric heroism, there followed an incident of dropped letters, mistaken addressees, and vendettas opposing the Beaufort/Vendôme/Montbazons supported by their relative, Mme de Chevreuse, to the finally victorious Condé/Longuevilles.

The great salon hostesses became involved: Mme de Rambouillet, who reigned from the chambre bleue of the hôtel she had herself designed, and Mme de Sablé, the most neurotically hypochondriac.[23] The novelist Mme de La Fayette used the incident of the dropped letters for the plot of *La Princesse de Clèves*, and La Rochefoucauld, by turns lover of Mme de Chevreuse and Mme de Longueville from the opposed factions of the major aristocracy, but by now dis-enchanted by Anne of Austria's lack of interest in his early infat-uation with Mme de Chevreuse, finally burned in the queen's presence the letters which had been gratuitously thought by Mme de Montbazon to have been addressed by Mme de Longueville to Maurice de Coligny.[24]

Mme de Motteville is very funny about the word-by-word effort which Mme de Montbazon and Mazarin, witnessing for the regent the scene of Mme de Montbazon's apology on 8 August at the hôtel de Condé, put into Mme de Montbazon's letter of excuse, after a day (5 May 1644) which saw the interchange of thirteen letters on the subject. Mme de Montbazon apologized to Mme de Longueville with defiance, and had to be made to go back to the beginning because she could not be allowed to get away without the initial address, 'Madame'.

The matter did not end there. Mme de Chevreuse gave a reception beside the Seine[25] to which the regent was delighted to come with the princesse de Condé on the assurance that Mme de Montbazon would not be there. She not only was there, but as Mme de Chevreuse's step-mother,[26] she presided, and refused to leave on the regent's request. It was the five-year-old king who banished her,

> The unhappiness which the queen, Mme my mother, has at the lack of respect you showed her, forces me to send you this letter . . . written to give you to understand that you will go to your house at Rochefort and that you will stay there until you receive further instructions from me . . .

A plan was made to assassinate Mazarin, as must have been expected as soon as losers emerged from the round of office-giving and pardons in the summer of 1643. The first attempt was to be made when Mazarin first left the hôtel de Clèves in the morning and then when he left the Louvre as usual to return home on 30 August, but he took care never to be alone when leaving the house, and seems on the second occasion to have been warned by the guard. As was to be expected, Madame de Chevreuse and the Beaufort faction were behind the assassination attempts.

On 31 August Beaufort attended a reception at Vincennes given by Chavigny for the regent, who apparently behaved quite normally. She was in the Louvre with Mme de Chevreuse and Mme de Hautefort as usual on the evening of 2 September when Beaufort came after hunting to pay his respects. He was well received and recounted his day's hunting. When Mazarin came in, he took Anne aside to an adjoining room. Beaufort was quietly arrested by Guitaut, the captain of the guards, and taken to Vincennes after one night in the Louvre. According to her *femme de chambre* as recounted by Mme de Motteville, Anne is said to have wept on the night, three days earlier, when the arrest had been decided. She had mastered the art of face-to-face dissimulation.

Mme de Chevreuse agreed to leave Paris only after 200,000 livres of debt had been paid, but Mazarin took the opportunity to rid himself of the bishops of Limoges and Lisieux together with Beauvais, all associated with the Beaufort faction, if not directly with the attempt on Mazarin's life. The pretext was that Mazarin was merely following the advice of Gaston d'Orléans and of Condé. Everyone had been surprised that Mazarin had been so firm, and that he had turned down the offer of private guards such as Richelieu had had. True to his characteristic gentleness and guile he was, however, no firmer than he needed to be, and he did bring in Italian guards, but had them disguised as servants, and never put them on parade. The Swedish and Venetian ambassadors wrote home to say that Beaufort's imprisonment meant the defeat of the party wanting immediate peace with Spain at any price. Peace negotiations had in fact been started in 1643, but it was to be some years before they were to bear fruit in 1648 in Westphalia.

After the first challenge to the regency had passed with the defeat of Beaufort and the 'cabale des importants' as it was called, of which he was the leader, the upbringing of the young king, rising five, could be expected to take place in circumstances of greater stability. Everyone who has left a portrait admiring Louis's later military aggression has emphasized the childhood interest in playing soldiers with his companions, and echoing the sound of drum beats. By the age of seven Louis could competently handle a gun and had begun the career which would make him an excellent shot.

Mazarin was early to initiate him into the work of the council, and in addition to his instruction in horsemanship, fencing and dancing, he was having a relatively solid musical education. As soon as he was eleven, his mother wrote to the Jesuits, from whose ranks the royal confessor was traditionally chosen, and picked from them Charles Paulin to be the king's confessor. The letters to Rome left by Père Paulin, naturally more interested in Louis's spiritual welfare, contain comments on the boy's progress, chiefly concerned with his physical prowess.[27] Père Paulin, using the *Catéchisme royal* of Antoine Godeau, bishop of Grasse,[28] prepared Louis for his confirmation and first communion. After he had been confirmed by the bishop of Meaux, brother of the chancellor Séguier, on 3 November 1649 in the private chapel of the Palais-Royal, Louis and Philippe made their first confessions on Christmas eve, followed by their first communions at midnight mass at the parish church of Saint-Eustache. Mazarin was present. It was made an event of some public splendour, doubtless in the hope of defusing public tension which within days would result in the arrest of Condé, Conti and Longueville. Then on 25 March, the feast of the Annunciation, in 1650 Louis renewed the dedication of France to the Blessed Virgin first made by Louis XIII in December 1637.

As soon as possible Mazarin took Louis to short council meetings, or to brief parts of longer ones, encouraging him to ask questions and take a serious interest in what was going on. He was present when his mother formally received foreign diplomats and was taken by her to parades of guards on their exercise grounds in the Bois de Boulogne and the Bois de Vincennes. When he had been taken by Mazarin and Anne to bolster the morale of the troops in Flanders, the purpose of the tour had been as much to interest him in the military generalship which was intended to be among his future roles. Following an understanding between the Spaniards and the Dutch allies of France, the military situation had been going badly for France, but the tour ended with popular acclaim in Dieppe, where the young Louis took part in the pretence of a naval battle. Mazarin was carefully moulding him into the monarch he wished him to become.

Louis and his brother Philippe, now known as 'le petit Monsieur' except by Louis, who called himself Philippe's 'petit papa', were involved in Anne's stylized, baroque religious practices, including visits to numerous shrines, like the chapel Anne had had built at Val-de-Grâce and the magnificent cathedral at Chartres. Anne's own piety was sincere, her devotion warm and her religious practices assiduous. Louis was brought up in a hot-house atmosphere of pious observances, rites to be performed without any real understanding of their significance.

What remains difficult to disentangle is the relationship between the emotional fervour of Anne's devotional life, supported by alms-giving and developed with the aid of the whole repertory of visual aids to Spanish baroque religious fervour, its images, relics, elaborate reliquaries, ornamented sacred vessels, monstrances and other holy objects, and the strict sexual morality taught by the church, if not always strictly imposed by its canonical discipline. Louis was himself to become a victim of norms of sexual morality which tightened as the century progressed, and even to have his attention firmly drawn to the lamentable state of real need which his wars imposed on the citizenry, but his fervently pious devotional upbringing in childhood and adolescence did not impinge strongly on the moral values to which he was being formed.

From their move to the Palais-Royal in October 1643, Louis and Philippe called on their mother when she awakened at mid morning. A little later, unusually for seventeenth-century courts, when Louis was thirteen he, at least, took his meals with her. There was a first childhood infatuation for Marie de Hautefort. Isaac de Bensserade, a little-esteemed poet but an important author of court entertainments commemorated Louis's emotional fixation in verses, written in the first person, in which Louis declared that he had inherited his passion for Marie from his father. Louis XIII had in fact had an emotional fixation on her. In the meanwhile Mazarin's public intimacy with Anne was growing closer as he slowly weaned her from other sources of pressure, like the 'conseil de conscience' which had been the intermediary for royal almsgiving and the bestowal of benefices and the convents which were also the source of pro-Spanish political pressure.

The years since Rocroi and Thionville had seen a further succession of victories for French arms, chiefly under Enghien, from 1646 Prince de Condé, and Turenne, but also under Gaston d'Orléans, at Freiburg and Philippsburg in 1644, Nördlingen in 1645, Dunkirk in 1646 and at Lens in 1648. Victories in Flanders, Franche-Comté, Bavaria and south of the Danube at Zumarshausen did much to crush Spanish power in what had once been the duchy of Burgundy and opened the routes to Germany. Mazarin had organized the military successes and completed his political domination.

Abroad he successfully exercised pressure on the new pro-Spanish pope Innocent X, elected in 1644. Innocent had tried to degrade Mazarin for his secular employment but Mazarin, with even more than his usual skill, finally extracted from him a red hat for his brother. It had taken a threat of schism from the *parlement*, and Mazarin had needed to send naval forces in 1646 and 1647 to take the Spanish bases in Tuscany, giving France control of regions immediately adjacent to the papal states. He also cemented the Turkish alliance as well as that with Poland whose king, Ladislas, married Marie-Louise de Gonague, daughter of the duc de Nevers, in 1645.

Finally in 1648 Mazarin successfully concluded the all-important treaties of Westphalia as a result of the congresses held in Westphalia from April 1644, in Münster for the Catholics and in Osnabrück for the Protestants, which embodied the post-reformation political division of Europe practically along the sectarian divide. The partition lasted more or less until the era of Napoleon. The treaties limited the power of the emperor, forcing him in important matters to seek the authority of the diet, now an advisory coalition of princes and cities, and left France with the Rhine for its border except at Strasbourg, which remained a free city, and except for certain French outposts on the Rhine's left bank, including the three bishoprics of Toul, Verdun and Metz.[29]

Unhappily for Europe, the only son of the king of Spain died suddenly in November 1646, leaving the infanta, Maria-Teresa heir to all Spanish territories, and any projected marriage between her and Louis apparently too great a risk for the Spaniards to run. It could have resulted in a French king to whom Spaniards owed allegiance. The French and Dutch therefore signed a formal treaty on 30 January 1648 with the Franco-Spanish situation still unresolved. The French were still at war with the Spanish, who had begun to claim important victories at Lérida in Catalonia, in Naples and in the Milanais.

What Mazarin and Anne together tried to pass on to Louis was a sense of responsibility to God for the use of the sovereign authority bestowed on him, and even a respect for the customs, rights and structures by which the kingdom had been governed a century and more earlier. It was under Henri IV that his great Huguenot chief minister, Maximilien de Béthune de Sully, who had begun to centralize the administration and strip the princes of the blood of their authority just after the turn of the seventeenth century. Richelieu and now Mazarin were to continue the process, but Louis XIV was left by Mazarin with a strong consciousness of the need to respect the structures of customary constitutional law.

Louis in his *Mémoires* tries to make it clear to his own son that the king is only the repository for the time being of sovereign power, which it is his sacred duty to pass on intact. When Louis is later at such pains to seek to legitimize his extension of French frontiers with reference to the laws of inheritance, by implication considered constitutional and therefore of divine instititution in early modern

France, it is because he wishes to believe that the derivation of his sovereign authority directly from God justifies his war-making, however scant a part the desire to enforce divinely bestowed rights may actually have played in Louis's motivation in going to war.

Mazarin saw his own greatest achievement as saving for Louis the Bourbon inheritance threatened by Louis's uncle Gaston and cousin Condé. Péréfixe wrote that Mazarin's biographers would find nothing more greatly to praise in him than his education of the young king. By the early 1650s Louis was being received by Mazarin for an hour or so on most days to be instructed in how the domestic and foreign matters arising each day should be interpreted and dealt with. Louis was discussing the daily despatches with Mazarin from the age of fourteen, and was made by Mazarin to write essays on the issues they raised. By the last years of Mazarin's life Louis had already started to preside at council meetings, although he left the decisions to Mazarin.

Unfortunately, Richelieu had left France with about three years' future income already spent and Mazarin's domestic policies were determined by the need to find money for the war against Spain. France's annual expenditure had remained manageable without penal levels of taxation until preparations for the Spanish war began in 1634, when it rapidly increased fivefold. By 1643 the expenditure of the French administration amounted to over 124 million livres, exceeding income of under 71 million by 75 per cent, the value of 80,000 kilograms of gold.[30] By 1647, governmental borrowing alone had risen above 350 million livres.

The fiscal system was not only out of date, exempting the aristocracy from much direct taxation on the grounds that they were deemed to absolve their contribution by donating their blood in battle, but it was also unfairly administered and unfairly distributed geographically. The clergy were exempt in exchange for an annually voted 'free gift', amounting in 1645 to 4 million livres. A system of direct government tax commissioners and *intendants* with their own enforcement bodies, some of whom were also commissioners, was superimposed on the system of tax officials who, like the lawyers and judges of the *parlements,* had bought and could sell or bequeath their offices only as long as their functions were not usurped, making themselves redundant and their offices unsaleable. The regime of *intendants* naturally dismayed both the landed gentry from whom the provincial *lieutenants-généraux* directly responsible to the king had always been drawn, but also many of the tax farmers whose functions the *intendants* rendered otiose.

The system of *intendants,* used occasionally from early in the century, but systematically under Richelieu, was institutionalized by a decree of April 1643 and became the core mechanism of the fiscal 'absolutism' of the governmental administration of France. In addition the state borrowed money either from foreign bankers or financiers, or at home from tax-farming financiers who lent against the privilege of themselves collecting indirect taxes on such products as wine and salt, a system which under Richelieu sporadically and under Mazarin systematically, was extended to include the farming of direct taxation.

Tax farmers sublet their territories, and at each stage collectors made substantial profits while the peasants were subjected to some-times extreme pressures, and the state extracted further funding from the creation and sale of new offices. Further civic loans or *rentes* were arranged by local government 'sur l'Hôtel de Ville', like modern local authority bonds, with interest payments and other state debts falling due to individuals rapidly declining into arrears by the late 1640s. Meanwhile the value of the existing financial offices diminished as their number multiplied.

This was the problem that led to the first great disruption in the life of Louis XIV. It was brought about when the 1648 treaties of Westphalia ended the Thirty Years War, and when the Fronde broke out in Paris in 1648, eventually forcing the regent and her sons to flee the capital. That event made a deep and enduring impression on the young king, although the nature and extent of the trauma are still debated. Whether or not it bred in him a horror of Paris and urban life is not clear. It certainly did lead him to harbour deep wells of distrust and his extraordinarily developed skills of dissimulation.

Mazarin would succeed in bringing about peace before he died in 1661, his own enrichment having been largely due to the skill and assiduity of Colbert, who held power under Louis, and under whom prosperity, made possible by peace, was to return to France. Louis, however, during the all-important last ten years of Mazarin's life, when between the ages of fifteen and twenty-two he was being daily inducted by Mazarin into the affairs of state, learned only how to administer a country which needed to win a war and was desperately short of funds. One of the difficulties left for the historians of his reign to resolve is the extent to which he was to misapply the relative easing of the financial burden. Did too much money go on territorial aggrandizement, or securing frontiers, or on great architectural enterprises? Was he justified in refusing to release convicts after serving their sentences to increase the number of galleys, unless they could buy replacements for themselves to row them? African slaves could not be employed, because Colbert, peace-loving and humane as he often appears, thought they died too quickly.

4

The King Comes of Age

When the Fronde proper broke out in 1648, Louis was still nine, quite old enough to be made aware of the broad outlines of what was at stake, although not to discriminate intelligently between the positions of the various participants. His perception of affairs will have been filtered down to him overwhelmingly through the eyes and attitudes of Mazarin and Anne.

It has been said that the Fronde 'began as a work-stoppage by government tax officers who refused to carry out their duties',[1] but that is scarcely true even in a narrow, technical sense. It was not the paid government officers who went on strike, as well they might have done for arrears of stipend. The Fronde started as an urban protest, sparked by the *parlement,* but was carried on a wave of provincial uprisings against increases of taxation or changes in the mode of collecting taxes which stretched back to a series of sporadically violent protests, like those of the *croquants* and of the *nu-pieds* between 1636 and 1639.[2] These had taken place over different local taxation issues in different parts of France, but had intensified since taxation was tripled between 1630 and 1635, and few of the French population, perhaps at this date rather lower than 20 million, had been unaffected.

On the appointment of Anne as regent, the *parlement,* in May 1643, had been encouraged by her promise to take greater heed of its advice in exchange for breaking her late husband's will. There followed the plots to detach Anne and Louis from Mazarin and to transfer power back to the nobles. When they failed, the regent's dependence on Mazarin came under pressure from a resistance to new governmental fiscal measures which had begun building up since Particelli d'Emery, *contrôleur général* and then from 1647 *surintendant* of finance, had begun introducing them in 1644 and 1645. The increasing use of tax commissioners was by-passing the system by which the *parlement* had to register, and could make representations about, new fiscal exactions.

Emery's edicts mostly concerned the taxation of the previously exempt, like royal office-holders and owners of Paris houses built outside the city walls (the *toisé*), and were followed by further measures to increase tariffs on goods imported into Paris, unenthusiastically registered by the *parlement* only after a year's delay. The value of *rentes* on the Hôtel de Ville began to decline, interest payments fell into arrears, and the salaries of judicial officers were cut.

Mazarin had been forced by the reluctance of the *parlement* to register d'Emery's decrees to withdraw or soften some of them, but on 23 March 1645 the *parlement* sought to reinforce its protest by holding a meeting of all its eight chambers, Grand' Chambre,[3] five of *enquêtes* and two of *requêtes,* with the other sovereign courts, but this was forbidden by Anne. There ensued a guerilla war between Mazarin, always acting through Anne, and the *parlement,* which culminated early in 1648 when Anne went so far as to hold an ill-advised and authoritarian *lit de justice* on 15 January to create twelve new saleable posts of the senior judges who presided over the *cours de requêtes* and were known as *maîtres des requêtes.* Mazarin had reduced the number of new creations from twenty-four, in addition to the existing seventy-two, valued at 180,000 livres each, but the body of existing *maîtres des requêtes* demanded reconsideration of their registration by the *parlement* two days later.

Séguier formally presided over the *lit de justice.* As in 1643, Louis forgot the lines with which he was to open the proceedings, and the stress forced him to tears. Only the fact of the tears is reliably recorded, not their cause, but they can scarcely have been occasioned by mere stage-fright in one already so used to public appearances, and it is unlikely that they were tears of frustration at the outrage and indignation he shared with his mother at the refusal of the magistrates personally to submit to such measures as the renunciation of gilded ornamentation on carriages.

The king was nine and a half, but appeared still to appear 'small, bashful, withdrawn and silent'.[4] The tears must surely have sprung from an unusual lack of self-confidence in a very confused small boy. This was the occasion on which the advocate general, Omar Talon, went on to deliver the famous oration which might well have given Louis cause for alarm. Talon spoke against the abuse of the *lit de justice*, originally intended as a forum for consultation, and against court expenditure on luxuries while peasants starved and their furniture was auctioned.

Court expenditure was becoming generally perceived as intolerable. Mazarin for instance had brought back Italian players to entertain Anne and the court, and to play the comedy *Orfeo* with music by Luigi Rossi at the Palais-Royal for the 1647 carnival.[5] With its numerous changes of scene and complex stage machinery it had cost 400,000 livres without salaries and travel, and employed 200 men to build the scenery alone. The *Gazette* recounts that Louis wanted to see the entertainment a third time, although it lasted six hours, and he must have been tired after the preceding day's ball, which he had opened with a *courante*.[6]

The other sovereign courts, Grand Conseil, Chambre des Comptes and Cour des Aides, made an alliance with the *parlement,* and for three months declarations, ordinances and edicts were imposed, rejected, delayed, amended, appealed and obstructed. Talon's speech on 15 January had been published in edited versions which stimulated resentment in the provinces, and made the Dutch think that the French administration was on the point of disintegration.

The foreign extractions of both the regent and of Mazarin made it difficult for them to impose the stern measures invoked by Richelieu under Louis XIII, more clearly backed by royal and divinely derived authority. The only such authority currently represented in France was vested in a nine-year-old, and France was at the expense of its peasants conducting a war unsustainable without a fiscal regime which was already sporadically igniting revolution.

In England, the parliament would not actually execute Charles I until 1649, but his wife, Henriette de France,[7] sister of Louis XIII and aunt of Louis XIV, had already taken impoverished refuge in France, where she had been given living quarters in the Louvre. France was not gripped by a Cromwellian wave of religious zealotry, but in 1648 Anne, touchy about all matters concerning royal authority, visibly anxious to reassure potential lenders of continued royal credit-worthiness and aware that the threat to the English monarchy had started with parliament, did not appear as the likely saviour of the strong monarchy established by Richelieu.

The *maîtres des requêtes* had ceased work as a result of the proposals to increase their numbers. The agreement had run out the preceding December whereby office-holders of the *parlement* and the sovereign courts every nine years paid the *paulette*, a sum equivalent to a sixtieth of the value of their office, in return for the right to sell or bequeath it, in this way preventing the right of nomination, or effectively resale, from reverting to the crown.

On 30 April a royal decree renewed the agreement at the added cost to all office-holders except those of the Paris *parlement* of doing without wages for four years. After some hesitation the Paris *parlementaires* turned the exemption down, and on 13 May 1648 the courts autonomously decided in an *arrêt d'union* to send deputies to a new assembly to be known as the Chambre Saint-Louis, which Anne immediately but vainly declared illegal. On 18 May the royal power abolished the decree of 30 April, with the technical effect of leaving no legal basis for the sale or bequeathing of the expensive but lucrative offices, now technically vacant crown offices to which no re-appointments had been made, and on 23 May it declared illegal the creation of the *arrêt d'union*.[8] Between 29 and 31 May four officers of the *parlement* and two from the Cour des Aides were arrested.

None the less, on 15 June the new body was allowed to meet. Between 30 June and 9 July the Chambre Saint-Louis produced a twenty-seven-article charter, rehearsing all the old grievances, but also demanding the prosecution of the financiers and the tax farmers, the abolition of the *intendants,* and, most importantly of all, a veto over tax legislation. On 9 July 1648 Mazarin sacrificed Particelli d'Emery, who had at least had the confidence of the bankers, replacing him with the inept maréchal duc de la Meilleraye, and on 18th the abolition of the *intendants* and a diminution of 12 per cent in the annual *taille* tax levied on individuals for the year were decreed.[9] However, as Mazarin conceded more and more, so the demands of the Chambre Saint-Louis increased.[10] At a new *lit de justice* on 31 July, Mazarin and Anne had to accept the essential demands of the *parlement* and the law officers. The annual deficit was touching 50 million livres, and on 18 July the French state defaulted on between 80 and 120 million livres of debt. On 22 August the Chambre Saint-Louis, acting as an assembly of courts, initiated measures against the financiers.

Anne of Austria, Mazarin and the aristocracy were now forced to sell jewellery, and the royal table was cut back. It is true that Turenne had scored an important military victory at Zumarshausen in Bavaria, but the unpaid army in the north-east was demoralized by the departure of its Dutch allies in accordance with the Westphalian treaties. Then on 22 August the young Condé in the Spanish Low Countries won at Lens the considerable victory on which Mazarin had been counting. Louis, not yet ten, was already well enough informed, doubtless by Mazarin himself, to realize how displeased the *parlement* would be at the consequent relief of pressure on Mazarin.

The young king was right, but the victory made the court over-confident and sparked off the civil war which was to follow. Mazarin profited from the solemn *Te Deum* at Notre-Dame on 26 August to order the quarter sealed off and the arrest of three leading members of the *parlement,* including the incorruptible and much respected Pierre Broussel, who had been part of a delegation to the Palais-Royal on 24 March 1645 and who, being ill, had not been present at the ceremony. By the time he was dragged from his sick-bed, all Paris knew what was happening and was in uproar. On hearing the riot as La Meilleraye attempted to arrest the leaders of the protesting *parlementaires,* the coadjutor bishop of Paris, Jean-François-Paul de Gondi, later cardinal de Retz, dramatically rescued him and took him to Mazarin and Anne at the Palais-Royal.[11]

The *parlement* and members of the sovereign courts were out of order on several technical counts, not least in claiming to act under the authority of the king in order to save the monarchy from Mazarin's clutches. They were in effect attacking the jurisdiction flowing from the authority, which had been delegated by Louis to his mother, under which they purported to act. The point is not merely pedantic because, in spite of the immense amount of time and ink spent on legal arguments to justify the positions being held, what was happening neither rested on nor required more than the flimsiest patchwork of legal legitimization. Without necessarily knowing it, the instruments of government in France were part of a Europe-wide ripple in political organization of which uprisings in

England, Ireland, Spain, Portugal, Germany, Italy and the Ukraine in the 1640s and 1650s also formed part.[12] It was an early incursion into national governance of what would later after huge setbacks develop into the flow of liberal democratic forms of government.

Mazarin had become distrusted and was thought of as the Italian interloper. Parallels were seen between him and Concini, assassinated on the orders of Louis XIII, whose body had been disinterred and dismembered by the crowd in 1617. Mazarin had, also alongside the *parlements* and the courts, three principal potential personal opponents in the series of domestic socio-political struggles normally referred as *frondes*.[13] They were the 'grand Condé', the victorious general of Rocroi and Lens; Gaston d'Orléans, brother of Louis XIII and uncle of the young king; and finally Jean-François-Paul de Gondi, coadjutor bishop of Paris with the title archbishop of Corinth and the right of succession to the Paris see.[14] Gondi was the most dangerous, but Condé, the easily bored, arrogant hero of the battlefield, impatient of all intrigue, was to hold the balance between the subtle Italian-blooded Gondi, impetuous, but lucid and calculating in pursuit of power, and the even more Italian, crafty and infinitely patient Mazarin. All three – Condé, Gaston and Gondi – were in 1648 still cooperating with Mazarin and the regent.

Gondi was a skilful dissimulator. He was also ambitious, wanted a red hat, had spies everywhere, and thought he would make as good a first minister as Mazarin, of whose real advantage, the true relationship with the queen and probably with the young king, he appears however to have been unsuspicious. Gondi's early prowess as lover and duellist masked a high intelligence, but was eclipsed in the public eye by his reputation as a reforming prelate and preacher of renown. Gondi was gauche, myopic, and ugly. His duelling and numerous concurrent liaisons with the wives and daughters of the great, virtually bereft of emotional content on either side, must be regarded as manifestations of a frenetic determination to boost his self-confidence by proving that in spite of his appearance, he could both please others and impose himself.

He had to borrow 48,000 livres for his episcopal bulls. A fortnight after they were signed on 5 October 1643 he took his doctorate in theology, and preached on 1 November, the day after he received them.[15] Only in the course of November did he take holy orders, becoming a priest prior to his episcopal consecration in Notre-Dame on 31 January 1644. On 25 August 1648 Gondi had spoken out before the court against the taxation of ecclesiastical property, the day before he presided over the formal *Te Deum* in Notre-Dame.

Gondi, who was known for his not necessarily disinterested distribution of alms to the poor, left the cathedral after the *Te Deum* still in his vestments to discover the city in uproar at the arrest of Broussel.[16] He found La Meilleraye, still grand master of the artillery as well as *surintendant des finances*, leading some guards and being harassed by a stone-throwing crowd. He blessed the mob, rescued La Meilleraye, whose wife's lover he had once been, and took him to the Palais-Royal, where Anne and Guitaut, captain of the guards, had been joined by Mazarin, Longueville, Condé and Gaston.

Omar Talon estimated that about 1,260 barricades were put up within hours. Further barricades were put up overnight alongside the chains blocking street entrances put in place by the Paris authorities to control mob movements. Gondi would at this point willingly have taken on the governorship of Paris, but the crisis which would have made that possible was averted when his advice to conciliate the crowd was followed. Peace was momentarily restored on the promise to release Broussel, although disturbance continued the next day, when the chancellor, Pierre Séguier, accompanied by his brother, the bishop of Meaux, and his daughter, on his way to the Palais de Justice to suspend the *parlement*, found his carriage blocked by a barricade, was recognized and pursued by the crowd, and ordered his coachman to stop at the first open courtyard on the Quai des Augustins. All three hid undiscovered while the house was ransacked, and were eventually rescued by La Meilleraye, but there were three deaths in the ensuing violence. The crowd must somehow have been disciplined, since the goods stolen from the house were spontaneously returned.[17]

The *parlement* suspended its own sitting after two hours, and marched *en masse* to the Palais-Royal followed by a crowd, said to be of some 20,000. The situation remained inflammable, with pockets of suspicious townsfolk ready to break into violence at even unconfirmed rumours of retributory repression. Elements of the populace demanded the handing over of the king into their safekeeping. It was the *parlement* which ordered the dismantling of the barricades, as the court had lost all authority. Chavigny, the governor of Vincennes from where Beaufort had escaped on 31 May, was arrested on 18 September because, Olivier d'Ormesson suggests, he was a possible replacement for the hated Mazarin.

Mazarin had spent the night of 26 August 1648 preparing for the royal party to flee. He turned down an offer of help from Christine of Sweden, but it may well have been known that he was recalling troops from the German front. News spread not only by word of mouth, but by hastily printed pamphlets and placards. The citizens of Paris had become easy prey for trouble-makers of any motivation, including Spanish infiltrators, of whom there were certainly some. By 29 August Mazarin realized that it was essential to remove the king and the regent from Paris, but when they did go briefly to Rueil, the Parisian reaction was such that Mazarin realized that any future departure from the capital would have to be conducted in secrecy.

On Condé's return from Lens, his support was solicited by both Mazarin, whom at bottom he despised, and by the *parlement,* which invited him to collaborate in reactivating the prohibition of 1617 forbidding foreigners any ministerial role in the government of France. He twice dined with Gondi, nearly doing a deal with him involving a cardinal's hat for his own brother, Conti. However, Condé was not fully committed, Gondi was afraid that the *parlement* would act precipitately against Anne, and Mazarin thought he might be able to avoid civil disturbance until the peace with Germany was signed in Westphalia.[18]

Condé, Gaston and Mazarin managed to restrain Anne's hawkishness and on 22 October she signed a document handing over taxation rights to the *parlement,* to be registered two days later at a *lit de justice.* Chavigny was freed and the court recalled from Saint-Germain to Paris. When, as the *parlement* had demanded, the regent returned on 31 October to the Palais-Royal, Mazarin had already reached an agreement with Condé to reestablish royal authority in Paris. He planned, however, for Anne, Louis and Philippe to leave on 6 January.

Gaston, Condé and Gondi were all cooperating with Mazarin and the regent. Gaston in particular, drawing 1 million livres from the royal treasury in 1648, had presided over a series of conferences at the Luxembourg palace between 13 May and 26 August, seeking to make the officers of the *parlement* aware of the country's financial situation and to delay the revocation of the *intendants.* But, in the eyes of the *parlement* and the populace who, like the *parlement,* regarded the government of Anne and her minister, Mazarin, as tyrannical, perpetually returning to the fact that both were foreigners, all three of Gaston, Condé and Gondi offered advantages as potential regents in place of Anne. Gondi was ambitious for power based on his populism, his outrage at the regent's behaviour, and his contempt at Mazarin's social and intellectual inferiority. Gaston was edging closer to the *parlement,* and Condé was moving more clearly into the regent's camp.

The life of the young king had not yet been totally disrupted by the Fronde in Paris, and still less by its manifestations in Bordeaux, Rouen and Aix, although he must have felt the furious intensity of his mother's feelings and the general sensation of serious menace in the atmosphere. Together they no doubt sowed the seeds of his later heartfelt dislike of the *parlement,* and perhaps of the Paris that the *parlement* had come to signify for him. It is not fanciful to trace to 1648 the roots of his later preference for a court in the countryside in which, apart from the magnificent amenities he could create or enhance, he could exercise absolute royal control without impediment, in which he could conceal his diffidence and hesitancies behind the liturgical minutiae of complex ritual, and which was geographically removed from the instruments of obstruction to his government, the *parlements,* its courts of law and its office-holders.

It is certain that, even if much worse was to come, Louis at ten was already bound to be over-committed to the position of the mother to whom he remained so close, and must necessarily have been becoming aware of the political forces within his kingdom with which he would one day have to deal. It is finally worth noting that his total loyalty to his mother and Mazarin was itself an essential element in the political situation. Were he to have yielded to any blandishment to connive at Mazarin's dismissal, the history of seventeenth-century France would have been different. Mazarin and Anne needed to make certain of his loyalty and if possible to ensure that no such blandishments reached him.

The alliance in Paris between the populace and the office-bearers of the *parlement* broke down over the winter. Neither had been hostile in principle to the authority of the monarchy, although both disliked the way it was being exercised, and Louis had learnt the need to be wary of each. Then on the eve of the feast of the Epiphany, 5 January 1649, Mazarin's plan was put into operation. Anne, Louis, Philippe and her immediate entourage left the Palais-Royal for Saint-Germain.

Dissimulation had been total and totally successful, with twelfth night games before Louis and Philippe went to bed. Mazarin went to a supper party given by the maréchal (later duc) de Gramont. The boys were woken at two a.m. and the party was joined at Cours-la-Reine by Gaston, Condé, his brother Conti and his brother-in-law Longueville. Condé's sister, Mme de Longueville, pregnant with La Rochefoucauld's son and nearing term, stayed behind, but Mazarin, who stayed late gaming at Gramont's party, sent his servants and three nieces, with important papers and small items of large value, like jewels.[19]

Saint-Germain was, as usual when not in use, totally unfurnished. Two camp beds had been brought and two more were found. They were allocated to the king, his mother, Gaston and Mazarin. Everyone else slept on straw in the palace whose windows had not yet been glazed. It was a particularly harsh winter, and a night Louis XIV was never to forget. As soon as the court's flight was discovered, the gates of Paris were closed. The *parlement* was exiled by royal order to Montargis, just over 100 kilometres south of Paris.

Condé's troops blocked access to Paris, and Turenne was ordered to bring his troops back from Germany. Gondi, ordered to join the court, pretended that he could not get out of Paris, and the *parlement* prepared to defend the city which Mazarin obviously planned, with the help of Condé's troops, to blockade into starvation. Anne consulted her confessor to ascertain whether she might in the circumstances, and knowing that the plan would entail deaths, besiege Paris without sin. He said she might.

A hesitant Longueville and a resolute Conti returned from Saint-Germain at two a.m. to join Gondi, and on 11 January Conti, whose deformed spine prevented him from cutting a military figure, was appointed military leader of the Fronde. Longueville was despatched to rally forces in Normandy, and a squadron of Gondi's regiment, called Corinth after his see, raised at his own expense, was defeated on 28 January in an action to open a route by which Paris might be provisioned which became known as 'First Corinthians'. In France, Normandy, Poitou, Guyenne and the south were entirely disaffected, and the *parlements* of Brittany and Languedoc followed Paris in proscribing Mazarin. Mazarin, however, disliked the idea of a battle with the forces joining together to oust him, always preferring the slow, less overtly violent tactics of the blockade, which allowed time for consideration and negotiation, to those of the pitched battle.

Condé, who preferred battles, did however win one at Charenton on 8 February, when the Fronde army again attempted to break open a route through the blockade. Condé murdered his prisoners and left no route by which Paris could be provisioned. Turenne, brother of the rebel Bouillon, now declared himself for the Fronde, but Mazarin, anticipating the defection, had made sure of buying over his troops with money borrowed from Condé and 1.5 million livres raised from the banker Barthélemy Hervart. Turenne himself had to flee to Holland at Stenay. Peace, signifying victory for the court, was signed at Rueil on 11 March 1649. Gondi accepted its provisions only in May, and on 13 July went to Compiègne to invite the court in the name of the citizens to return to Paris. The regent and Louis, not quite eleven years old, returned on 18 August, but the young king's traumas were not yet over.

Mazarin said that he amused himself by collecting such of the vast collection of pamphlet attacks on him known as 'Mazarinades' as he could get hold of.[20] No one knows whether Louis saw any of the Mazarinades which Mazarin boasted that he had collected, but it is difficult to see how he can have been kept unaware of them. They varied from the learned to the violent and the vilificatory, via the pointed and the poetic, the accusatory and the witty. Some were almost pornographically obscene, attacking Anne of Austria in the vilest of terms, often for the relationship with Mazarin which they supposed, as well as calling for Mazarin's murder. None was anti-royalist. Many gave rise to popular songs, and Mazarin's paternity of the king was openly chanted in the streets. Louis must have known about the accusation, and he can scarcely have failed to have reflected later in life on the possibility of its truth, even if he had not been told so.[21]

The populace, whose hostility towards Mazarin remained undiminished, welcomed the king back with noisy acclamation when he returned to Paris on 18 August 1649, congratulating Anne on returning their king to them. Gondi made his peace with Mazarin, although he offered his support to Condé as soon as Condé's rift with Mazarin became apparent. For the moment, however, although tension slackened in the summer of 1649, Gondi was only lying low, and the threat to the government from the nobility was predictably leading towards renewed hostility. Mazarin's political acuity was never more skilfully deployed than in the summer of 1649 when, in addition to prosecuting the war with Spain in the Low Countries and quietening the unrest in the south, he successfully fomented antagonism among the former *frondeurs*. His first concern was to make certain of a reconciliation between Anne and both Mme de Chevreuse and Gaston d'Orléans.

The difficulty was Condé's inordinate demands for reward for services rendered during the siege of Paris. He now wanted the return of the overlordship of France's maritime commerce, which his wife's brother had held until his death without heir in 1645, and which had subsequently been retained by the crown. He also demanded the principality of Montbéliard, which would have made him an imperial prince as well as the senior prince of the blood in France.

In addition, he wanted a cardinal's hat for his brother Conti, a place in the *conseil d'en-haut* for his brother-in-law Longueville, and his own appointment to govern the fort at Pont-de-l'Arche in Normandy, which would have commanded the road from Paris to Rouen. Mazarin genuinely tried to acquire Montbéliard from Württemberg to please Condé, but he felt that Longueville, governor of Normandy and in command of the forts of Caen, Dieppe and the Vieux-Palais at Rouen, already had sufficient power in Normandy. Longueville was also sovereign prince of Neuchâtel, and Condé was governor of part of Burgundy and Champagne. Between them, Condé, Conti and their sister's husband governed about a sixth of France.

In June Mazarin had wanted Condé to lay siege to Cambrai, but Condé, as always preferring direct attack, turned down the command, which was given to the comte d'Harcourt. He was forced to lift the siege after ten days on 3 July. As a result Mazarin was forced to make further compromises, giving the fort at Pont-de-l'Arche to Longueville, and undertaking in a document signed on 2 October neither to make any senior appointment nor to arrange advantageous marriages for his nieces without Condé's consent. Condé, who wanted Mazarin's ministerial position for himself, if not indeed to share the monarchy with the young king, began to behave insolently towards the cardinal. The final rupture was predictable, and did not appear to be far off.

There was a multitude of incidents, of which the most important was Condé's success in imposing a wife of his choosing on the young duc de Richelieu, still a minor but governor of Le Havre under the tutelage of Richelieu's niece, and of achieving his retention of that important position in spite of Anne's order replacing him. Mazarin was even forced to declare on 16 January 1650 that he would defend the Condé interests whenever the occasion might arise.

Mazarin's way of dealing with the situation was to ally with his former enemies, the *parlementaires,* and to have Condé, Conti and Longueville arrested in the north-east on 19 January 1650. In spite of his heroic stature, the Parisians had not forgiven Condé, whom they blamed for trying to starve them to death in 1649. Of the three only Longueville, Condé and Conti's brother-in-law, was not a prince of the blood. The conditions of arrest were not physically unpleasant, and the three princes had their suite of servants, but mass was said in French in case a message was slipped into the Latin that the princes would understand, but that their guards would not.

Condé's carriage had been fired at on 11 December 1648 and, although it was empty, a lackey had been killed in the following carriage. Condé blamed Gondi and Beaufort, a duke and, as grandson of Henri IV, a prince of the blood. Condé arraigned them before the *parlement,* alone competent to try dukes and princes of the blood, but found the still resentful *parlement* unwilling to act. Gondi and Beaufort were forced to seek Mazarin's protection, although by November 1650 Gondi was attacking Mazarin again, and working to ally the *parlement,* Gaston d'Orléans and the three princes. Gondi and Beaufort were much assisted by Mme de Chevreuse, whose former lover, Châteauneuf, was to recover custody of the seals from the chancellor Séguier.[22] Gondi was to be put forward for his red hat, and the maritime *surintendance* would go to Vendôme with its reversion to his son, Beaufort. Vendôme's elder son, Mercœur, would have the vice-regency of Catalonia.

Mazarin flaunted the arrest of the princes as a sign to foreign powers that order was restored in France. In France itself, the alliance between the court and the *parlement* was fragile, and *intendants* were still carrying out Mazarin's orders, by-passing the governors who owned their offices. Neither Anne nor Mazarin could be assured of any loyalty in the French provinces, although all sympathizers with the uprisings against centralized power acknowledged their reverence for divinely originating royal authority and for its repository, the king himself.

Louis at the age of eleven was accordingly taken by his mother and Mazarin during the first part of 1650 to rally support for the government on a tour of the provinces, where recently ceded forts, which had been distributed between the three imprisoned princes and their supporters, were quickly taken back into royal control. Mme de Longueville, Condé's sister, had tried and failed to raise Normandy against the regent, and after a series of adventures took temporary refuge in Rotterdam. Mazarin thought she had plotted his death.[23] After a three-week morale-boosting journey through Normandy and a fortnight's respite in Paris, on 5 March, Louis was taken by Mazarin and Anne to Burgundy.

Condé's arrest had entailed stripping him of his governorship of the province. He still had loyal followers, and a month's siege was required to reduce the fort of Bellegarde (today Seurre, to the east of Beaune and south of Dijon) to subjection. It was Louis's first scent of battle, and the enthusiasm he inspired among the soldiers as well as the trappings of battle exhilarated him. Mazarin wrote to Lionne on 11 April 1650 that even the soldiers of the besieged fort shouted 'Vive le roi', fired in salute, and said they would abstain from firing on the king's army for the day.

Anne had to travel again to Normandy, before going to the west for the pacification of Guyenne, where after a blockade she and Louis entered Bordeaux on 5 October. This time she broke down with fatigue, her health no doubt worsened by being bled four times in an effort to restore her. She had to be carried home in short stages, and Mazarin had to leave her in Paris when he left on 1 December to deal with Spanish pressure on the north-east front in Champagne. Turenne had re-aligned his allegiance with the court after deserting the regent in 1649, but the imprisonment of the princes made him rejoin the Spaniards in the Low Countries, and Mazarin, along with forces commanded by du Plessis-Praslin, was lucky in achieving a severe defeat of the Spanish army at Rethel late in December. Turenne was forced to flee again to Stenay, where he rejoined Mme de Longueville. The attachment he had formed to her was not strong enough to prevent him now from rallying again to the regent's cause.

The Spaniards had encroached far enough into France from the Low Countries for Mazarin to fear that they would attempt to liberate his valuable hostages, the three princes, who were accordingly moved away from the front, at first to Marcoussis and then to Le Havre. The *parlement* was becoming restive at their treatment. They had not been charged or tried, and increasing support was being found for them.

At the end of January 1651 a series of alliances known as the Union des deux Frondes[24] was signed by the forces aligned against Mazarin, specifying the benefits which would accrue to Gaston, who would have the right to nominate members of the king's council, to Gondi, who would get his red hat, to Condé, who would be given the recently abolished title of *connétable*, and to Châteauneuf, who would become first minister. Condé's eight-year-old son would marry one of Gaston's daughters and Conti would marry the daughter of Mme de Chevreuse. When Mazarin returned to Paris, exhausted, on 31 December, he was not immediately aware of how precisely planned the attack on his position had become.

During January 1651, Gaston, and then Mathieu Molé, the chief justice, demanded the release of the princes. Anne was not yet sufficiently recovered to be moved from Paris, as in January 1649. On 1 February Gaston declared that he would not appear at the council again until Mazarin was dismissed from it. He called together the marshals of France to instruct them henceforward to take orders from himself alone. He was attempting to assume virtually royal authority, to which he had so often aspired during the lifetime of his brother, Louis XIII.

On 4 February Gaston and Gondi encouraged the *parlement* to demand not only freedom for the princes, but also the dismissal of Mazarin. On the 5th the members of the provincial nobility in Paris formed an illicit assembly and demanded the convocation of the Estates General, with countrywide representation from nobility, clergy and populace. The clergy assembly, in session since May 1650, also demanding the liberation of the princes, refused to vote its customary 'free gift' to the crown. Gaston's demand of the military authorities that they should take orders from him alone was now echoed by the *parlement*, which issued the same instructions to the senior civil officers. Anne would not use military resistance within Paris on account of the danger that the king would be taken from her. Late on the evening of 6 February, Mazarin left the Palais-Royal on foot and in disguise to make his way to the Paris gate where horses and an escort awaited to accompany him to Saint-Germain, where Anne, Louis and Philippe were to join him the next day.

Unfortunately for Anne, Mme de Chevreuse told Gaston d'Orléans that Anne intended to follow Mazarin with the king, and by next day on Gondi's instructions the Palais-Royal was being watched, and was then surrounded. The anti-Mazarin coalition was not going to let Louis escape. The captain of Gaston's guards slept in Louis's room, where the presence of the king had to be vouched for by a delegation from the Parisian crowd. Gondi even proposed abducting the royal sons and putting Anne into a convent, but Gaston thought there was no need for quite such drastic measures.

On the 8th, Anne was constrained to commit herself to excluding all persons of foreign origin or allegiance from her government. That included cardinals, and precluded the possibility of a ministerial post for Gondi if he were to be made a cardinal. On the 9th the *parlement* ordered Mazarin to leave the country within a fortnight with all foreigners in his household. On the 10th Anne was obliged to consent to Mazarin's exile and to freeing the imprisoned princes. She managed, however, to get word to Mazarin to whom she had earlier secretly given full powers to act as he thought best in the matter of the princes. Mazarin reached Le Havre where he was allowed to see the princes, although only without any escort.

He released the princes, trying to persuade them that they owed their imprisonment to Gondi and their release to Anne, and with a diminishing entourage made his way with the humiliating help of a Spanish passport and escort to the Brühl château of the archbishop-elector of Cologne to whom Anne had already written. Mazarin was given an enthusiastic official welcome. Mazarin may have been the enemy of Spain, but he was after all the faithful servant of the king of Spain's sister, and the Spaniards did not miss the irony of the situation any more than Mazarin himself, although they naturally relished it more. At his mother's behest Louis signed the letter ordering Mazarin into exile. It was accompanied by as tender a note from Anne as was possible in such public circumstances. Condé returned to Paris and was met on 16 February at Saint-Denis by Gondi, Gaston and Beaufort. Condé was restored to all his former offices and privileges, and Pierre Corneille's *Nicomède*, first played towards the end of February, reflected the still growing public sympathy for him.

The anti-Mazarin coalition soon split. Mazarin was to point out that Gondi had changed sides six times in eighteen months. Anne had agreed to the convocation of the Estates General, but she had agreed with Mazarin to defer it until after the king's majority on his thirteenth birthday, 5 September 1651, when Louis could annul anything that was decided.[25] The nobles, however, wanted the Estates to be convoked before the majority, and the majority itself to be deferred until Louis's eighteenth birthday. During the intervening five years Anne would have a council of twenty-one members charged with implementing the decisions of the Estates.

This proposal implied a major constitutional upheaval, and would have frustrated the ambitions of Gaston, reducing his power to that of one vote among twenty-one, of Condé, who still hoped that his house might one day to succeed to the crown and rule by divine right, and of the *parlement*, which wanted sole control. The assembly of nobles was accordingly dispersed, with the net result that the spectre which it had evoked of a monarchy limited by a representative council in fact ensured the country's acceptance of its polarized alternative, the absolute monarchical power which Louis was to inherit.

Even before Richelieu's death Mazarin had begun to surround Anne with highly placed advisers on whom he could rely. They came to include Lionne, secretary of the queen's commands, Servien and Le Tellier, members of the *conseil d'en-haut*, the retired British diplomat Montagu and maréchal du Plessis-Praslin, the governor of Louis's younger brother, Philippe. There were others, too, including Mercœur, who went through with a secret marriage to Laura Mancini, Mazarin's niece, at Brühl in July 1651, and Millet de Jeure, employed by Richelieu and now Mazarin's faithful retainer, made Philippe's under-governor to facilitate his access to the regent. He was to be the principal agent securing the conduct of the secret correspondence between Anne and Mazarin.[26]

Mazarin and these advisers successfully adopted the strategy of allowing Condé's arrogance and ambition to sweep him further than the other aspirants to authority would eventually regard as tolerable. Condé was allowed to exchange the governorship of Burgundy, where he nevertheless retained certain posts, for that of Guyenne. He supported his sister, Mme de Longueville in breaking off the marriage preparations of his brother Conti with the daughter of

Mme de Chevreuse, who immediately offered her services to Mazarin.[27] Condé obtained for Conti a promise of the governorship of Provence, with large sums of compensation for himself, Conti and his brother-in-law, Longueville.

The route between Paris and Brühl was naturally watched. As far as is known, the correspondence between Anne of Austria and Mazarin stayed secret. Ciphers were no doubt changed, and a variety of pseudonyms used. Hundreds of private letters must have been burnt. Such letters were seldom entrusted to couriers travelling directly and Mazarin's correspondence went more often via the military government of Sedan, or via the merchants of Antwerp or Liège. From writing a letter to receiving its reply took at least three weeks, and Anne could write and read only when she could guarantee being left undisturbed, as when she went into her chapel ostensibly to pray.[28] The letters were long, several sheets each. Only two close associates were able and permitted to help in the deciphering.

In spite of the frequency and intimacy of the correspondence, Mazarin worried. He also underestimated the emotional pressure being put on Anne and the seriousness of the threat that she would not only be deprived of the regency, but that her children would be removed from her custody. He knew that her political judgement was weak, and that her nature dictated that she would in his absence be tempted to turn her affections elsewhere, although in fact she did not.[29] There is in fact no suspicion of any infidelity to Mazarin from at least as far back as the death of Louis XIII in 1643. Mazarin's own judgement is clearly distorted in his letters by what he had been through and by the uncertainties of his present situation. He gives Anne detailed but quite unrealistic instructions about things to do, things to avoid, attitudes to adopt, and is horrified to hear that the young king has danced a ballet at a court entertainment, or that Anne has brought back Mme de Beauvais, dismissed for connivance in a plot contrived by Condé to give the impression that Anne had another lover.[30]

Unless Le Tellier was lying to please him in a letter of 20 February, Mazarin learnt that at the mention of his name Louis would break into tears, and that he had told his mother that he would recall Mazarin when he reached his majority five months later, on 5 September 1651. Yet nothing consoled Mazarin, or calmed the anxieties which gnawed at him. Predictably, however, his strategy was unwinding itself successfully. Anne was obviously straining very hard to get to him sums of the money of which he was alarmingly short.

By July 1651 Condé's insupportable pretensions had alienated everyone, and most importantly Gondi, who is said to have contemplated the assassination of his former ally, and who had several late and long sessions with Anne, whose female sensibilities he did not neglect to flatter. Anne again consulted her confessor, but drew back from further violence against Condé, or even a second imprisonment. Condé had initiated a pamphlet war against Gondi in which he sought to unveil Gondi's considerable political ambitions, and he was already making overtures to the Spaniards, who were profiting from Mazarin's absence from France, and from the preoccupation of the noble *frondeurs* with their own quarrels.

Gaston and Anne were reconciled, although Gaston still wanted a meeting of the Estates which could postpone Louis's majority, and was shocked when, calling on his nephew on 26 August, less than a fortnight before Louis attained his majority, he was told by Louis, not quite thirteen years old, that he had ten days to decide whether he wanted to belong to his nephew's party or to that of Condé. To Gaston's muttered expression of loyalty, Louis replied that he wanted proof.

Political events reached crisis point on 17 August 1651, when Anne had a series of charges against Condé read by the chancellor to deputations from the three sovereign courts and the *parlement*. Gaston stayed away. On 21 August, both Condé and Gondi came to the *parlement* with an armed force. Uproar nearly ended in open battle. Condé sent La Rochefoucauld, who was siding with him, to withdraw his men from the antechamber, and Gondi went out for the same purpose.

As he came back there occurred the famous incident in which La Rochefoucauld closed the door on Gondi, pinning him to the doorpost and calling on his assistants to stab the coadjutor. Parliamentarians intervened, but Gondi, facing La Rochefoucauld's swordsmen, was also in danger from the room at the back. One of Gondi's attendants stepped between Gondi and the leader of Condé's men, and the son of Molé, the chief justice, persuaded La Rochefoucauld to let Gondi go. Swords had been drawn on both sides, and only the captain of the guards prevented an affray.

This extravaganza of baroque posturing was not yet over. Gondi accused La Rochefoucauld in the chamber of trying to murder him; La Rochefoucauld said he deserved it; Gondi replied that La Rochefoucauld was a coward, and the duc de Brissac, who had left the service of Gaston to align himself with Gondi and was married to one of the archbishop's ex-mistresses, challenged La Rochefoucauld to a duel. La Rochefoucauld accepted, but Gaston prevented it from taking place.

Gondi was forbidden to return to the chamber and Condé remained downstairs next day when the debate resumed. When Condé left with his escort he met Gondi leading a procession in the opposite direction. Fighting almost broke out, but, as convention demanded, Condé descended from his carriage and knelt to receive Gondi's blessing. Gondi bestowed it, and bowed deeply. The script dictated by ecclesiastical protocol had vindicated its superior importance over power squabbling among the aristocracy, and Anne held matters where they were until the declaration of the king's majority, which took place a fortnight later, on 7 September.

It was a splendid occasion. Anne had prepared opinion by communicating to the *parlement* a letter discharging Condé from all the accusations against him, but insisted that the letter should not become public until after the king's majority had been proclaimed. She also had a further declaration against Mazarin registered. It fooled nobody, but drew from Mazarin a deeply stylized protest at the pain that it had inflicted on him and an elaborately posturizing plea to save him from the profound shame into which he had been plunged. Condé alone of the great figures of state was absent from the ceremony. He sent a note which was handed by Conti to Louis just as Louis was about to mount his horse. He passed it to Villeroy, his governor, without opening it, or even looking at its seal. Louis's uniform was smothered in gold braid. Behind him in a carriage came his mother, his younger brother, still briefly the duc d'Anjou for a few minutes longer, although now also known as 'le petit Monsieur', and Gaston, still 'Monsieur'. The crowd went wild with joy.

Louis as king opened the proceedings with a brief speech. Anne gave a short speech resigning the government of the realm into the hands of her son two days after his thirteenth birthday. He replied by thanking her and appointing her after himself as 'chef de mon conseil'. Louis prevented his mother from following all others present in bending a knee in homage. The declaration of the majority was followed by public celebration, including tournaments and ballets. Louis danced his first ballet in public and for the first time was allowed to play cards for money. There is a sense in which nothing was outwardly to change. Anne, still referred to as queen until Louis's own marriage in 1660, continued as if she had still been regent, and her relationship with Mazarin remained unaltered.

What did change was almost impalpable, but none the less real. Government was now conducted directly in the name of the king, the repository of the divinely bestowed authority to govern, and not merely in the name of a regent, who in the hierarchy of authority had never been more than his mother and delegate, and a foreigner at that. That considerably changed sentiment in the nobility, in the government, among the parliamentarians, and even in the country at large. It incidentally changed criticism into lèse-majesté and insurrection into treason, both capital offences.

However illogical, the hardship imposed by poor harvests and war taxation was more tolerable when it was directly authorized by divinely appointed authority than when, with whatever legal legitimacy, it came from Anne and Mazarin, neither of whom was even French by birth. Condé, for instance, wanted to prevent the entry into the council of Châteauneuf, Molé and La Vieuville, which Anne had agreed with the *frondeurs*. Two months earlier Anne would have had to yield. Gaston agreed with Condé, and threatened to absent himself if the new appointments were made. Louis, however, simply ordered the seals to be taken from Séguier and given to Molé, in spite of his technical disqualification as first *président* of the *parlement*. He also commanded Châteauneuf and La Vieuville to appear at the council, which they did as early as the next day, 8 September. Anne's agreement with the *frondeurs* was thereby honoured.

Gaston had even attended his nephew's ceremonial *lever*. That ceremony marked Louis's majority and was the first time he 'held court'. The nation was predictably to suffer for elevating so young a boy into such a position of ostensible power, both because it was impossible to avoid inflicting psychological damage by bestowing such apparent authority on such inexperience, and because it created a power vacuum which invited a struggle for real control.

Gaston had allied with the Fronde only to rid the kingdom of Mazarin. The difficulty for Anne now was to bring Mazarin back without so alienating Gaston as to drive him to join Condé, who had left Paris to rally forces of rebellion in Guyenne, the Bordeaux region of which he had just become governor and which was largely loyal to him. Mazarin was anxious that his own position as Anne's principal adviser should not be usurped by Châteauneuf. Both Anne and Louis wrote to Mazarin promising his immediate recall, but Anne, who could not rely on the council, and who was operating among a flood of hostile and often ribald pamphlets, had to rest her hopes on a small number of Mazarin's friends. The strategy had to be for Mazarin to earn his return by achieving victory over the Spaniards.

Immediately after his majority, Louis was taken by his mother on a tour to re-establish royal authority in the kingdom. On 26 September 1651 they left with 4,000 men for Bourges intending to destroy in Berry, one of Condé's governorships, the authority of Mme de Longueville and her brother Conti, who fled with Nemours to the fort at Montrond. On 7 October the royal party was welcomed by Bourges, where the thirteen-year-old Louis, having attained his majority, was taught how to develop friendly relations with the populace by ordering that the Grosse Tour, long a symbol of their subjection, should be demolished. On the same day he signed the declaration against Condé, Conti and Mme de Longueville, together with Nemours and La Rochefoucauld. The *parlement,* corporately hedging its bet, found reasons not to register the queen's accusation of treason against Condé, Conti and Mme de Longueville.[31] The friends of Mazarin, now a little nearer France at Huy on the Meuse, thought it might be the moment to bring him back, although Anne and Louis intended to move on to counter Condé in Guyenne, to which Gaston controlled the routes from the Meuse.

Anne deferred her departure for Guyenne with Louis until Mazarin's arrival at Poitiers on 28 January 1652, where the king himself met him and escorted him to his lodgings, and where he was left alone with Anne. Châteauneuf did not await the conclusion of that initial interview to resign. Gondi needed at all costs to keep Gaston from supporting Condé's rebellion. Realizing now that Anne's affection made Mazarin's eventual recall inevitable, Gondi had already started to negotiate with Mazarin, using the princess

Palatine as an intermediary.[32] He offered to facilitate Mazarin's return in exchange for the coveted red hat, although the cardinalate would have to precede Mazarin's return which, if allowed to take place first, would inevitably have compromised it. Meanwhile Turenne and Bouillon defected from Condé's cause to serve the queen, the title to which she reverted now that the regency was over.

In fact the invitation of Anne and Louis to Mazarin to return, dated 31 October, was botched by Anne's acceptance of advice to inform Mazarin's Paris friends. As a result the governors and commanders controlling the route from Huy to Bourges were unlikely to honour any governmental orders to allow Mazarin a safe passage in case rebel forces finally prevailed. The safe passes were drawn up in secret and signed by the thirteen-year-old Louis, who clearly enjoyed exercising his new power. As soon as Mazarin entered France on 24 December 1651, the *parlement* rather pointlessly put a price on his head equal to the proceeds from the sale of Mazarin's library of 40,000 volumes whose sale they began. Mazarin would have been in real danger had sentiment in the country not been swinging behind the court, and against both Condé and the recalcitrant *parlement*. Gondi at least had already realized that it was not in the end possible to establish stability of government without consent, and that legitimacy lagged far behind in the fight for power.

Two attempts were made to kidnap Gondi in November 1651. They were organized by La Rochefoucauld in Condé's interest. Gondi escaped by chance, once by taking an unaccustomed route home to give other people a lift from the Chevreuse residence, and once when the hired watch had slipped off to a tavern when Gondi left his mistress. Gondi was able to dispense large sums, perhaps of Spanish origin, in pursuit of the cardinalate, and some of his support was from Jansenist clerical sympathizers, hostile to Mazarin. The consistory of the sacred college was finally held on 19 February 1652, and Gondi heard the news on 1 March. From now on, he is the cardinal de Retz.

The civil war continued. Mazarin arrived in Poitiers on 28 January at the head of 1,500 horse and 2,000 foot soldiers and immediately took charge. Louis supplied the necessary authority. Condé, with whom Gaston had signed an alliance on the 24 January, instructed Beaufort, and Nemours at the head of Spanish troops, to join him in the Bordeaux region. Rohan had raised an insurrection on behalf of Condé in Angers, but royal troops led by Turenne retook Angers on 28 February and moved through Tours, Amboise and Blois to approach Orléans from the south.

The city had wanted to stay neutral, but was about to admit royal troops when Gaston's daughter, la grande Mademoiselle, rowed round the barricaded city, found an open gate, entered and made her way to the central square. She was loyal to Condé and already twenty-four years of age, but aspired to marry Louis, her first cousin and still thirteen. She now governed the town for a month and a half on behalf of her father, admitting Nemours and Beaufort.[33] Their plan to seize the Loire bridges at Gien was foreseen by Turenne, and they were defeated at Jargeau. Condé, worried about Retz's influence over Gaston, left his own troops to Conti and rode with La Rochefoucauld in nine days from Agen to Orléans. After defeating Turenne at Bléneau, he rode with La Rochefoucauld, Beaufort and Nemours to Paris, where Gaston had never succeeded in imposing authority. Paris was exhausted, with one in seven of its citizens destitute, and it was now almost unanimously royalist. Condé's party arrived on 11 April 1652. Against the advice of Retz, the populace let him in.

Both armies grouped near the city, that of Turenne, loyal to Anne, at Saint-Denis and Condé's rebellious troops at Saint-Cloud, hoping to reach the Porte Saint-Honoré by way of Charenton and the Bois de Boulogne. Gaston, although in merely nominal control of the city, allowed Condé to send only baggage through the town, forcing his army to pass round the walls to the Porte Saint-Antoine, where Turenne pushed it from the south to the trap he had laid for it by blocking the road to Vincennes. The trap was closed at dawn on 2 July, pinning Condé's army against the city walls in the Faubourg Saint-Antoine. Mademoiselle herself had the city gates opened to the wounded and had the Bastille canons fired in support of Condé while the remnants of his army entered the city. She had one last salvo fired off in the direction of the royal party, which included Mazarin, out of range on a hilltop. She had saved Condé and, as Mazarin pointed out, immediately ended all hopes of marrying Louis.

The battle had exacted its price. La Rochefoucauld lost an eye and was blind for months. Mazarin lost a fifteen-year-old nephew. Anne had spent the time praying in the Carmelite chapel at Saint-

Denis, later helping to tend the wounded. Beaufort killed Nemours, his sister's husband, in a duel arising from a serious quarrel about strategy at Orléans, and on 9 August, Bouillon died. On 19 August Mazarin went voluntarily and temporarily into exile again to show that it was not his presence, but the inability of the *frondeurs* to govern, which was the cause of continuing domestic violence.

First from Sedan and then from Bouillon, Mazarin continued to govern France. The Paris *parlement,* guided by its more moderate leaders Mathieu Molé and Fouquet, had been transferred by a royal edict of 31 July to Pontoise, where it registered a declaration of Mazarin's innocence of all the crimes of which he had been accused. His private letters to the queen leave no possible doubt that they were lovers, although they are less overtly passionate than the surviving eleven from Anne herself to Mazarin, starting in January 1653, plus a copy of a last letter, as passionate as its predecessors, dated 30 June 1660, when Anne was fifty-nine.

Retz stayed on in Paris, heavily barricading Notre-Dame against possible attack by Condé, his own populist instinct having turned him into the leading advocate of peace. In September he went to Compiègne, invited Louis to return to Paris and restore order and harmony, and received his cardinal's hat on 11 September from the king, just turned fourteen. But although Retz was hissed by the Parisian crowd for failing to bring back peace, Condé left Paris. Louis and the court entered the town on 21 October. Louis held a *lit de justice* on the 22nd forbidding the *parlement,* now re-established in Paris, any participation in the affairs of state, and on the 25th Gaston signed an act of submission to his nephew.

Louis wrote to Mazarin recalling him on the 26th, and Mazarin insisted on the removal from Paris of Retz, although he did not finally return to Paris until 3 February 1653. Condé and Conti were declared guilty of *lèse-majesté,* and Retz, after waiting undecided to consider his options, burnt most of his papers, salvaging some to stuff into his pockets in case he was making a mistake, and visited the Louvre on 19 December, accompanied by only a small retinue. There, he underwent what looks almost like a choreographed arrest, playing his part in the end of the Fronde like the rest of the cast.

He was arrested in an antechamber after having seen both Anne, who was glacial, and Louis, who was friendly and apparently in good spirits. Retz was supposed to accompany Louis to mass, but apparently became anxious at the end of the interview and made to leave through the antechamber, where the maréchal d'Aumont, in spite of his rank still captain of the guards, showed him the order for his arrest.[34] Of all the major characters in the Fronde, only Mazarin and Anne, and with them Louis XIV, had emerged fully victorious.

5

The *Sacre*, Marie Mancini and Marriage

Whatever the 1374 ordinance presumed about the moral and intellectual endowments of French princes, the majority conferred on Louis at thirteen did not make him an instant adult. In July 1653 Mazarin left with Louis for the front.[1] He was not yet fifteen. He considered that Louis needed the experience of seeing from close at hand the army preparing for actual battle, and Louis's personification of authority by divine election with his boyish presence among them did undoubtedly encourage the troops. He became fascinated by Turenne's defensive tactics and by the logistical problems of moving and supplying troops and hundreds of horses who would need daily to be fed and watered in a fortified camp. Mazarin was to visit the front line each year until the Peace of the Pyrénées finally ended the war, although he did not always take Louis. Anne was always impatient of these absences, and it was during them that the couple frequently wrote to each other more often than once a day.

The documentary evidence we have of Mazarin's decisive influence over the young king generally dates from the early 1650s and from the letters of his mother to the cardinal.[2] But it is clearly justified to speak of Mazarin as Louis's 'surrogate father' and even to speak of Mazarin's 'fatherly pride' in Louis's youthful achievements, as have many historians who simply did not entertain the possibility of Mazarin's physical paternity.[3] Mazarin could even write to Anne that she had no need to hear from both Louis and himself 'since she probably could not tell which one was writing', so close were her son and her lover, as by 1653 it is universally admitted that Mazarin must have been. To others, Mazarin referred to Louis in private letters as 'the best friend I have in the world'.[4]

It is probable that much of the practical advice passed on by Louis XIV to the dauphin in his *Mémoires* derives from Mazarin,[5] and it is certain that Mazarin behaved towards Anne and Louis in private as the child's father. The letters between Anne and Mazarin contained coded references to their passionate affection for one another, and to their common care for Louis. Anne's handwriting and spelling are very poor, and the signs of love littering the bottom of her letters are like the kisses of an unrestrained and untidy teenage girl, but her rather gauche expressions of intense affection read sincerely enough, as do Mazarin's rather more refined but equally passionate expressions of love to her.

Anne's biographer, Claude Dulong, has convincingly shown that the wax seal of the folded paper containing the few letters from Anne which have been preserved carried the interwoven initials of AA (for 'Anne d'Autriche') and JCM (for Jules, Cardinal Mazarin), partly encircled by a series of the letter S repeated four times with an oblique vertical line through each, originally signifying the four qualities of love 'sabio, solo, solicito, secreto', a cipher which Anne has also added to the end of two of the eleven autograph letters which are still extant.[6] Mazarin is always careful, 'I would like to say a thousand things about [my] feelings for [you], but I think it is better to do it by word of mouth,' and 'I won't write to you about [yourself] or [myself] or of [your feelings] or of [mine], because the letters run great risk of being intercepted.'

To disentangle the feelings being expressed in guarded and to modern taste stilted seventeenth-century letters, always heavily coded, would necessarily deprive them of the astonishment they provoke. Anne, however, is sometimes almost forthright in alluding to love-making to come. She writes in January 1653:

> I don't know when I can expect you to return . . . All I can say is that I suffer from the obstacles which keep you from coming back, put up only impatiently with the delay, and if [you] knew all [I] suffered from it, I'm sure you would be much moved. I am moved so strongly at the moment that I haven't got the strength to write

for long, and really don't know what I'm saying. I have been
receiving your letters nearly every day, and without that I don't
know what will happen . . . For the delay blame me, who am a
million times yours, and to the last breath. The child[7] sends you
every greeting. Goodbye, I can't go on, and [you] know why . . .

If Mazarin was Louis's father, did Louis know it? He must have known
by his early teens that his mother and Mazarin were lovers, and he
must have suspected from Mazarin's very closeness to him and the
intensity of their relationship that the cardinal was more than just
his godfather and his mother's lover. A great deal in his later attitudes, but especially his attitude to the memory of Louis XIII and
his extreme distaste for homosexual behaviour, reinforces the ante-
cedent probability that he knew that Mazarin was his true father.
The evidence, particularly although not exclusively the letters, is at
any rate simply too strong to admit any cynical hypothesis that
Mazarin was merely using either Anne or Louis, and it would need
to have been both, to satisfy his own ambition.

Louis and Mazarin became very close to one another during the
1650s, travelling annually together to the front, sharing letters to
Anne, who would, when necessary accept a letter from either as her
daily missive. Sometimes, between them, Mazarin and Louis wrote
four on a single day. Anne, who became frightened that she was
importuning Mazarin with several letters a day, is told that Louis
embraces Mazarin nightly and that Mazarin has shown Louis her
letters. He must therefore be presumed to have seen the ciphers
and certainly saw the signs of passionate affection which all the
extant letters contain. On the 13 August 1655 Anne wrote: 'This is
the second letter today . . . I am not writing to the king, since he
knows that this letter is for both of you', and in August 1658, when
Louis, almost twenty, had stayed with the court, Anne wrote to
Mazarin at the northern front: 'The king is not writing to you
because you don't recognize the difference between our handwriting, any more than between our feelings, which for you are the
same.' Such a proclaimed identity of handwriting suggests that Anne
was virtually congratulating herself on the continued over-mothering
of Louis, the reasons for which the Fronde makes comprehensible.
Even if, on a particular day, there was only one letter, Anne's heart
and the king's were joined together in affection for Mazarin,

although the affection of the fifty-four-year-old woman cannot have been of the same quality as that of her nineteen-year-old son.

The literary register of these letters is that of the love letter between mature partners whose liaison is of long standing. It surpasses the simple domestic intimacy of routine family correspondence rather as the letters of Mme de Sévigné to her daughter surpass the normal feelings expressed in letters from mothers to daughters. Anne's letters contain strong private expressions of fondness and of longing, while treating the now near-adult king as still in need of proper training.[8] It is significant that Anne does not mention Philippe. Her attitude towards her children differed markedly in a way which cannot entirely be explained by the greater importance of Louis as heir to the throne and her apparent fidelity to Mazarin. It seems likely, as already suggested, that Anne was frightened that Philippe would come to challenge his elder brother's position as dauphin, and later as king, as Gaston d'Orléans had never ceased to challenge the position of Louis XIII. Abetted or initiated by Mazarin, Anne may well have made some blinkered attempt to avoid any such danger by starting to treat Philippe as if he had been a girl.

Philippe was probably effeminate by temperament, but Anne did whatever she could to encourage this element in his psychological make-up, in particular by encouraging his close friendship with the extraordinary François-Timoléon, abbé de Choisy, whose regrettably unreliable memoirs probably tell the truth when they tell us how he was himself dressed as a girl, with ears pierced and beauty spots, to the extent that he says he felt that he was genuinely female.[9]

Philippe at the age of twelve or thirteen was a constant caller on Choisy, as were Mazarin's nieces and some other young ladies of the court. They would dress Philippe up and groom his hair. Choisy asserts that Philippe, too, would have liked to dress as a woman, but was inhibited by his public position. Only in the evening could he relax with earrings and beauty spots. Later on, he was to be seriously lacking in self-confidence and to indulge his taste in lace, ribbons, jewels and trinkets. Mme de La Fayette remarks with gentle perceptivity in her 1659 portrait on his extreme effeminacy and an accompanying narcissism. It appeared to render him incapable of being attached to anyone except himself. Nancy Mitford is less perceptive but more forthright, 'In spite of being one of history's most famous sodomites, Monsieur had two wives, a mistress and eleven legitimate children.'[10]

Louis in his *Mémoires* tries to make it clear to his own son that the king is only the repository for the time being of sovereign power, which it is his sacred duty to pass on intact. When Louis is later at such pains to seek to legitimize his extension of French frontiers with reference to the laws of inheritance, by implication considered constitutional and therefore of divine instititution in early modern France, it is because he wishes to believe that the derivation of his sovereign authority directly from God justifies his war-making, however scant a part the desire to enforce divinely bestowed rights may actually have played in Louis's motivation in going to war.

Louis is reliably thought to have disliked studying from books. In spite of the care lavished on providing him with textbooks written especially for him, the custodians of Louis's education, allowing him privileged access to approved grandees, whether military, religious or civil, successfully achieved in him mindsets, attitudes and assumptions which might, had all gone well, have strengthened his self-confidence, but which needed to be reinforced by a liberal education.

The memorialists naturally give a gilded account of the educational accomplishments of the young king, in whose name even a sumptuously bound French translation of Caesar's *Commentaries* was published in 1651.[11] The truth however appears to be that to his regret he never properly mastered Latin, the language of culture and international diplomacy, but he did learn his catechism, and a smattering of elementary mathematics, drawing and Italian. Mazarin was having him trained primarily in the disciplines required for statecraft and kingship, cultivating both his interest in military matters and his sense of rank. By the time he was twelve, Louis could write reasonably good French, although his handwriting was inelegant. His smattering of Latin was not enough to translate even Caesar on his own, but he excelled at dancing, fencing and, above all, horsemanship. In music, he was attempting to master the spinet after the lute and the guitar. Desmarets de Saint-Sorlin designed a pack of playing cards to teach him the elements of classical mythology.

It was necessary that however Louis's tastes and interests developed – and much could be done about that – Louis should at least unquestioningly adopt the values required of him to implement what remained essentially Richelieu's view of France's potential, and that

[81]

meant unintentionally enhancing the insecurities. Louis's role was to be far too important to be left to be determined by his own ideas.[12] He was going to be brought up unable to disavow an upbringing, what is still referred to in France as a *formation,* contributing to ostentious display at home and a drive for conquest abroad, with appropriate disregard for the necessary cost in suffering and death.

Louis was in many ways a man who meant well, was intelligent and perceptive, whose instincts were often humane, and who could be kindly. The more unpleasant and sometimes aggressively insecure character traits he was to develop, are wholly due to his upbringing. The unusually severity of the insecurity that very early became apparent was no doubt the unavoidable result of the need from earliest youth to play, and even to grow into a public role, and to dissimulate his true circumstances and natural feelings, which were strong and gave rise to bouts of bad temper.

What has to be of concern in his biography is how it might be possible to reconcile a real concern for his people, which he deluded himself into believing that he had, with the pursuit of a policy so belligerent as inevitably to add to the effects of the natural disasters mostly of failed harvests, which in the *Mémoires* he constantly blames. Why was he later, in 1668, at pains to have records of decrees promulgated against royal authority during the Fronde simply expunged from the records of the *parlement*?[13] The need of all-powerful rulers to re-write the past is perhaps better recognized for what it is today than it was then, but it was always a danger signal.

The key to the enigma of Louis's personality must lie in the involuntary but all-pervading self-deception, perhaps boosted by Mazarin but masquerading as self-justification in the *Mémoires.* There are occasions when the extraordinarily self-satisfied text lapses into a language which suggests that Louis did regard his position as close to divine. In view of the Christian scriptural image and devotional topos that the faithful are members of the body of which Christ is the head, it is, for instance, disconcerting to find Louis dictating, 'We should think of the welfare of our subjects much more than our own. They seem to be a part of ourselves, since we are the head of a body of which they are the members.'[14] Did Louis really think of his subjects that 'it is only for their own good that we should give them laws', a power 'exclusively intended to enable us to work more effectively for their happiness'. It is not necessary to have recourse to any hypothesis involving hypocrisy to see the power behind the self-deception.

Did Louis really believe that the specific character of the French monarchy was 'l'accès libre et facile des sujets au prince'?[15] It is true that later, at Versailles, once a week a table would be put out for members of the public to deposit requests or complaints, and that these requests would be passed to the relevant departments of state for comment, after which Louis would grant or deny them, or much more often procrastinate with the celebrated 'Je verrai', by no means inevitably a polite way of denying a request.

Yet provision for getting a written request on to a table at Versailles once a week cannot be regarded as more than the merest token, a concession to the tradition of easy familiarity built up between Henri IV and his subjects and between Louis XIII and his soldiers. It also required the mediation not only of someone physically present at Versailles, but of someone who could write. Louis did seek the fair adjudication of grievances which arose between his subjects on civil matters, but his anxieties about the administration of justice were confined to situations in which his own supreme authority was not being even remotely challenged.

The encouragement of the excitement aroused in Louis during his youth by military matters, equestrian feats, and glorious moments in the history of France was the result of deliberate policy. There were more important things for Louis to learn than those contained in the pedestrian textbooks written for him by La Mothe le Vayer.[16] The system was, as we shall see, to fail not in the matter of religious education, which made of Louis an orthodox, pious, and committed Christian, obsessive rather than saintly, after the model of his mother's baroque Catholicism, but when, especially during young manhood, it provoked clashes with the allure of sinful sexual attachments.

It also barely, if at all, avoided sowing the seeds of arrogance. When in January 1652 a delegation of *parlementaires* led by Pomponne de Bellièvre called on him at Poitiers, Louis simply took the document of remonstrance and declared that he would put it before his council. When Bellièvre tried to explain that the *parlement* had itself the right of direct access to the council, the king, aged thirteen, simply dismissed him, 'You may go, sir. I have spoken.'[17] Time would show how educationally dangerous it was to allow a thirteen-year-old to exercise that sort of power in that sort of way. And the divine right which made Louis king did not extend to a licence to be ill-mannered or disrespectful to his seniors.

On 7 June 1654, the fifteen-year-old king was finally crowned king of France in a ceremony, the *Sacre,* with its incorporation of liturgical elements from an episcopal consecration. The *Sacre* did in fact still confer ecclesiastical status, the tonsure, and the minor 'orders' associated with the sacrament of order.[18] The coronation no longer conferred the already inherited kingship, but it displayed it, and ostentatiously signified the bestowal of the divinely originated spiritual authority inseparable from the medieval monarchy. Even if it had spasmodically been eroded since the high middle ages, Louis needed some form of spiritual authority to appoint bishops and regulate the behaviour and civil rights and obligations of the clergy.

None the less, in the circumstances of 1654, the ceremony was intended to manifest, particularly in front of the recently rebellious great feudal overlords, that royal authority was being re-asserted and was sacerdotal as well as secular. Louis prostrated himself like any candidate for ordination to the priesthood, and was anointed in accordance with ancient practice in Reims cathedral with the holy oils kept in Reims at the abbey of Saint-Rémy and by tradition sent down from heaven to Saint Rémy for the consecration of the founder of Gaul, Clovis, in AD 496.

The ceremonial was also exploited for its potential for pageantry. The cathedral was full by six a.m. and a procession led by the bishops of Beauvais and Châlons hammered liturgically three times on the door of the royal apartments to demand Louis XIV 'whom God has given us for king'. Louis was then led in a magnificent procession to the decorated cathedral, where the high altar was partitioned off by the spectacular Reims tapestries, now mostly still in the Reims museum, where a special balcony had been constructed for all the grandest personnages of the realm, although Gaston did not come, Condé was in rebellion, and of the princes of the blood only the king's brother and Vendôme, son of Henri IV and Gabrielle d'Estrées, attended.

Gaston's daughter, la grande Mademoiselle, who had thrown in her lot with Condé, was not invited, and was contemptuous of those who had to be asked to replace the absent princes of the blood, but the twelve peers of France were present, six lay – the dukes of Burgundy, Normandy and Aquitaine, and the counts of Flanders, Champagne and Toulouse – and six ecclesiastical – the archbishop of Reims and the bishops of Laon and Langres, all three of whose sees carried dukedoms, and the bishops of Noyon, Beavais and Châlons, who were also counts. Since the archbishop of Reims was not in holy orders, the ceremony was carried out by his senior suffragan, the bishop of Soissons, and since neither Laon nor Langres had yet been consecrated, their functions were filled by the archbishops of Bourges and Rouen. The ecclesiastical proprieties were as a matter of course meticulously observed.

After the ceremony alms were distributed, and Louis's curative touch exercised on some 200 of the sick. At least half a dozen pamphlets were issued to describe the grandeur of the setting and the ceremony, which was not, however, followed by the traditional joyous return to Paris and the triumphal entry into the city. Mazarin and Anne had organized a deliberate snub of the city which had behaved so antagonistically during the Fronde, which it had originated and during which it threw itself behind Gaston, half-favourable to Condé. In due course Louis, although he never much liked Paris, was to have his quotient of squares, statues, arches and monumental buildings erected there, but he did not consent to a formal triumphal entry until he returned with his bride in 1660.

Mazarin, Anne and Louis continued to constitute in each other's eyes a family unit. Mazarin took care to initiate Louis into the mysteries of statecraft, including domestic administration and diplomacy with foreign powers, inviting him to attend inceasingly lengthy and complex council sessions, and only rarely spending any length of time apart from him. Louis's essays turned into drafts of written solutions to some of the problems discussed, and Mazarin was deeply concerned to make Louis assiduous in preparing for the moment of Mazarin's death when, as Mazarin repeatedly told Louis, he should personally take over the active governnment of the kingdom. Indeed, the intensity with which Mazarin prepared Louis to take over after his death the functions which he was himself meanwhile exercising, and the promptitude with which in 1661 Louis made clear after Mazarin's death that he would henceforward act as his own first minister, further bolster the argument for Mazarin's paternity. Mazarin's position, which made him morally irreplaceable, does nothing to weaken the arguments for the assumption that it was founded on a physical relationship.

Richelieu had heavily promoted moral, social and religious elevation of serious, scripted French drama, and had conferred respectability on it, hoping that its vogue would replace that for the slapstick comedy of the Italian companies. Mme de Motteville explains that the elevated sentiments displayed and promoted in Pierre Corneille's plays were a positive encouragement to virtue 'parmi les occupations vaines et dangereuses de la reine'. What Mme de Motteville considered to be the queen's dangerous diversions is not entirely clear. They are quite likely not to have included her compulsive passion for gaming, but obviously referred to her taste for Italian *commedia dell'arte*, and must have referred to her flirtatious disposition as well as the intimacy with Mazarin of which Mme de Motteville disapproved.

Anne's attachment to the Italian comedy, generally dependent on mime and music, frequently bawdy, sometimes satirically topical, often played in the smaller of the two theatres built by Richelieu in what had become the Palais-Royal, was so great that, even during her period of mourning after the death of Louis XIII, she would attend in disguise. A staircase direct from the queen's rooms gave private access to her box. The popular Italian comedy had in practice been banished from Paris during Richelieu's ascendancy.

During the years following the *Sacre*, while the war with Spain dragged on as France emerged from the Fronde, the French, now under Turenne, increasingly achieved military supremacy. Louis had himself been undergoing what might reasonably, if anachronistically, be regarded as the Sturm und Drang of his late teens. In 1655, Louis was to become seventeen. Mazarin and Anne were still relying on Montagu to patch up their occasional lovers' quarrels, like that occasioned by Mazarin's willingness to rehabilitate Condé. In addition to Louis's religious formation in the care of his mother, and his mostly practical training in administrative and military matters at the hands of Mazarin and Turenne, even the court diversions of these years were designed to prepare him for the role he was being prepared to play, the Roi soleil.

In fact, of course, the more magnificent the splendour with which Louis was vested even in the great series of *ballets de cour* mostly devised and written by Isaac de Bensserade,[19] the easier it would be to place Louis on a remote pedestal to be a spectacular visible symbol of a real power wielded by someone else. The first of Bensserade's ballets to be danced by the king was the 1651 private 'Ballet de Cassandre',[20] played on 26 February when the king was twelve, and given at least four performances, presumably to distract the king from Mazarin's exile to which Anne had just been forced to consent.

The *ballets de cour* seldom had anything approaching a plot, although they might have had a central theme. They were composed generally of about a score of *entrées,* ballets or moving tableaux in up to half a dozen of which the king and his immediate family might dance. The scenery was often highly elaborate, moved about with the help of heavy machinery which also enabled chariots to cross the sky, winged horses to disappear behind clouds or monsters to emerge from raging seas.

Bensserade, who was a dramatist before he acquired the virtual monopoly of *ballets de cour* from 1651 to 1669, lacked any sort of personal or literary refinement. His manners were worse than un-gracious, his verse inelegant, and his humour coarse, but he was clearly to be shoe-horned into the Academy by the king in 1674 and he won the favour, too, of the king's brother, Philippe. He was given annual pensions of 3,500 livres, and died in possession of a large number of minor benefices.

It was Bensserade who was reponsible for the *Ballet de la nuit* for the 1653 carnival. The Venetian ambassador, at that time Giovanni Sagredo, had noted the previous Christmas eve that the king was applying himself all day long 'exclusively to learning this ballet'.[21] He also alleged of Louis that 'gambling, dancing and the comedy are his only concerns.' The ballet opened with the moon, dressed in a black robe, being drawn by an owl across the sky in a chariot accompanied by the twelve yellow-skirted hours of the night. The seventh *entrée* changes to a street scene, and the fourteenth to a yard in which the maimed and lame are healed.

Still to come were the descent of Venus in a machine, a witches' sabbath, and a house on fire. The climax came when Philippe, play-ing the morning star, announced the arrival of the sun, 'c'est le jeune Louis'. The Sun King finally appeared in a gold costume radiating light and crowned with ostrich plumes. The public was admitted, and there were more than half a dozen performances with forty-three *entrées.* The king danced six roles in all. Mazarin was successfully attempting to bestow on Louis an allure of untouchable magnificence, using the young king's agility to help create his iconography.

Louis danced different roles in the various *entrées* and the ballets invariably received favourable notices in Renaudot's *Gazette* which had remained faithful to Mazarin during the Fronde. Its point of view, although not necessarily commanding sympathy, is at least identifiable, and it is useful in gauging the sentiments of the literate public. Loret's *Muse historique,* which appeared in octosyllabic doggerel from 1650 to 1655, also attracted a subsidy from Mazarin, but printed a mixture of gossip, scandal, announcements, reviews and social and political reportage of which certainly elements appear to have been paid for, making it less reliable as a reflection of opinion. Loret's notice of the *Ballet de la nuit* had to be compiled on the basis of the programme, because he had had to queue for a rather bad seat. He was given a place in the parterre for 6 March.

The propagandist intention behind these court entertainments seems incontestable, although by no means all the roles played by Louis were deities or stars. Some were of the lowliest condition, but that, too, was of course part of the propaganda, cementing the relationship of king and people, themselves elevated by his grandeur. The entertainments were open to the public at least until Vigarani's new house was opened at the Tuileries in 1662, after which access to court functions became less easy. Mostly the *ballets de cour* were put on during the carnival week preceding Lent. In 1654 the cast of *Les Noces de Thétis et de Pelée* included roles for two of the children of Charles I as well as parts for the woman who was soon to become Louis's first love, Marie Mancini, and for Françoise-Athénaïs de Rochechouart-Mortemart, the future Mme de Montespan.

Louis danced in some of his roles with Giovanni Battista Lulli, the composer and director of music. He appeared as a Fury, as Apollo, as an allegory of the sun, and as War.[22] In 1655 there was a *Ballet du temps* in which Louis played The Golden Century, and in the *Ballet des Plaisirs de la Ville et de la Campagne* Louis, referred to as a demi-god, took the part of the Genius of Dance. There were also more private entertainments into which Bensserade slipped discreet allusions to other members of the court as well as to the numerous female objects of the royal interest.[23]

Sumptuous entertainments at which Louis danced, although they helped him to develop his athletic grace and poise, were, however, on the whole only annual events. We are told by the loyal Marie du Bois, Louis's *valet de chambre* from April 1557, about Louis's day-to-day existence. He recited the office of the Holy Spirit on waking, and said his rosary, studying either the scriptures or the history of France before rising and making use of the *chaise percée* (or commode, more properly known as the *chaise d'affaires*), on which he remained for half an hour, in the alcove in which he had slept and in the presence only of two valets and an usher, issued with a *brevet d'affaires* which allowed them entry.

At his formal *lever* in his bedroom, he greeted the princes and other important personages in his dressing gown before washing hands and face and removing his night-cap. All then knelt while he prayed by his bed, before having brought to him the clothes in which in an adjoining room he performed his physical exercises. After practising his dancing, he returned to the bedroom, changed and breakfasted. He then went to see Mazarin, who would remain alone with him before generally summoning a secretary of state to discuss some aspect of the country's affairs for over an hour. This is the stage at which the affection between Mazarin and Louis has been described as 'almost like that of father and son'.[24] Du Bois makes it clear that Mazarin was thorough in instructing the king in the affairs of his country and the mechanisms of government as well as turning him into an *honnête homme*.

After his hour or so with Mazarin, Louis would go riding before attending mass with his mother, with whom he also generally dined, further marking the unusual intimacy of their relationship. Thereafter he talked to ambassadors before greeting members of the court and perhaps attending a council meeting. There was a different routine for the frequent hunting days. Hunts did not normally last more than half a day and therefore did not preclude all other activities. Sometimes the king would attend a play in the evening, before supper and dancing, perhaps followed by cards, parlour games or billiards. He would retire to bed before his mother, and the night-time *coucher* was as elaborate as the morning *lever*, with prayers, a solemn undressing and further use of the *chaise d'affaires*.

His female social companions were automatically to be found in the circle of Mazarin's nieces, the 'Mazarinettes' now living in the Louvre and treated by Anne as if they were her own close relatives. At a private soirée given by his mother in 1655 for Henriette de France, sister of Louis XIII and still queen of England, and her eleven-year-old daughter, Henriette d'Angleterre, Louis's intimacy with Mazarin's nieces was such that it seemed natural to him to offer to partner one of them, Laure-Vittoria in the first dance, his childhood friend since 1647, passing over the daughter of the guest of honour. Protocol was understandably firm, and his mother intervened.

Mazarin none the less, now fast amassing wealth, used his nieces skilfully to promote both the political interests of France and his own social position. It is not even as impossible as historians have thought that there could ever have been any question of marrying a niece to the king. The *mésalliance* would doubtless have stretched perhaps to breaking point the tolerances of a still powerful nobility, and, more importantly, France could not afford to abandon the political advantage to be gained from marrying Louis to a politically appropriate bride.

But there was an additional difficulty, no doubt the greatest, which should not be discounted. Such a marriage would almost certainly have been a marriage between first cousins, Mazarin's son and the daughter of one of his sisters. That would have required for validity a public papal dispensation, and therefore, unlike the other possible marriages to Marguerite of Savoy and Maria-Teresa of Spain, only apparently Louis's first cousins although daughters of sisters of Louis XIII, disclosure of the clandestine consanguinity and Mazarin's paternity. The consequences of formal disclosure are incalculable, but would certainly have led to challenges to Louis's kingship, Mazarin's ruin and Anne's disgrace.

Mazarin had himself been the eldest of six children. In 1655, when he became fifty-three and was in a position to advance the interests of his family, three of his siblings survived with him, the prioress Anna-Maria, to die without issue, and two widowed sisters, Laura Margherita, comtesse Martinozzi and Geronima, baroness Mancini. Of Laura Martinozzi's two daughters, the elder, Anne-Marie, had in 1654 married Condé's brother, the prince de Conti, in a union intended to seal the rehabilitation of Condé himself and which gave Anne-Marie the rank of a princess of the blood. Laura's second daughter, Laure, married in 1655 Alfonso IV d'Este, heir to the duchy of Modena. Laure's own daughter was to marry James II of England.

Geronima Mancini, Mazarin's youngest sister, had nine children between 1636 and 1649, two of whom had by this date died. One

more was to die in 1658. To Condé's outrage, Mazarin had negotiated the marriage at the age of thirteen of the eldest, Laure-Vittoria,
to the duc de Mercœur, future duc de Vendôme and a prince of the
blood. Geronima's second daughter, Olympe, pretty but not
intellectually well endowed, was the object of Louis's own serious
amorous attentions for two years before she was married in a
Genoese galley in 1658 to Eugène-Maurice of Savoy, for whom the
Soissons title was renewed. It carried with it the privileges of a prince
of the blood.

It was after 1655 that Geronima's three remaining unmarried
daughters, Marie, more astute if less well-favoured than Olympe,
Hortense and Marianne (or Marie-Anne) began to appear at court.[25]
They had been brought to France in 1653 and, after eight months
at Aix with their sister, Mme de Mercœur, Hortense and Marie
finished their education at the Visitation convent in the Faubourg
Saint-Jacques. Geronima's fourth child, Marie, next in order to
Olympe, was Olympe's willing successor in Louis's affections.

Louis's sexual initiation appears from several reliable sources to
have been undertaken by Mme de Beauvais, Anne's first lady of the
bedchamber, in her late twenties and blind in one eye. According
to the journal of the king's health kept by Antoine Vallot, his
personal physician from 1652, Louis caught gonorrhea from Mme
de Beauvais in 1655.[26] She had been brought back into Anne's court
after being dismissed at Mazarin's insistence on account of her part
in Condé's conspiracy to compromise Anne with at least the
appearance of a young lover, and Louis was to accord her a pension
for the rest of her life.

Strong and agile, he was soon to prove he had a voracious sexual
appetite. As early as 1655, before he was seventeen, he became
seriously attached to Olympe Mancini, in whose honour he organized in the following year a magnificent tournament, using an Italian
motto to surround the image of the sun on his shield. Mazarin
married her to the heir of the duchy of Savoy early in 1657. Only
then, according to Mme de Motteville, did Mazarin bring Marie 'on-
stage (sur le théâtre)'.

Louis, remaining 'demi-enchanté' by Olympe, was also, much to
his mother's anxiety, more dangerously showing signs of infatuation
with one of his mother's ladies-in-waiting, Mlle de la Motte
d'Argencourt, who had on that account to be dismissed.[27] Louis, who

was on several occasions seriously rebuked by his mother, had certainly attempted to go further than mere flirtation, and his obsession came close to dominating his mind, diminishing the intensity of his interest in other royal pursuits like sports, hunting and military affairs.

However, Marie Mancini, born in 1639, while notoriously ill-favoured and physically undeveloped as a thirteen-year-old, whom her mother had wanted to leave in Italy destined for a convent, was also clever, lively and ambitious enough to set her sights on the king. Her education at the convent had turned her into a linguistically accomplished, widely read, and, if still a little cheeky, a sophisticated young woman.[28]

Her mother, about whom Marie's *Apologie* has little good to say, fell ill late in 1657. As Mazarin's sister, she was almost certainly the king's aunt, and Louis dutifully took to calling on her, drawing closer to Marie, who appears to have waited for him after his visits to her dying mother. After her mother's death, Marie, now an attractive eighteen-year-old, was much more freely able to move in court circles, and immediately took her place in the intimate entourage of Anne of Austria. A portrait by Mignard shows her now as a dark-eyed beauty. In June 1659 Loret, the gazetteer, and in 1660 Somaize, the satirical social commentator on *préciosité*, both draw attention to her wit as well as her eyes. A pen-picture of her as 'Maximiliane' by Somaize in 1661 is fulsome not only about her wit but also about her breadth of culture. She knew enough about *galanterie* to keep Louis's approaches furtive even at the height of his passion for her, and she became the great, and perhaps the only romantic passion of his life.[29]

In 1658, it was also time for Louis to marry. Since the birth in Madrid of the Spanish infanta, Maria-Teresa, a few days after that of Louis, their eventual marriage had seemed the obvious way of resolving Europe's major political tension between Habsburgs and Bourbons. In 1658 Spain and France were still at war.[30] Spain hoped that the Fronde and the defection to it of Condé might open the way to an easy military victory.

But the ending of Turenne's defection, his military successes during the 1650s, and the brilliance of Mazarin's patient diplomacy had given France a position of relative strength. Mazarin had contrived to lead France into the alliance with the generally hated Cromwell at the treaty of Paris of 3 March 1657, thereby rendering nugatory Spanish hopes of outright victory. The only peace acceptable to Anne of Austria involved the marriage of Louis and Maria-Teresa. Tentative suggestions that the war might be ended in this way were made at Mazarin's instigation in Madrid in 1657 by Hugues de Lionne, nephew of the pro-Mazarin minister, Abel Servien, and himself later a minister close to Louis XIV. They had broken down on the Spaniards' insistence that the French should rehabilitate Condé, although he had put his forces at Spain's service.

Louis's marriage to Maria-Teresa was not achieved easily. After Louis's *sacre* at Reims in June 1654, Mazarin had needed yet again to raise money for the war, and on 20 March 1655 had arranged for the king to hold a *lit de justice* to register the creation of seventeen new posts, the stipends for which would involve further taxation. When protests came in, Mazarin sent Louis to address the *parlement*, which he famously did on 13 April, the occasion on which he did not in fact say, as alleged, 'L'Etat, c'est moi', but on which he did make a more effective rebuke by disrespectfully coming in his hunting clothes and addressing the *parlement* directly, rather than having his announcement made by the chancellor, as custom demanded.

Louis ended by announcing one imprisonment and nine exiles, no doubt thinking that he was beginning to exercise an authority which his whole upbringing had been designed to make him believe was his. In fact the carefully nurtured appearance of real political authority on this occasion was merely a façade such as would characterize French governance throughout the reign. The subsequent acquiescence of the *parlementaires* was brought about by Mazarin's patient negotiating skills, remission of the punishments so publicly proclaimed, a liberal scattering of bribes and the support of Fouquet, both the *procureur général* of the *parlement* and *surintendant des finances*, and as such directly responsible to the king alone.

In the late May of 1658 Louis, no more than close friends with Marie, left Paris to join the army in the Low Countries. To Mazarin's annoyance he stayed at Mardyck, just to the west of Dunkirk, where his entourage consumed supplies which Mazarin needed for the troops, and where there was a shortage even of water. Thanks partly to support from Cromwell's troops,[31] Turenne, advancing north into the Spanish Low Countries, what is now Belgium, carried off a spectacular victory against Condé at the battle of the Dunes on 14

June, allowing him to force the surrender of Dunkirk on 25 June and of Gravelines on 30 August.

Whether or not on account of the heat at Mardyck, or of the decomposing bodies not properly buried, or for some other reason, Louis contracted a serious fever on 28 June. He attempted to conceal it, but it was too strong, and Mazarin ordered the king to be taken to Vallot, who was at Calais, ready with the inevitable enema. He drew three bowls of blood from the king's right arm. Louis became delirious and broke into a rash of violet spots. His tongue thickened and turned black, his body became puffed up, and he became convulsive and incontinent.

We do not know how near he came to death, as contemporary accounts vary from the dismissive to the alarmist, but Patin, disapproving of Vallot, wrote to a friend that the popular Forty Hours devotion, in which the Blessed Sacrament was exposed for adoration and to which baroque France had invariably turned in times of crisis under Richelieu, was being held in every church. On 5 July, Vallot, following Montpellier practice, administered antimony, in the form of three ounces of emetic wine, but without effect. On 6 July a letter from Calais to Gaston d'Orléans reported that the doctors had given up hope.

On 7 July a medical consultation was held. Vallot told Mazarin that only a 'master stroke' could save the king, but the *Gazette* did not report the illness until 9 July, after recovery had set in, while Mazarin was playing down the symptoms as trivial on 3 July, when they were still getting worse. No one relished the complexities and dangers of arranging for the peaceful succession of Louis's brother, the effeminate Philippe, if Louis were to die. Philippe was not trained or experienced enough to take his brother's place, and he was not considered likely to continue tolerating the ascendancy of Mazarin, who must have felt his own position threatened. Anne of Austria said that she would spend the rest of her life in the convent at Val-de-Grâce if Louis died, even though he would be succeeded by her second son.

Louis received communion on 6 July, begging Mazarin to tell him when he was close to death, but he did not receive the last anointing, which meant that he was not thought to be *in extremis*. The crisis passed on the night of 7 July. After a total of eight bleedings, four purgings and an uncertain number of enemas, Louis left Calais on 22 July in the company of Marie Mancini to convalesce at Compiègne, where his mother awaited him. Mazarin remained with the army, suffering badly from gout, almost permanently and unbearably painful from 1658, and on 3 August Anne wrote him an intensely affectionate letter, longing for reunion. What she wanted almost as much was peace with her native country, Spain, which effectively meant the marriage of Louis to Maria-Teresa, and the king's recent illness had shown the urgency of an heir. While everyone had been considering the problems of the succession, Marie Mancini meanwhile had been sobbing, apparently with genuine concern for Louis's welfare.

Mazarin, always a gambler but never impatient, now took some of the greatest political risks of his life. He not only negotiated an alliance with Puritan England but, in order to jolt the Spaniards into renewing the proposal that their infanta should become Louis's bride, he also made serious preparations to marry Louis to princess Marguerite of Savoy, daughter of Chrétienne, sister of Louis XIII, already passed over by the Elector of Bavaria in favour of her younger sister. Maria-Teresa was the daughter of another of Louis XIII's sisters, and therefore a cousin of both Marguerite and Louis, but if the Spanish were unwilling to marry her to Louis, there was not only Marguerite, but there were also serious possibilities in one of the daughters of Gaston d'Orléans by his second marriage, half-sisters of la grande Mademoiselle,[32] and in the princess of Portugal, whose country virtually relied on its French alliance to retain its independence from Spain.

Louis was no doubt touched by the sincerity of Marie's concern for him during his illness, but she may not yet have been as obsessed by him, or he by her, as they were both to become a little later. It seems certain that Mazarin's strategy was to jolt Spain into a marriage between Louis and their infanta, who might still have inherited the Spanish throne although her father, Philip IV, now had a son by his second marriage, and her succession was by no means inevitable. But it is possible that Mazarin did regard the Savoy marriage as a fall-back, and he certainly allowed the Savoy court to believe that the proposition of a marriage between Louis and Marguerite was sincere.

Louis set out from Paris on 26 October with Mazarin and the court to meet an apparently reluctant Marguerite. Marie chose to ride alongside him, in dignified solemnity in towns, but in wild gallops in open country, disdaining the jolting shelter of a coach. Marie's memoirs say that she never thought that the marriage with Marguerite would take place, teasing Louis about how ugly Marguerite was, and there are reports that Louis was frigid towards Marguerite at their first meeting, although he apparently told his mother that he liked her well enough and argued against Anne, desperate for Louis to marry Maria-Teresa, when she pronounced the proposed marriage to be a *mésalliance*. La grande Mademoiselle reports that Louis entertained Marguerite with conversation about the organization and achievements of his army when they drove with her.

Louis, now twenty, wanted to marry, needed an heir and professed himself ready to marry Marguerite, although he was not distressed when the Spanish instantly reacted, letting Mazarin know, even before the court arrived at Lyon on 24 November, that they were sending an emissary. They had chosen Antonio Pimentel, formerly Spanish ambassador to Sweden and object, before her 1654 abdication, of Queen Christina's unseriously flirtatious attention. When, after a few days, Pimentel arrived, Mazarin had to closet himself with Marguerite's distraught and livid mother to excuse the calling off of the wedding. Anne expressed her sympathy not with Marguerite's mother, her late husband's sister, but with Mazarin, landed with so delicate a task. Fouquet had to find half a million livres to fund the expedition to Lyon and the pay-off to Savoy.

Louis accepted the prospect of Maria-Teresa as bride just as he had accepted Marguerite de Savoie. He would do his duty, but already appears to have intended to try to keep Marie in his life. When the Savoy court left Lyon, Louis and Marie spent the whole day together once the king had exercised with his musketeers and talked to Mazarin, whose gout was causing him ever-increasing pain. Olympe's husband, Soissons, was furious at the way Louis had dropped his wife for her sister. Anne spent her time at her devotions, with Mazarin, and gambling, but there is no indication that, in spite of her strong desire for the Spanish marriage, she was as worried as she should have been about the growing attachment of Louis to Marie. She presumably thought that, just as Louis had consented to marry Marguerite of Savoy despite his earlier dalliances, especially with Olympe Mancini, so when the time came, Louis would leave Marie.

La grande Mademoiselle recounts that, after Anne had retired for the night, Louis would escort Marie back to her lodgings, at first following her coach, then acting as coachman, and finally travelling in the coach with her. There were moonlit promenades *à deux* round what a century later de Cotte would rebuild as the Place Bellecour at Lyon. Pimentel followed the French court back to Paris and expressed to Mazarin in January Spanish doubts about the practical possibility of separating Louis and Marie. It was only when back at the Louvre in Paris that Anne could no longer ignore the whispers of the couple in her own presence.

According to Marie's memoirs, the five months following the return to Paris were given over to entertainments of all sorts, parties, balls, festivals, *galanteries*, promenades, 'no one ever had a better time . . .' Mme de La Fayette, famous author of *La Princesse de Clèves*, tells us that Marie even recounted to Louis what was being said about his mother's earlier love life, and her relationship with Marie's own uncle, Mazarin. Even if Louis had not previously known about his mother's relationship with Mazarin, he was now being told by Mazarin's niece. It would be surprising if they did not discuss their likely consanguinity, and the need for it to be divulged if they were to obtain the papal dispensation which would allow them to marry. Marie was now acting as if sure of her future with Louis, who even proposed to dance a ballet with her in Lent, provoking a quarrel with his mother, who threatened to absent herself for the whole penitential period. Mazarin had to dissuade the king.

Then on 4 June Mazarin signed the preliminary peace document with Pimental at Paris, which included as article 23 the marriage of Louis and Maria-Teresa. Mazarin's negotiations had proceeded successfully enough for him to be ready to go to Saint-Jean-de-Luz to sign the peace treaty, including the marriage clause, when Louis came out with a final act of defiance to his mother and Mazarin. He loved Marie, would never love anyone else, and intended to marry her. There are indications that Marie might have become intent on being Louis's queen, but had not been willing to allow him to become her lover. The only way for Louis to keep Marie in his life seems to have been to marry her.

Marie and her sisters were immediately sent to Brouage, near La Rochelle, of which Mazarin was governor. There was a long and tearful interview between Louis and his mother on the eve of Marie's departure. Louis was in tears when he escorted Marie to her carriage on 21 June. Marie's farewell is legendary, 'You are crying; you are the master, and I am going away.'[33] Racine uses it in *Bérénice,* when the queen of the title heroically renounces the emperor, whom she loves, but who had for political reasons repudiated her: 'Vous êtes empereur, Seigneur, et vous pleurez!'

Marie departed, Louis embraced his mother, and then left alone for Chantilly, recently re-confiscated from the Condé family. Mazarin and Louis exchanged letters with a philosophical tinge about the need to control the passions, regarded since the outbreak of the religious wars in the sixteenth century as the cardinal point of ethical achievement. Mazarin, himself emotionally torn, was movingly but vainly concerned to comfort and encourage Louis, whom he nearly pushed into dismissing him. In the end, Mazarin's patience won the day. What he did that was unpardonable was to allow Olympe to follow the court, with access to the king, while Marie remained confined to Brouage.

Mazarin, of whom his contemporaries left nothing unpleasant unsaid, was himself suspected of having wanted to make Marie Louis's queen, but she was his least favourite niece. She has been seen as spoiled, selfishly ambitious and scheming. She has been unfavourably judged for her willingness to wreck her uncle's assiduously achieved success, the crown of her uncle's career, the paix des Pyrénées, ending the long hostility between Spain and France. But she must sincerely have loved Louis, and have felt encouraged by the failure of Mazarin or Anne to attempt to inhibit her growing intimacy with him.

There is no evidence that she would ever have consented to become his mistress, and nothing has yet been discovered in Mazarin's letters, our only major source, to suggest that he or the queen were worried by what they saw of the couple's relationship, and what was being widely remarked by the court, during the five months between the return from Lyon and the inevitable crisis. Did they imagine that Louis and Marie might conduct a semi-clandestine relationship until finally they were shocked into awareness of the strength of Louis's passion?

What is of immense importance is the effect that the experience had on Louis. His relationship with Marie has been seen as largely responsible for his courtesy, *galanterie* and his artistic tastes, even for overcoming his aversion to books. The letters from Mazarin show the sacrifices, the control, the ethical values and the standard of external behaviour which his position imposed on him. In the face of the flat refusal of Mazarin and Anne, even the urgency of his passion did not make rebellion, with the political and domestic catastrophes it would entail, really possible. The possibility did little more than cross his mind. His attachment to Marie had, however, been allowed to grow too strong for renunciation not to have been deeply painful.

Mazarin, having successfully pushed Richelieu's policies to success, now followed Richelieu's tactic with his recalcitrant master. Like Richelieu, he made a genuine offer of resignation. Like Richelieu's, Mazarin's offer was more than half a threat. He knew without joy, again like Richelieu, that he had won. What had to be, would be. Louis's brief and discourteous replies to Mazarin's moral sermons, stammering in their defiance, show that he had been too carefully educated to rely on the certainties of Richelieu's value system to be capable of setting himself suddenly and totally adrift from his upbringing. It was Marie in the end who rejected the connivance in external pretence in which Mazarin and Anne had taken refuge for themseves, but, by 1659, Louis was simply unable to play any other role than that for which he had been so carefully groomed.

The couple were at first allowed to correspond and then found ways of continuing when communication was officially forbidden, although the correspondence between Louis and Marie, all of which has been lost, presumed destroyed, never quite ceased. The supervised correspondence was arranged so that Jean-Baptiste Colbert passed Marie's letters to the king. Colbert's cousin, Colbert de Terron, passed Louis's to Marie. Anne even allowed the couple to meet again, on 13 August at Saint-Jean-d'Angély, leading Marie into fits of rage, despair and folly.

Mazarin remained suspicious, particularly of the influence on Louis of Louis-Victor de Rochechouart, comte de Vivonne, brother of the future Mme de Montespan, already in trouble for holding irreligious festivities at his house at Roissy on the preceding Good Friday. They had been attended among others by Bussy and Philippe Mancini, Mazarin's nephew, exiled for the offence. Mazarin, who suspected Vivonne of inciting Louis to revolt, wrote to Louis pointing out that refusal to submit would unavoidably lead to resumption of the war with Spain.

Mazarin spent from late June to early November 1659 negotiating the wedding with the Spanish first minister, Luis de Haro, insisting himself on regulating the last details, and relying on Jean-Baptiste Colbert to undertake the necessary commissions in Paris. Yet further contributions towards the expense were sought from the major French towns, the 60,000 livres offered by Lyon being judged insufficient against the 100,000 from Rouen, and the 150,000 from Paris slight compared with double that sum being raised by Philip IV from Madrid. When deciding who should offer his hand to whom, the rights of a prince of the church crippled by gout had to be weighed against the protocol entitlement of a Spanish grandee. The balance was too fine, and Mazarin's recourse to 'l'expédient du lit' by which he pronounced himself in too much pain to rise, was employed so frequently as to arouse suspicions. No preliminary meetings took place at all.

Then there was the question of where the negotiations should take place. That should have been easy, because the river Bidassoa, which separated France from Spain at the western foot of the Pyrénées, contained an island, the Ile des Faisans, of which both countries claimed ownership and on which half a century earlier, on 9 November 1615, Anne of Austria, about to marry Louis XIII, had been exchanged for Louis XIII's sister, Elizabeth, about to marry the future king Philip IV of Spain. But the Spanish lawyers discovered an act of 1510 which implied ownership of the island by the French, who then could not renounce their claim to it without losing fishing rights.

Money passed between lawyers, and the island was declared neutral territory, costing tedious delays while each side built bridges to it and shelters on it, as well as between French and Spanish shelters a ceremonial tent, the qualities of whose wall-hangings, to be provided by each side, had to be stipulated and matched, like the number of nationals, including soldiery, who had the right to be present from each country on the island at any given time. Publicly, and to Pimentel, Mazarin gave out that he did not care about such trifles. Privately he boasted to Michel Le Tellier that the quality of his entourage and equipment was greatly superior to that of the Spaniards. Mazarin's biographer generously concedes a draw, largely because don Luis had had his mules' blankets embroidered.[34] On the other hand, if the Spanish offered feasts on more precious crockery, the French catering was so good that even the grander

Spaniards pocketed left-over game birds, and don Luis had to ask Mazarin to moderate the gastronomic prodigality in case the Spaniards grew to expect similar standards of culinary excellence.

The minutiae of the arrangements for the peace had already been argued out and ratified in Paris and Madrid, but they had now to be gone through once again, the Spaniards knowing that politically, personally and financially, Mazarin could not afford either to fail to bring back peace or even to stay away too long from Paris. Further delay meant more French concessions.[35] On the other hand, Spain, with 8 million inhabitants against 20 million French, had drained itself of wealth, losing 300,000 on the battlefields, and 4,000–5,000 a year more young men to colonize the Americas. Economically even more damaging to Spain was the expulsion of the talented Jewish and Islamic communities and the oppression of the converted members of each. The sticking point came from the precise details of the rehabilitation to be accorded to Condé. Without his support Spain might have lost much more than it did of the Low Countries, and it still owed him for the upkeep of his army. It was, Mazarin realized, in the interests of France to buy back Condé's loyalty by paying off the debt to him incurred by the Spanish during his treasonable alliance with them.

After the protracted histrionics, sulks, threats and occasional shouts of the bazaar negotiation which the talks resembled, and at which both Mazarin and don Luis excelled, it was agreed that Condé should recover the government of Burgundy, but with only one fort, Dijon. His son would become *grand maître* of the king's household. France would receive, in addition to what had been agreed in Paris, Mariembourg and Philippsburg, both in today's south Belgium, and Avesnes, now in France a few miles from the Belgian border.[36]

The real difficulty remained the residual possibility that Maria-Teresa might inherit the Spanish throne unless, in return for her dowry, she renounced all rights to the succession on her marriage to Louis, as Anne of Austria had renounced her own similar rights on marriage to Louis XIII. The Spanish king's eldest son by his second wife had just died, and his second son was sickly from Habsburg in-breeding. In Spain, the succession could pass through the female line, and, were the second son also to die, it would pass to Maria-Teresa. No one could predict that a third son, later to become Carlos II, was at this date still to be born in 1661.

Maria-Teresa did make the solemn renunciation, explicitly excluding the Low Countries from it, in exchange for an increased dowry of territory recently captured by the French, and the sum of 1.5 million livres. This was the same sum as had been the dowry of Anne of Austria, but to be reckoned not in still falling Spanish currency, but in gold, and with the renunciation of rights to the succession dependent on the actual payment of the dowry in its agreed instalments. Constitutionally, it was in fact doubtful whether a renunciation of rights of succession to the Spanish throne could ever be valid, even if they came through the female line, since they were God-given. Even if valid, it could be argued that a renunciation could not affect the rights of unborn descendants of their holder.

Anne of Austria's dowry, calculated in Spanish currency, had not been paid, and had anyway lost half its value since her marriage. Making the renunciation of the rights to the succession dependent on the payment caused predictable difficulties, but it became clause 4 of the marriage contract inserted into the seventy-four articles of the treaty of the Pyrénées. It was proclaimed by Maria-Teresa in the episcopal palace at San Sebastián on 2 June, and again on the wedding day itself, 9 June 1660. Technically, the renunciation, even if it had been legally valid, became void when the Spaniards missed the first payment of a third of the 1.5 million livres d'or on the eve of the marriage. It did not matter very much at the time, since the dynastic Habsburg–Bourbon alliance was more important than the money to Anne, Mazarin and Louis.

Negotiations were over by 11 November 1659, and the necessary papal dispensation for the marriage between cousins was obtained. A French delegation headed by the duc de Gramont, governor of Béarn, was already in Madrid to ask officially for the hand of Maria-Teresa, appearing in multi-coloured finery before the stiffly restrained Spanish grandees arrayed in formal black. Mazarin, Anne and Louis spent the winter in Provence raising money. Condé joined them in January at Aix, where news arrived of the death of Gaston d'Orléans. Sensitively received and pardoned by Louis at Aix on 27 January, Condé was rehabilitated by letters patent, not only ending the last feudal challenge to royal authority and the last threat of France's subordination to a foreign power, but also cementing the Habsburg–Bourbon dynastic alliance. Condé, who had discreetly declined a courteous invitation to Louis's wedding,

commissioned a large painting by Lecomte for Chantilly, entitled
Le Repentir.

Louis's bride was neither intelligent nor handsome, and even Mme
de Motteville finds it necessary to temper her moderate praise with
criticism of her features. Velázquez's famous portrait in the Louvre
allows something of her dull backwardness to appear, and her
appearance in stiff Spanish dress and wig created something near
polite consternation in the French court. She was also extremely
repressed, unable to express any emotion about the man she had
always supposed she was destined to marry, or indeed to put together
enough words to make a sentence to any male other than her father,
on whose bidding she was absolutely dependent. She had, however,
cultivated an affection for Louis's portraits sent by his mother, her
aunt.

Since a Spanish princess had by custom to be married before she
left Spain, and a French king had to marry in France, a first ceremony at which don Luis de Haro married Maria-Teresa by pro-
curation was held on 2 June at Fuenterrabia, in a chapel decorated
by Velázquez for the occasion, where the Spaniards played down in
attire and gifts what for the French was an occasion for rejoicing.
When the time came, Maria-Teresa, dressed in white satin, asked
her father's permission to say yes to her marriage vows. Tears came
into Philip's eyes as he gave his consent, and when Maria-Teresa had
pronounced her assent, Philip IV lifted his hat to the new queen of
France. The new queen and her father then dined in separate
apartments.

Anne was not allowed by her brother, Philip IV, to kiss him when
on 4 June she crossed the river to pay her compliments, and the
conversation between them was as stilted as everything else about
the occasion, and as was after all to be expected after a separation
of forty-three years, more than half of which had been spent with
their countries at war with one another. Louis performed some
spirited equestrian manoeuvres to show off to the royal party across
the river, and Maria-Teresa proclaimed herself fittingly impressed.
The cultural differences between Spaniards and French were again
made clear when the Spaniards, who seemed to the French so stiff,
dowdy and ridden with protocol, sat lightly enough to ecclesiastical
regulation to serve meat on a Friday, and then presented plays in
which Spanish comedians parodied religious ceremonies. Anne,

however, clearly enjoyed the regression to the culture of her youth, Spanish chocolate, iced drinks, guitar music and irreverent theatre. At Anne's request, Philip IV sent Spanish troupes to play before her every evening at Saint-Jean-de-Luz.

At this stage in her life, Louis's mother, having largely renounced make-up and the pleasure she had once taken in dancing, together with the excessive Spanish-style use of rouge, being proud of a complexion so nourished as not to require disguise, had not yet given up the flamboyantly Spanish aids to devotion, statues, images in extravagant frames, paintings, relics in elaborate reliquaries, rosaries in exotic materials, which decorated her chapel, or her more worldly secular pursuits, which included the love of gaming and the theatre.

The two kings signed the treaty in an elaborate and lengthy ceremony on 6 June, and on 7 June Maria-Teresa left Spain in a French carriage for Saint-Jean-de-Luz, the prosperous whale-fishing town where householders had been evicted to harbour the French court which had arrived on 8 May. The 8 June was spent preparing for the wedding ceremony, and is memorable chiefly for the train of tittle-tattle which it has left concerning the tetchiness about precedence and protocol which inevitably invests such occasions. The *Gazette* printed flattering reports, but we have several other accounts of different parts of the proceedings, including those of la grande Mademoiselle and of a canon of Le Mans, Matthieu de Montreuil.[37] Louis forbade Maria-Teresa to kiss anyone except his mother, so drawing her in to the tight family circle of Mazarin, Anne, Louis and now increasingly his brother, Philippe.

The second wedding ceremony took place with all possible liturgical solemnity at a high mass on 9 June, celebrated in the small town church of Saint-Jean-de-Luz, decked out with tapestries and, in a chapel for the king of Spain and his daughter, cloth of gold. Louis wore a suit of cloth of gold covered with black lace and Maria-Teresa a cape of red velvet embossed with golden fleur-de-lys. She wore a golden crown. The young couple supped in public with Anne and Philippe before Maria-Teresa was prepared by her ladies-in-waiting for the marital bed and an impatient king. Anne of Austria closed the curtains on them, and the marriage was consummated that night.

6

Mazarin's Death and the Fall of Fouquet

Primi Visconti, an Italian nobleman and shrewd observer of Louis's court, assures us in his memoirs that Louis never abandoned marital relations with the queen, with whom he conversed as if he had had no mistress, with whom he ate, and to whom he afforded all the honours of her rank. Despite Louis's multiple infidelities, he always came back to the marital bed at night, however late he had stayed up 'studying papers'. Marital relations were interrupted only for a period of some months when the queen withdrew in protest at Louis's affair with Louise de La Vallière. The queen mother had to intervene before normality was restored.

The return to Paris after the wedding proceeded slowly, with the queen mother and the new queen resting, while Mazarin took the opportunity of showing Louis western parts of his kingdom which he had never hitherto visited. Brouage and the province of Aunis were included in the itinerary. Mazarin was its governor but there is no record of whether or not Louis and Marie met again on this journey. It was while Mazarin and Louis were absent from Anne who had remained at Saintes, that Anne wrote the last letter we have from her to him. Dated 30 June 1660, Anne's letter alludes to the similarity between the affection between Mazarin and herself and that between Louis and Marie and is as passionate as any which preceded it.[1]

Mazarin had wanted Anne to dismiss from her service someone whose name is now unknown but who had stolen the box containing Louis's correspondence with Marie Mancini, potentially damaging to both Mazarin and Anne. The letters were subsequently recovered and destroyed.

The court set out from Saint-Jean-de-Luz on 15 June, and took a month to reach Fontainebleau by way of Bordeaux and Poitiers, with the *Gazette* selectively reporting the journey. Louis went hunting during a 48-hour stop at Richelieu, the château in Poitou built by Mazarin's predecessor. There were stops at Amboise, Blois and Chambord, which had reverted to crown ownership with Gaston's death, before the arrival at Fontainebleau on 13 July. Mazarin and Anne returned to Paris, but Louis and Maria-Teresa stayed at Vincennes while the triumphal entry into Paris and the three days of festivities were prepared.[2]

The entry took place on 26 August 1660. More or less discreetly supervised by the government, the entry was supposed to be the city's official welcome at which the *prévôt des marchands,* heading the commercial community, handed the king the symbolic keys to the city. The role of the *parlement,* in deference to memories of the Fronde, was much less than might otherwise have been expected.

At the far end of the Faubourg Saint-Antoine the king and queen, enthroned on a platform eighteen steps above the street, listened to addresses, harangues and other expressions of loyalty, receiving the professions of homage and allegiance of the major corporations and city companies. Then at two p.m. came the entry itself, a solemn procession of unimagined magnificence, headed by representatives of the monastic houses and orders of friars, after whom came other members of the university, then guards, then governing officials of the city, and then the merchant corporations, with the tailors to be the first on horseback. There followed in increasingly colourful order the archers, the officials of the sovereign courts and Mazarin's retinue, the largest of all with its seventy-two silver-muzzled mules, their saddle-cloths of red velvet trimmed with gold, leading the nobles and princes of the realm. Pages held parasols to shelter the ageing chancellor, Pierre Séguier.

The king, shining with gold and silver, was on horseback, preceded by musketeers, pages, the heralds and officers of the household. Mme de Motteville marvels at the quality of his mount and at the crowd's rapture at the sight of the queen, much bejewelled in a chariot drawn by six horses. The future Mme de Maintenon was entranced, particularly with the schooled leaps of the horses of the

Grande and Petite Ecuries, 'I believe that nothing so beautiful could possibly be seen', but she ends her long private letter, 'The king knows perfectly well that he cannot afford expenses of this sort.'[3]

Most significant was the absence of Mazarin from his coach, whose curtains were down. This, as even the crowd was now acknowledging, was really his triumph. He had been hugely rewarded in money and lands by the king at Toulouse in December 1659, was suffering very badly from his gout, now aggravated by kidney stone, and his general health was plainly deteriorating, not helped by the radical purges and emetics administered by his doctors. Health is however unlikely to have been the reason why he did not take his seat in his coach. He preferred to appear with Anne on the balcony of the Hôtel de Beauvais to watch the procession in public with her. It was an act of self-vindication, even perhaps of defiance.

After the entry, the court returned to the Louvre. Mazarin, no doubt conscious of impending death, intensified his efforts to prepare Louis to take over the government, and had to settle problems connected with the Stuart restoration in England, with the recently concluded peace with Spain, and with the negotiations which ended war in the Baltic and with Poland. He lived in the Louvre and it was in his apartment there that, on 30 October, Molière achieved his successful return to Paris with *L'Etourdi* and *Les Précieuses ridicules*.

In a highly perceptive report of 9 June 1660, written soon after Louis's marriage, the Venetian ambassador Giovanni Batista Nani wrote:

> The young king looks up to his mother with the greatest respect and never distances himself from her authority and her advice. He is to the highest degree in love with his wife, and loves his brother with great tenderness; but all his affection seems to be devoted to the cardinal . . . There is a deep sympathy, a submission of minds and intellects.

He reports that the king sees Mazarin 'several times a day', starting as soon as he has dressed, waiting if necessary, and leaving again if the cardinal is giving audience to ministers. Generally the visits 'last several hours during which the cardinal brings [Louis] up to date with everything, teaches and trains him.' Among Louis's qualities is his love of secrecy and his capacity for 'dissimulation totale', so brilliantly exhibited in the escape from Paris at the beginning of the Fronde.

Court life, recovering from the war and inspired by the marriage, revolved round the young king and his queen, with gaiety, parties, excursions, balls and other organized pleasures which dazzled its chroniclers and future historians. Its spirit was about to be epitomized by Louis's obsession with the hunting lodge at Versailles and everything that went on there, but it ignored something much more important that had already taken place in the higher echelons of French society.

Mazarin, whose confident personal morality prolonged the values of the first third of the century, had been determined to uproot 'Jansenism', failing to see it for the reaction to the exuberant baroque values of early seventeenth-century French culture which it was. As a spirituality rather than as a theology, it had already been an early manifestation in religious life of a general reversal of the cultural euphoria which can be traced during the early seventeenth century in all the imaginative work in France, and especially the literary and visual arts. In devotional matters it showed all the characteristics of a strong reaction to the excessively optimistic values which had invested French culture between the formal end of the religious wars in the very late sixteenth century and the late 1630s. It would go on to fight its corner through the period of Pascal, Racine, La Rochefoucauld and Bossuet until, in the eighteenth century, belief in the congruence between a rational ethic and human instinct and confidence in the harmony between man and nature and became the defining characteristics of eighteenth-century rococo.

In the broadest sense the clash between the new values and the old was reflected in the *Querelle des anciens et des modernes,* although not all the positions of factions and personalities in the literary *Querelle* accord with the appropriate ideological alignments. We find for instance the baroque spiritual optimism about human nature of the Jesuits castigated by Pascal going hand in hand with an educational system which was based on the study of antique classics rather than modern, or even antique Christian authors, while the spiritually austere *solitaires* of Port-Royal undertook advanced experiments which promoted the birth of modern science, and were sympathetic to the philosophy of Descartes, which regarded animals as mere machines.

It is necessary to remain aware of the value clash because it largely explains how the flourishing of the arts under the Sun King failed for so long to establish the victory of the modern era over which he presided, and which was reflected in the rise of opera and in the Quinault–Lulli cooperation over the spirit of remorseless Greek tragedy favoured by Racine, Boileau and the religious devotees of Augustine.

What affects any understanding of the reign of Louis XIV, and the unparallelled grandeur with which Louis was himself vested, is that his iconic status rested on the contention of the *modernes* that the modern era was in all things superior to antiquity. It is not without significance that there were firm bonds linking the authors, painters and thinkers, the early optimism of devout baroque, the literary champions of the *modernes* and the political allies of Fouquet, or that the austere Colbert, nineteen years older than Louis, and the reactionary Chapelain, Colbert's manager for literary affairs, should by and large represent a more restrained opposing con-servative system of political, literary and devotional values, in spite of the need to build up the image of Louis in the 1660s as invincible Sun King.

Louis's *Mémoires*[4] were written only after peace had been restored in 1659, and they do not advert to the horrors of French peasant life depicted by Jacques Callot in his famous series of engravings.[5] During the 1660s, while France was recovering from the Spanish war and Colbert was re-establishing the state finances, the condition of the rural economy was becoming less harsh. The king would later forcibly be told about the true state of the French peasantry, but widespread and life-threatening hardship would scarcely deviate much from the normal vagaries brought on by bad harvests or inept administration before the outbreak of the Dutch war in 1672. In the *Mémoires* Louis is more concerned with the principles of governance and the necessary offices of state.

At the date of Louis's wedding, all that can be said is that the picture was not uniform. Nearly everywhere, but worst in the Paris region, there were some extremes of sometimes judicial cruelty, as well as suffering and death by starvation. In some places it was even worse, and whole villages-full of peasants could escape the rampages of the military only by fleeing to the woods where slow death from starvation was certain. The armies, often unpaid, inevitably left behind them a citizenry which had been subjected to pillage, murder and rape.

Louis cannot of course be held personally responsible for the state of France in 1660, but the situation was bad enough for whole new religious congregations to have sprung up to relieve the oppression and the poverty, the terrible half-life of those condemned to the galleys, the starving, the injured, the sick and the derelict. Consciences were being stirred, and with the new *hôpitaux*, compassion was moving into embryonic forms of corporate organization. Military hospitals, 'Les Invalides', were set up in Paris and Marseille. That in Paris, replacing a former arsenal and powder factory, consisted of twelve courtyards, covering ten hectares, and contained 300 beds, only 4 or 5 to a ward and each with only a single occupant. The institution was intended to reflect the grandeur and gratitude of its creator as much as to alleviate the sufferings of former 'officers and soldiers'.

Louis was to sign the document of foundation in April 1674, after the beginning of the Dutch war, having already signed that to rebuild the Salpêtrière for the homeless in April 1656. Spontaneous acts of individual rather than institutional kindness are increasingly re-corded as Louis aged, but they are counterbalanced by such inci-dents as the whipping of a woman who shouted insults at him after her son had been killed during the building of Versailles, or the hanging of an old Frondeur discovered by a court party which had got lost hunting in the forest, and which he had welcomed and fed.[6] The members of the hunting party who had related the incident were appalled.

Compassion was the prerogative of officialdom and the charitable organizations, mostly ecclesiastic. The alleviation of distress could not, as a policy, take precedence for Louis over other, more pressing political objectives affecting the wealth and standing of French political and military might. Racine and Corneille would write pieces about the clemency of princes, but for them clemency was a private virtue which might indeed adorn a monarch. They did not investigate the values of more general compassion among their always socially elevated tragic figures.[7]

When Louis does skirt what subsequent generations have regarded as social problems in his *Mémoires*, the real purpose of which must have been to justify himself to himself under the guise of guidance to his son, the tone is robustly reliant on a pre-ordained social caste system. When he details the effects of the failed harvest of 1661 upwards through the 'ordres de l'Etat' from social group to social group, he simply moves without thinking from 'le peuple' to the 'personnes de la plus haute qualité'.

He will give 'alms' to the poor of Dunkirk, but only to prevent their destitution 'from tempting them to follow the religion of the English'. The charitable gesture here is neither politically nor socially motivated, nor can it plausibly be regarded as a measure whose primary purpose was to snatch the inhabitants of that city from the jaws of hell. Louis had been obliged by the terms of his alliance to cede the town to the English after Turenne had taken it for the French in 1658. In 1662 Louis bought it back from the indigent Charles II, who could not afford its upkeep, in an attempt to strengthen his frontiers. But to anyone sharing the values of his culture, it would not have seemed implausible that Louis's motive, while not the product of social concern, may yet have contained a genuine, if ill-founded religious element.

When in 1662 Louis goes on to speak of the great Paris carrousel of 5–6 June in front of the Tuileries in what thereafter became the Place du Carrousel, and of his need to cultivate the affection of his subjects by such expensive diversions, it is again 'surtout les gens de qualité' who matter to him. The court's familiarity with the king, elevating it into a 'société des plaisirs', not only gives pleasure to the people, whose spirits were no doubt genuinely elevated by public celebration, as they had been at the news of Louis's birth, but its extravagance creates in foreigners an 'impression très avantageuse de magnificence, de puissance, de richesse et de grandeur'.

This was the mindset into which the twenty-three-year-old had been formed. The thinking behind it derived from Richelieu, but had been developed under the tutelage of the plebeian and populist Colbert, always timidly conscious of his family's lowly origins, and himself elevated not by birth, but by high intelligence, attention to minute detail and exceedingly hard work. He was quick to understand the mechanisms of social power, the means of manipulating them and the way to gain advantage from the caste system.

When Louis refuses clemency to tax rebels he feels not that he is God's agent but that, like God, he is acting in virtue of a greater good, a view which reveals something of what he has been taught to believe about the nature and origin of his own power, but which also says a great deal about his religion.[8] When in 1667 Louis admits that princes can do wrong, and warns his son against the repercussions of scandal, he insists that, however evil the deeds of the prince, rebellion is criminal:

> He who gave kings to men wanted them respected as his lieutenants, reserving to himself alone the right to examine their conduct. It is his will that whoever is born a subject should obey without discrimination . . . There is no principle more firmly established by Christianity than this humble submission of subjects to those who are put in authority over them.[9]

Oliver Cromwell, Louis's adversary across the channel until the mid-1650s, was generally detested in France, but he might well have agreed that civil authority was to be regarded as the instrument of divine justice. There are, however, other ways of interpreting the New Testament, and Louis's theory of sovereignty is as baroque in its static hierarchy of divinely ordained authority as is his concept of fixed social orders in his view of society. The 'gens de basse condition' have inferior moral standards, the 'vulgaire' is more easily led away from the paths of reason, and each 'profession', ploughman, artisan, merchant, financier, judge, 'contributes in its way to maintenance of the monarchy.' It is by regression to an earlier, obsolescent set of social values, that Louis acknowledges some complicity with the secret preference which 'âmes généreuses' have for the profession of arms. Their moral standards must none the less be properly maintained.[10]

Louis's own justification of his Dutch wars was to be that they enabled him to establish the peaceful conditions in which he could apply himself to the government of 'un Etat puissant et riche'.[11] The mistake which subsequent historians have not avoided is to assume that Louis's spectrum of social values and his concept of himself as the mediator of divine authority arose out of some coherent political theory on which were founded baroque attitudes, when in fact it was the values themselves that generated the political and social theory which bolstered them. It is when the practice crystallized into the theory which it generated that its defective assumptions became obvious.

Louis was rehearsing his part for a ballet in the 'galerie des rois' of the Louvre early in February 1661 when a candle was unfortunately knocked over, causing a serious fire. Mazarin had to be taken to his palace in the rue Vivienne then known as the Palais Mazarin, and later to become the Bibliothèque Nationale. Mazarin's collections were kept there, and it is there that Loménie de Brienne famously heard Mazarin say repeatedly before he left: 'I'm going to have to leave all this.'

Mazarin wanted to die at Vincennes, a crown palace of which he had become governor on Chavigny's death, and of which he wanted to make a royal residence grander than Fontainebleau. He was having it improved by Le Vau and decorated by Giovanni Francesco Romanelli, whom Mazarin had first brought over from Rome in 1646 to decorate the Palais Mazarin. Mazarin was also stocking the estate at Vincennes with game and exotic animals for Louis to hunt. Unhappily the fruit trees planted there did not flourish, and Mazarin ended up buying in the fruit which he sent to Anne, purporting its provenance from the Vincennes estate. He had an apartment in the château with five principal rooms, but during the rebuilding lived briefly in the governor's former lodgings.

On 28 February Mazarin's favourite niece Hortense married Armand de la Porte de la Meilleraye, son of the marshal La Meilleraye related to and favoured by Richelieu. It was Armand who became Mazarin's residual legatee in exchange for undertaking to assume the Mazarin name and arms on the cardinal's death. Mazarin had feigned to leave all his possessions to Louis, no doubt partly as a posthumous defence against too rigorous an enquiry as to the manner in which he had come by them.[12] Declaring that he owed to the king everything he possessed, on 3 March Mazarin left his entire estate to Louis, but expressed the hope that Louis would dispose of it according to Mazarin's own wishes, expressed in a will dated 6 March.

He nominated as executors the *surintendant des finances,* Fouquet, the secretary of state for war, Le Tellier, the bishop of Fréjus, Ondedei,[13] the *premier président* of the Paris *parlement,* Lamoignon and Jean-Baptiste Colbert, effectively manager of Mazarin's personal affairs from 1648. The same day, Mazarin added the codicil forbidding any inventory to be made of his papers and possessions, and the king, having read both documents at Vincennes, renounced the legacy. On the following day Mazarin in a new codicil, lengthened the list of individual legacies, including those to members of the royal family.[14]

The court, which had gone to Saint-Germain after the fire, now came to Vincennes, from where the cardinal went out only when carried in his chair. Anne called daily and spent some hours with him, as also did Louis. Mazarin's confessor persuaded him to give up secular literature for more pious reading. On 22 February Anne left his room weeping, and on 3 March the confessor spoke of viaticum. There was fluid in the lungs. On 5 March Anne ordered the forty hours' exposition of the Blessed Sacrament, normally reserved for royal sickbeds, to be held in Paris churches, and on 7 March Mazarin took leave of the royal family, asking them not to return so that he might not be distracted in his preparations for death.

Colbert[15] had taken charge and told Anne, who was again in tears, that Mazarin was unlikely to survive the night. He had remade his will after hearing, as he no doubt expected, that Louis had refused the gift of his estate, which included the eighteen enormous diamonds known as *les Mazarins* together with the pictures, books and other beautiful objects which Mazarin had collected with re-markable success partly in order to attempt to form Louis's taste. Anne, to whom his will left, among other items of extraordinary value, the fourteen carat 'English Rose' diamond, spent the night in Louis's room to avoid hearing Mazarin's cries of pain from her own. That evening Extreme Unction was administered, and on the 8 March Mazarin asked to hear mass, expressing contrition for his faults. Until near the end he had toyed with the idea of taking holy orders, and dreamt of being elected pope.

He died piously, feeling that he had fulfilled his Christian obligations and prepared to deliver himself back into the hands of his creator. It happened a little after two o'clock on the morning of 9 March 1661. He was fifty-nine. Anne went to Val-de-Grâce to console herself in prayer.[16] The bond of love between Anne and Mazarin had remained undiminished to the end. By midday, Louis and the court had left Vincennes for Paris. Louis ordered full court mourning, the first and last occasion on which such a measure was taken for a non-royal person. Anne had already promised to care for Mazarin's nieces, giving the *surintendance* of her own household to Anne-Marie Martinozzi, princesse de Conti, and that of Maria-Teresa to Olympe Mancini, comtesse de Soissons. Anne would shortly marry Marie Mancini to the duc de Bouillon.

On the surface level, the death of Mazarin itself appeared to change comparatively little, even if it immediately liberated Louis from much constraint, and allowed him over a broad range of issues to confront his mother, to whom he remained deeply attached but with whom he was none the less capable of quarrelling. Structurally, however, Mazarin's death produced a choice which would profoundly affect every aspect of France's administration. The inevitable power struggle between Fouquet and Colbert concerned administrative structures as well as personal animosities. It had in fact been fought and won while Mazarin was still alive, and by the date of his death its public outcome was inevitable. Mazarin knew that it would reveal and unleash some of the pent-up social, religious and political forces which he himself had been holding in check.

In spite of Colbert's ambition and bitter dislike of Fouquet, he could not denounce what he regarded as Fouquet's flamboyant malpractice while the cardinal still lived without endangering Mazarin. The manner in which Mazarin, and after him, Colbert, acquired huge fortunes, the way in which Colbert protected Mazarin by refusing to denounce Fouquet before Mazarin's death, and the different philosophies of fiscal administration and artistic patronage represented by Colbert and Fouquet and between which Louis had to choose, are all important. Before Mazarin died, Louis had no real choice between alternative philosophies of governance. He had to follow Mazarin.

On Mazarin's death, Louis could theoretically choose between the opposed attitudes of Colbert and Fouquet to administering France and formulating its policies. Colbert and Fouquet, their behaviour, character, policies and personal styles were radically inimical to one another, with an incompatibility approaching absolute. One or other was necessarily going to face disgrace. But, in order to protect the reputation of Mazarin, it was Fouquet who would have to be removed. So much would have been clear before Mazarin's death to any outside observer who knew the facts.

To understand the choices which Louis actually made in 1661 it is necessary to appreciate the constraints which determined them. Louis's choice of the brilliant administrator, Colbert, over the highly competent money-raiser, Fouquet, might even reasonably have been made without involving considerations about Mazarin's reputation, although such considerations are certain to have been dominant in Colbert's mind since well before Mazarin's death. The disgrace of Fouquet in favour of reliance on Colbert, inevitable before and resolved no later than immediately after the death of Mazarin, determined the administrative style into which Louis would continue to be forced, as in fact he was, virtually until the moment of Colbert's death in 1683.

Louis, in accordance with Mazarin's wishes, and without realizing what was at stake, now gave the government of Brittany to La Meilleraye, duc de Mazarin since the cardinal's death, forgetting that it actually belonged to his mother, whom he did not bother to consult. Anne objected; Louis accepted her objection, and Hortense's husband had to content himself with a lieutenancy. But the incident presaged future tensions, and Anne's political voice, weak even under Mazarin, further diminished. Anne lost political standing with Louis. That in turn meant that Fouquet, who had been counting on Anne's protection, would even more certainly be defeated in the struggle for power by Colbert, who had already used Mazarin to undermine the king's confidence in him.

Mazarin had died rich.[17] If we accept a margin of error of the order of a third, Mme Dulong, his biographer, believes that we can reasonably say that Mazarin left a heritable fortune of around 35 million livres.[18] That we have even a reasonably reliable, if incomplete account of Mazarin's affairs is largely due to the devoted book-keeping of Colbert, in charge of Mazarin's personal affairs from 1648, but formally appointed to his service only in 1651, and the fact that the exile of 1651 had meant the submission of accounts which would never otherwise have been put on paper, even in encrypted form.[19]

From around the time of Louis's birth, Mazarin had set out to make himself rich. Colbert's difficulty from 1648, when he unofficially became Mazarin's financial steward, was to disgrace Fouquet, mostly because of the flamboyance of his personal style and his cavalier attitude to running the nation's indebtedness, without compromising Mazarin, to whom Colbert became fiercely loyal. Mazarin's refusal to allow an inventory of his belongings confirms his desire to protect his own posthumous reputation as well as his heirs.

Mazarin had in fact been trading on his own account with crown money diverted from its designated destination certainly as early as 1641, and in very large amounts indeed by 1645, when he took over a loan of 1,050,000 livres to the Gonzague family, secured by its lands, on the occasion of the marriage of Marie de Gonzague to the king of Poland. The money came from the the king and his bankers.[20] Mazarin made extensive use of borrowed names, but not everything in nominee names was returned to him after the Fronde and the 1651 exile, when finally he was recompensed for his declared losses.

His principal banker before 1651 had been Thomas Contarini, himself also bankrupted by the Fronde. Contarini had been a co-accused in 1651, and a member of a commercial banking consortium to which Mazarin belonged. When he minimized Mazarin's revenues for the years 1641–8, putting them at nearly 7 million livres, a cursory scrutiny of the registers led the hostile *parlement* to raise that sum by another million livres. Mazarin was luckier in the dramatic under-valuation of his already breath-taking collections, many of the old masters from which had been hidden during the Fronde in the Palais-Royal, which was not searched.

After the Fronde, Mazarin was terrified of any possible renewed destitution. He used nominees like Jacques Tubeuf, one of the eight *intendants* of finance in France and *surintendant* of Anne of Austria's monetary affairs, for acquisitions and sales, but it was the sharpness of Colbert, who had by now become formally attached to Mazarin's service, that raised Mazarin's annual revenue to some 2 million livres. Some of it came from Mazarin's own offices, notably his governor-ships and the *surintendance* of the education of Anne's two children and of her own household, but some also came from participation on Richelieu's model in subsidized commercial enterprises, especially those concerned with overseas trade, shipping, fishing and other maritime activities, and from the subsidiary offices which Mazarin had the right to sell, like all those pertaining to the household of Anne and of her younger son, Philippe.

His private purchases and sales, of luxury goods for the perfume trade for instance, were supervised by Colbert and undertaken in the greatest secrecy. He acquired a mountain of copper against the probability that France would introduce a copper coinage, and in the end nearly doubled his money even though it did not. We know that a secretaryship in the Anjou household, carrying social prestige and ennoblement, cost 30,000 livres, but that a candidate for one such post, Charles Bonneau,[21] was prepared to pay Mazarin an extra 100,000 livres to obtain the appointment. One group of financiers offered to pay him 90,000 livres for his support in 1657. Mazarin accepted, providing the sum was paid in cash and in advance.

To these immensely lucrative sources of income must be added gifts from Anne, who connived at Mazarin's self-enrichment. Sometimes she gave him ransom payments, sometimes confiscations and captures. Sometimes Mazarin could sell advantages of status, as of Franche-Comté's rights to neutral status in the war with Spain. When the annual payments of 100,000 livres ceased with the peace of the Pyrénées, Mazarin demanded and received a compensation of 1.5 million livres. When it came to the exploitation of public power for private gain, Mazarin's behaviour was both more corrupt and closer to malversation than Fouquet's. That is why he did not move against Fouquet at Colbert's prompting, and why Colbert found it difficult to topple Fouquet without incriminating Mazarin himself when alive, or his reputation posthumously.

Colbert was occasionally stretched to disguise from the treasury just what it was that Mazarin was doing, as in the matter of equipping boats to fish in the Atlantic. Sometimes the treasury knew, but could not prevail against Mazarin's virtually sovereign power. Very often, however, the initiative in revenue-producing activities came from Colbert himself. If, like Richelieu, Mazarin lent money to the crown, which on more than three occasions he is known formally to have done, he did not, like Richelieu, need to be careful to channel his revenues through benefices and appointments, the administration of his lands and commercial enterprises. He could rely on Louis's loyalty and Anne's powers, in practice sovereign even after Louis's majority, to legitimize where necessary what might otherwise have been regarded as his predations.

On the morning of Mazarin's death, Louis called a meeting for the following morning of the principal persons concerned with the government of the state to take place in Paris. Among those present were the secretaries of state, the *surintendant* Fouquet, the chancellor and Lionne. It was at that meeting on 10 March 1661, that Louis made his famous speech, almost certainly written by Colbert, making known his wishes, as protocol prescribed, through the chancellor. The chancellor was not to use the seal, nor the secretaries to sign anything, not even so much as a passport, except with Louis's express authority. Fouquet was to act through Colbert, and the president of the clergy assembly was to address himself directly to the king. It would no longer be necessary for Anne d'Autriche to attend council meetings.

Mazarin had inherited a vestigial administrative system which separated issues concerning finance, foreign affairs and war. At his death, the three areas had developed into what were virtually departments of state: finance, headed by Fouquet; from 1642 by Le Tellier, later to be succeeded by his son, Louvois, for the military; and by the diplomat Hugues de Lionne for foreign affairs.[22] All three were extremely capable and, as Saint-Simon was later to note with disgust, of relatively modest birth.[23] Of the three only Fouquet appeared to covet Mazarin's vacant position. He was close to the queen mother, had an extensive network of spies, and was invariably successful at borrowing money when it was really required. He took care that Anne was in a position to satisfy her whims.

These three, heading what had once been the *conseil étroit* of Louis XIII, came immediately to be known after Mazarin's death as the *conseil d'en haut*[24] and, with Louis, these three and their successors ruled France until the death of Louis XIV. None of the old aristocracy, and not even the queen mother, was ever invited to join it. Occasionally others, like Turenne, were invited to a particular discussion, but its formal number increased to four only in the 1670s and to five in the 1690s, to revert again to three in 1714. In fifty-five years, Louis appointed only seventeen ministers to the *conseil d'en-haut*. Five were from the Colbert family and three were Le Telliers. In addition, Colbert's family came to count an archbishop, two bishops, intendants of the police and the marine and three generals. All his daughters married dukes, two of whom also became ministers. Richelieu had led the way in socially elevating his family, but both Mazarin and Colbert profited from his example.

Only members of the *conseil* were entitled to be called ministers of state. Below them came the secretaries of state, and the *conseil des dépêches*, dating from the Fronde, over which the king himself presided, which contained the chancellor, the ministers, the secretaries of state and such councillors as were required. It dealt with correspondence between central government, regional governors and *intendants* and home affairs involving more than one secretary of state. From 1661 it met twice a week, but was gradually phased out until, after 1691, it met only every second Monday. The chancellor, although head of the judiciary, was not involved in policy-making. He presided over the *conseil des parties*, the lowest tier of the king's council, concerned with administrative matters like the posts, royal expenditure, military supplies and judicial business reserved to the king.

The evidence that Mazarin gave Louis directly to understand that it would be better not to appoint a successor to himself as first minister is not clear, although Mazarin had obviously trained Louis to understand and undertake the creation of policy and the supervision of government. That advice may have been only implicit. Its ultimate source was Colbert, who no doubt envisaged for himself a position in the king's service analogous to that which he had filled for Mazarin, making him a sort of royal *intendant*.

It must have been Mazarin, continuing the course set by Richelieu, whose memory lay behind Louis's decision to annul the old constitutional right of the princes of the blood to share in the government of the nation. On Mazarin's death he simply ignored, and thereby abolished, the right of any member of the nobility, however closely related, to share even in the counsels, let alone the power of government. There was consternation at the French court, to which Mme de Lafayette and Ezechiel Spanheim, the Prussian minister, both testify, at the announcement that Louis intended himself to govern without a first minister, but the court was not aware of quite how strong and numerous were the links which made Mazarin simply irreplaceable, and the professionalism of the training in government which Louis had received.

Anne's court ally, Nicolas Fouquet,[25] the *surintendant,* was born in January 1615 of a pious family of ennobled bourgeois. Most historians have accepted the accusation of malversation against him, although more recently some have written in his defence. Of the twelve siblings out of fifteen to survive infancy, all six girls became nuns, and of the boys two became bishops, one became a priest, while the other three also received the tonsure. It was a devout family. Their father was an important lawyer, intelligently and piously devoted to good works and an early member of the Compagnie du Saint-Sacrement.[26] Fouquet's mother, Marie de Maupeou, also from a distinguished legal family, led the lay support for the charitable work of Vincent de Paul.

Nicolas, a Jesuit-educated lawyer, was early trusted by Richelieu, becoming in March 1633 a *conseiller* at the new sovereign court of Metz, for which he required a dispensation of age, as again when the judicial post of *maître des requêtes* was bought for him a year in advance of its creation in December 1635. He joined in the maritime and colonial enterprises of his father, who was to die in April 1640, the year of Nicolas's marriage into the Breton magistracy. In February 1641 Fouquet bought the run-down château at Vaux-le-Vicomte, halfway between Paris and Fontainebleau, and its *seigneurie* which made his nobility permanent.[27] He was moving from the nobility awarded to the senior administrative officers of the magistracy to the landed aristocracy. His wife died that August, leaving him with a six-month-old baby.

By October 1643 he was lending the crown 61,000 livres, and on 29 August 1646 he invested part of his daughter's inheritance from her mother by buying a property and *seigneurie* at Kerraoul in Brittany. His political ascendancy had followed swiftly on the death of Louis XIII, with important commissions, as he attached himself to Anne of Austria. There had been setbacks, and Fouquet was briefly dismissed by Mazarin for criticizing the level of taxation required by the Spanish war. By 1646 Anne had reinstated him as *intendant* of the northern army, and by 1648 Mazarin had appointed him *intendant* of Paris. That July he lent 22,000 livres to Mazarin.

When the Chambre Saint-Louis successfully demanded the abolition of the *intendants*, Fouquet was crucially left in a powerful position to mediate between the *parlement* of which he was a member and the crown, whose servant he was and against which the *parlement* was about to enter into open rebellion. A person of great charm, Fouquet successfully helped to mediate while serving the crown against the princes in 1650, switching roles at will between his parliamentary function and that of royal official and supplier to the military commissariat.

In the autumn of 1650 Fouquet was crucially made *procureur général* of the *parlement*.[28] He was a 'creature' of Mazarin, an officer of the crown, and the necessary intermediary between the regent and the *parlement*, of which both his non-ecclesiastical brothers were members, although one was to die in 1651.[29] Then on 4 February 1651 he remarried Marie Madeleine de Castille, the only child of very rich parents with a banking background which was to prove invaluable to him. Officially, he was now acting for the *parlement* against Mazarin during Mazarin's second exile, but in fact Fouquet connived with his brother Basile to keep Mazarin informed of what was being planned against him, and even succeeded in obstructing the seizure of Mazarin's property.

On the sudden death of La Vieuville on 2 February 1653 Fouquet's chance came. Jointly with Abel Servien, while still retaining the office of *procureur du parlement*, Mazarin appointed him *surintendant des finances* on 8 February. Servien would be in charge of spending and Fouquet would raise money. Since the *surintendance* was a commission and not a saleable office, Fouquet was enabled to retain his parliamentary office.

The respective functions of the two *surintendants* was altered at the end of 1654 when the state had already borrowed against the revenues for 1655 and 1656, and Servien was falling out with both Mazarin and the financiers. On 17 February 1659, Servien died. Fouquet was left in sole charge. He was particularly useful to Mazarin because, as *procureur,* he could act powerfully to achieve the necessary registration of financial edicts by the *parlement.* It was partly by sporadically satisfying them that Fouquet ensured the retention of his *surintendance* until support for him vanished with the cardinal's last breath. By failing to ensure that due interest on Mazarin's loans to the crown was paid on time, Fouquet had allowed Colbert's animosity towards him the chance to build in Mazarin a suspicion and distrust of the profligate personal style of his protégé.

Both Colbert, acting on behalf of Mazarin, and Fouquet had been supported by their relatives and taken part in vastly profitable commercial enterprises. Mutual suspicion and dislike had set in early. Colbert was the more focused, aggressive, and deceitful, Fouquet the more ambitious, easy-going, devout and financially skilful. Fouquet's gentle policy towards the financiers was the one which France, driven by the Spanish war to the edge of a renewed bankruptcy, needed to follow. Colbert had already undermined an unsuspecting and brashly self-confident Fouquet's standing with the king, insinuating the view that the *surintendant* was outdoing the king himself in ostentatious luxury, in patronage and in style, and flattered Louis's desire to break away from his mother's attempts at maintaining some tutelage over him, best achieved by showing the inefficacy of her protection of Fouquet.

Colbert more than insinuated that Fouquet must have come by so much wealth in the course of manipulating the nation's financial affairs, thereby in effect stealing from the king, and is normally, probably rightly, supposed to have reinforced the king's resolve by pointing out discrepancies and exaggerations in Fouquet's presentations of the state's accounts. Choisy tells us that Fouquet never believed that the young king would for long take on the onus of presiding in any detail over the government, and that he fed Louis an exaggerated account of state expenditure and a diminished account of revenues, making things seem even worse than they actually were. Fouquet's disgrace was inevitable before Mazarin died. Louis must have taken the formal decision to ruin him within three or four weeks of Mazarin's death. It is quite likely to have been only days.

Louis gives us an account in the third section of the *Mémoires* for 1661 of his dismissal of Fouquet. It is an extraordinary passage of self-justification based on an uncritical acceptance of Colbert's hatred and fear of Fouquet which, by Mazarin's death, had become near clinically paranoid. It cannot have been based on the perceptiveness for which Louis gives himself alarmingly generous credit, and it goes well beyond any view that Mazarin might ever have nourished. The self-deceit is so blatant and so complacent that its ultimate source must lie deep within Louis's personality, no doubt, like his need to conquer women, ultimately deriving from his search for self-confidence, for the desire for personal reassurance and the imperative internal need to free himself from his mother, with whom his relations were now erratic. As it stands, it does no credit at all to Louis's political antennae, to his emotional need for self-deceit, or even to his intelligence.[30]

It is known that the *Mémoires* for 1661, in Louis's twenty-third year, were edited with the help of notes by Colbert in 1669 or 1670, when Louis was thirty-one.[31] He attacks the *surintendant* for the 'vastes établissements' he projected, the 'insolentes acquisitions' he had made and the 'dérèglement de son ambition'. Fouquet is accused of seeking to deceive him, of bad faith, of excessive expenditure, of forming cabals and of buying offices at the king's expense for his friends in the hope of soon making himself 'l'arbitre souverain de l'état'. Louis goes on to recount his decision to arrest Fouquet and the difficult summer (of 1661) he had while dissembling his intention, before congratulating himself for taking on himself the onerous duty of managing the state finances.[32]

The means available to Louis for avoiding a repeat of the king-dom's financial failure of 1648 were limited.[33] Taxation had already risen to the intolerable levels which had occasioned the uprisings of 1631 in Paris, Bordeaux, Poitiers, Marseille, Orléans and Aix, and the Languedoc insurrection of 1632. Direct *per capita* taxation then tripled between 1637 and 1645, and was to rise again by a third between 1654 and 1655, while indirect taxation on selected products, goods, and services, confided to tax 'farmers', more than doubled between 1634 and 1644. Bad harvests meant real starvation, and the government's income was still far from financing the war.[34]

The expedients available to Louis ranged from the comparatively orthodox loans and advances which Fouquet had charmed from the banking community by means of promises of profit, rates of interest up to 20 per cent, and confident reassurances about solvency, to inventive creations of hereditable and saleable offices and the imaginative exploitation of the difference between the nominal value of the currency, which could be augmented, and the metal content, whose value could be diminished.

Fouquet was intransigently set against the debasement of the currency because it undermined the confidence which underpinned national solvency, but he relied heavily on borrowing against the future instalments of the three main forms of revenue, direct taxation (or *la taille*), the indirect taxation levied through the farmers, and the *affaires extraordinaires*, largely the sale and letting of offices and rights, and the sale of 'royal domain', property and rights which the crown retained the right to buy back at the sale price.

It is true that Fouquet's own commercial maritime ventures were considerable, and partly concealed by the use of borrowed names. In September 1658 he acquired from the indebted duc de Retz, and with strong encouragement from Mazarin and Louis, the Belle-Ile, an island off the entrance to Quiberon bay, with a mandate to fortify it to protect France's base for New World ventures. It was a large, strategically important island off the west coast of France, slightly to the north of the mouth of the Loire, an easily defended base, ideal for multiple maritime enterprises concerned with fishing, trading, transport and even processing, and a jumping-off ground for expeditions to the New World.

Fouquet built there the equivalent of a small industrial town as well as a naval construction yard and a port. Further acquisitions round the mouth of the Loire gave him control of the access to the Atlantic of an important region of west France. During his later prosecution, a sketch plan for the fortification of Belle-Ile, the 'projet Saint-Mandé',[35] was made to seem a sinister threat to the northern part of France's Atlantic coast and the hinterland of the mouth of the Loire, then a much bigger waterway than it is now. The document became the basis for an astonishing accusation of *lèse-majesté*, conviction for which seemed the easiest way of securing the death penalty.

Three months later Fouquet established a Paris-based company to trade with Spain and the east. It had the vast capital of 1,050,000 livres, made of three equal contributions, one of which was from Fouquet himself under the name of an intimate collaborator, and another from one of Fouquet's senior subordinates. Fouquet had his own small armada, bought and sold ships and cargoes, fortified his island and appeared to become altogether too rich and powerful for the comfort of a government which Colbert was intent on controlling. Colbert was poised to become the grand architect of Louis's image as all-powerful Sun King, and Louis, whatever his sentiments towards his mother and the 'old court' whose members came from her generation, was also reacting in the way Colbert required.

Colbert's chief weapon, endlessly reiterated to Louis and Mazarin, was the inference that the *surintendant* and *procureur général* must have connived with the hated but indispensable bankers to enrich himself to the impoverishment of the crown and its subjects. Belle-Ile, ran Colbert's whispers, the maritime enterprises, the huge sums spent on the two private palaces of Vaux and Saint-Mandé, the immense amounts spent on patronage of the arts, and even the vast sums lent on his own account to Mazarin, required the complicity of the bankers on whom Fouquet relied, but to whom he was in a position to grant favours, notably in assigning state assets against individual state loans. Fouquet was in a position to negotiate with the bankers the interest levels on state loans and to regulate their commerce in the state debt.

The further step followed logically that malversation was involved, after which the sentiment of an often starving peasantry, to say nothing of the country's 15–20 per cent of resentful bourgeois and minor nobility, could be relied upon to support an extension of the accusation to *lèse-majesté* and peculation, understood as trading on one's own account with crown money. Peculation, if proved, also carried the death penalty as well as confiscation of goods. Colbert needed and came near to successfully pressing for the death penalty.[36] Louis was not uninterested in acquiring the estates.

Colbert first manoeuvred an unsuspecting Fouquet, unaware of the imminence of any serious attack on his position, into selling his parliamentary office of *procureur général*. Colbert knew that the parliamentary office would have entitled Fouquet to trial by the *parlement* and would have prevented the use of the extraordinary jurisdiction which Colbert needed for the death penalty, itself required to ensure that Fouquet would have no opportunity to substantiate any accusations against Mazarin that might emerge from the trial. Mazarin's reputation needed to be safeguarded.

The *parlement*, if it had convicted him at all, would certainly not have imposed the death penalty, and only from a special judicial commission might greater compliance be expected. Louis had an understandable, if exaggerated fear of re-starting the Fronde, and did not want another serious quarrel with the *parlement*. He intended to let the death sentence stand if it was passed, and certainly, from his subsequent treatment of those responsible for refusing it, intended that it should be.

However, before Fouquet had any idea that he was under threat, Louis required a loan from him of 1 million livres, and there was more money-raising business which Louis needed Fouquet to complete before he could safely have him arrested. The trap was carefully engineered. Fouquet owed his brother 400,000 livres, so it was agreed that he should sell the office of *procureur* to Achille de Harlay for 1.4 million livres. Fouquet, whose fondness for grand gestures was flattered by the king's request for a loan, was thereby removed from the protection of the ordinary jurisdiction of the parliamentary courts, and the danger of re-igniting the Fronde clash between court and *parlement* was removed from his projected arrest.

The haste with which Louis formally decided on Fouquet's disgrace immediately after Mazarin's death no doubt owes something to Louis's petulant desire to disconcert his mother for her display of outrage at Louis's first infidelity after his marriage. On 1 April

1661, three weeks after Mazarin's death, the king's brother Philippe, 'Monsieur' since the death of Gaston d'Orléans, had married Henriette d'Angleterre, to be known at court as 'Madame', daughter of Charles I of England and Henrietta-Maria, and the favourite sister, 'Minette', of Charles II. Maria-Teresa had been pregnant since February, and was to give birth to the 'grand Dauphin', to be known as 'Monseigneur', on 1 November. On 20 April Louis took the court to Fontainebleau, where it remained until 4 December.

By May, less than a year after his marriage, and not much more than a month after that of his brother, Louis was ready to start an affair with his brother's seventeen-year-old wife, who had already inspired passion in the heart of the young duke of Buckingham, the son of Anne's own former admirer. His mother considered Louis's infatuation incestuous. Louis's marital infidelities, from which he could not be restrained, were a major reason why his mother did not retire from the court when her presence at the royal council was declared unnecessary.

In fact Louis's brother, Philippe, Henriette's husband, although jealous, was too effeminate in upbringing, appearance and inclination to pay Henriette much attention. His emotions were engaged with younger male members of the court, notably the chevalier de Lorraine, while Louis's own pregnant wife, Maria-Teresa, was unable and unwilling to ride or participate in her husband's favourite outdoor pastimes. She was less enthusiastic than he was about wide-open windows in freezing rooms and inadequately sprung coaches.

Louis's extra-marital partners would divide into those with whom he had a relatively long-term relationship, sometimes lasting years and productive of offspring who, if they survived infancy, were later legitimized, and the simple *écartades* of a few days or a few hours, or less. Both sorts tended to be taken from his wife's maids of honour. The duchesse de Navailles, the queen's lady-in-waiting, was in charge of their behaviour. Courted by Condé while he was still the duc d'Enghien, she later married and acquired a strong reputation for virtue.

When at Saint-Germain she risked much by asking the king to choose his friends from outside the circle of maids of honour. Louis had been obliged to take to clambering over the roof to visit Mlle de la Mothe-Houdancourt. Mme de Navailles, who had married a marshal of France, had grills put on the windows. In spite of Anne's pleas, the Navailles were in 1664 eventually dismissed and, when Anne reproved Louis for punishing them for their virtue, was herself publicly cut by her son.

Le Tellier, Colbert and Montagu all had to intervene to put matters right between mother and son, but they could not get Louis to restrain his roving eye and obsessive need to conquer. Henriette had rivalled in his affection Mlle de la Mothe-Houdancourt. She in her turn would be rivalled by Louise-Françoise de la Baume-le-Blanc de la Vallière, who had first been taken up as a smoke-screen for the relationship with Henriette, and by whom Louis was to have five children, of whom two survived to adulthood.[37] Louise was at least unmarried, and she was not Louis's sister-in-law. Court life continued to give his mother plenty to worry about, and she never did have the opportunity to retire from it. She felt that she needed to exercise a restraining influence on Louis, then fell ill in the summer of 1663. From December 1664 until her death on 20 January 1666, she was to suffer from breast cancer.

The court was at Fontainebleau, the magnificent château embellished round the old castle successively by François I, Henri IV and, most splendidly of all, by Louis XIII. It was named after its principal water spring, the Fontaine Beleau, itself called after the hound which unearthed it. Louis spent the summer of 1661, following Mazarin's death, succumbing there to the political manoeuvres of Colbert against Fouquet, and to the charms first of Henriette d'Angleterre and then of Louise de la Vallière. It was as early as this summer that Louis also became deeply fond of the small hunting lodge at Versailles, where he used to entertain his young friends, their ages averaging less than twenty, away from what remained, for all its fêtes, parties, entertainments, excursions, gambling, feastings and high spirits in that summer of 1661, the constraining court ambience of Fontainebleau.

Henriette d'Angleterre, vivacious animator of the joyousness of the younger court, became Louis's natural partner. Typical of her sense of mischief is her role in the clash of the two plays about Berenice. Friday was the traditional day for a first night. On Friday, 21 November 1670, Racine's *Bérénice* was given its first night at the Hôtel de Bourgone in Paris. The following Friday, 28 November, Molière's rival troupe put on *Tite et Bérénice*, by Racine's hostile ageing rival, Pierre Corneille. The subject contained a clear allusion to

Louis and Marie Mancini, and the clash was neither a challenge nor a coincidence. Both Fontenelle and Voltaire (twice) say that Henriette put the rival dramatists up to writing on the same subject for the rival companies without telling each that she was also approaching the other. It was the sort of behaviour the young court enjoyed, and it is reasonably certain that Henriette was the culprit.

Louis was bored by his wife, who had been pregnant since February, and Henriette's husband's infatuations with his male companions left her in need of an outlet for high spirits. Maria-Teresa's affection for Louis seems briefly to have been returned at the beginning of their marriage, although she was herself to remain genuinely in love with him throughout her life. The frequency with which Louis abandoned his mistresses for their replacements as their pregnancies advanced was to become a characteristic of his love life.

The *Muse historique* tells us that Henriette went swimming every day, going by coach on account of the heat, but returning on horseback, accompanied by her ladies, Louis and the whole young court. The mutual attraction between Louis and Henriette, ordinarily, as Mme de Lafayette, more a *moraliste* than a novelist, observed, 'the precursor of great passion', was quickly obvious. The queen mother was seriously concerned; Philippe felt, if not jealous, at least insulted, and Henriette's mother, who arrived at court on 6 July, was upset. Louis and Henriette agreed that Louis should cover their affection by a simulated relationship between Louis and one of the queen's ladies-in-waiting. The first choice, Mlle de Pons, was swiftly removed by her parents; the second choice, Mlle de Chimerault, declined the role; the third was the sixteen-year-old Louise de la Vallière, one of Henriette's ladies-in-waiting.

Mme de Lafayette remarks on the restraint shown by Louis and Louise as their strong real relationship came to replace the pretence. Louis would not see Louise in Henriette's apartments, nor on the daytime excursions, but in the evenings he would steal away from Henriette to visit Louise, neither a great beauty nor a great wit, but with blue eyes, blonde hair and a modest grace. Several commentators praise her complexion, but criticize her teeth and the fact that she was thin to the point of emaciation. Louise became Louis's openly declared mistress and, like Louis, knew that she was living a life of sin. Also like Louis, she rather ineffectually wished that she could do something about it.

At some deeper level, Louis retained the piety instilled in him by his mother, whose own flamboyant devotional life had, as Louis must have known, been compatible with retiring to her private chapel to read Mazarin's love letters. Louis acknowledged the contradictions between his principles and his behaviour, and was even sporadically overcome by bouts of shame. After having privately determined the fate of Fouquet, he was not inclined to go out of his way to remain on speaking terms with his mother, but he apparently dissolved into tears when he underwent her reproaches and explained his ineffectual efforts to restrain his passion for Louise. Colbert reports that Louis ordered his ministers to inform him if they noticed that he was being unduly influenced by any woman, promising to free himself within twenty-four hours. If he did indeed make any such promise, it can only have been fired by a mixture of bravado and guilt.

The contradiction within him, common enough, affords an important key to his character and later behaviour. The mistake is to see both in terms of youthful disregard for moral norms followed by later conversion.[38] Respect for the church meant formal observance of the proprieties and the avoidance where possible of open scandal, but it seems certain that in practice, and certainly during the earlier years of the century, public perception of the theological malice of sexual sin did not reach as far as the church, despite its moral theologians, taught that it should.

It may seem outlandish, but it also seems more than possible that Louis, who remained devout and would not have dreamt of repudiating the authority or integrity of the church's moral teaching, was simply unable to experience as mortally sinful his consensual sexual liaison with the unmarried Louise. Louis, quite probably in this, too, like his mother, remained aware of, and no doubt regretted the sinful nature of his behaviour. The state of mind of neither was defiant, and it is difficult to believe that either of them thought that, should they die, their illicit liaisons would be punished by eternal damnation, although they knew that that was the teaching of the church.[39]

The high point of court life in the summer of 1661 was the inaugural fête which Louis asked Fouquet to lay on for him at Vaux-le-Vicomte, where Louis and his bride had already briefly stopped on their way back from the south-west to prepare at Vincennes for the solemn entry into Paris. Fouquet's fall had already been decided, and an appropriate moment for the arrest was being awaited. It needed to be well away from Paris and access by Fouquet to his papers at Vaux and Saint-Mandé, and could not take place until after the sale of the parliamentary office and the negotiation of the loan to the king. Even after the famous fête at Vaux on Wednesday, 17 August, Louis was to betray no hint of his intention. It was after the fête, for instance, that he appointed Fouquet's brother to mastership of his private chapel.

Exaggerated interpretations of the Vaux festival have long been current, but it is indeed true that it cannot have been far from Louis's mind when he complained in the *Mémoires* that, at the beginning of his reign, payment of his personal debts remained delayed, or defrayed from credit, while the bankers displayed 'un luxe insolent et audacieux'. The queen mother had written a week beforehand of Louis's envy at the magnificence of Vaux, with the conclusion that the money had been taken from that which by right should have been his own. But Louis had himself proposed the inauguratory celebration, and was still putting up a front of grateful reliance on the *surintendant*.

Fouquet, a notable patron of the arts, perhaps indeed the most notable in Fance, close friend of Mme de Sévigné, and patron of La Fontaine, aligned with the incipient movement of the *modernes* and had made a magnificent success of his château. He had commissioned Le Vau for the rebuilding in August 1656, and it is Le Vau who must chiefly be responsible for the famed relationship between the gardens and the house from which the celebrated large canal crossing the main axis cannot be seen. The gardens themselves were designed by André le Nôtre. The shell of the house was largely completed within a year by a work-force of 18,000.

Le Vau developed the plan from one he had already used at Raincy, exploiting his liking for triple arches, used for entry into the rectangular entrance hall from the courtyard, for the passage from entrance hall to oval salon, and for the exit from the salon to the garden. The profusion of water works, canals, lakes, and fountains was said to surpass anything in Italy, but the interior decoration, for which Le Brun had used a restrained version of Pietro Cortona's baroque which he had studied in the Pitti palace in Florence, was not quite finished on the date of the festivity. Like the Pitti, it used a mixture of stucco, gilding and painting, but it avoided illusionism, foreshortening and the merging of painting and sculpture. Le Brun also used 143 tapestries, for whose manufacture a small factory was established nearby. It was later moved to Paris and has become known to history as the Gobelins.

Louis and his party set out from Fontainebleau at about three in the afternoon, arriving some three hours later. Louis then emerged into the garden from the oval salon only at dusk to walk in the gardens before returning to the house for supper. The maître d'hôtel was the already famous François Vatel, later to move to the service of the Condé family, where he is generally, but unreliably, said to have committed suicide by ramming himself against his sword. He thought that insufficient fish had arrived for a great feast, the evening after two tables had already gone short of roasts.

The service at Vaux was French style, that is a buffet rather than a series of dishes, with frequently recharged platters of every imaginable fowl and fish together with the roasts, the fruit and the sweet dishes. Then came the comedy-ballet with the candle-lit stage set in one of the clearings in the park, *Les Fâcheux*, by the fashionable but still struggling newcomer, Molière, with help from Pellisson, a décor by Le Brun and music directed by Lulli. It was essentially a series of ten satirical sketches exaggerating the external mannerisms, or *caractères*, of different social types, with mime and ballet and with Pellisson's prologue spoken by a naiad who ordered the trees and the pillars to speak.

Fouquet was in a hurry and wanted both a comedy and a ballet in a fortnight, to be staged together. There were not enough dancers, and those there were needed time to change between *entrées*, which had therefore to be interspersed with scenes from the comedy. So came of age the *comédie-ballet*. Molière, in ordinary clothes, stepped forward into a classical décor at the start to excuse himself for being without actors for the king's entertainment. An ornamental shell then opened up to reveal a pretty naiad who spoke Pelisson's prologue, after which the trees opened to reveal dryads, fauns and satyrs, among whom appeared satirical likenesses of recognizable social characters, possibly modelled in part on well-known contemporaries, some of whom may have been present and whose meetings and caricatures make up the almost unconnected series of scenes.[40]

Louis himself indicated to Molière the marquis de Soyecourt as a potential additional 'fâcheux'. Molière put him in as a hunter for the second performance at Fontainebleau. The prefatory 'Au Roi' to the published version shows Molière pretending to take himself more seriously than he did, and also seriously respectful, but quite at ease with Louis.[41] The Vaux entertainment was followed by a firework display made famous by La Fontaine's description, tracing figures in the sky and along the canal, with whale-oil lanterns illuminating buildings and statuary in the foreground. For Louis this degree of sumptuousness of luxury and magnificence of spectacle confirmed the impression that a grandeur rightfully his alone had been usurped. Fouquet had indeed in that metaphorical sense committed *lèse-majesté*.

Louis's self-justificatory remarks on the arrest of Fouquet have been mentioned in connection with the *Mémoires*, but it was Colbert who planned the arrest in meticulous detail. It would take place at Nantes where Louis would go to preside over the opening of the Estates of Brittany in early September, and was planned for Monday 5 September, Louis's twenty-third birthday. Heavy military cover would prevent any attempt at a retreat to Belle-Ile, which would be seized immediately after the arrest. Fouquet and Lionne left Fontainebleau on 24 August by coach for Orléans where they took a barge, followed by one containing Le Tellier and Colbert. Louis arrived at Nantes on Thursday 1 September. On the 4th, Fouquet did Colbert a favour by procuring money required by Colbert for the navy against his personal credit. The king sympathized with the bout of fever from which Fouquet was recovering.

The arrest was planned to take place during a meeting between Louis and Fouquet on the morning of the 5th. The arresting officer was to be d'Artagnan, and a memoir by Colbert to which Louis must have been privy specifies the pretext of a hunt so that musketeers would be mounted and carriages ready. The memoir even names the valet and the doctor who should accompany Fouquet to prison. There was some delay before Louis saw d'Artagnan arrive with the musketeers, and, as he wrote to his mother on the 15th, he had to fill time with Fouquet until their arrival, 'pretending to look for papers until I saw d'Artagnan in the court through the window'. Fouquet, finally suspicious, did try to elude capture, but got no further than the town square. Pellisson, an employee of Fouquet, was also arrested, and their houses were sealed.

Early in November a tribunal was set up to seek out malpractice in financial administration going back to 1635. Over 4,000 financiers were to be indicted and all but a small handful 'amnestied' on payment of fines fixed by a new *conseil des finances* over which Colbert presided. Some were condemned to death, but none was executed. On 15 November the names of Fouquet's judges were disclosed, most of them believed or certainly known to be hostile to him. Fouquet's own trial started with the investigation early in 1662 and lasted until the completion of the brief formal trial at the end of 1664. The worst that could be proved against Fouquet was untidy accounting, and the failure, copied from Mazarin, to keep separate his private accounts from those of the state in times of desperate need. Fouquet argued well, pointing out that Séguier, the chancellor, who was interrogating him, had been on the side of the *parlement* during the Fronde, while he had himself supported Louis throughout. Public opinion turned to his support.

Among Fouquet's papers were compromising letters from great ladies he had seduced, which he may have been keeping as an insurance policy. That caused some consternation, but was not treason. Almost certainly to protect Mazarin, an inventory of whose own possessions at death had been expressly, and indeed repeatedly forbidden by the cardinal on account of the many awkward questions it might have raised, no inventory of Fouquet's possessions, such as Fouquet knew would help to exonerate him, was allowed to be taken. One had in the end been prepared for Mazarin during the Fronde, but that was in an attempt to incriminate him. Fouquet was taken by surprise, and could have hidden nothing. The refusal of an inventory can scarcely be explained other than by fear among his enemies that anything an inventory might have disclosed could be matched from the possessions and enterpreneurial activities of Mazarin or by now even of Colbert himself.

It was largely due to fierce pressure from the political Catholic party, those close to the now suppressed Compagnie du Saint-Sacrement who had prayers for Fouquet said in all the Paris churches, that the final verdict, not delivered until 20 December 1664, just avoided a majority for the death penalty. Fouquet had not been found guilty of either peculation or of *lèse-majesté*, but it was a political trial, and he was not acquitted, either. He had committed formal irregularities and should be convicted of 'malversations et abus'. The vote was nine of the commissioners for execution, with the mitigation of beheading rather than hanging, and thirteen for banishment in perpetuity. Colbert was beside himself with rage. Louis, furious, changed the sentence of banishment to the much harsher sentence of life imprisonment, and banished Fouquet's family.

Louis, perhaps genuinely frightened either that Fouquet might have tried to replace Mazarin or that he might have had too much to reveal, and anyway impelled by Colbert to break with the old order associated with his mother and Mazarin, simply imposed life imprisonment under conditions that were at first, on Louis's continuing and detailed instructions, exceedingly strict.

Fouquet, escorted by 100 musketeers, left Paris on 27 December 1664. for the fortress of Pinerolo, where he would die in 1680. The most surprising revelation was that, as measured by the scale of Mazarin, or even, a little later, by Colbert, and subtracting his debts from his assets at the date of arrest, he was himself barely solvent, and not a rich man at all.[42]

7

The Young Ruler

When Mazarin died, Louis had declared that he would govern without appointing a first minister. When Fouquet was arrested, Louis pronounced his intention of himself assuming the burdens of the office of *surintendant,* simply abolishing the title.[1] In fact, acting on Colbert's advice, he established a *conseil des finances* composed of the chancellor and four others, one of whom was the *intendant* who took minutes, acting in modern terms as administrative secretary, a position assumed by Colbert until 1665, when he became *contrôleur général,* and the frequency of meetings was reduced to two a week. Although Colbert replaced Fouquet as minister alongside Le Tellier and Lionne, Louis also dropped the custom of appointing ministers by letters patent. Henceforward, all those summoned to advise the *conseil d'en-haut* were entitled to be known for life as ministers, although they had neither office nor function, but only title, when once the summonses ceased.

The *conseil d'en-haut* now met in principle seven times a fortnight before dinner, which was at one o'clock. Louis presided from a *fauteuil* and the *conseil* consisted only of ministers, seated on *tabourets.* The *fauteuil* had wooden arms, and the *tabourets* were upholstered chairs without arms. Meticulous protocol at court regulated who had the right to a *fauteuil,* who to a *tabouret,* and who had the right to be seated at all, in what order senior courtiers might be seated, and in whose presence.

No one dressed up or took notes. The pretence was that the king, exercising his personal sovereignty, merely discussed matters of state privately but regularly with whomsoever he pleased. It was, however, a principle for him never to discuss political affairs outside the council or with others than its members. Government was in the hands of a very few, all of them dependent day-to-day directly on Louis for their positions, which does not mean that Louis did not also become dependent on them, obviously for information, advice and executive action, but also, particularly in the case of Colbert, for knowledge, strategic planning and moral support.

The *conseil des dépêches*, where Louis also presided, met much less frequently than the *conseil d'en-haut*. It consisted of the chancellor, the ministers and the secretaries of state, who could buy and sell their offices with royal permission, and could be forced to sell them. Colbert, a member of all three councils (*finances, dépêches,* and *en-haut*), now effectively held more political power than had either Richelieu, whose thought he embraced and extended, or Mazarin, whose private affairs he had managed with such spectacular success. He was required only to be careful to father his decisions on Louis and to persuade Louis, always neurotically touchy about even potential erosion of his authority, that he had originated them himself.

In a well-known letter of 24 April 1671 to Colbert from Chantilly, Louis congratulates himself on his restraint, says that he is writing so as not to give Colbert the chance to react in a way which might further have displeased him, and continues, 'do not risk annoying me further, because when I have heard your arguments and those of your colleagues, and have given my opinion on all of your claims, I never wish to hear more about it'.[2] Colbert, stung by the rebuke which ended in a veiled threat to remove from him control of maritime affairs, immediately went to call on Louis, who sent him next day a pacifying letter, assuring Colbert of his continued friendship and gratitude. J.C. Rule draws attention to Louis's habit of teasing Colbert in council about Colbert's fidelity to Richelieu's policies, 'Colbert, here, is going to say to us again, "Sire, the great Cardinal Richelieu, etc . . . ."'[3]

Colbert, born in 1619, was above all an admirer of Richelieu, extending the cardinal's quest for an independent France to an attempt to establish self-sufficiency. He was cold, brutal, highly intelligent, often depressed, but extremely hard-working. He firmly believed in the superiority of seventeenth-century French culture

Louis XIV on horseback

Cardinal Mazarin

The mother of Louis XIV, Anne of Austria, and his wife, Maria–Teresa, infanta of Spain and his mother's niece

Detail from Versailles 1668, the Cour de marbre

Louis XIV outside the Marly estate (1724)

Presentation by Colbert of members of the Académie des sciences to Louis XIV

Mme de Montespan   Louis XIV in stage costume dressed as the sun

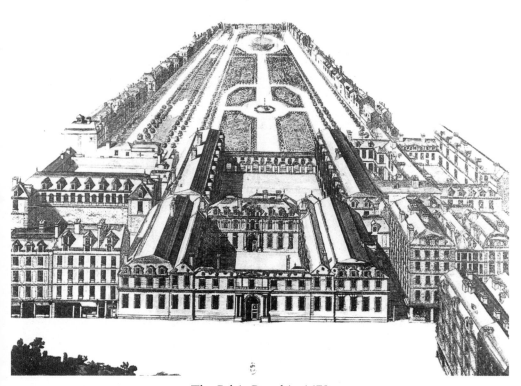

The Palais-Royal in 1679

Versailles 1668

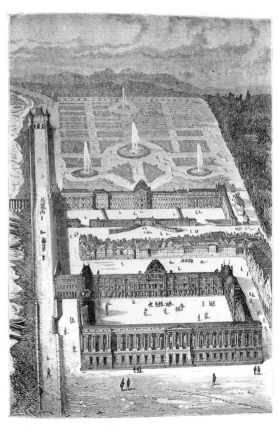

The Louvre and the Tuileries
(Seine flows up the left hand
side of the picture)

over anything created in antiquity, and set out both to exalt and to control it. Historically, his reputation has seen extreme swings. Bitterly hated during his lifetime, his illiberal fiscal policies and principles of government were rejected by the eighteenth-century liberals before they were rehabilitated for restrained admiration by the revolutionary generation, generally hostile to Louis XIV. Elevated in the nineteenth century as the supreme example of devoted service to the state, Colbert has more recently been seen as the super-bureaucrat who, in addition to engendering and administering foreign, domestic and commercial policy, supervised in great detail the Sun King's public image. The strategy for Louis's reign designed by Colbert was to glorify France itself through the elevation of its divinely appointed king to a quasi-divine status of his own.

While purporting in all things to be merely the faithful servant of the king's commands, at the height of his power Colbert was to run the country's finances as controller-general of finances from 1665, to regulate its commercial activities, to organize Louis's building programmes and artistic patronage and to oversee France's maritime enterprises.[4] After taking over from Fouquet what was henceforward known as the intendancy of finance in 1661, Colbert took over the superintendancy of buildings and general superintendancy of commerce in 1665, and became secretary of state in charge of the navy, rivers and forests, commerce, and with some part of responsibility for the fortification of coastal towns in 1669. By 1671 he was also in charge of the clergy and of the royal household.

The mere list of his discrete responsibilities, which he often began to exercise before the necessary authority was formally bestowed on him, indicates the vast role Colbert played in the running of the country, no doubt as great as that of Mazarin at the height of his power. He originated and implemented policy, reformed the country's administration, and imposed an inquisitorial accountability on its fiscal system. It is he who actually exercised the power of government, with the complexities of which Louis could never really bother himself, preferring to manage the intricacies of court ritual.

What Louis required was the final say on all important issues. He trusted Colbert, and could not easily deviate from the path dictated by Colbert's briefing. He also needed the illusion and the appurtenances of power, and the revenues required to finance his personal projects. He was content to preside over the *conseil d'en haut* two or three times a week, and sometimes the principal lesser councils, and rigorously to enforce the complex minutiae of court protocol.

It is commonly, if erroneously, asserted, following Saint-Simon, that there were only three instances subsequent to 1661 when Louis manifested 'extreme anger', once each with Colbert, Lauzun, who wished to marry the grande Mademoiselle, and Louvois, minister for the army. Louis was in fact prone to anger, but none the less cultivated an image of fastidious courtesy. He could be brutal, insensitive and unfeeling, but he became careful never to be impolite. In spite of his aggressive military ambitions, the sometimes teasing and sometimes grotesque way in which he held on to and brutally exercised supreme power, and above all for his self-image as God's appointee, it has sometimes been possible to regard Louis primarily as the wealthy head of the landed gentry, seriously interested in horsemanship and hunting, a lavish and considerate host, and a courteous but firm enforcer of court ceremonial. There was a side to him which this role fitted well.

Louis's dependence on Colbert reached the stage that he could write to him when he was unwell not to come back until he really was fit: 'I order you to do nothing that will prevent you from serving me when you arrive.' Colbert's closeness to Louis is well illustrated by Louis's contribution of 200,000 livres to the dowries of each of Colbert's daughters, two of whose marriages were arranged only with the direct intervention of Louis.[5] While his mother was alive, Louis was understandably coy about his illegitimate children, so that when Louise de la Vallière became pregnant in 1663 with a son, who was in fact to die in infancy, Louis charged Colbert with making arrangements for the confinement and the care of the newly born infant. He was placed with former servants of the Colbert family.

The closeness of Louis's reliance on, and cooperation with Colbert often makes it difficult to know what was the individual input of Louis into the overall strategy which was Colbert's creation. The strategic aim derived from Richelieu, who had died in 1642 and had both trusted and trained Mazarin, and from Mazarin who daily devoted hours to training Louis during the 1650s, and during the same period came to have an absolute trust in Colbert. It cannot therefore surprise that Louis and Colbert, both products of Mazarin's tutelage, came to share assumptions, points of view, grand aims and the general strategies by which they would be achieved.

A carefully selected presentation of the evidence from the decade following Mazarin's death can, however, make Louis seem either on the one hand totally subservient to his role as trustee of the glory of France and its people or, on the other, as so insecure as to need to delude himself by the grandeur of the demi-god figure he was forced to assume. Externally, he did, however, begin to behave as if genuinely convinced that the attributes of the roles in which he was metaphorically cast were his by right. Understandably but indeliberately, he confused his divinely bestowed but artifically projected royal mask with his merely human functional status.

As early as 1661, Louis was allowing Colbert, nineteen years his senior, to write in his name and on his behalf to the provincial commissioners and governors, and to train the *intendants* by sending them on a series of missions before appointing them to their *intendances*. All orders were given in the name of the king, but there was a working balance between the authority conferred by royal rank and that with which age, experience, intelligence and success vested Colbert. Colbert left huge left-hand margins in his drafts and letters to Louis, which invariably came back allowing him full tactical discretion. If the strategy was both inherited and agreed, the tactics were Colbert's.

For all that, the king and Colbert did not altogether agree. It is a tribute to the attitudes of each to the other that, if in November 1662 Louis could write to the *intendants* informing them that in future they could learn his wishes from Colbert's instructions to them, in 1666 Colbert, trying to restrain Louis's war expenditure, could write of the people's 'disgust' at the ravages wrought by endlessly passing troops, 'His Majesty has made a mixture of his recreation and his warfare.'[6] Louis was naturally always addressed in the third person.

With the breaking of Fouquet in September 1661, Colbert had become leader of the victorious party in the enterprise of making France prosperous as well as independent. For a score of years Louis was to play Colbert off against his rival and enemy, Louvois, made secretary of state for war in 1668 and Chancelier des Ordres du Roi in 1671. There is one famous occasion on which Colbert appears to have complained openly at a council meeting of a preference given to his rival, Louvois, appointed to the vacancy for a chancellor of the king's orders which Colbert had coveted, and which Mme de

Montespan had begged Louis to give him. The Savoy ambassador reported back on the incident, showing the court interest in the Louvois–Colbert rivalry.

Louis's attitude, personal animosities apart, preserved only the illusion of serious political power in the government of France. Its executive reality was abdicated, in the first instance to Colbert, in spite of the occasional favour shown to Louvois in what must be regarded as Louis's failed attempt to keep a balance between two rivals. The year after the favour accorded to Louvois in the matter of the chancellorship of the king's orders, the succession to Arnauld de Pomponne, disgraced largely at Louvois's instigation as minister for foreign affairs, was given to Colbert's brother, and not to Louvois's candidate, much to the amusement of the court.

It was Colbert who held the greater and wider power. His aim, developed from that of his admired Richelieu, was at the root of what has been called his 'mercantilism', the strategy of keeping as much bullion as possible circulating within French borders, promoting French self-sufficiency wherever possible, and increasing the money supply, and with it he hoped the tax base, by exporting as much and importing as little as possible.

Choisy, who believed that the scattering of raw materials in territories belonging to different countries offered Europe the necessary basis for building prosperity on peaceful trade and cooperation, is strongly critical of Colbert's quest for self-sufficiency, precisely because it was based on the view that a country's prosperity, and its ability to pay taxes, was measured by the store of precious metal in circulation. The enrichment of one country meant the impoverishment of another.

France had neither gold nor silver mines of its own, and needed therefore, according to Colbert, to manufacture whatever it could, to attract bullion from elsewhere, and to erect high tariff barriers. He would have liked to prevent the importation of silks from the east, cloth from the Low Countries, horses from England, or wool from Spain.[7] What Colbert was not against importing was expertise, whether by inviting foreign craftsmen to France, or by sending French workers to be trained abroad.

Colbert's aim included emphasizing the grandeur, indeed the quasi-divine image of the king, particularly among the artistic and literary communities. What started off as almost disinterested patronage soon became a system of rewards for singing the glories of the king. Its recipients were told what was expected of them. The crown had become one of the comparatively few potential large-scale sources of artistic patronage left in France, and Colbert the mediator between the king in his role as patron and the potential recipients of his patronage. It was his responsibility as the *surintendant des bâtiments*, one of the posts whose functions Colbert exercised before he occupied it from 1 January 1664.

Alongside the medals and monuments, he wished to use the arts and the sciences for the glory of the king, to this end establishing a spectacular series of academies, artistic and scientific foundations, reformed the Académie française, and re-organized the theatrical life of Paris, reducing the number of permanent companies from three to two, and then merging them into one. He elevated the status and income of craftsmen by changing them from guild members into members of academies in return for control over their activities, and established such manufactories as the Gobelins for wall-hangings and furniture and the Savonneries for carpets, over whose production he could exercise total control. Every pattern used at the Gobelins had to be officially approved.

Louis was to manifest a personal interest in matters concerning benefactions to men of letters, and had himself depicted visiting the Observatory and the Académie des Sciences in paintings that have become well-known.[8] At his re-organization of the Académie française after the death of its protector, Séguier, in 1672, Colbert ensured that Louis was himself made protector in 1673, and that the Académie met henceforward in rooms set aside for it in the Louvre. Meanwhile, however, the Gobelins was constituted from the original manufactory established by Fouquet at Vaux, amalgamated with several other workshops in a property on the faubourg Saint-Marcel, acquired for 40,000 livres by Colbert. Charles Perrault says that Colbert had 'foreseen', or already knew, that he would be appointed to the superintendancy of buildings.

The speed with which the new strategy was put into execution as soon as Fouquet had been removed from office on Louis's twenty-third birthday suggests that Colbert had been meditating on it during the 1650s. Louis himself can have contributed little, since he was an adolescent for most of that decade, although his interest in the theatre was already keen. When he was just eighteen and too impatient to wait, he went to see Thomas Corneille's *Timocrate,* which only purports to be a tragedy and was the century's most commercially successful play, in one of what were then the two public playhouses in Paris. All Paris was said to know it by heart and it had an unheard-of run of over eighty performances at the Marais. Louis took a large party on 12 December 1656, before seeing it again at Philippe's residence in January.[9]

Since we know that Colbert was working to undermine Louis's trust in Fouquet well before Mazarin's death, and that Mazarin almost certainly had reasons to want any action over Fouquet suspended until after his own death, it seems likely that Mazarin was himself a contributor to Colbert's elaboration of Richelieu's plans for the creation of a strong, independent France under a glorious monarch, to be achieved partly through creating strong centralized cultural institutions. The models were no doubt to be strengthened versions of Richelieu's by now semi-somnolent Académie française and Mazarin's 1648 foundation of the Académie de Peinture et de Sculpture, which the opposition of the pre-renaissance guilds had made less than totally successful.

Richelieu had had great difficulty in founding the Académie française,[10] and we know from the 1655 discours on reception into the Académie of his doctor, La Mesnardière, that by the end of his life Richelieu had intended to make the Académie the engine for the unification of all cultural activity in France. He intended to use it to found a college much grander than what Mazarin was to achieve with the Collège des Quatre Nations. Under the direction of the existing Académie, whose members would become salaried, the new college would appoint 'illustrious' professors, including specialists in the physical sciences. Richelieu had apparently acquired a property with his 'great college' for the study of 'les belles sciences' in mind, and was counting on an annual budget of 100,000 livres.

The group which was turned into the Académie française in 1637, and may have been meeting as early as 1629, had on the whole been hostile to accepting the letters patent erecting it into a formal consultative group. The only member in favour was Jean Chapelain, author of an *Ode à Richelieu* published, as ameliorated in draft by Richelieu himself, in 1633, of several more odes to grand personnages and of a long patriotic poem, the slow, digressive and glacially monotonous *La Pucelle,* earlier parts of which had been annotated by Richelieu himself. It was Chapelain, a Richelieu sycophant and a poor but pompous and over-ambitious poet, although a perceptive, if conservative, critic and first-class administrator, who acted for him in the complex matter of the foundation of the Académie, and was paid by him bi-annually from 1633 until the payments became an annual pension in 1636.

It was on Chapelain, who was to die in 1674, and to a lesser extent Charles Perrault, brother of the architect Claude, that Colbert was largely to rely to implement his cultural policy, centred in good measure on the thurification of Louis. Chapelain's famous sonnet, 'Quel astre flamboyant sur nos provinces erre', comparing Louis XIV to Mars, Jupiter and the sun, set the tone, and Chapelain had the advantage for Colbert of a publicly known hatred of Fouquet and the financiers, and an association with the court faction during the Fronde. He was officially employed by the Longueville family, whose ancestry his epic *La Pucelle* attempted to glorify.

He also had a proven ability to appear to take both sides at once in several major literary disputes. As early as 1662, Chapelain, who had ingratiated himself with Mazarin and Colbert, was asked by Colbert in connection with the appointment of a new royal historian to draw up a list of 'living men of letters', with comments on their abilities, from among whom one might be chosen for appointment, but which would also contain names of writers suitable for other functions. The promotion of a consciousness of French history was a lynch-pin in Colbert's grand plan for the glory of Louis, and had been at the core of Louis's own education.

Chapelain submitted a non-partisan list of ninety-eight names, including all forty members of the academy and, among the other fifty, twenty who had published only in Latin. Other such lists were apparently called for, and Mézeray was appointed *historiographe,* an earlier provisional appointment having been cancelled because the appointee, Perrot d'Ablancourt, was a Huguenot. Then, as early as 3 February 1663, Chapelain was invited by Colbert with three others, including Charles Perrault, to form a group which met at Colbert's residence on Tuesdays and Fridays and which developed into the *petit conseil* before it became the Académie des Inscriptions et Belles-Lettres. Louis wrote to them that entrusting his *gloire,* 'the thing which is the most precious in the world', to them was a manifestation of the high esteem in which he held them.

From 1663 Chapelain was also directly concerned with the distribution of royal literary patronage, indicating what was expected of them to prospective recipients in the unlikely event that they did not already know. To one who did not, the Italian poet Girolamo Graziani, Chapelain explained that Louis granted 'gratifications', as they were called, not because he wished to be praised, but simply to act 'royalement'. However, the paeans of praise would seem more spontaneous if they were printed abroad. As he said to Colbert, the benefactions would appear more noble, the more disinterested they looked. Other foreign beneficiaries were advised on dedications and flattering mentions of Louis.[11] Officially appointed chroniclers of the reign multiplied and, in spite of the preference for Mézeray on religious grounds, benefactions were at first also made to Huguenots.

The formal 'gratifications' paid to authors appear to have started as early as March or April 1663, going from 800 to 3,000 livres, with Chapelain awarded the top figure and referred to as 'the greatest poet there has ever been, and with the best judgement'.[12] Louis himself took a serious interest in attracting to Paris an international group of scientists, mathematicians and scholars, and Colbert was particularly successful in executing this part of the programme, drawing the Dutch physicist Huygens to Paris for 6,000 livres annual 'pension', and paying the Italian astronomer Gian-Domenico Cassini 9,000 livres a year.

Colbert had set the total budget at 100,000 livres a year, but only 77,500 livres were distributed in 1663, with fifteen non-French nationals included in the list. The distributions grew to 110,000 livres in 1669, and then declined steeply to 49,000 livres in 1674 during the Dutch war, dipping to 40,000 in 1688 before they were abolished in 1690, their purpose in establishing Louis's munificent patronage accomplished. In 1663 the benefactions came in a silk purse, but in 1664 the purse was leather, and from 1665 the beneficiaries had to collect their gratifications from the treasury of the department of buildings. Perrault's memoirs complain of delayed payments: the years began to have fifteen or sixteen months. There were additions and deletions to the list, but about forty men of letters or learning, of whom about ten were non-French, received annual pensions from 1663 to 1690.

Colbert's literary strategy, entrusted to Chapelain for execution, at first nearly back-fired. When, on 28 May 1663, Louis showed the first symptoms of the measles which could at this date be fatal and which he caught from Maria-Teresa, he recovered within a week. Chapelain nevertheless urged all the recipients of benefactions to celebrate the cure. Some, not on the original list, earned their place by their pieces. The young Racine sent via an intermediary an ode which Chapelain sent back for improvement. The young Turks of the literary world, omitted from the list, took to satirizing the whole organization of benefactions, and some, like the young Boileau-Despréaux and his fellow-frequenters of La Croix blanche corporately ridiculed Chapelain himself in the scurrilous *Chapelain décoiffé*.[13] In spite of a mock conversion from satire to praise, Boileau-Despréaux continued in his seventh *Satire* to attack a list, mutable from edition to edition, of conformist recipients of official subventions.

Colbert's cultural campaign moved swiftly. Louis's own principal interest had resulted in an Académie for teachers of dance founded by letters patent in March 1661, the month of Mazarin's death. By 1663 he had integrated the Académie française, the Académie Royale de Peinture et de Sculpture and the future Académie des Inscriptions into the great enterprise of working to the glory of the Sun King. Le Brun was appointed director of the Gobelins in Paris in March 1663, and in 1665 the *Journal des savants,* with reviews, obituaries and accounts of experiments was founded, largely to advertise Paris as the world's intellectual centre and the munificence of the French king. Its director was Pierre de Carcavy, Colbert's former librarian.

It can be argued that the academies established in the first dozen years after the death of Mazarin ended up by reducing spontaneous artistic creativity to adherence to a set of rational and eternal rules, stifling real creativity. Such an outcome might indeed even have been foreseen and welcomed by those, mainly the partisans of the *anciens* in the *Querelle,* who thought that there were discoverable rational norms underlying the beautiful, the tasteful, the artistic, the moral and the true.

The proximate purpose of the academies was, however, to bring the activities over which they presided into a chorus of praise for the transcendant figure of the Sun King. The Académie de Peinture started to admit new members on the acceptance of a work dealing with the history of the king, and from 1663 offered prizes for statues or paintings of the king's heroic actions. Several academies employed composers to write music in the king's honour, and the Gobelins produced the famous tapestries of the history of the king. From 1671 the Académie française offered an annual prize for a panegyric of the king.[14]

Charles Perrault sent a memorandum to Colbert in 1666 suggesting that the four major academies, Académie française, *petit conseil*, Académie des Sciences and Académie de Sculpture et de Peinture, should be made the kernel of a vast 'académie générale'. Colbert's aim was not only to glorify Louis, but also to bring all cultural activity under royal control to serve the glorification of the king.[15] He did not, however, favour the rigorous monopoly control of the academies on which Louis himself was to insist.

The right to elect a director was removed from the Académie de Peinture et de Sculpture at the end of 1663; the Académie Royale des Sciences, created in 1666 with fifteen fellows at a pension of 1,500 livres a year, received formal statutes only in 1699, leaving the government itself in charge for over thirty years. In 1672, Perrault had the method of recruitment to the Académie française changed, giving the king the power to control membership. When Séguier died on 28 January 1672, and Colbert had Louis made its protector, he had himself named as vice-protector.

From 13 January 1673 Perrault also had the sessions at which new members were received, and gave their now traditional discourse, made open to the public. Colbert had the meetings made more frequent than the customary twice a week. They were to last precisely two hours. Minutes were kept; *fauteuils* were introduced in place of chairs; academicians were given a *jeton* for attending if they arrived on time, reimbursable for cash; those whose primary interest in the proceedings was the cash became known as *jetonniers*. Work on the dictionary was slowed down by the length of the deliberations on whether the letter 'a' was a noun or not and, if it was, what was its gender.

From 1666 the French artists sporadically supported to study in Rome were formed into the Académie de France à Rome at the Villa Medici, with six painters, four sculptors, and two architects, and in 1667 the Observatory was begun. The Académie des Sciences was to be founded in 1669, although the term was being used three years before that. Then in 1669 what became the Académie Royale de

Musique and was first known as the Académie d'Opéra ou réprésentations en musique was founded. Entrusted to Lulli, who bought it in 1672, it took over the larger of the two theatres in the Palais-Royal on Molière's death in 1673. In 1671 Colbert established the Académie d'Architecture.

Paris itself was not neglected. Colbert, as minister for Paris, persuaded Louis that the lax policing of Paris needed to be re-formed, and instigated the appointment of Gabriel-Nicolas de La Reynie in 1667 to a new post of lieutenant of police in Paris. La Reynie became very close to Louis and remained in charge for thirty years, until in 1697 he was succeeded by Marc-René de Voyer d'Argenson. He acted as head of the political as well as the criminal police, who had hitherto been the responsibility of the Châtelet, the highest court in France under the Paris *parlement,* from which he was technically supposed to take instructions. His first major step in 1667 was to tighten the censorship regulations. Crime, security, roads and street-lighting came later.

Paris was to be turned into a glorious capital for a glorious king. Since raw sewage was being dumped in the river from which drinking water was being taken, it was imperative to create fountains from which safe drinking water could be drawn, and the second half of the century saw the completion not only of fountains but of the Observatory, the Louvre, the Gobelins, the Invalides, the Institut, the Porte Saint-Denis, the Porte Saint-Martin, the Place Vendôme, the Porte des Victoires, the Pont-Royal and the Tuileries.

Colbert hoped that Louis would make the Louvre his main residence, but Louis made it clear in the year following Mazarin's death that he did not intend to spend much time there. In the spring of 1661, however, Louis was not yet twenty-three, and might yet be prevailed upon to fall in with Colbert's scenario for the reign. It was not until Anne of Austria died on 20 January 1666 that a sense of full emancipation in this, as in so many other matters, can be sensed in Louis's actions. Even when he had rejected Colbert's preference for making the Louvre his centre of government, Louis was not yet definitively committed to Versailles. Rueil, Saint-Germain, the Tuileries and Fontainebleau were still possibilities, although they became increasingly improbable. The Louvre was largely turned into private apartments, allocated as grace-and-favour residences, and into administrative offices and meeting rooms, as for the Académie française.

Colbert's undoubted achievement did not go as far as carrying out the root-and-branch reform of the whole fiscal system, which is what was required. What he did achieve, much aided by the peace he inherited from Mazarin, was the restoration of some equilibrium in the state finances. All types of military expenditure were reduced, and he had the added bonus of a diminution in the pillaging and rape of the countryside and its inhabitants by a dissatisfied soldiery. At the same time the investigation of the 4,000 financiers by the *chambre de justice* brought back to the treasury huge sums in back taxes and misappropriated funds, allowing for some slight diminution of taxation and for the building up of the navy.[16]

For most of the 1660s the king was still in his twenties. His own indifference to the vagaries of the weather and to physical discomfort means that he cannot exactly be said to have been considerate towards the more delicate and often sickly Maria-Teresa, but it was primarily for her sake that he went to some lengths to keep his relationships with his mistresses private. In spite of attempts to alert her, particularly in the celebrated anonymous 'Spanish letter' of 1664 in which the marquis de Vardes[17] was the prime mover, Maria-Teresa appears not to have been aware of the nature of the relationship between her husband and Louise de la Vallière until about 1666, when she was informed by the former Olympe Mancini, now comtesse de Soissons, and still jealous of the woman who had won Louis's affections.

The story of the seduction of Louise de la Vallière by Louis is normally printed as part of the *Histoire amoureuse des Gaules* by Bussy-Rabutin, cousin of Mme de Sévigné. When she fled from the court on 24 February 1662 two days before Bossuet's sermon on adultery, Louise had had to be brought back from the convent of the Visitation, but since she had made it clear that that was where she was going, her flight seems not to have been intended to be a definitive break. In fact, she clearly relished many aspects of her privileged position, using it to obtain for clients favours from the king numerous enough to attract comment, and for which she expected the usual monetary reward.

Pious and passive, Maria-Teresa accepted, apparently without serious complaint, the fate which God had chosen to send her, offering up to him the successive deaths of her infant children. She even appeared relieved to see them spared the agonies to which their roles would have subjected them in the dynastic politics in which

they would have been pawns. The grand Dauphin, born on 1
November 1661, was to be the only one of her six children to survive
into adulthood. One, in 1664, may have been stillborn, and Maria
Teresa nearly died giving birth. At court she liked the attentions
which courtesy demanded should be paid to her, and she gamed,
generally losing, sometimes excessively. It is alleged that Louis
sometimes had to settle her debts and that once, in November 1675,
she lost 60,000 livres before noon, and missed mass in an
unsuccessful effort to win the money back.[18]

The court was still small, scarcely a hundred or so persons,[19] but a
wider public rejoicing was called for at the birth to Maria Teresa of
the dauphin, a healthy male infant whose gender vastly diminished
the prospect of a disputed succession such as had prevailed in France
for the score of years before Louis's own birth. Louvois, the son of
Michel le Tellier, who had begun to work with his father earlier in
1661 and whose rivalry with Colbert went back to the beginning of
his career, is said to have suggested to the king that the celebration
should take the form of a tournament or carrousel, with much public
display of equestrian skill, accuracy and grace, as the riders galloped
in such medieval feats of military skill as piercing a suspended ring,
or hitting the suspended effigy of a Turk's or an African's head or a
Medusa mask with a lance.[20]

They were on this occasion teamed into five 'quadrilles', each
representing an ancient civilization. Louis, who excelled at all
equestrian sports and led the first quadrille, was dressed as a Roman
emperor, with his brother and Condé among the other quadrille
leaders, dressed as Persians, Turks, Indians and Americans. Louis
could be expected to do well, and Louvois knew that Colbert would
be much embarrassed to find the money for the festival of which
the medieval jousting and tilting competitions were the high point.
It has been suggested that Colbert resolved the financial problem
by commandeering the proceeds of what amounted to the Parisian
sales tax for the royal treasury, and then postponing the fête for a
fortnight, keeping high-consuming visitors in Paris to pay for the
festivities with the extra tax.[21]

In the mind of Louis, the carrousel of 5 and 6 June 1662, inspired
by a famous festivity of exactly half a century before in 1612, in what
was as much a pageant as a series of competitions, became an
opportunity to display his equestrian prowess before Louise, and a

semi-feudal chance to consecrate any victory to her. The procession, which included musicians and performing animals as well as the competitors, and was intended to have the air of a carnival, took the lengthy route across Paris from the Arsenal to the tilting ground, a square opposite the Tuileries still today known as the Place du Carrousel, to enhance the opportunity for public exhibition and celebration.

Louis's team did not win the competition, but the event did at least show his awareness at this date of the need to cultivate some rapport with the Parisian population.[22] Quite importantly in view of the re-importation into Paris of the Italian comedy by Mazarin and Anne immediately after Richelieu's death, elements of the pageantry were Italianate. A renewed recourse to Italian inspiration was to become characteristic of architectural and artistic work in France in the 1660s.

Indeed, paradoxically, Louis and Colbert diverged in taste and inclination precisely over Colbert's inheritance from Richelieu of the overriding desire to promote all that was French and modern, including the pre-eminence of its king. Louis, following Mazarin's native Italian taste, leaned towards a love of Italian artistic and architectural achievement.[23] It was Colbert, aided by his assistant Charles Perrault, the champion of the *modernes,* who wanted Louis to make the Louvre the centre of government. Colbert became pre-eminent in directing the massive mid-century rebuilding that took place in the capital, while Louis succeeded, no doubt partly by employing as architect Le Vau, to whom Colbert was resolutely hostile, in imposing a perceptibly Italian character on Versailles, which had at least started out as his own semi-private project.

The Louvre fire of 1661 had left Colbert with the opportunity of rebuilding what he hoped would be the principal royal palace. Jacques Lemercier, Richelieu's principal architect, and, after his death in 1654, Louis Le Vau had already been working on the east side of the Louvre, and Le Vau had been commissioned to design for Mazarin's executors the Collège des Quatre Nations, now the Institut de France, on the left bank of the Seine. His magnificent design for the Institut, derived from Pietro da Cortona and Borromini, incorporated the two great symmetrical wings of the central block, which itself squarely faced across the river the axis of the Cour carrée of the Louvre. The north-south axis of the Cour carrée was intended to be extended to a grand bridge joining the Collège to the Louvre. To the shame of Paris what was actually built was the feeble nineteenth-century Pont des Arts.

Le Vau's plans for the east side of the Cour carrée had to be scrapped when Colbert became *surintendant des bâtiments* in January 1664. An attempt to commission François Mansart failed, and various Paris architects were asked to criticize Le Vau's designs before submitting their own. Forced to turn to Italy itself, Colbert immediately turned down three of four designs, leaving that of Bernini, who was invited to make a much heralded but largely futile visit to the French capital, arriving in June 1665.

His design, remarked Colbert, contained splendid opportunities for ballrooms and grand staircases, but did not improve on the king's current accommodation, or meet the practical needs of a royal palace. The kitchens were too far from the banqueting hall, and there was a shortage of privies. Colbert's assistant, Charles Perrault, ensured Bernini's speedy return to Rome. He left behind only the spectacular marble bust of Louis XIV now at Versailles.[24] Louis, who is known to have inclined towards Bernini's second plan, and who, like Bernini, thought grandeur more important than comfort, so disliked the poor horsemanship displayed on the equestrian statue he commissioned from Bernini to be completed in Rome that, when it arrived nineteen years later, he had it altered by Coysevox and banished to the end of the park.

The east side of the Cour carrée was eventually confided to Le Vau, the first architect, with Le Brun, the first painter, and Claude Perrault, brother of Charles and an amateur with a serious interest in architecture and engineering. Although the groundwork was almost certainly done in Le Vau's studio, the rejection of Bernini's plans and the committee solution represented a victory for Colbert's persuasive powers over the personal taste of the king, perhaps happy to concede now that his interests were concentrated on Versailles.

It was partly the need to keep his pleasures and his parties private that attracted Louis to the small château of brick and stone, a courtyard surrounded by three wings, which Louis XIII had had built at Versailles in 1624. Louis XIV was first struck by the attractions of what was little more than a hunting lodge when he took his wife there on 25 October 1660, and between 1661 and 1663, before Colbert became *surintendant des bâtiments,* Louis spent 1.5 million livres on improvements, mostly to the gardens. He was later himself to write a small guide to the gardens and occasionally took privileged companions there, but what at first he intended to build was primarily a love nest for Louise and himself. The gardens were planned with seduction in mind, and it is no serious exaggeration to say that they were designed, with a heavy input by Louis himself, as coded invitations to romantic pursuits, perhaps especially the 'unlimited vista' round the axis on to which the château opened on the west, away from Paris.

Everything at Versailles, from the social organization of the court to the livery of the domestic servants serving food at the great feasts, and the form of the food itself, with pâtés of châteaux encased in gelatine, would contribute to the illusion that Louis XIV had transformed the real world into an enchanted fairyland, inhabited by himself and his friends, elevated to the level of the allegorical figures from ancient history or mythology with which they mingled. Louis could create at least a fantasy environment within which he felt secure.[25]

After Fouquet's arrest, Louis had plundered Vaux-le-Vicomte of tapestries, curtains, silver, statues and over a thousand expensive orange trees on the self-deceiving grounds that they have been paid for with money that was rightfully his.[26] He also moved the Vaux-le-Vicomte team of Le Vau, Le Nôtre and Le Brun, 'premier peintre du roi' from 1663, to work at Saint-Germain, and he now transferred them to work on Versailles, where Le Vau constructed the orangery, and Le Nôtre created the magnificent gardens, differing from Louis only in preferring parterres decorated with patterns of dwarf shrubs to flower beds, but at one with him in the delight he took in complicated water systems. Water drained from the low marshy ground was used for the pools and canals as well as later for fountains.

The kitchen garden was left until later and planned and directed by an ex-lawyer called La Quintinie, ennobled by Louis, who was fond of him. He wrote a knowledgeable book on kitchen gardening and was an expert on pear trees, of which he lists the 500 best in the Versailles garden.[27] Blooms were confined to the Trianon de Porcelaine, built to a design by Le Vau for Athénaïs de Montespan, for whom Louis also had Clagny erected, a small château north-east of the main building and very close to the Versailles château itself.

The cost was prodigious, 1.5 million livres in the three years 1661 to 1663, but twice as much was still being spent on Paris until 1670, when 1,633,000 livres were spent on Versailles, to become 2,621,000 in 1671.[28]

Louis wanted to preserve the old lodge, and Colbert wanted to save the cost of replacing the accommodation it contained, so the new château was built round its three wings, north, west and east. The inner façades of the three wings inherited from Louis XIII still survive in the Cour de Marbre, the present entry from the Paris road. Louis started with a commission to Le Vau to erect two wings of *communs* in the forecourt for the domestic staff, and only very gradually gestated the ambition to move the whole court there.

Work did not start in earnest until after the peace of Aix-la-Chapelle, which ended the 'war of devolution' and was signed on 2 May 1668. Even then it was not immediately obvious that removing the court and the major officers of state to cramped quarters in the country, where scope for plotting was curtailed, where the comings and goings of court members could be regulated, attendance rewarded, absence punished and high-ranking foreign dignitaries impressed, was the best way of governing France. The arrangement had the immediate advantage of keeping the *parlement* physically as well as hierarchically removed from government, but that, in the long run, may have been a mistake.

Both the aged chancellor, Séguier, and Colbert felt that he should live in a refurbished Louvre, and Colbert certainly begrudged the money Louis was spending on what everyone, including Louis, thought at first might at best one day become an elegant country retreat. None the less, Colbert could write as early as September 1663 about the king's affection for Versailles, and his intention to use it to receive foreign royalty and ambassadors. He singles out for mention the furnishings, particularly those of the apartments of the queen mother, who was especially fond of jasmin, and of Chinese gold and silver filigree, 'the daily balls, ballets, comedies, music . . . promenades and hunting'. Christopher Wren on the other hand criticized the feminine fashions and knick-knacks he found at Versailles in 1665, preferring the 'masculine' furniture of the Palais Mazarin. Everyone to whom an apartment was allocated at Versailles found it furnished, with the king providing food, candles and firewood as well as furnishings.[29]

There was what amounted to an inaugural fête at Versailles in May 1664 when for the first time Louis gave an entertainment there for more than half a dozen courtiers. He had originally intended it to be a quite small affair. Formally dedicated to the queen and the queen mother, it was called *Les Plaisirs de l'Île enchantée* but was in fact devised to show off the king's peacock feathers to Louise de la Vallière. Louis himself, true to his fashionable Italianate taste, chose the theme from Ariosto. The duc de Saint-Aignan, a boyhood friend of the king who also belonged to the circle of Mme de Sévigné, was the master of ceremonies, organizer and choreographer of the display. He had been promoted duke, was from 1644 in charge of a cavalry regiment, and was also well known in the world of letters. Molière used him as the model for Oronte in *Misanthrope,* and Racine dedicated *La Thébaïde* to him.[30]

The entertainment was intended to run from 7 to 9 May 1664, but ran on, despite a severe squeeze on space. Some of the 600 invited courtiers were sleeping in cottages and barns. The lavishness of the display had surpassed anything previously imagined. The gardens were illuminated by 4,000 candles and innumerable flambeaux, with the whole park drawn up into the fairy-tale illusion in Ariosto's *Orlando furioso,* of an enchanted island which had mysteriously appeared off the coast of France, from which Roger and his knights, held under a spell by which Alcine had bound them, came in a grand procession to entertain the ladies of the court.

The cavalcade, preceded by a herald, three pages, four trumpeters and two drummers, was led by Guidon, played by Saint-Aignan, after whom came Roger, preceded by eight trumpeters and two drummers, and played by the king, now twenty-five. The procession of magnificently mounted male members of the court was closed by Roland, played by Condé's son. After the procession came Apollo's eighteen-foot high golden chariot carrying four centuries, Python, Atlas, Time and various allegorical animals. It was pulled by four horses. It was escorted by the hours of the day and the signs of the Zodiac.

The first night was devoted to a tournament after a display of horsemanship by 'Roger'. It was won by Louise de la Vallière's brother who was presented with the prize sword by the queen mother. The service of supper was a virtual ballet and was set to a 'Rondeau pour les violons et flûtes allant à la table du roi' written for the occasion by Lulli, who headed a large band of musicians. The servants were dressed up for rustic roles as if they were dancers, and moved in time to the music. Supper was served on an eight-sided table with the food presented within architecturally sculpted forms as a feast first for the eyes.

On the second night, the 8 May, Molière, as much impresario as playwright, who had presided over the service of supper the night before, presented *La Princesse d'Elide,* best described as a *comédie galante,* a mixture of music and dance taken from a well-known Spanish comedy by Moreto set in a conventional Greece and offered by Alcine to her noble captives. It is a hasty piece, starting in verse but ending in prose, published not on its own, but only within the limits of an account of the whole three-day entertainment. Molière is said to have stolen the evening with his buffoonery in the first *intermède,* as Lyciscas, but today's printed text, which was certainly not adhered to, gives Lyciscas only one short appearance.

On the third day, the setting was Alcine's palace. More ballet music by Lulli led to the appearance of Roger who broke the spell, whereupon Alcine's palace disappeared to a clap of thunder and a brilliant firework display. The effects were master-minded by Torelli's rival and, in a sense, successor, Vigarani *fils,* who caused a rock to rise from the waves to form an on-stage island, flanked by two others.[31] Three monsters emerged as well, one carrying Alcine and the other two carrying nymphs. There followed greetings in alexandrines for the queen mother and a ballet of giants and dwarfs, Moors, knights, monsters and jugglers, before Roger was given the wand which set Alcine's palace on fire.

The court mostly stayed on, tilting in the dry moat, and eating in the park. The great event was the first performance of the first three acts of Molière's *Le Tartuffe* by which Louis was much amused. The furore it caused was such that the play, vigorously defended by Condé, none the less had on account of the apparent religious implications of its satire on spiritual directors to be banned. The final entertainment from Molière, confirming his closeness to Louis and the court, and explaining the rent-free availability to him of the Palais-Royal theatre, was *Le Mariage forcé,* in which Louis had once danced a role. It had been written in a hurry for 29 January 1664, called an 'impromptu' by Loret in the *Muse historique,* with a ballet for Louis to dance and *entrées* between the scenes. It was given in the apartments of the queen mother. Lulli and Beauchamp were this time working to Molière's directions, but there had been no professional dancers. The female dancing roles were taken by male courtiers. The court finally moved on to Fontainebleau on 14 July.

Two years before *Les Plaisirs de l'Ile enchantée*, the ambitious thirty-four-year-old Bossuet, whose aspirations were teaching him that it was more important to please the Gallican court than to please Rome, had preached the famous Lenten sermon against Louis's adulterous life in 1662. Unhappily, we do not know exactly either what he had threatened to say, or what in fact he did say in denunciation of the king's way of life. The 'texts' even of the famous *Oraisons funèbres* are only rough drafts, sometimes indicating rhetorical structures which Bossuet presumably considered using. Born in 1627, he was hubristically to see himself as the new Augustine, to specialize in placing a coterie of ecclesiastics close to him as tutors in the houses of the great, and belonged to the first generation of important moralists to adopt the severe new ethical values to which the second half of the century turned. They are to be discerned appearing in the secular as well as the religious spheres, are connected with *préciosité,* tragedy (but not opera) and the novel, and can be found in the secular moralists like Boileau, La Rochefoucauld, La Bruyère, Mme de Layette and Madame de Sablé.

Bossuet's sermon can have done nothing to assuage Louis's self-doubt, although Versailles may have helped him to mask it. But in 1664, the year of his inaugural fête, Louis, no doubt under pressure from his mother, admitted that he could not receive the sacrament at Easter on account of his sinful relationship with Louise. It is possible, in view of the lengthy list of annulments and dispensations actually given to members of Europe's royal families, that a few years earlier some special rule for monarchs might covertly have been elaborated, freeing them for an extra-marital monogamous relationship once their dynastic duty had been accomplished, as Louis's had been with the birth of the dauphin.

The attitude of the period towards sins of the flesh, the church's norms for absolution included, must be understood in context. Louis was a lot stricter about the minutiae of the prescriptions for fasting and abstinence. Partly, but by no means wholly on account of Pascal and the jansenizing moralists, moral norms would become stricter in ten years' time.[32] Meanwhile, in 1664 Louis took advantage of the absences due to illness of the queen and of the queen mother to introduce Louise to formal court life. Her third pregnancy already obvious, Louis placed her at a table with his brother and Henriette d'Angleterre in the gaming rooms of the queen mother.

It was later in the year that had seen Louis abstain from fulfilling his Easter duties and had been marked by *Les Plaisirs de l'Ile enchantée,* that Anne of Austria developed breast cancer. Louis, once so close to her, put aside any feelings of resentment at her reliance on Fouquet and at her moral disapproval of his behaviour, and became assiduous in his attentions during his mother's long drawn-out and painful illness. It quite soon became apparent that it was terminal, and by 18 January 1666 no posture could relieve the severe pain throughout her body. Her almoner, the bishop of Auch, suggested the time had come for a general confession, which was followed the next day by the last anointing.

Anne saw each of her sons alone first. Her sons, with the queen and Henriette, followed by other senior courtiers, then went in procession to collect the oils for the last anointing. The archbishop carried the Blessed Sacrament for viaticum. During the administration of the sacrament Anne admonished Louis to do what she had told him, without revealing to the others present what that had been, and the whole room was in tears. Louis, Maria-Teresa and Mme de Motteville remained with the archbishop until late, when Louis retired, apparently to spend the night in tears.

Prayers were said throughout the kingdom, the forty hours' exposition ordered in the Paris churches, and the relics of Saint Geneviève were carried in procession for veneration in the streets of Paris. Before she died, early on the morning of 20 January 1666, Anne had consented to receive Louise. In her will she left money for the saying of 10,000 masses for the repose of her soul, and a daily mass to be said in perpetuity for the same intention at Val-de-Grâce, whose cupola Pierre Mignard had just finished painting. The convent also received the reliquaries which Anne had kept nearest to herself.

After his mother's death, Louis left the Louvre immediately for Versailles, where he received deputations of condolence. The funeral was on 12 February at Saint-Denis, where the embalmed body was taken on 28 January, less the heart, which went in a silver box to Val-de-Grâce, and the intestinal organs, which went to the Paris

Carmelite convent. From the 29 January, when high mass was sung by the bishop of Auch, until the day of the funeral, 12 February, a hundred masses were said each day in the basilica for the repose of Anne's soul, and 150 livres were daily distributed to the poor of Paris.[33]

A touching letter of Louis to his own son, the grand Dauphin, on Anne's death asserts not only his distress at that time but also that his custom of keeping only 'one household and one table' with her, and of seeing her several times a day 'was not a law . . . but a mark of the pleasure that I had in her company'. The strength of Louis's affection for his mother during his adolescent years and his grief at her death in 1666 on the other hand must seriously affect any evaluation of the emotional turmoil caused in him by her attitude towards his relationships with women.

After his mother's death, Louis felt able openly to appoint Louise his mistress and a duchess, and to have his children by her legitimized. Their first child, who did not survive, was born on 19 December 1663. Marie-Anne de Blois, born in 1666, was the first to survive beyond infancy, and was legitimized when her mother was made duchess of Vaujours la Vallière by letters patent registered by the *parlement* on 14 May 1667. She married the prince de Conti, Condé's nephew, in 1680, when she was thirteen, and died in 1739. The second to survive was the comte de Vermandois, born at Saint-Germain on 2 October 1667 and legitimized in February 1669. He was made an admiral that October, but died late in 1683, still an adolescent.

Four months before Anne's death, Maria-Teresa's father, Philip IV of Spain, had died on 17 September 1665, leaving to succeed him Carlos II, a sickly and feeble-minded child of four, son of Philip's second wife, Maria-Anna of Austria, his sister's daughter. The new king of Spain was still being breast-fed, could not walk, and was also backward. He would be unable to read or write at nine. Against expectations, he was to survive as king until 1700, when his death without issue would provoke the war of the Spanish succession. Philip had made his second wife regent, with the proviso that, were the male line to be extinguished, his thrones, which included those in the Low Countries, should pass to her daughter Marguerite of Savoy, Mazarin's fall-back choice of bride for Louis, promised to the emperor Leopold and half-sister to Maria-Teresa, Philip's daughter by his first marriage.

Maria-Teresa's renunciation of all rights to the Spanish throne on marrying Louis XIV had been almost as an after-thought when the contract was drawn up, made conditional on the payment of the dowry, and the dowry had not been paid. Since the law of part of the Low Countries allowed for the succession to pass to the children of the first marriage irrespective of gender before entitling those of the second, it could be, and was, tenuously argued that Maria-Teresa's claim to the Spanish sovereignties took precedence over those even of her half-brother, Carlos II.

In fact the customary law of Brabant applied to private law alone, and so could not be alleged to resolve matters of dynastic succession. None the less, since Louis wanted to extend his boundaries, and Maria-Teresa's claim allowed him to give the European chancelleries legal bones to gnaw at, Louis claimed in lieu of the unpaid dowry the fiefdoms of fourteen provinces, much more than he actually expected to get.[34] Much was left to Lionne's diplomacy. He had to threaten Spain without frightening England and the United Provinces into a Protestant anti-French alliance.

In late April 1667, there was a conference at Breda to consider the political position involving English, French, Dutch, Swedes and Danes, and very nearly resulting in the feared Anglo-Dutch alliance. Turenne reviewed the French troops, and Louis came to watch manoeuvres. Colbert complained about the cost. The dauphin, Maria-Teresa's son now aged five and a half, marched in front of his regiment. In May 1667 the French, reviewed by Louis but directed by Turenne and Sébastien le Prestre de Vauban, the brilliant military engineer, began the assault, taking possession of what they claimed, tongue-in-cheek, to belong to the queen by right. A treaty was signed on 31 July.

Louis XIV was probably by nature and certainly by upbringing inclined to the pursuit of military glory as conferring or demonstrating the highest form of human honour. Richelieu and then Mazarin were anxious to extend France's fiefdoms in the Low Countries. Under the impulsion of this policy, which Louis did nothing to restrain, Le Tellier had created a well-trained army, part of which was kept always ready for service. The preferred method of pursuing French policy was the slowly built-up menacing readiness of its army and navy. France had already by this means acquired Marsal in 1663, important for the defence of Metz and Nancy, at no greater cost than a parade of strength with drum-beating and a review by Louis XIV of front-line troops.

The 'war of devolution', as it was called, referring to the devolved sovereignty claimed by Louis on Maria-Teresa's behalf, was more a pre-ordained succession of surrenders than a series of battles. Although there were casualities, they were few, and Louis could mostly play the role of a hero out of Ariosto. When he was reviewing, supervising, or planning, with his entourage present, he slept in a tent of Chinese silk, but when military action was foreseen, the queen, Louise, Mme de Montespan and the other elegant court ladies who accompanied him were despatched to Compiègne. According to one commentator who was present, the marquis de Saint-Maurice, Louis went to bed only at dawn, slept on straw under canvas, performed prodigious feats of endurance on horseback, and spent half-hours waxing his moustache.

Europe was alarmed. The English and Dutch, later joined by the Swedes did ally early in 1668 in an attempt to get France to give up some of the conquered territory. But the emperor, Leopold I, now married to Marguerite of Savoy, was persuaded to accept a 'partition treaty' on 19 January, without Spanish consultation and expensive to France only in bribes. This was a secret treaty between France and the emperor according to which, should Carlos II of Spain die childless, France would acquire the Spanish Netherlands, Franche-Comté, Navarre, Naples and Sicily. The remainder, Spain, its other European possessions, and its New World colonies, would go to Marguerite. Louis's next move was to seize Franche-Comté, a task given by Louvois to Condé, the province's governor. From 7 to 15 February 1668, when he arrived at Dijon, Louis was there, collecting surrenders and receiving oaths of loyalty, with the inhabitants of Besançon, Dôle and Dijon anxious only for neutrality.

The acquisition of Franche-Comté sealed the victory in the Low Countries, and Louis himself led the party containing Le Tellier, Colbert and Lionne which, against the advice of Louvois, Turenne and Condé, followed a policy of graciousness in victory at the treaty of Aix-la-Chapelle on 2 May. Franche-Comté was handed back to Carlos II of Spain, but Louis retained many important towns in Flanders, including Armentières, Oudenaarde, Tournai, Courtrai, Ath, Douai and Lille, where, incidentally, there was no law of devolved succession to the female children of a first marriage. The towns were quickly fortified by Vauban.

In spite of the treaty of Aix-la-Chapelle, the embers of the hostile attitudes between France and Spain were kept glowing by France's desire to achieve an impregnable north-eastern frontier. There was certainly a lull in actual warfare, and the thirty-year-old Louis profited from it chiefly by creating his castle and his court. Versailles was prepared to become the magnificent gilded cage which finished by imprisoning the flower of aristocratic France, making its rigid social hierarchization with corresponding gradations in the possibility of preferment and enrichment a creation in its way even more impressive than the buildings themselves.

Louis had taken with him to the front Maria-Teresa, whose rights he was purporting to vindicate, and Louise de la Vallière's succcessor as his mistress, Françoise-Athénaïs de Rochechouart de Mortemart, marquise de Montespan. Louise de la Vallière, whose duchy was registered on the legitimization of her surviving children on 13 May, had been left at home on account of her pregnancy. When she realized the danger of her position and galloped to join Louis, she received a cool reception and was sent home. She had been paid off with the duchy which produced little revenue, and cruelly had nothing more to look forward to from her relationship with Louis. Her presence was none the less humiliatingly still to be required at court in the hope that it might help to conceal to the rest of Europe, and to all but the king's intimates in France, the new liaison with the beautiful and stylish Athénaïs. Louis even had to pass through the apartments of Louise, whom he was pretending to visit, in order to reach Mme de Montespan. He once tossed a pet dog to her to keep happy for him while he was with Athénaïs, an act of contempt for a discarded mistress which was to become not untypical of him.

Nothing supports the view that Athénaïs de Montespan was merely an ambitious money-grabber who did not genuinely care for the king, although she was clear-minded, and historians have raked up occasional instances of hard-heartedness. She never felt morally guilty in quite the way in which Louise did. Although she did finally go to a convent, she did not become a nun or feel the need to do penance like Louise, who left a work of devotion, *Reflections upon God's Mercy*, published in 1680. What remains unclear is how much she was motivated from the beginning of her relationship with Louis more by fear of losing him than by genuine love for him. Their liaison started when she was taken with the queen to Flanders, leaving Saint-Germain on 16 May 1667.

Athénaïs, witty, intelligent and beautiful, also had a sense of fun and appears to have been a shrewd and amusing mimic. She knew how to use her position, obtaining favours for herself and her family, but not pestering the king with small requests on behalf of those seeking to exploit her hold over Louis.[35] She was also generous with charitable donations and artistic patronage, and her piety appears to have been sincere. Like Louis, she picked and chose among the commandments, and remained acutely aware of the apparent incongruity of combining double adultery with meticulous observance of the Lenten fast.

Because Louis was married, his liaison with Louise had been adulterous. But Athénaïs was also married, as Louise had not been, which made Louis's liaison with her doubly adulterous. Fornication, and both single and double adultery were mortal sins, although of different degrees of theological malice, but they all, if unrepented at death, entailed damnation. Hell was not considered to contain gradations of the type envisaged by Dante's epic poetic fantasy. The difficulty from both the ecclesiastical and the civil points of view did not lie in the heightened sexual malice of a double adultery, but derived from the added malice of the liaison with Athénaïs, that it entailed the usurpation of the rights of her husband, the marquis de Montespan.

The degree of outrage actually felt by the marquis is not clear, but he certainly started to turn the situation to his advantage by laying demands on Louis, who simply sent him to his estates in the south with orders to stay there. The marquis, however, refused to keep quiet, and held a mock funeral for his lost wife. In spite of repeated requests, it took Louis almost six years to get the *parlement* to issue in the spring of 1674 an edict legally separating the marquis de Montespan from his wife.

Ecclesiastical rights in the matter of Athénaïs's husband were even trickier. Her father did not object to her position as royal mistress, but her uncle felt strongly that her husband's rights were being disregarded, and he was archbishop of Sens, in which diocese lay Fontainebleau. He reacted by imposing public penance on a woman living in concubinage in his diocese, and published the church's teaching on adultery in all its parishes. When the king ordered him not to leave Sens, he defied the ban and went to Fontainebleau, threatening to excommunicate the king if Louis prevented him from carrying out his duty of visiting the parish churches of his diocese. The court did not again visit Fontainebleau during the archbishop's lifetime.

Louise, whose enforced retention at court was a constant humiliation, ran away for a second time on Ash Wednesday 1671, and Colbert had to fetch her from the convent of Sainte-Marie at Chaillot. By this date her liaison with Louis had long finished. She was finally to be given permission to become a Carmelite at the convent of the Incarnation in 1674, when Louis no longer required her to mask his liaison with Mme de Montespan whose legal separation from the marquis de Montespan had finally been registered by the *parlement*. The marquis could no longer claim custody of his wife's, and Louis's children. Louise made her religious profession as Sœur Louise de la Miséricorde, and died a Carmelite in 1710. So many of Louis's ex-mistresses ended up in convents, that most of his biographers have repeated the quip by Bussy-Rabutin that to have lain in the king's arms must have been the most secure way for a woman to assure her path to salvation.

Louise's 1671 attempt to run away from the humiliations had followed the formal recognition and provision for her son. When in 1674, after the separation came through, she was finally free to leave, she generously allowed her husband to keep her dowry, obtained pensions for her mother, her married sister and her servants, and gave her jewellery to her children. If the story is not a product of baroque attitudinizing, she also asked forgiveness on bended knee of Maria-Teresa, and was entertained by Mme de Montespan before entering the convent on 14 April 1674. Bossuet preached at the veiling ceremony, and among those who attended, according to the *Gazette,* were the queen, the king's brother and La grande Mademoiselle, daughter of Louis XIII's rebellious brother, Gaston d'Orléans.

The last great celebratory act to be held by the old peripatetic court at Saint-Germain was the baptism of the dauphin son of Louis and Maria-Teresa, born on 1 November 1661. The baptism was on 25 March 1668. Galleries were erected in the courtyard of the vieux château and the music was entrusted to Lulli. The pope, Clement IX, was godfather, represented by the Cardinal de Vendôme assisted by the pope's *legatus a latere*,[36] Antonio Barberini, and the godmother was Henriette de France, represented by the princesse de Conti, Mazarin's niece. The massive font was made of silver.

Meanwhile the victorious peace of Aix-la-Chapelle had been celebrated at Versailles. The court ballet in which comedies were intermingled with ballets was slowly being replaced by opera or, briefly, tragedy. Molière himself was to die in 1673, and the 1670s became the decade of Racine. Colbert oversaw the absorption of the members of Molière's company into one or other of the remaining two. The last of the ballets, the *Ballet des ballets*, was staged at Saint-Germain in 1671. The entertainments, comedy or tragedy, but increasingly at Versailles, continued until 1682. Molière's troupe was to spend ten days at court each October for over ten years, starting in 1662 and lasting until Molière fell out with Lulli in 1672, when Lulli obtained the legal ownership of any printed words to which he had set the music, which included Molière's plays, and other theatre companies were restricted to two voices or other instrumentalists and six violins.

To celebrate the peace in 1668, and no doubt also the ascendant star which was Mme de Montespan, a great celebration known as the *divertissement* was held at the new palace of Versailles on 18 July. It cost over 150,000 livres. From midday until six in the evening the château was open, and at six the king led parties of courtiers round the gardens, where a magnificent reception had been prepared and, in a theatre prepared by Carlo Vigarani, Molière gave his *George Dandin ou le Mari confondu,* with ballets and intermezzi inserted from *Les Fêtes de l'Amour et de Bacchus,* for which Molière had written the words and Lulli the music for a hundred musicians. Supper was served in tents and outdoor buffets, and was followed by a dazzling ball and a firework display launched from seventy-two points, ending with Louis's monogram made of fireworks shining in the night sky. Louis would not again attempt to rival his own entertainments until 1674, although lesser displays did take place, not only at Versailles, but also at Chambord, at Saint-Germain-en-Laye and at Fontaine-bleau.

Gradually Versailles had come to command Louis's affections as more than a resort for love and leisure, and irrespective of his waning concern for Louise de la Vallière. The grand canal was dug out in 1668, and Louis himself determined on the extension to the west, still leaving the Louis XIII château, and especially its east-facing façade, more or less intact. The extension was to be built no longer of brick but of stone, imposing, decorated with columns, of loosely classical aspect, and quadrupling the interior floor space by building outwards on the three wings enclosing the Cour de Marbre. The reconstruction of the ground floor had been completed by the early summer of 1669. Le Vau was to die in 1670 having scarcely begun the grand interior staircase which Le Brun would eventually decorate.

Louis's own grand apartment was begun in 1670 but was not inhabitable until November 1673. Le Brun took charge of the queen's apartments, almost as grand as the king's. The quarters assigned to Mme de Montespan were designed by Le Vau at the top of the grand staircase, with access to the king's apartments. Despite her later disfavour, she continued to occupy these rooms, with five windows looking on to the Cour royale, for sixteen years, no doubt the result of an act of kindness, also at least not untypical of Louis, which permitted her to remain near her children, although from 1685 to 1691 she lived in the splendidly decorated 'appartement des Bains' on the ground floor. Baths were a novelty, and the actual 'cabinet des bains' contained an octagonal bath cut from a single piece of marble with hot and cold running water. It cost 15,000 livres.

8

Public Policies, Private Pleasures,
Poisons and Punishments

There are ways in which Louis himself is always going to remain an enigma. Astonishingly, we do not really know how tall or short he was. Reports about his physical appearance, routinely filed by foreign ambassadors, not only differ, but contradict one another. Louis clearly wished to appear tall, but only inaccurate conclusions can be drawn from guessing which reports about him were the product either of awe at the grandeur of the staging or, if for domestic consumption, of a desire to please. He certainly wore wigs designed to make him appear taller in public than he was, and the best guess must be that he never attained the physical stature he deemed appropriate. He was of medium height.

Whatever must be said about the insecurities bred by Louis's up-bringing and exacerbated by his idolization, and by the clergy-fuelled guilt induced in him by the clash between his religion and his illicit liaisons, he was, in spite of the state to which his wars and prodigal expenditure were to reduce the country, by nature a sensitive person, capable of kindnesses and vulnerable to grief. Yet he was too aware of the need to maintain his dignity for even his greatest admirers to be able to quote more than a handful of instances of private kindness, the occasional apology, a letter to Colbert's widow.

The gentler side of his character is to be found above all in his concern for the starving, the beggars, the suffering, the deprived,

the sick and above all for those injured in his service. His compassion, as attested by Mme de Maintenon, took the form of keeping
himself informed of the state of deprivation of his people, of worry-
ing about it, and even of straining to relieve their distress in so far as
this was compatible with achieving glory for France and providing a
palliative for his own insecurity. His recorded concern took forms,
however, which also enhanced his own grandeur, the creation of vast
institutions, for the homeless, for the sick, for those wounded in
battle, for whom Les Invalides was built. These foundations may well
have been prompted by Colbert.

Some indeed, like the 1656 Hôpital Général for vagrants, vaga-
bonds and beggars, were founded before Louis himself was old
enough to have played any part in their foundation. The purpose
was largely to clear vagrants from the streets and they became liable
to arrest once refuge was available. More characteristic of Louis's
concerns was his habit of occasionally walking the streets to see that
the laws governing the disposal of refuse, daily by tumbril, were being
observed. A special inspectorate was created to ensure that the con-
tractors, paid for by a special tax, used the agreed number of
tumbrils. Louis did have a strong sense of personal justice and would,
where he could, prevent exploitative injustice from being perpetrated in his name. His sense of fairness was strong, even if based
on a social system which was already out of date.

By the end of the 1660s France was again in full economic bloom.
Confidence, killed off by the Spanish war of 1635 which had lasted
until 1659, was being reborn, but in a way which at every turn
enhanced central control of the French economy and of French
culture, organized and financed with a Colbertian gloss to thurify
the glorified Louis as its pinnacle and as its personification. It was a
dangerous way to treat a monarch. Agriculture was left alone, but
invention and enterprise of all sorts were encouraged and protected,
with the proviso that they could be integrated into Colbert's overall
plan for state magnificence.

Colbert had actively sought to bring both the provincial
administrations and the nobility which so often enjoyed a privileged
position in them, under central control. Louis never called the
Estates General to meet, but the provincial estates had considerable
autonomy in fiscal and administrative matters, especially Languedoc
and Brittany, to which Colbert did not dare send out the *intendants*

by which he effectively centralized the administration of most of provincial France.[1] Nonetheless in 1665 Louis again strengthened his prerogative to assume the totality of civil jurisdiction into his own hands by allowing for a *lit de justice* to be held in his absence. In 1673 he would force the courts, no longer referred to as 'sovereign', to register his edicts before they made representations about them, so removing the power of the *parlements* to delay his acts of jurisdiction. They remained, however, powerful bodies, conscious of their status as bodies professionally competent to impede monarchical despotism.

With respect to provincial administration, Louis again strengthened his position. The 45,000 office-holders who owned offices which could be bought, sold and bequeathed remained a brake on any tyrannical tendencies, but the king still had 150 major offices in his own gift, appointed the *premiers présidents* of the once sovereign courts, promoted senior lawyers to the rank of *maîtres des requêtes*, and chose from among the eighty of those the thirty who would oversee the fiscal regimes of the financial districts into which France was divided. He also appointed the highest officers of the army and navy, the regimental commanders and all officers down to the rank of colonel.

The provincial nobility were swiftly made to conform to Louis's will when assize courts responsible to Séguier, reestablished in the winter of 1664, pushed ahead at Clermont in 1665 with executions where hitherto there would have been connivance between magistrates and condemned members of the nobility. The *intendants* saw to it that the judges at the 'grands jours' showed mercy to the poor, but rigour to the nobility. Condemnations of nobles to death began to take place and actual exemplary executions did take place.[2] In June 1665 an investigation responsible to Colbert was begun into titles of nobility for fiscal exemption. The legal codes were slowly being reformed. A new civil code came into force in 1667, a criminal code in 1669 and the commercial Code Savary in 1673.

In August 1664 the East India Company was founded and a royal tapestry manufactory was established at Beauvais. In September customs tariffs were imposed, and by February 1665 an edict had authorized the establishment of metal-work manufactories. That July, letters patent re-established the tapestry manufactory at Aubusson; in August a patent was issued for the manufacture of gold braid; in

[171]

October for glassware and crystal at what was to become the Saint-Gobain company and for the manufacture of fine cloth at Abbeville; in March 1666 for soap manufactories. Craftsmen everywhere were forced to trade creative freedom for the status, security and financial rewards of state employees, their guilds neglected or disempowered. Regulations for the length, breadth, quality and dyes of cloth were imposed. In October 1666 construction of the Canal du Midi was authorized, and in 1667 the customs tariffs were stiffened. In March 1669 Marseille was to become a free port, and in June the Compagnie du Nord was founded for trade in the North Sea and Baltic countries. The pace of Colbert's administrative reforms and innovations was breath-taking.

He was also busily re-organizing France's maritime affairs. From 1661 he had taken control of the Atlantic and Mediterranean fleets, although his full authority over maritime affairs came only in March 1669 after the superintendancy of buildings (1664), the controller-generalship of finance (1665), and the responsibility for the affairs of Paris, the king's household and the clergy (February 1669). In 1661 Colbert had still had to appear to defer to Hugues de Lionne, directly responsible for the navy to Louis, but with his establishment of the *conseil de commerce* in 1664, Colbert could amalgamate his ambitions for French commercial dominance with his aspirations for French maritime supremacy, and became official director of the maritime department, at the same time as he took responsibility for commerce, the consulates and the companies of the Indies.

Richelieu had seen the importance for France of a strong navy and of commercial fleets in the Atlantic and the Mediterranean, but all had been neglected by Mazarin who, in 1651, could muster only six warships. By 1656 navy expenditure had sunk to 300,000 livres, and in the early 1660s Colbert could report to Louis that the navy was down to two or three war vessels out of a total fleet of only a score of vessels in all. All the navy arsenals were completely empty. Louis dreamed of overseas dominions for France. Colbert sought to establish colonies with all the panoply of metropolitan administrative structures. He re-equipped the hospitals in the major ports, re-built the arsenals at Toulon and Rochefort, opened schools of marine engineering and hydrography, and by 1677 had a navy of 140 ships, with a galley fleet of 34 vessels. At the same time, with Colbert's encouragement, the commercial fleet increased by a third between

1664 and 1688. The cloud on the horizon became heavier on account of the overlap between Colbert's responsibility for coastal fortifications and Louvois's responsibility for the much larger body of army engineers.[3]

In Paris, for which Colbert also had overall responsibility, La Reynie quickly commanded universal respect. His main achievement was to impose a single unified policing authority, which meant no longer leaving each *quartier* to provide for itself, and putting the arrest and punishment of criminals and the prevention of crime under the same authority that was responsible for health, the cleanliness of the streets, sewers, lighting, security and the regulation of public behaviour. Robbers roamed the streets by day as well as night; purse-snatching and various forms of mugging were commonplace.[4]

La Reynie replaced the local nightly watch, the *Guet*, with a uniformed corps, doubling the pay and tripling the size of the force. Louis insisted that they should constantly patrol, always changing their routes, so that their appearance was unpredictable. Punishment was by death, the galleys or imprisonment, but in prisons as in the galleys convicts still needed to bribe those in possession of orders for their release or stay where they were.

Provision was beginning to be made for the homeless, the starving and the seriously ill, and La Reynie, with Louis's strong backing, contrived to introduce some order into the administration of criminal justice. He was also in charge of extinguishing fire. When London had burnt down in 1666, the only remedy had been the immediate destruction of all neighbouring property. Construction workers, like slaters, carpenters and masons were therefore in Paris obliged to register to be called on as necessary. La Reynie did not get hold of thirteen pumps that could send strong jets of water to rooftops until 1699.

An order of 7 June 1670 provided for a single long tree-lined promenade on the Paris right bank, the Cours de Reine developed from a Florentine model, with two boulevards, a word originally meaning fortifications, crossing it at right angles and then crossing the river. Commercial activity was concentrated at the four geographical corners, with large buildings or enterprises outside the existing walls marking new boundaries to which the town might expand: the glass factory in the faubourg Saint-Antoine, the Savonneries to the west, the Gobelins on the Bièvre, a tributary of the Seine, the Observatory to the south, the Salpétrière to the south-east, and the Invalides to the south-west.

Meanwhile Mazarin's Collège des Quatre Nations was going up on the south bank from 1662 to 1672.[5] The old defensive walls were crumbling, and served little useful purpose. Their removal now allowed the town to open up outwards. The wall extending from the Bastille to a fork on the river downstream from the Tuileries was made into a wide boulevard, edged on each side by elms. Paris was to be allowed by Mazarin to develop from a defensible enclave to a prosperous commercial city, just as the Loire châteaux had already been converted from forts to palaces. Colbert was very swiftly to become active in this transformation almost from the moment of Mazarin's death, at least initially with Louis's own full backing.

Colbert's chief interest was the Louvre, but he was also much concerned about the provision of green spaces, commissioning Le Nôtre to design the Champs Elysées. In 1662 the Vigaranis had completed the Tuileries theatre, capable of holding 6,000 spectators and of staging the most complex of baroque ballets. Efforts to prevent the emptying of chamber-pots through windows or to stop butchers from throwing offal into the river were not entirely successful, but street lighting was installed and improved from 1662.[6] The quality and size of pavements was regulated, and Colbert exploited new springs at Vaugirard and Saint-Cloud to provide Paris with water. He constructed a new fountain at the Pont Notre-Dame, and was to order the repair of the capital's twenty-two public fountains and the construction of fifteen new ones in 1671.

In Louis's private life court gossip was commenting as early as 1666, the year of his mother's death, on the king's ill-concealed interest in Athénaïs de Montespan, about to become twenty-five, lady-in-waiting to the queen, and mother of two children. A Mortemart, one of France's greatest families, Athénaïs first came to court in 1660 and was maid of honour at the wedding of Henriette d'Angleterre to Louis's brother, Philippe. She was married in 1663 at the age of twenty-three to the indigent and eccentric marquis de Montespan, with estates in Gascony. Her real name was Françoise, but she considered Athénaïs more flattering.

Primi Visconti tells us that it was because Louise de la Vallière was so taken by her, and spoke of her so often, that Louis, whose eye was settling on the princess of Monaco, wanted to meet her. When

Visconti wrote that there was no lady of quality who did not want to become the king's mistress, he was, obviously, light-heartedly exaggerating, but Louis, known for his *écartades*, must have represented a challenge to the *gloire* of the young, high-spirited and beautiful women who surrounded him. It was an environment in which religious sincerity did not exclude a lax attitude to chastity or even a belief in and recourse to love potions. In fact, in spite of her husband and her uncle, Athénaïs's father felt that Louis's interest in his daughter bestowed honour on the family.

We do not know how many lovers Louis had. There would be a period at the end of Mme de Montespan's reign when there were a number of more than casual partners, Mlle de Fontanges and Mme de Ludres, but certainly also Mme de Soubise, and if even only the more sober of the gossip-mongers are correct, there was also a stream of ladies-in-waiting and domestics.[7] What is important for any estimate of Louis's character is that fidelity, whether to the queen or to the mistress *en titre*, was not part of it. The lovers came not in series but in parallel. Casual intercourse with a domestic was not unknown.

The reason why we do not know their number is also important. Even after the death of his mother, to whom he had wished to save pain, and still motivated by what was at least courtesy towards his now portly wife, Maria-Teresa, Louis, still driven by insecurity, was successful at secrecy, buying discretion with lavish rewards. He was also able and willing severely to punish those who broke his trust. The marquis de Saint-Aignan was never indiscreet, and was often Louis's confidant in personal matters, but the twenty-year exile of the marquis de Vardes, who had tried to warn Maria-Teresa about Louise de la Vallière, was harsh.

The marquis de la Fare tells us that Athénaïs was skilful enough both to cultivate the queen's good opinion of her by communicating weekly in her presence, and to become a close friend of Louise de la Vallière, through whom she frequently saw Louis, and whom she outshone in wit, grace and beauty.[8] She even claimed to rely on Louise to put the finishing touches to her attire. Loret, who was adept at wringing money out of the *Muse historique* both by putting things in and by keeping them out, may have had his own reasons for flattering sources of gossip for his doggerel scandal sheet, but he was lyrical in his praise for the mental and physical attributes of Athénaïs when she first arrived at court 'more angelic than human'.

Years later, when recalling that she had attended the Versailles *Divertissement* of 1668 with her friend Mme Scarron, in due course to become Mme de Maintenon, while Louise de la Vallière sat next to Louis, knowing that her successor was the *raison d'être* of the proceedings, courtiers referred to the simultaneously present three most important royal partners of the reign as the past, the present and the future.

In the context of obtaining love potions that would make Louis love her, and even of procuring whatever powders or diabolic pacts were deemed necessary to alienate Louise from the king's affections, it is frequently suggested that Athénaïs became the client of Catherine Monvoisin.[9] Known as 'La Voisin', Catherine Monvoisin was fortune-teller, purveyor of aphrodisiacs, love potions, poisons and abortions, and able to arrange blasphemous rites, claimed to include black and otherwise sacrilegious masses. There is plenty of evidence about the use of aphrodisiacs and poisons but, unsurprisingly, nothing reliable to support fantasies about satanism and black masses.

There is no need to suppose what is often alleged, that Athénaïs's relationship with Louis was, either from her first arrival at court or from her return there after abandoning her husband, the fruit of a carefully elaborated strategy to replace Louise in the king's bed by ingratiating herself with her. Although possible, it seems unlikely. The most probable scenario involves an element of marital disillusion with her plainly half-mad and openly semi-bankrupt husband, and after her return to court a slowly awakening awareness that Louis was beginning to find her more attractive than Louise. At that point the cultivation of Louise, with whom her friendship was mutual and genuine, would ensure frequent meetings with Louis.

Louis's physical relations with Athénaïs lasted a dozen years, from 1667 to about 1679, during which she bore him eight children, of which four attained adulthood.[10] The eldest was Louis's favourite, the duc du Maine, born in 1670. Louis had had re-built for her by the young Jules Hardouin-Mansart the house at Clagny, which left Mme de Sévigné wide-eyed in admiration in a letter to her daughter of 7 August 1675.[11] She was regarded by Colbert as a serious source of expenditure. Not only was the 1668 *Divertissement* held for her, but, alongside Clagny, Louis built for her the bathroom suite at Versailles and the porcelain Trianon. Her husband came to Paris every year. Perhaps it was guilt that allowed him to create Montespan's son by his wife a duke and peer.

Louis was fond of his children, happy when they came and sad when so many failed to survive. The legitimization of those born to Athénaïs was bound up with dynastic considerations aimed at excluding Louis's brother, Philippe, from the succession, but Louis wanted them treated in youth as a single family with his children by Louise de la Vallière, who was still at court for the birth of Athénaïs's first three children by Louis. Primarily as a courtesy to the queen, they were removed from court at birth. The nursemaid chosen to care for them was the widow of the burlesque poet, dramatist and novelist, Paul Scarron, who developed his reputation for wit and his genuine literary taste as a canon in the household of the bishop of Le Mans, Charles de Beaumanoir-Lavardin, still half a soldier, and a well-known eccentric.

In 1638 Scarron began to be a victim of the terrible disease, presumably rheumatoid or tubercular in origin, which ended by totally crippling him, paralysing him with great pain in a deformed position which he himself considered ridiculous and described as 'Z-shaped'. He was not to die until 1660, but by 1640 he had become impotent. Anne of Austria gave him permission to call himself 'the queen's invalid' and an annual pension of 1,500 livres, cancelled when in 1651 he published an attack on Mazarin.[12] He had returned from Le Mans to Paris in 1641.

In 1652 he married Françoise d'Aubigné, daughter of the prison governor of Niort jail, who had been seduced by the impoverished and imprisoned son of the poet Agrippa d'Aubigné. On release he had taken his wife and family to Martinique, where Françoise met a future neighbour of Scarron. When her father died, Françoise returned to France, presuming that she would be relegated to a convent, but met Scarron through the neighbour she had known in Martinique. She married Scarron in 1652. Françoise was painted by Mignard, and the couple were surrounded by literary friends, including many who had associated with Fouquet, notably including Mme de Lafayette and Mme de Sévigné. They appeared pseudonymously in Madeleine de Scudéry's *Clélie* and the satirical *Dictionnaire des précieuses* by Somaize.

After Scarron's death in 1660, Françoise at twenty-six found her circumstances again reduced, but, a Catholic again after a brief

Huguenot episode, frequently visited from her convent base the Hôtel d'Albret and the Hôtel de Richelieu, in the salons of which she soon met and became friendly with Athénaïs. An indigent, literate, well-born widow, innocent, devout and knowledgeable, Mme Scarron was exactly the person for whom Athénaïs would be looking to take care of the child to be born in 1669. Mme Scarron had to consult her confessor before agreeing to care for a royal bastard, and Louis was chilled by her attitude of disapproval. She was however the granddaughter of Agrippa d'Aubigné, the staunch Huguenot colleague of Louis's own presumed grandfather, Henri IV, before he became a convert to Catholicism, much admired by Louis, who had little regard for his own presumed father, Louis XIII.

Ironically it was Mme Scarron's connection with the blue-stocking world he found disagreeable which would lead Louis to enjoy her company. Almost certainly it was in 1683, and quite probably soon after the return of the court to Versailles on 10 July but before the beginning of Advent in November of that year, three or four months after the queen's death on 30 July, that, as Mme de Maintenon, Louis would marry her.[13] Everything makes one suppose that she was still a virgin until she met Louis.[14]

Athénaïs, who had been feigning an affair with a young guards captain known as Lauzun to divert attention from her liaison with Louis, enlisted Lauzun's help to smuggle her new-born daughter into a carriage in which Mme Scarron was waiting, and transferred to the house built, equipped and staffed just outside Paris on the road to Vaugirard. Louis was lucky that Mme Scarron was also discreet.

Mme Scarron was personally responsible for the infancies only of the 1669 daughter who died, and of Louis-Auguste, created duc du Maine on legitimization. There were at first different houses for the other different children until they were brought under one roof where Mme Scarron had general supervision. Mme Scarron might be up all night with a sick infant in one house, leaving next day, fully dressed, by carriage from her own front door to carry on with her social life which, to avoid suspicion, had to remain unchanged. On occasion that meant using disguise and her own back door. The discretion paid off in another, unforeseen way. It was some time before Athénaïs realized that her close friend and the governess of her children was attracting the predatory attention of her lover.

Unfortunately the 1669 baby, a girl, did not long survive, but other infants came in 1670, 1672 and 1673. Louis had them legitimized by letters patent registered in December 1673, in this way making it easier to bring them back to Saint-Germain in 1674. 'The widow Scarron' became a member of Mme de Montespan's household and Louis twice gave her 100,000 livres with which she bought Maintenon on the Eure, near Chartres. She had not even visited it, but was totally captivated when she did.[15]

In January 1675 she was exultant: the king had given her permission to style herself Mme de Maintenon, and himself referred to her as 'marquise'. Her letters to her confessor and others show her determination to retain her spiritual detachment and to remain indifferent to the grandeur of her new status. The later pacifism, the attachment to education, the passivity in prayer, the prepared-ness to overlook Mme Guyon's vulgarity, the readiness to undergo Fénelon's influence and the detachment from the good things of this world are all already there. They mistakenly suggest a certain early dowdiness. Surviving portraits reveal that Mme de Maintenon might have distressed a fashion editor, but was a very pretty woman indeed. She was also competent, sensible, intelligent and interested in things of the mind and spirit. She was undoubtedly pious.

Strains in Mme de Maintenon's relationship with Mme de Montespan began to manifest themselves in brief outbursts in February, August, and September 1675, more likely at that date to have been caused by Mme de Maintenon's relationship to the children, which had become much closer than that of their mother, than by Louis's increasing interest in Mme de Maintenon. Mme de Maintenon, who had noticed signs of maternal jealousy as early as September 1674, was however urging Louis to think of his immortal soul, and to break with Athénaïs. It is conceivable, but unlikely, that Louis began a physical liaison that year with Mme Scarron, just as it is conceivable but on the whole unlikely that the physical liaison did not begin before the queen died and Louis was free to marry Mme de Maintenon, as she then was, in 1683.

Easter 1675 was critical. The stricter moral norms associated with Saint-Cyran and Port-Royal had begun to permeate French society, and both Louis and Athénaïs had been more and more seriously worried about their spiritual states. For the sake of avoiding public scandal, senior ecclesiastics began to concert an assault on Louis's relationship with Athénaïs. Both sought to satisfy their Easter duties by going to confession and communion. Athénaïs was refused absolution by a simple curate at Versailles, probably but not necessarily primed by higher authority. An appeal to the parish priest led to his refusal to put pressure on his curate. Louis's own confessor, the unsubtle Père de la Chaise, not held in high esteem even by his Jesuit colleagues, could not find a suitable time to hear his royal master's confession.

Mme de Montespan was obliged to retire to her own house at Clagny. The Jesuit preacher, Louis Bourdaloue, frequently regarded as the greatest preacher of his generation and often invited to preach at court, delivered a pointed sermon on Easter Sunday, after which Louis, congratulating him, told him that he should be pleased with him, as he had sent Mme de Montespan to Clagny. Bourdaloue is said to have replied bluntly that God would be happier if Clagny were forty leagues from Versailles. Both Louis and Athénaïs confessed and took communion, and Louis rejoined the army in Flanders without saying goodbye to his mistress. Bossuet wrote him a number of letters to strengthen his resolution to give her up, and called, in semi-disguise, on Athénaïs to fortify her resolution to occupy herself in charitable works. Clagny was still occupied with 1,200 workmen, and Athénaïs spent much time playing cards with Louis's brother, Philippe, and went briefly to take the waters at Bourbon. She was already having to struggle hard to stay slim. Both lovers showed what contemporaries regarded as genuine signs of repentance and of resolution. Maria-Teresa called on Athénaïs at Clagny and stayed longer than was demanded by a simple courtesy visit.

The eldest son of Louis and Athénaïs, the duc du Maine, had developed a lameness which was beginning to deteriorate. Mme de Maintenon left for Barèges in the Pyrénées with him on Sunday 28 April, a fortnight after Easter, hoping to find some alleviation in the healing waters there. The doctors tried to stretch the shorter of his legs. What had happened must have been poliomyelitis.

Some amelioration did take place, and in a letter to her daughter of 10 November Mme de Sévigné wrote from Brittany that Louis had been delighted with the progress when Mme de Maintenon returned, and Louis saw his son walking without support, but holding Mme de Maintenon by the hand. Mme de Sévigné had already reported to her daughter on 16 October that the king's son was walking. Mme de Maintenon was to repeat the journey to Barèges in June 1677, where the waters no longer helped, and she nearly gave up hope for the life of the duc du Maine during a further medicinal visit that September to Bagnières.

Athénaïs had the right to attend court with her children, and Louis gave permission for her rooms at Versailles to be prepared for her against his return from Flanders. It had been agreed that they would meet only in the queen's quarters. The first person he met was Bossuet, whom he swept aside, and when he did meet Athénaïs again it was only in her apartment which was full of other ladies. The meeting was obviously emotional. Mme de Caylus tells us that Louis drew his mistress into a window recess where they whispered together for a long time. There were tears. They made a deep bow to the carefully chosen chaperons and withdrew to a neighbouring room. On 2 July 1677 Mme de Sévigné wrote that 'Quanto' [Mme de Montespan] and her lover were more strongly attached than they had ever been and had re-awakened the passion of their early years. No empire was ever more firmly established. Athénaïs was to bear the king three more children.

It is impossible to gauge how serious the renunciation had been. Bossuet and Père de la Chaise had been convinced. Madeleine de Scudéry, the novelist author of *Clélie*, who possessed a mimosa-like sensitivity in these matters, had thought the renunciations sincere, but that temptation would win once the lovers met again. She was right. It is possible that the king was sincere but weak, and that la Voisin called at Clagny with love potions ordered by Athénaïs during the king's absence. It is also possible that the sincerity of the king's renunciation of Athénaïs had something to do with the first stirrings in 1674 of at least an emotional fixation on Mme de Maintenon and that Athénaïs, sensing this, had gone to Bourbon in 1675 primarily to diet. Mme de Sévigné remarked on her return that her weight had halved. Later in life an Italian diplomat, having seen her enter a carriage, swore that her upper leg was the size of his waist.

What is unlikely is that any love potions which Athénaïs may have acquired were the effective agents in re-kindling the king's passion. What she just may successfully have acquired is some kind of appetite-suppressant. During the 1680s, when the affair was over, she was to become so overweight as to be ungainly, and we know that Louis's tastes favoured the young, slender and boyish, a Marie Mancini, a

Henriette d'Angleterre, a Louise de la Vallière, described by the Savoy ambassador as slim and by Olivier Lefèvre d'Ormesson as emaciated, or a Marie-Angélique de Fontanges.[16] Mme de Maintenon, three years older than Louis, also appears in her portraits at this period as very slim-waisted. Louis's eyes tended to rove during the later stages of the pregnancy of a current mistress.[17] It would soon become clear that the poisons available were much more efficacious than the love philtres.

It is possible that in 1675 and perhaps later Mme de Montespan, desperate, employed love powders to re-arouse the king's passion for her, but love philtres generally involved no more than gentle amusement in and around the royal court. The difficulty was that the source of supply was to be found among those generally able to tell fortunes, procure abortions, make up lethally effective poisons, and obtain the service of priests prepared to use the consecrated elements for grotesquely immoral purposes. It was, however, believed that the most effective love potions were those with a supernatural charge, and one hears about powder made from parts of dried toad being passed by sacrilegious priests under consecrated chalices.

This was of course dealing with a world in which the reality of the after-life, heaven, hell, demons and divine intervention in human affairs were taken for granted, and in which it was universally known that arsenic and antimony were poisons which could be administered in enemas. The poor, who could not afford pharmaceutical products, were in this respect better off with the herbal remedies of tradition than the well-off, whose doctors we know to have killed them as often as did their illnesses, treating most manifestations of ill-health with bleedings, emetics, or purgings. Astrology, at times and places regarded as an academic discipline complementing white magic, was in Louis's France still popular and respectable. The lines drawn between genuinely medicinal remedies of herbal origin, relatively harmless or downright fraudulent substances, such as those sold to increase male potency, and potentially lethal poisons were very thin. The lines between superstition and devotion were not always very much clearer. And there was a whole low-life world of defrocked priests, witches, black masses, infant sacrifices, abortions and 'satanism'.

The actions and reactions of ordinary French people were, around 1680, partly conditioned by their belief in the reality and activity of the world of spirits in which lay power over human affairs and human destinies. They were still less than 200 years away from the 1486 *Malleus Maleficarum*, the immensely popular handbook for witch-hunters, and less than a hundred from Bérulle's participation in the horror of the political Catholics at the Edict of Nantes, manifested in his ill-considered work wrongly maintaining the diabolic possession of Marthe Brosse, his 1599 *Traité des Energumènes*. The mass hysteria of the Ursulines considered to be possessed at Loudun in 1634 was less than half a century before the poisons scandal about to break in Paris, and to occupy Louis personally. The Siècle des lumières, with its enhanced trust in the union of reason and instinct was in 1680 not yet fully foreseen.

Much was harmless. When the marquise de Langey, quarrelling with her ultra-eccentric husband about a legacy, accused him of impotence, he demanded a formal 'congrès' before the *lieutenant civil* and the necessary dozen witnesses.[18] Langey had to change his shirt twice during the allotted time, because 'the drugs he had taken made him hot'. Tallemant's *Historiette* spares us no detail of Langey's failure in July 1660 and of the hilarity of all Paris, including the vaudevilles and bawdy rhymesters. Mme de Sévigné was in a carriage two doors away, and her laughter was heard at the end of the street.

Love philtres are also certain to have played a part in the second marriage of the king's own brother, Philippe. He was so famous for sodomy, which carried the death penalty, that Louis was unable to undertake against it the campaign he wanted to. Philippe did have a mistress as well as two wives and eleven legitimate children, eight of them by his first wife, Henriette d'Angleterre.[19] After her death, Philippe then married in 1671 another close relation of the English royal family, Elizabeth-Charlotte von Wittelsbach, princess Palatine, known as 'Liselotte'. She had to become a Catholic and renounced her rights to the English succession. Nancy Mitford describes her accurately enough as 'a great blonde Teutonic tomboy'[20] and no doubt equally accurately recounts Philippe's despair at the prospect of conducting a marital relationship with her. There can be little doubt that any available aids were used.

Married by proxy at Metz, the new Madame, as the wife of the king's brother was always called, arrived in Paris in November 1671. Philippe attached holy medals to his genitals and kissed the fingers of the chevalier de Lorraine, his principal male lover, before retiring with Liselotte, and they had three children before moving to separate beds. Liselotte was a prolific and indiscreet letter-writer, contemptuous of Mme de Maintenon of whom she was jealous, hostile to the iniquities of Versailles, to the grand Dauphin, and the comte du Maine.[21] She was not glamorous, but was fond of hunting, enjoyed spending all day in the saddle, bristled with prejudices, retained her German Protestant likes and dislikes, and let it be known that she had fallen in love with Louis, unaware that La Reynie was showing him the more succulent parts of her letters.

It is improbable that la grande Mademoiselle was ever actually in love with Louis, although she had certainly aspired to marry him before having a cannon turned in his direction during the siege of Paris on 2 July 1652. She had been exiled and lived on her estates at Saint-Fargeau until she was reconciled to Louis in 1657. An attempt was made to marry her to the pretender to the throne of Portugal, then to the duc de Lorraine, and finally to Louis's brother Philippe, thirteen years her junior, on the death of Henriette d'Angleterre, in 1670. Louis had said simply 'There is a place vacant', but Philippe preferred Liselotte, and la grande Mademoiselle was already in love with the marquis de Puyguilhem, commonly known as the comte de Lauzun, one of the captains of the king's guards, and universally thought as unattractive in appearance as he was in character. Half a dozen, or perhaps eight years her junior (no one is sure), he was an impoverished cousin of Saint-Simon, who finds nothing good to say about him, except that he was attractive to women.

La grande Mademoiselle was forty-three, and immensely rich. When she asked Louis for permission to marry Lauzun he accepted the idea with some amusement, but thought his uncle's daughter old enough to know her own mind. She should, as friends advised, have married Lauzun immediately, but she wanted a court wedding, and delayed a week, starting to bestow on Lauzun wealthy properties. The court was scandalized, particularly at the dissipation of all that wealth. Mme de Sévigné wrote one of her best letters on the subject, panting with amazement and wide-eyed with incredulity. Dated Monday 15 December 1670, the letter announced to her daughter the astonishing news of the wedding to take place 'on Sunday'. Louis would have preferred to see the money go elsewhere, to his children by Mme de Montespan, for instance. Others had eyes on it, Philippe for one of his daughters, and the Condés, although they were in no particular need of it.

Instead of pushing ahead with an immediate marriage, Mademoiselle gave Mme de Montespan and Louvois time to marshal their opposition. Louis, alarmed by the hostility the proposed marriage was arousing, then decided to forbid it, on the pretext that the couple had put it around that they were marrying not with his tacit consent, but at his express wish. There was an interview in which Mademoiselle certainly shed tears, and Louis is said to have, but it is not at all clear what happened thereafter. Lauzun gave back the lands and titles, and it is probable that Louvois and Mme de Montespan conspired to have Lauzun imprisoned, and if so, on the grounds that a wealthy Lauzun and Mademoiselle, heroine of the Fronde, might again represent a danger to Louis's own position.

The final rupture came in October 1671. There is another improbable story that Lauzun, having confided to Mme de Montespan his desire to captain a particular guards regiment, hid under her bed while she spoke to the king about the matter, urging him not to grant Lauzun his wish. Lauzun that evening escorted Mme de Montespan to the ballet and repeated to her verbatim her conversation with the king. Athénaïs, incensed, told Louis, who thereupon summoned Lauzun to account for his behaviour, whereat Lauzun lost his temper, snapped his sword in two, and said he would not use a sword again in the service of a king who broke his word at the bidding of a whore.

It may well not have happened. Saint-Simon and Segrais give quite incompatible accounts and dates, but Saint-Simon says that the king then performed 'perhaps the finest action of his life'. He threw his cane out of the window saying he would have regretted having struck a gentleman. But on 25 November 1671 Lauzun was arrested and taken for ten years to Pinerolo to join Fouquet.[22] Lauzun was to be released only in 1681 on payment by Mademoiselle of a large sum to the duc du Maine, Mme de Montespan's eldest child by the king. Mademoiselle and Lauzun appear to have married privately but, if so, it did not last longer than weeks. Mademoiselle provided for Lauzun financially.[23]

This was one of three occasions on which Louis is said to have become extremely angry,[24] although many more can be counted in the pages of this book. The point, however, is that Louis is caught

[185]

here in several characteristic poses in a single incident, indulgent, even kind, to his uncle's rich daughter who had once been his entrenched enemy, but had also wanted to marry him; less characteristically weak and vacillating under court pressure, probably reinforced by Athénaïs just as she gained power over him, in withdrawing his consent and imposing his control over his immediate family; quite apt to bully those unable to resist him in his punishment of Lauzun's presumed impertinence; and yet able to restrain himself from an act which would have detracted from his chivalresque obligations, if only at the cost of a pointlessly flamboyant gesture, approved of only by Saint-Simon, snobbish defender of an out-of-date caste system.

Poisons were more sinister than love potions, even if supplied from the same sources. In the Paris of 1679 the difficulty is to disentangle the allegations from the realities, fantasies from actions, the murders and attempted murders from dabbling in the occult, and in the present context to understand the constraints placed on Louis. To palliate Athénaïs's jealousy of his latest favourite, Mlle de Fontanges,[25] Louis had given her the honour she had coveted since 1671, the post of *surintendante de la maison de la reine*, but Athénaïs none the less left Saint-Germain on 15 March 1679, according to Mme de Maintenon, still jealous. Her relationship with Louis had been over since her final pregnancy in 1678, but Louis still called on her daily, although they were now never alone.

Mlle de Fontanges died at Port-Royal on 28 June 1681. Liselotte was certainly wrong when, in one of her letters, she accused Mme de Montespan of murdering her with poisoned milk, but two of Mlle de Fontanges's servants had just died 'and it was said openly that they were poisoned'. Louis was sufficiently worried after her death to oppose an autopsy on Mlle de Fontanges, but by now not even Louis could safely step in to stop a post-mortem without sacrificing credibility. Before the poison scandal was over, it would cause Louis himself much worry.

The poisoning had started long before it became public. A society lady, the marquise de Brinvilliers, it would later turn out, poisoned her father over eight months in 1666, during which she also devotedly nursed him, and then on 17 June 1667 poisoned her brother, the *lieutenant civil* in charge of the Châtelet prison, who was replaced by La Reynie in his more powerful post. The marquise killed another brother in September, and attempted to kill her husband. He survived because her lover, who did not wish to marry her, supplied him with antidotes. The marquise was kindly, busy in good works, visited the sick, but tried out her poisons on them. Colbert's ordinance on criminal procedure of August 1670, apparently partly aimed at stopping witch-hunts and at a more humane prison system, might have appeared at a more appropriate moment.

The sudden unexplained death of a healthy adult was by 1670 almost always attributed in the public mind to poison. Racine's mistress, Thérese du Parc, who died in December 1676, was almost certainly poisoned, and in November 1679 La Voisin was to accuse Racine of the murder. Louvois wrote to the examining magistrate on 11 January 1680 saying that he could have the order for Racine's arrest as soon as he liked. It was never issued, which suggests protection at the very highest level.

Soon after La Reynie's appointment, he was warned by a priest at Notre-Dame of an alarming increase in confessions of murder. This did not link a penitent with a sin, and so did not break the seal of confession. Then the marquise de Brinvilliers, condemned to death in her absence in 1673, was arrested in 1676 in the Low Countries. The *parlement* dragged matters out from 29 April to 16 July, reluctant to be dealing with one of its own class. Mme de Brinvilliers apparently underwent a religious conversion at the end, was tortured, and beheaded the day after sentence before her body was burnt. She had appeared to confirm the proliferation of poisoning with her dying words. The arrest had been on the orders of Louvois, but the trial had apparently implicated the financier Reich de Pennautier, *receveur général du clergé*, a protégé of Colbert released for lack of firm proof, so that the Colbert–Louvois hostility was now involved.

Then a lawyer came to La Reynie with the report of a dinner hosted by a Mme Vigoureux at which a drunken Mme Bosse had boasted about the amount she was making by poisonings in the highest ranks of society. She needed three more before she could retire. La Reynie sent an emissary to Mme Bosse to buy a bottle of poison by which to rid herself of a cruel husband. Mme Bosse, Mme Vigoureux with her son and two daughters were all asleep in the same bed when they were arrested. Mme Bosse and Mme Vigoureux talked cooperatively. They were, they claimed, fortune-tellers who lived in the penumbra of the court, lodging with junior staff occupied with laundry or hunting, who had easy access to the court and the palaces. They drew up horoscopes to find ways for people to make themselves irresistible. Mme Monvoisin had helped them to experiment with chemicals. A frequent client had been the pretty Mme de Poulaillon of a noble family locked up in a convent by a rich husband who suspected her of trying to poison him.

So far, no doubt so bad. But it was still only murder in high society, if of disturbing frequency and broadness of base. High-born clients with murder, rich marital partners, or simply desirable lovers in mind, were being supplied with the necessary means to achieve any desirable demise by low-caste 'fortune-tellers'. Deplorable, of course, but it was all to become very much worse because of the twin pressures predictably produced by an official religion which for too long had tolerated rampant superstition round its edges, surrounding ideals of genuine sanctity with means to ends which short-circuited the moral system, and by Louis's susceptibility to the acceptance as God-given of an obsolete caste system.[26]

The old military *noblesse d'épée* was by now so mingled by inter-marriage with the new *noblesse de robe,* that the distinction was fast disappearing outside a few ultra-conservative sensibilities, but it remained strong in Louis's mind, as the *Mémoires* show. On 12 March 1679 the police, alerted by Mesdames Bosse and Vigoureux, arrested La Voisin on suspicion of witchcraft. Five days later, they arrested Adam Cœuret, known as the abbé Le Sage, although he was not a priest. He pronounced the magic formulas while another associate who was a priest, and whose mistress, Françoise Mariette, dealt professionally in poisons, passed La Voisin's potions underneath the consecrated chalice. A second priest was involved, Etienne Gibourg from the central Paris parish of Saint Eustache.

La Reynie consulted Louvois, and both, close to Louis, consulted him. Louis's immediate reaction, in which the others concurred, was that the competent tribunal, the *parlement,* which had already dragged out the trial of the socially acceptable Mme de Brinvilliers, would not adequately deal with a situation which involved so many accusations against members of the social caste from which its own members were drawn. A special commission should be appointed to look into the Bosse–Vigoureux allegations, now increased by those of La Voisin and Cœuret. The first pressure on the administration of justice had begun to be felt. The special commission met in the Arsenal on 10 April and decided to sit in secret. Technically the

Commission de l'Arsenal, it has been known ever since as the Chambre Ardente. Between 10 April 1679 and 21 July 1682 it met 210 times, heard 442 cases, ordered 367 arrests, imposed 34 death penalties, sent 5 men to the galleys, and exiled 23 more.

The second pressure militating against justice stems from La Reynie's uncritical acceptance of the wildest allegations, including those of pacts with the devil and black masses. La Voisin claimed to have buried 2,500 children in her garden. On 26 June 1680 Gibourg admitted to have said mass on the naked stomach of a woman. A baby was sacrificed. Astaroth and Asmodeus were invoked, and the woman then said that she demanded the friendship of the king, and that he should abandon La Vallière. The evidence that the admission was made is incontestably in the archives of the Bastille. What is harder to accept is that the eminent and intelligent members of the commission, and everyone else concerned, were sufficiently super-stititious to find this farrago of fantasizing believable.

Their belief survived what they supposed was a reasonably rigorous procedure whereby La Reynie should arrest anyone he thought suspect and submit their interrogation to the *procureur général*, who would decide whether to proceed. If he did proceed, the suspect would be confronted with the other accused and a report on the confron-tation sent to the commission, which would then decide either to liberate the suspect or to continue with the interrogation. If the interrogation was continued, its detailed report would again be submitted to the commission, which would acquit or again proceed, this time to interrogation under torture. On the result of this final interrogation sentence would be passed. There was no appeal.

Arsenic, cantharides, nail cuttings, crayfish powder and other supposed aphrodisiacs were found in Mme Bosse's house. At their confrontation, La Voisin accused Mme Bosse of three murders, that of her husband, that of the husbands of Mme Dreux, a cousin of one of the judges, and Mme Leféron, whose husband had been a judge of the *parlement*. Mme Bosse was now married to her lover. Mesdames Dreux, Leféron and de Poulaillon were sent, to the horror of Parisian society, to join the other accused at Vincennes. In the end the three of them were sent to end their days in convents in the Low Countries. Caste had counted. La Voisin was a professional abortionist, child kidnapper and murderer. She survived torture and was burnt alive with Mme Bosse. Mme Vigoureux died under torture.

Duchesses, princesses, viscountesses and countesses were all being named and, what was worse, so were Mlle des Œeillets, by whom Louis had a child, the duchesse de Vivonne, Athénaïs's sister-in-law, and two of Mazarin's nieces, the king's former lover Olympe, now comtesse de Soissons, accused of murdering her husband, and Marie-Anne, duchesse de Bouillon, accused of poisoning a valet who knew too much about her love life, and of trying to poison her husband. La Reynie, horrified, exclaimed that men's lives were up for sale. The king tipped off Olympe de Soissons, who fled to Brussels with another noble suspect, the marquise d'Alluye.

What most concerned Louis was the mention by several suspects of Mme de Montespan in the summer of 1680. In December 1679, Louis was still demanding the strictest justice 'without any distinction of persons or of rank or sex'. In July 1680 La Voisin's daughter and a woman called Filastre made statements that 'fearing some diminution of the king's good graces', Athénaïs had had dealings with Mme Monvoisin, who had had sacrilegious masses celebrated and provided Mme de Montespan with powders. Louvois showed the transcript to Louis, and passed it to La Reynie, who appears to have believed the accusations, saying the king wanted them properly examined. Louis's liaison with Athénaïs had been over for some time, and the duchesse de Fontanges was now showing herself the recipient of the royal favour by receiving courtiers from her bed. On 6 April 1680 Mme de Sévigné wrote to her daughter that Athénaïs was in tears over the matter.[27]

Colbert consulted an eminent lawyer, who pointed to various discrepancies, and on Colbert's advice the whole matter was hushed up. Colbert wrote to the king pointing out the implausibilities of the accusations against his former mistress. On 6 October La Reynie advised Louvois not to mention Mme de Montespan, and Louis forbade the clerks taking depositions to use ledgers. They should stick to loose sheets. Louis abstracted those on which Athénaïs's name appeared, and burnt them in 1709, two years after Mme de Montespan's pious death, forgetting that a copy was (and still is) in the police files. La Voisin never mentioned Mme de Montespan even under torture. The king kept her at Versailles until 1691. Athénaïs was almost certainly innocent of any idea of murder. On the count of acquiring and administering aphrodisiacs, her innocence is less certain, but the crime a lot less grievous.[28]

When the accusations against Athénaïs surfaced, then multiplied, the trials collapsed. To drop the accusations against Athénaïs alone would be too manifestly unjust. La Reynie refused to have the trials stopped and all the dossiers destroyed. Most of the suspects were acquitted, happily admitting to consulting La Voisin for horoscopes. The special commission became a laughing-stock The duchesse de Bouillon, asked by a member of the commission what the devil looked like, is said to have answered 'small, dark, and ugly. Just like you.' Louis exiled her for contempt.

On La Reynie's suggestion the remaining prisoners were kept in custody by *lettres de cachet,* more usually used against recalcitrant sons and daughters refusing to entertain dynastic marriages. Had La Voisin and her two intimate companions not already been executed, they would have benefited, too. As it was some 150 prisoners, most of whom may well have been guilty of serious crimes involving murder or sacrilegious 'satanism', were imprisoned for life in solitary confinement and forbidden to speak to their gaolers. Some must have been innocent.

It is difficult not to have some sympathy with Louis. Accusations of murder by poisoning had begun to smack of a corporate hysteria. It engulfed La Reynie and was threatening Louis, forcing him into the volte-face about equal severity for all. Insecure as ever, he was worried that Mlle de Fontanges may have been poisoned, that Mlle des Œeillets, mother of his child, and two of Mazarin's nieces may have been guilty of murder, and that his former mistress, Mme de Montespan was somehow criminally involved.

To tip off one of Mazarin's nieces in time for her to flee to Brussels, to forbid the use of ledgers to take records of depositions, and to have destroyed all the loose sheets on which Mme de Montespan was mentioned, were tyrannical interferences with the process of law, but it would be surprising if worse things were not being done to keep the Sun King's chariot in orbit. Louis in the end had the consent of Louvois and La Reynie as well as the organizational brilliance of Colbert behind him. The glory of his reign was still climbing, although it was nearer to its apex than Louis and Colbert probably imagined. What Louis did was what was necessary to protect the caste system around which the court revolved. He could go on shoring up his self-confidence in the fantasy world created for him by Colbert.

9

'Sans vue, sans bois, sans eau': Versailles

Colbert's achievements were magnificent, and he died rich, but his triumphs, especially in domestic policy and admittedly during a score of years which started with a dozen without serious war, came at a price. He failed to make Paris the true capital of France and, shortly before his death in 1683 was driven to despair by the renewed war expenditure and its consequences, while Louis had become seriously concerned only to finish the works at Versailles without apparent regard for the financial consequences. In an undated letter of sometime in 1680, Colbert warns Louis that his lack of consultation is leading him to disaster. Louis's expenditure 'is so extraordinary as to be without parallel'. Then on 8 June 1683, he writes again that expenditure authorized by Louis exceeds receipts by 3.6 million livres. Louis replied that the high expenditure grieved him, but that 'some of it was necessary'.

Louis had by then finally overruled Colbert to make Versailles rather than Paris the place of formal royal residence, the home of the court and the seat of government. The decision had been taken quite gradually, and Colbert still held out hopes of victory virtually up to his death. The irony is that it was Colbert, who wanted peace and had opposed the wild extravagances of Versailles, who incurred the opprobrium for excessive taxation to sustain the war at the end of his life, rather than Louis, who was responsible, but the maintenance of whose image of irreproachable magnificence was Colbert's most prestigious achievement.

Colbert found himself in the end edged into allowing Louis the money from an already bankrupt treasury to boost his sense of untrammelled authority by creating Versailles. The creation of Versailles was an act of chutzpah surpassed only by that of Peter the Great at Saint Petersburg, but otherwise unequalled in the history of European monarchies. It was perpetrated, like Saint Petersburg, to which it is in all respects inferior, at huge cost in money, hardship and lives, by a monarch in a position to impose what was essentially a fantasy over the whole of his immediate environment.

Louis's domestic comportment depended on the exercise of rigid control over a subservient court. Its members were advised whether they had earned their chances of preferment or lucrative benefaction through an intricately devised and punctiliously observed but complex code of behaviour, encompassing invitations to the *lever* at the top end to exile at the bottom, and passing through privileges conferred at table or the hunt and a graduated series of tiny distinctions such as those between intrinsically insignificant invitations, or modes of greeting, ignoring and reprimanding.

The great manifestation of the self-image Louis almost involuntarily acquired, the château of Versailles, went well beyond what Colbert, and almost everyone else, considered reasonable. Affordable, it certainly was not.[1] Comprehensible, barely, and then only if regarded as a magnificent garden, with a château to service it. Ian Dunlop makes the trenchant point about Le Nôtre's garden that its features are described from the vocabulary of a domestic interior, *Galerie, Salle, Cabine, Appartement,* even *Tapis, Buffet,* and *Broderie.*[2] The château itself was never properly designed as a single unified building, and to this day impresses by its sheer mass rather by any exterior architectural elegance.

The garden was designed for the recreational aspects of corporate living. True, the concept is anchored to its period. Its figures are formal and geometric. The dominating lines are straight, the angles often ninety degrees. It is not the sort of extension of the country house that the ha-ha would soon make possible, to be seen from the warmth and shelter of bricks and mortar, creating the eighteenth-century illusion of continuity between house and estate. Le Nôtre's garden could be taken in only if you moved round it and experienced its vistas and bosquets.[3] It then became a work of art in its own right. Too many zeros defeat the imagination, but in 1685 just short of 3 million hornbeam plants alone were transferred from the Forêt de Lyon to create the backdrops Le Nôtre needed, and he is said to have had 1.9 million flower pots.

Abstracting from furnishing and decoration – fountains, ponds, canals, statues, urns outside, and tapestries, paintings, exquisite furniture, silverware, cabinets, tables, chairs, *objets d'art* and carpets within – at all stages of its early existence the garden intentionally gave greater aesthetic pleasure than the architecture of the grandiose house. Louis's personal hand-written guide to his garden showed how proud he was of it.

The house was from the start subject to the addition of wings here and there as needs arose or changed. It successfully set out to provide living quarters which from the outside looked imposing rather than aesthetically pleasing, and to harbour such ancillary conveniences as were required to house the Sun King's horses, hounds and deferential court, to impress the world with the magnificence of its occupant, and, almost as an afterthought, from which conveniently to administer the country. As late as 1667 Louis still described Paris as 'le lieu de notre résidence ordinaire'. At least until his mother's death, he was still intent on enhancing the grandeur of Paris.

Set in the bleak, unfriendly countryside described by Saint-Simon as 'sad and bare', with 'no view, no water and no woods', what the Versailles ensemble of garden and house does do perfectly is reflect the personality of its creator, Louis himself. Asked by Colbert whether, while campaigning, he wanted long or short accounts of the Versailles works, Louis notoriously answered, 'De longs, le détail de tout.' It is true there was already the triple-winged hunting lodge which all the successive architects wanted to pull down. But for reasons no doubt of family sentiment and memories of escapes from Fontainebleau with Louise de la Vallière, Louis was determined to keep the old lodge, threatening to re-erect it if anyone did pull it down. This meant that the fourth side facing east towards Paris, the front court, had to remain open to create a courtyard entrance, and that building had therefore to start by constructing an envelope round the three existing wings. The axis of the garden had therefore to lead westwards from the middle of the west wing.

Saint-Simon, described Versailles as 'sans vue, sans bois, sans eau' in his celebrated *Mémoires* written well after the death of Louis XIV, between 1739–1751. He had huge prejudices and had a political career which eventually failed, but was a sharp observer, and the *Mémoires* contain some brilliant pen portraits. He talks in terms of 'tyrannizing nature', jumbling the beautiful and the ugly. Voltaire is equally brutal about all aspects of the house except the west front.

Although he manages to admire the fountains, the aspect of the building seen from the garden and the craftmanship of the chapel, his view of the immense superiority of Saint-Germain leaves Saint-Simon with only disparaging comments about Versailles, from the marsh and bog on which it is built, to the view of the evil-smelling privies afforded from the rear of the royal apartments. Overall the building is left looking 'like a tomb' because the chapel, where the element of interior design is derisory, was put where it was on account of Hardouin-Mansart's attempt to force the king to build a whole extra storey.[4]

Saint-Simon's comment that the château had among the 'drawing-rooms heaped on [horizontally, *en enfilade*] one another' no theatre, no banqueting hall and no ballroom, suggests that Louis XIV had actually planned to hold his large functions in the park, as they had been held in the great outdoor celebrations of 1664 and 1668. In a sense the grandest rooms were out of doors. Louis's love of hunting, shooting and outdoor activities generally is well known. In ferociously cold winters he appeared immune to cold, and his habit of always flinging windows wide open inflicted considerable hardship notably, later, on Mme de Maintenon. He may well have considered outdoor entertainment possible for most of the year.

Louis now asked Le Nôtre to prepare the plan for the town of Versailles, stretching out to the east of the château. Louis was following the example set by Richelieu at the town of Richelieu adjoining the Richelieu family property. Richelieu, too, had left intact what his father had done but enormously enlarged the building and created a town over which the house and park appeared to preside. Like Richelieu, Louis allowed people to acquire parcels of land providing that they undertook to build to definite specifications.

It was in 1668 that serious building work started with what Colbert referred to as the '*Enveloppe*' round the existing wings and behind them, after Louis had decided that an enlarged service building rather than a grand palace was what he wanted, a *château* rather than a *palais*. He himself kept his private apartments within the old walls, and that is where he was to die in 1715. At the end of 1668 work on the 'Enveloppe' was begun, and it had reached about twenty feet, with a ground floor gallery nearly completed when, according to Charles Perrault, Louis decided that he disliked it sufficiently to have work stopped in June 1669. New designs were called for, and at least four were submitted. In Le Vau's design, which may initially have been accepted, the Louis XIII triple-winged château would have been pulled down after the new wings had been erected, leaving a new, bigger structure, on three sides of a square with large pavilions in the two western corners.

That design was scrapped, and the idea of the 'Enveloppe' re-instated, with wide spaces between old and new wings on the north and south. It took half a dozen years to decide on the form of the grand staircase, and the form of interior spaces was still being considered after the roof went up in 1670. The building was conceived as an adjunct to the park, for which a tall structure was thought to be appropriate. An Italianate articulation was devised for the west (garden) front, allowing an extra full floor to be built.

This was the stage at which the king's suite was built at the north end of the west wing, looking out over the garden, with the bathroom suite below, and living rooms in the north wing itself, enabling Louis to keep an eye on the comings and goings in the Paris-facing Cour de marbre. Only those who had the right to drive into the Louvre's Cour carrée were admitted: princes, dukes, the highest military officers and ambassadors. The design was by Le Vau, whose success in incorporating architecturally supportive features from 1668 has been regarded as brilliant. He died unexpectedly in October 1670, and after an interregnum during which his office appears to have remained in charge, Mansart was appointed the king's architect in 1679. There were plans for separate buildings for an opera house and for entertainment near the château but in the park. The ground floor of the south wing was designated for Philippe and his family, and the first floor for Maria-Teresa.

Enough drawings survive to make clear that among numerous plans for the building, some construction which actually took place in the early 1670s was later pulled down.[5] The sculptural decorations of the façade, entrusted to Le Brun, linked the château to the elaborate mythological figures and statue groups in the park, to the two buildings planned to be erected opposite the facades, and even to the specific tree plantings they faced nearby in the park.

[197]

They were intended to bring house and park into a visual unity, joined by a common, often allegorical theme, with Le Brun taking his inspiration from the Italian guides to the symbolism of emblem books, notably Cesare Ripa's 1593 *Iconologia*, of which a French translation had appeared in 1644. Even the keystones of the arches on the façade were linked to the sun or the general mythological scheme.

Just before 1674, when building was sufficiently advanced for the king, his wife and his mistress to spend long periods there, and there was room for ministers to work, Colbert ordered twenty-eight marble statues greater than life size to be designed by Le Brun for the western parterre. Twenty-four, in six groups of four, were to be of single figures, and four of famous rapes from classical antiquity inspired by Gianbologna and Bernini. The written plan has been lost, but the single figures allegorized the sun's court and the groups the elements which bound the universe together: earth, air, fire and water.

At this date the decoration of the interior of the château was also sun-obsessed, with months in the octagonal salon, while the seven rooms of the king's *appartement* were named after the seven planets, culminating in the 'Salon d'Apollon'. The inspiration came from the Pitti palace in Florence, where Pietro da Cortona had framed historical pictures with figures representing the gods and goddesses after which the planets were named. The complexity of the Louvre paintings was such that in 1678 the *Mercure galant* printed one and invited explanations of it from readers, offering to print them for the erudition they contained even if they were wrong.

There is an account of a Saturday spent at Versailles in a letter of Mme de Sévigné of Wednesday, 29 July 1676. They attended the queen's *toilette*, went to mass, and assisted at the royal dinner, assembling in the king's *appartement* at three. Everyone was there, the king and queen, Philippe with wife and daughter, all the princes and princesses, Mme de Montespan and her entourage, all the courtiers and ladies, the court of France. It was not in the least too hot, there was no overcrowding: 'everywhere is divinely furnished; everything is magnificent.' There follows a paragraph noting who is sitting where for cards, and who is winning. There are no *jetons*. Only gold is on the table, and Mme de Sévigné is clearly awe-struck by the size of the stakes.

Mme de Sévigné continues to her daughter, 'I curtseyed to the king as you taught me. He returned my greeting as if I had been young and pretty.' The queen asked after her health as if she had just given birth, and talked to her about the daughter to whom she was writing, Mme de Grignan. Various other members of the court spoke kindly to her, and 'Mme de Montespan spoke to me about Bourbon, asking me to tell her about Vichy, and how I got on there. She said that instead of curing her knee, Bourbon had given her toothache.'

There follows a long description of Mme de Montespan's attire, jewellery and hair, 'her waist is not half as big as it used to be, without harming her complexion, her eyes, or her lips . . . a triumphant beauty for the ambassadors to admire.' The king absents himself to read his mail, but comes back. There is music the whole time. At six everyone got into carriages and 'went to sail in gondolas on the canal, where music was played, and on the return at ten, there was a play. Midnight chimes. There was supper. That is how I spent Saturday.'

Expenditure at Versailles had had to be curtailed during the Dutch war of 1672 which ended with the series of treaties in 1678–9, not all of which involved France, collectively known as the Peace of Nijmegen. The wars require lengthier consideration, but Louvois, now more important than Le Tellier, his father, as minister of state for war, and Colbert, who had not opposed the war, were able to present Nijmegen as a victory. Louis's personal reputation at home and abroad reached its apogee about 1680, the year in which Paris solemnly gave him the title 'le grand' and in which, on 7 March, the grand Dauphin married Marie-Anne-Christine-Victoire von Wittelsbach. Henceforward all inscriptions referred to the king as 'Louis le grand'.

Colbert's 'enveloppe' building at Versailles was, however, now too small. Louis wanted to have with him not only his brother and the dauphin, but also his whole extended family, including Mme de Maintenon, Mme de Montespan and Mlle de Fontanges, together with his principal ministers, administrative staff and the whole of his court, to many of whom he wanted to offer accommodation. Le Vau's collaborator, François d'Orbay, was to build the great 'Escalier des Ambassadeurs', to be magnificently decorated by Le Brun, but d'Orbay was passed over for Mansart in the second stage of the construction of the château undertaken by Louis after Nijmegen.

The integration of château and park was forgotten. The Galerie des Glaces and its adjacent salons desecrated Le Vau's garden façade, filling the terrace and creating the unsightly architectural chaos of which Saint-Simon complained. Two large wings to the north and south of the main block more than trebled the length of the garden front, simply extending on each side Le Vau's Ionic order for the existing principal storey. Perfectly suitable for Le Vau's façade, the endlessly repeated Ionic order over the 600 metres of the extended west front now gave it its visually monotonous inadequacy.[6] What the surviving drawings reveal is a large variety of different ways of adding to the accommodation, either by continuing in the low-rise style hitherto favoured by Louis or by adding height with cupolas, roof, and chimneys, a French solution recently adopted by Le Vau at the Tuileries, which Louis was inhabiting while the Louvre was under reconstruction.

The final architectural solutions were entirely determined by the king's decision to replace a projected depiction of the labours of Hercules on the ceiling of the grand room which was to replace the terrace on the west front with a visual representation of his victories in the Dutch war. What counted architecturally was the provision of light sufficient to see Louis's military glories on the ceiling in a room well enough proportioned to befit the glorification of the monarch. Le Brun's assistant and first biographer, Claude Nivelon, tells us that, on hearing that a substitute for the Hercules paintings was required, Le Brun shut himself up for two days and produced the centrepiece for the ceiling devoted to Louis's exploits in the Dutch war, and was given the contract for painting the ceiling as a result.[7]

Mansart's solution, little short of genius, was to be a hall of mirrors, the Galerie des Glaces. It was eventually some eighty metres by twelve, with seventeen windows on one side and seventeen full-length mirrors on the other. He also provided a specifically French column capital requested by Colbert to the pilasters along the wall. He then revised the fenestration to admit as great an increase in light as was consistent with an adequately load-bearing structure, choosing a semi-circular top as in the Roman Colosseum, abolishing sills and creating French windows by taking the windows down to ground level. On the eastern wall of the hall went the mirrors, whose glass had to be made in Venice.

The graceful new window shapes were then also installed else-where, accentuating the Italianate appearance of the exterior of the building and providing more light inside. Colbert was anxious that Le Brun's ceiling should not offend foreign powers, and the whole plan was approved by Colbert in 1678. Le Brun's heavily mythologized paintings of the historical scenes specializing in contortions of face and torso expressing different sorts of pain, anger and other extreme sensations were painted as if to be seen at eye level, but placed in highly decorative and Italianate illusionistic painted frames.[8]

The difficulty created by this glorification of Louis's military prowess was that the Dutch war of 1672, the year in which Louvois joined the *conseil d'en-haut,* could be seen, even by the date of its concluding treaties of Nijmegen, to have been both catastrophic for France and, for Louis personally, doubly disgraceful, for its hideous cruelty as well as its disastrous political misjudgements. In fact it was worse than that, since it created the situation which would soon entail the destruction of France as a serious European military and political power until, just over a century later, Napoleon almost pulled it out of the political mire.

There is a paradox in the extreme inappropriateness of the iconography on which Louis insisted for the all-important ceiling which was the *raison d'être* of Mansart's glorious Hall of Mirrors. Louis, having just sown the seeds of France's eclipse, required in a secret meeting of the *conseil d'en-haut* that the Dutch war, lamentably fertile with the shoots of foreseeable disaster, should be celebrated by Le Brun's depiction of his glorious achievements. Among them was the assumption of the government of France on Mazarin's death with Louis depicted as Minerva, personifying wisdom, dressed as a French king in Roman armour.

The Hall of Mirrors proved so successful that Mansart added pavilions at each end, dedicated to war and peace, and extending the architectural scheme along the whole west façade, looking out over the three principal axes of Le Nôtre's park. The decoration of the stairway leading to the king's *grand appartement* must be contemporaneous with the decision to build the Hall of Mirrors. It shows the same misguided and dangerous self-satisfaction by celebrating events in the war.

Four illusionistic paintings, two on each of the long walls bordering the staircase and inspired by those in the Quirinal in Rome, showed figures from the four parts of the world looking down on visitors coming up, and gave the staircase the name of Escalier des Ambassadeurs.[9] Louis eventually changed the rooms of the *grand appartement* into a large suite of state rooms occupying the north and west sides of the 'Enveloppe', moving the chapel in 1681 to their east end. The king's own accommodation in the old Louis XIII château was ready for Louis's use by 1683, the year after the formal installation of the court at Versailles.

From 1678 to 1684, France was at peace. Between 1677 and 1679 expenditure on Versailles more than tripled. It was known in Paris by 1680 that Louis was going to make Versailles his residence and centre of government. Madeleine de Scudéry enthusiastically accepted Colbert's invitation to update her 1668–9 *Description de Versailles* and since neither the Hall of Mirrors nor the adjacent Salon of War was fully built, Louis decided to unveil at least the *appartement,* described in detail in the December 1682 number of the *Mercure galant.* Most remarkable, apart from the sumptuous magnificence of the furnishings, many of them made by Italian or Italian-trained craftsmen, was the creation of integrated interior decoration, so that the furnished room itself became a work of art over and above the individual works of art which were carefully placed within it.

When Colbert died on 6 September 1683, Louvois succeeded him as *surintendant des bâtiments, arts et manufactures.* At Versailles the Grand Commun, a 600-room block with 60 apartments for senior officials, had now been built to the south-west of the château, and the two stable buildings, one for hunting horses and the other for coach horses, had been erected. Each contained 600 animals, with the 500 couples of hounds and *manège* with the saddle horses in the Grande Ecurie, and 200 coaches housed in the Petite Ecurie, to the east of the Cour de marbre, flanking what is now the Avenue de Paris.[10] Beyond the Grande Ecurie was the Collège des Pages, also imitated from Richelieu's foundation at what had then been the Palais-Cardinal, where some 200 sons of the nobility were educated, with the emphasis on appropriate aristocratic pursuits. For acceptance they needed proof of nobility going back 200 years.

The Cour de marbre itself had by 1683 been rebuilt, creating buildings for the bureaucrats, and extending eastwards towards Paris in an increasing number of preliminary courtyards, the Cour royale and the Cour des Ministres. South of the Cour des Ministres and between the Grand Commun, which had its own chapel, and the princes' wing, finished with the *Aile du nord* in 1689, was the king's kitchen. Dining rooms were not yet usual. In the evenings, both the king and the queen normally ate in the ante-chambers of their suites, but the grand couvert, or midday meal, was normally served to Louis and Maria-Teresa together in the ante-chamber to her apartment, formerly a guards' room, and appropriately decorated for that function. A vast south wing had gone up, with a total of nineteen apartments, chiefly to house Louis's family, its western façade half as long again as the western façade of the château. The best apartments went to the dauphin and his wife, and to the Conti family. Where the wing joined the château a small theatre was built, and next to it the stairway of the princes, where a market was established for the courtiers.

One of the most beneficial side-effects of Louis's determination to create a small town for his own pleasure and convenience at so unpromising a location as Versailles was, perhaps not surprisingly, the boost it gave to technological developments. The Swedish royal architect, Nicodemus Tessin the Younger, kept an agent, Cronström, at Versailles to report on new technologies. Most important of all at Versailles was the provision of water, both for ornamental and for domestic use. The Francini family of hydraulic specialists were transferred from work at other royal residences and made part of the team at Versailles, where their work was early integrated into that of Le Nôtre's team. Their fountains used jets which combined to create shapes of bells and urns, and different sorts of vases in the air. Le Nôtre's plan called for 1,400 fountains. There are only 300 today.

Louis became obsessively concerned with the water supply for the fountains, at first mostly provided by drainage and ten windmills which worked a chain of buckets with the help of 120 horses. There were frequent breakdowns, and the supervisor had to make sure on pain of a fine that the fountains were working in whichever part of the park the king happened to be. The excavations had actually caused considerable loss of life, since the water beneath the surface soil was putrid from untreated sewage to the point of giving off poisonous exhalations. The larger fountains, with numerous jets, were turned on only when Louis was in that part of the park. From 1664 to 1690, the partial estimate for the two principal hydraulic projects came to over 13 million livres,[11] while painting, new pictures and gilding cost about 1.7 million livres, all new sculptures about 2.7 million livres, and all day workers in the château and park 1.3 million livres.

Colbert listened to every crank with an idea for providing water and to the serious engineers as well. Riquet, who had built the Canal du Midi, thought the level of the Loire might be raised, and a branch diverted to Versailles by canal, but the abbé Jean Picard of the Académie des sciences showed that the Loire was lower than Riquet thought. Smaller streams were considered, including the Etampes river.

It was the great Norman engineer, Sébastien le Prestre de Vauban, who suggested the feasibility of diverting the Eure from a point near Chartres eighty kilometres away, employing a system using a siphon. Louvois turned it down in February 1685, but in October 1684, Louis had decided to go ahead with an aqueduct above ground. Vauban accomplished the preparatory work in three months, and work on the scheme itself started in May 1685. The aqueduct was to be half a kilometre long, and carry water up to thirty-three metres above ground. Thirty thousand troops were put at the disposal of the con-tractor, and on 8 June 1685 Louvois was able to tell Louis that 1,600 arches of the 'Maintenon aqueduct' were under construction, some twice as high above ground as the towers of Notre-Dame. The project failed owing first to the incidence of disease among the workforce, and then to the demands of the 1688 war.

What did work to a limited extent was the monstrous-looking 'machine de Marly' which in 1681–2 succeeded in raising water some 160 metres from the Seine at Louveciennes. A working model demonstrated to Louis late in 1680 that water from the Seine could be raised to the level of the Saint-Germain terrace. Construction of fourteen water-wheels moving 221 pumps situated at intervals up the hill began near Bougival in 1681. The machine produced on average 3,200 cubic metres of water every twenty-four hours, but for the fountains to play, even at low pressure, twelve hours a day required some 13,000 cubic metres. For the fountains to play in full glory – Les Grandes Eaux – 3,800 cubic metres of water an hour were required. Meanwhile, pending the availability of water from the Machine de Marly, a system of canals and aqueducts had been devised and executed by Thomas Gobert and the abbé Picard, so that the park did have adequate water by 1683.[12]

Mme de Sévigné was enchanted by all that Louis accomplished at Versailles, and it is indeed true that the Hall of Mirrors illuminated by candles, the 100,000[13] candles illuminating the *appartements* when receptions were held, the 1,400 fountains playing at full strength, and the exquisite furniture, including the 167 items of solid silver counted by Tessin, must have been a marvellous sight. But some of the reactions we have reflect the awe of those at receiving invitations in the first place to a *Jour d'appartement,* held every Monday, Wednesday and Friday until the permanent installation of the court at Versailles, and thereafter on Tuesdays, Thursdays and Saturdays, and we must not forget the adulation assiduously pumped through the *Mercure galant.*

The Duke of Berwick thought there was in Louis 'no trace of pride except in his appearance . . . he had the art of putting you at once completely at ease with him.' Ezekiel Spanheim, the Prussian ambassador, remarks on Louis's ability in private conversation to strike a balance between grandeur and familarity, and Mme de Sévigné is the ideal guest, weak-kneed at being in the royal presence, lost in admiration at anything and everything to do with the king, and proud no doubt, too, at what her reports of high society would do for her daughter's social standing at Grignan, where she was married to the lieutenant-general of Provence.

But Louis's unbelievable prodigality in importing millions of bulbs a year, in forcing through the construction of Versailles, and in spending unspeakable amounts of money to flatter his own grandeur, before we even think of the wars, the peasantry and even the considerable loss of life in the construction works, suggest that Colbert's master-plan did not in the end work. Abstracting from the damage it did to Louis personally, to project him as Sun King for the sake of France may have seemed in the 1660s to make sense. By the later 1680s it was inducing something near to outrage in sections of the population and paranoia in Louis himself, who was spending vast sums of money on building, tearing up, and rebuilding ever greater monuments to his own grandeur. He was also creating what he intended to be an aesthetically pleasing and life-enhancing environment, luxurious, but also exquisite.[14]

It is really no surprise that Louis came to believe that there was something which really did lift him above ordinary mortals, that with the gifted team created for him he could construct an administrative

[205]

centre for France as well as an environment for gracious living grander than anyone else in Europe had dreamed of. It would be easier to regard the grimly determined obsessions as mere idiosyncracies to relax his moral tensions, give or take some doubts about his aesthetic judgements, had it not been for the hardships inflicted on Louis's subjects and his lust for even demonstrably pointless war. He disguised them with devotion and civility, but in the end they ruined France.

In 1681 a new orangery was being prepared in the park to the south of the château, and the huge excavation of the hillside was nearing completion. The financial situation plunged Colbert into gloom. When Colbert informed Louis that the *intendants* were rendering accounts which were full of the misery of the people, Louis replied on 8 June, 'Their misery causes me much grief. We will have to do all that we can for the relief of our people', following this letter with one of 10 June, 'Hasten all the works at Versailles because I might have to shorten this voyage by several days.' No doubt he meant merely to hasten the works necessary for his immediate personal requirements, but the obsessive obstinacy shines through, prepared to ride roughshod over everybody and everything in the interests of his personal convenience.

Guilt may have been about about to force him into at least the outward manifestations of relatively severe devotion, but it was not going to persuade him to abandon the self-delusion that his desire for grandeur was more than an arrogant whim which took precedence over the needs of his subjects, and the standing of his kingdom, and for which he himself was prepared to suffer. That is what Fénelon would be thinking about in the canonically formulated reproaches which would be contained in his 1693 *Rémonstrances* to the king. Louis needed to intensify the practices of devotion to innoculate himself against the feelings of guilt which proceeded from an insecurity he could not overcome. He had become psychologically dependent on his own artificial magnificence.

Mme de Maintenon had been openly urging Louis to return to fidelity to his wife, certainly since before the advent of Mlle de Fontanges, and the queen had been grateful for the increased attention. She loved the king, and her only other friend at court had been Anne of Austria, who had died in 1666, and perhaps at the end Mme de Maintenon, to whom she gave a diamond-framed portrait of herself. She was shy, meek, and remained rather childish, and would have liked the king, even though he slept in her bed, to have made love to her more often than the fortnightly pattern which developed. She always communicated next morning, and liked to be teased about it.

In May 1683 Louis wanted to inspect the army on the eastern front, and the queen accompanied him with Mme de Maintenon. In June the queen began to feel unwell and immediately after their return developed an abscess under her arm. The queen's doctor since 1680, Guy-Crescent Fagon, later physician to the royal children and, from 1693, to Louis himself, insisted on bleeding her, although her surgeon begged him not to. He followed this with a strong emetic about midday on 30 July. She died about an hour later, Louis himself having fetched from the temporary chapel the oils with which to anoint her. 'Poor woman,' he is said to have said, 'it's the only time she has given me any trouble.' If he did say that, it was not true. He had had more than once to pay off her gambling debts. In the traditional way, Louis left Versailles immediately after his wife's death. Mme de Caylus tells us that he went to Saint-Cloud on the Friday of the death, and then on the Monday to Fontainebleau.

Colbert fell ill that August. His most gifted son, Seignelay, wrote to the king at two a.m. on 2 September that the doctors had advised him to take communion that night and receive the last anointing. Louis replied that he was deeply touched, telling Seignelay to stay with his father as long as necessary. It is a genuinely warm letter, as is that Louis wrote to Colbert's widow after his death on 6 September.[15]

Louis remained at Fontainebleau until returning with Mme de Maintenon to Versailles on 9 October, probably marrying her in the old chapel there on the evening of their return.[16]

The three years following Colbert's death, 1684, 1685 and 1686 show the peak of expenditure on Versailles. In early August 1684, we are told that there were 22,000 men and 6,000 horses at work.[17] Louis had transformed the *maison de plaisance* at Versailles, where in the early 1660s he used to court La Vallière and hold small parties of young courtiers, into the vast acreage of the buildings which, when Mansart had finished, covered thirty hectares, had 2,143 windows, 1,252 fireplaces, and lodged within or near the precincts some 20,000 or perhaps even 25,000 persons. Le Nôtre's garden axis running west was about two thirds of a kilometre, with the north-south canal crossing it to lead south to the menagerie or north to the Trianon. The Grand Canal itself was projected to run for 1.8 kilometres.

Then, in July 1687 Louis decided to replace the Trianon de Porcelaine with the marble Trianon in order, the marquis de Sourches tells us, to give *fêtes* and *divertissements*.[18] He was intent himself on determining every detail, and characteristically designed the building to fit its garden rather than the other way round. He often passed the *après-dîners* there in a tent with Louvois, considering what instructions to give the architects. At first he wanted to retain the core of the building, as he had done at the Versailles château itself.

Then on 18 September Louvois wrote to Mansart that Louis wanted the garden side demolished and the roofs replaced with flat roofs above which chimneys were to protrude no more than thirty centimetres, even if that meant that they might smoke. On 2 October the court left for Fontainebleau. Louis wrote a series of letters specifying what he wanted down to the tiniest detail, and demanding haste. He made seven visits to the site in November. We know from later accounts of the delights of arriving at the new Trianon de marbre by canal and supping to Lulli's music, and if entertaining graciously is an art form, then Louis was a past master. But it was all dangerously expensive, as Louis would soon find out.

Louis notoriously and systematically noted who came to chapel, who made their Easter duties, and who was present at or absent from the entertainments and the *appartements*. Courtiers required leave to be away, except to rejoin their regiments, and advancements or favours took all these matters into account. A wedding or other special occasion might bring an indication from Louis that new and unaffordably expensive clothes were called for. There was a small townful of small traders and craftsmen to cater for the needs of courtiers. Courtiers had therefore to live by obtaining favours from the king on behalf of those who desired them and for which they would be paid by the recipients. Louis of course knew and exploited this situation. It put the court even more firmly in his power, but Louis now found that he again needed something smaller and more exclusive.

The system at Versailles had become too cumbersome. It was in November 1677, ten years before he decided to rebuild the Trianon in marble, that Louis, out hunting near Saint-Germain, came across Marly at the head of a valley surrounded by woods and with a vista widening on to the river. Work on a country-house, deliberately not called a château, for the whole royal family there had begun before the earliest plans which have come down to us were drawn up under the general supervision of Mansart in 1679. The new house, to be destroyed after the revolution, faced north, with a façade forty-five metres long.[19] Stretching from the entrance were two lines of half a dozen two-storey houses, linked by a trellis, and with series of falling terraces in front of each row. Louis's immediate family stayed in the Pavillon du Roi. Eleven of the linked two-storey houses each contained accommodation for two married couples, while the twelfth contained baths. The houses were placed at a considerable distance from each other in two lines stretching away from the Pavillon du Roi, dedicated to Jupiter.

The land in front of the guest pavilions, dedicated to lesser divinities, was formed into a series of descending terraces at right angles to the river, with ornamental ponds, the whole ensemble very carefully and expensively landscaped to afford calculated views as the house first became visible from the gate, and the landscape to the north gradually revealed itself. The northern façade was painted in *trompe-l'œil*, chiefly by Jacques Rousseau, a Huguenot who left France at the revocation of the edict of Nantes. Additions were made to Marly around 1700. Mme de Maintenon lamented that it would soon be another Versailles. The provision of pumped water alone was to cost over four and a half million livres.

The main buildings were completed by 1683, but Louis is not recorded to have slept there before 1686, having as at Versailles held his first parties in the gardens. He reserved his Marly parties for an inner circle of courtiers, and liked them to ask for invitations in public, as he passed down the Hall of Mirrors, saying yes to some and no to others, one way among thousands by which he made the degree of favour of any particular member of the court known both to the courtier and to everyone else.

Since Louis well knew that public indications of his favour were also signs that requests from courtiers so signalled out were more likely to be granted, the whole procedure smacked of bullying. The degree of inclination in a nod actually had implications for courtiers' ability to obtain favours for themselves or others, and thereby earn a living. Those not invited to Marly were thereby humiliated, and given an incentive to climb in the royal favour. Such a procedure unfortunately manifests again Louis's absolute determination to maintain his own tight control over all who came near him, whether by admitting to or excluding from various stages of the *lever* and *coucher*, rigidly enforcing the complex liturgy of who may or must remain standing or, if allowed to be seated, whether they may use a *fauteuil* or only a *tabouret*, and in whose presence who may or must wear headgear. Everyone was allowed to be seated at the gaming tables, even if the king was present. While the liturgical trivia of the etiquette are not important, for anyone seeking to understand Louis, his enforcement of them is.[20] It involves a degree of punctiliousness verging on scrupulosity, a psychological ailment, involving a neurotic, or sometimes even psychotic, lack of self-confidence.

A special etiquette obtained at Marly which Louis came to use as yet another source of control more than as somewhere he could himself relax, although he no doubt enjoyed getting away from the hammering and scaffolding at Versailles, and the atmosphere was more pleasant and relaxed. At the king's invitation gentlemen were allowed to remain covered in his presence. Whereas at Versailles only his brother ever sat down alone to eat with Louis, that privilege was at Marly extended to the grand Dauphin and, in due course, his three sons as well as Louis's nephew, the duc de Chartres, son of Philippe and Liselotte. Normally, however, at Marly the dauphin presided at a table of his own, the king had the women at his table, and the men sat at a third.

The etiquette could of course be amusing, as well as embarrassing. At Marly it was a sign of particular favour to have chalked on your door not only your name, but a prefixed '*Pour* M. Untel'. It was a place of intimate parties, elaborate amusements, hunting, outdoor games, mascarades, music and great enjoyment. There were plays, theatre, lotteries, opera and dancing. A relatively large element of entertainment was home-made, of the sort generated by dressing up under one pretext or another, or by playing charades. Physical demands were put on the male guests by outdoor activities, but intellectual and artistic demands made on the company were slight.

Even Liselotte, Philippe's new wife, and Saint-Simon have pleasant things to say about the entertainments there, although Mme de Maintenon disliked Marly, just as she disliked Versailles. The king took fifty or sixty guests there a dozen times a year, at irregular intervals, and always stayed three nights. Racine, appointed a gentleman of the bedchamber, was among those invited, as, frequently before her second disgrace in 1694, was Mme Caylus.[21] Louis himself at Marly retired to work for much of the time, but took great interest in the gardens, in their planting and upkeep, and in showing them off. That was another trait he seems to have taken from Richelieu, who was himself willing to reverse the natural characteristics of a large terrain to impose his own landscape in place of nature's.

The move of the court to Versailles took place in 1682, towards the end of the period normally considered to constitute the apogee of Louis's reign, roughly from the end of the Dutch war in 1678, yet to be considered, to the death of Colbert in 1683, the year in which by chance the main building at Marly was also completed, in which the queen died, and in which Louis married Mme de Maintenon. The immediate succession to the throne was already provided for in the person of the grand Dauphin, but Louis's own personal and domestic circumstances also underwent important changes, some of which had serious political repercussions.

On Louis's only legitimate son, the dauphin, also known as Monseigneur, born on 1 November 1661, depended the future succession of the senior branch of the Bourbon dynasty, and with it perhaps the God-given authority of the French monarchy. The dauphin was not given a training anything like as thorough as that Louis himself had received from Mazarin. He did, however, belong to the councils of finances and despatches from 1688, and was one of the three who replaced Louvois on his death in 1691. He was intelligent, courageous and cultivated, but his greatest contribution to his father's reign was his popularity. It assuaged some of the popular disquiet at Louis's absence from Paris. He was fond of music, enjoyed Paris and spent much of his time visiting it.

When he was twenty his father gave him 150,000 livres with which to buy pictures. He was also a collector of antiques, of paintings, of medals and of coins. Boulle, famous for his inlaid ebony furniture, designed a complete room for him. The dauphin hunted, for preference wolf, and often with Liselotte, now married to his uncle, Louis's brother. He took risks in the field and manifested inexhaustible energy. He is said after his unintelligent upbringing never to have read anything except the births and obituaries in the *Gazette*, and seems never to have reached full intellectual or emotional maturity as an adult. He was always terrified of his father.

[211]

He took over Meudon from Louvois, and married twice. His first marriage, in 1680, to Marie-Anne Christine-Victoire von Wittelsbach, was political, intended to secure, apart from the all-important succession to the French throne, the Bavarian alliance, partly because no suitable Spanish princess was available.[22] The marquis de Croissy, Colbert's brother, foreign minister from 18 November 1679 and an experienced diplomat, was sent to report on the proposed spouse, and his letter describing her is masterly in the excuses it offers for blemishes in her appearance.

Louis sent a painter to produce a faithful likeness, but the painting arrived back with a letter from Croissy saying that it was absurdly flattering. Louis became hesitant, but the dauphin was unbothered. Liselotte thought he chiefly wanted to get away from paternal tutelage. He won, and Princess Victoire, as she was known, came to the French court. The portraits do not show the sallow skin with brown stains, the red hands, the pale lips, the rotten teeth and the fat nose, but she had perfect French and Italian, and danced well. Mme de Maintenon was appointed one of her ladies, but the dauphine, like Liselotte, looked down on Mme de Maintenon on account of her deficient ancestry, a matter even more serious in her native Geman-speaking territory than in France. The arrangement was not happy.

After two miscarriages, the dauphine produced three sons, the duc de Bourgogne in 1682, the duc d'Anjou in 1683 and the duc de Berri in 1686. The birth of the duc de Bourgogne was particularly difficult. If male, and able to survive, this infant was destined to succeed the grand Dauphin as king of France, and the Bourbon dynasty looked secure. The king himself chose the wet-nurse, who had to be dark, healthy, intelligent and smell delicious. It was in an August heat-wave, and messengers were ready to take the news all over France. As well as being intrinsically so important, this was the first significant cause for celebration since the court had moved to Versailles.

When the contractions began the atmosphere became very excited. Louis had himself woken early, was told the delivery would be slow, went to mass, then at nine to council. The queen sent for relics for the dauphine to see, and Louis himself fed her food and wine before going to dine. The special delivery bed with bars to grip and a foot rest used by Anne of Austria and, before her, by Marie de' Medici, was brought in. It was an extremely painful delivery, with the dauphine becoming weaker all the time. It looked as if she might not survive and she made her farewells, fully expecting not to. Louis spent all night by the bedside saying he would rejoice even if the baby were a girl. From time to time the dauphine was bled, and was on the point of expiring when, at ten-thirty a.m. the duc de Bourgogne was born.

The dauphine, whose only real friend at court was Liselotte, with whom she spoke German, recovered. She was expected by Louis to play her part at court, where he appears to have counted on the civilizing influence of women close to himself or his family, and in 1684 she inherited the suite formerly occupied by Maria-Teresa. After the birth of her third son in 1686 she went into a decline, withdrawing more and more as if into clinical depression. The dauphin fell in love with a succession of her maids of honour, who had hastily to be married off. The dauphine's 'decline' proved fatal, and she died on 20 April 1690 of what proved to be massive ulceration of lungs and intestine, with gangrene in the stomach. It was only after her death that Louis heard of the jokes she shared with Liselotte at the expense of Mme de Maintenon, whom they found tedious as well as low-born.

She was not greatly mourned. The dauphin showed little interest in the three boys, whom he addressed by their full titles. They called him Monseigneur, and Louis himself took charge of their upbringing. The dauphin never got on with his eldest son, the duc de Bourgogne, and their respective coteries came to split the court. The dauphin himself married again Marie-Thérèse Joly de Choin, about whom we know almost nothing except that she was a dismissed lady-in-waiting of the princesse de Conti. The dauphin's letters to Mme de Maintenon, virtually the only source, suggest that the marriage was primarily to keep him virtuous. It looked as if, when he became king, he might live in Paris.

The grand Dauphin and his second wife slept in adjacent bedrooms at Meudon, except when Louis came and the dauphine moved downstairs, and they entertained, giving exclusive parties with great taste. Louis liked to come. The dauphin's real companion however was his half-sister, Louise de la Vallière's ravishing daughter Marie-Anne, married at thirteen to the prince de Conti, although she would have preferred his younger brother, a close friend of the dauphin, and let it be known publicly that her husband was a poor lover. They had no children.

The Conti brothers were princes of the blood, Bourbons in the Condé line. They were among the members of a new 'young court' who were bored by Versailles, and had joined a group of French volunteers fighting against the Turks in Hungary. In 1683 Louis was badly upset when the censored post from Versailles to the group showed up several homosexual relationships, and revealed that his liaison with Mme de Maintenon was regarded as a joke, that the court was now considered dull beyond belief, and that the princesse de Conti, Louis's daughter, found her obligation to drive out with Mme de Maintenon a tedious chore. Three young courtiers were exiled on account of that mailing, and Louis, on the eve of revoking the edict of Nantes, started behaving like the bully to which he so often reverted.

When the Conti brothers got back from Hungary, Marie-Anne, married to the elder brother, almost immediately caught smallpox, which she passed on to her husband. She recovered, and he seemed to be getting better. He was sitting up in bed, joking with her, when he fell back, dead. She was nineeteen and became the close companion of the dauphin, who took her to the opera in Paris, or played cards with her after the day's hunting. She never married again although there were several possibilities, and the dauphin finally married Mlle de Choin, one of her attendants, after Louis had bullied Marie-Anne by making her read out loud to him compromising letters she had written elsewhere which had been intercepted and passed to the king. She is said to have fainted twice during the ordeal.

Only a letter of 19 July 1694 from the dauphin to Mme de Maintenon has survived acknowledging that he remarried, and no one knows when or where the marriage took place. The younger prince de Conti, seriously compromised in the letters read by the king, was promised a pardon for serving under the chevalier de Lorraine only if he revealed some of the names alluded to but not spelled out in the letters. He refused to do this, and was not pardoned by the king until the day of the death of his uncle, le grand Condé, who had pleaded for his nephew, and who died on the evening of 4 December 1686.

By 1683, the year that saw the death of the queen and of Colbert, and the year of Louis's remarriage to Mme de Maintenon, the peak of Louis's reign had passed. The comte de Vermandois, brother of Marie-Anne, princesse de Conti, and Louis's surviving son by Louise de la Vallière, died that year in a garrison at the age of sixteen. He had been mixed up in a homosexual scandal as a young boy, after which Louis had callously taken no further interest in him. That year also saw the death of Louis-César, comte de Vexin, Louis's second son by Mme de Montespan.

That left surviving as direct descendants of Louis and the queen, the dauphin and his two children to date; the princesse de Conti, Louis's only surviving child by Louise de la Vallière; and by Mme de Montespan two boys, the duc du Maine (b.1670) and the comte de Toulouse (b.1678), and two girls, one of whom (Mme la Duchesse) was to marry the grandson of the grand Condé and the other, Françoise-Marie, who, much to her mother-in-law's outrage, was to marry Philippe's son by Liselotte, the duc de Chartres, later d'Orléans, regent after Louis's death.

No doubt, among these events, the most important for France was the death of Colbert and his replacement by Louvois. For Louis and his immediate entourage, however, the most important was the advancement of Mme de Maintenon, three years older than Louis and six years older than the elegant and handsome Mme de Montespan. She is generally depicted in sharp contrast with Athénaïs, dressed in black, severe, intolerant and dull, although in fact she made her way in society by her gaiety and wit, liked to wear blue, and was for three or four years the closely cherished companion of Athénaïs. She was undoubtedly pretty as well as pious, but she was neither a bigot nor an advocate of the revocation of the edict of Nantes, which she rightly blamed on Louvois. Her own Huguenot background and ancestry made it difficult for her to protest at the revocation, but she quite happily kept Huguenots on her staff after it. The king, said at first to dislike her coldness and severity, is also sometimes said to have been physically attracted to and rebuffed by her in 1673. That is unlikely and derives from the mistaken identification of two people referred to, but not by name, in a letter of Mme de Sévigné of 20 March that year.

For a period around 1676, when Athénaïs was still Louis's mistress, the relationship between the two former friends swung bewilderingly as they alternately stayed with one another, cut one another, travelled and laughed together, and refused to speak to one another. Whatever instructions Mme de Maintenon gave about the children were immediately reversed by their mother. Mme de Maintenon then complained to Louis, who took her side. Louis had Maintenon modernized and sent Le Nôtre to landscape it. It is at Maintenon that Athénaïs's daughter Françoise-Marie, the future duchesse d'Orléans, wife of the regent, was born. By this time, 1677, Mme de Maintenon was openly expressing the hope of restoring moral propriety to Louis's life.

This was the period when Louis's promiscuity was becoming quite open, most obviously with Mme de Soubise. The Soubises were poor, but Madame was pretty, and to help the family out she profited from husband's arranged absences, and would wear earrings to show Louis that the coast was clear. The Soubises became rich, and Louis is regarded as the probable father of the son of the princess, the cardinal de Rohan. When the beautiful nineteen-year-old Mme de Ludres,[23] a maid of honour in Liselotte's household and former mistress of Vivonne, came into the room, other ladies rose, an indication that she was publicly recognized as a favourite of Louis. Mme de Thianges, Athénaïs's sister, was rude to her. She had become a royal partner, as had Mme de Thianges herself. When the king moved on, she, like so many of the others, retired to the cloister.

Mme de Maintenon was unusually allowed to keep charge of the duc du Maine until he was ten. In 1677, when he was seven, she took him to Barèges again, and collected some of his letters to Mme de Montespan and the king. They must have been dictated, and were published in an edition of seven copies, dedicated to Athénaïs. Louis confided his last two children by Athénaïs, Françoise-Marie, born in 1677, and the comte de Toulouse, born in 1678, to Mme de Louvois to be cared for.

Although from 1678 Louis was spending more time with Mme de Maintenon, it was not yet generally imagined that he had fallen in love with her. She clearly found the king's infatuation with Mlle de Fontanges disgraceful, but was not so put out as Athénaïs when Mlle de Fontanges was made a duchess, and Athénaïs had to be appeased with the highest office available to a woman at court, superintendant of the queen's household.

Although Mme de Maintenon was attached to the household of the dauphine, who was still resting at Versailles after the birth of the duc de Bourgogne, she none the less accompanied Louis to

Fontainebleau on the court's annual visit in 1682. When, in 1683, Mme de Maintenon accompanied Louis and the queen on the journey to the eastern front just before the queen's death, she again left the dauphine at Versailles. Immediately after the queen's death, she went to Fontainebleau to await Louis's arrival from Saint-Cloud. It was on the return to Versailles that October that Louis married her. The ceremony was probably conducted by François de Harlay de Champvallon, archbishop of Paris, with Père de la Chaise and Louis's lifetime personal servant, Bontemps, as witnesses.

Mme de Maintenon's change in status was only semi-disguised. The king no longer addressed her by her title, but simply as 'Madame', the usage he had reserved for the queen. She occupied the queen's place in chapel, and took the head of the table at family dinners outside Versailles. She scarcely left her room to mingle with the court, but when she did so, it was to take her former modest rank. Her clothes were opulent without being fashionable, and the simple necklace and cross she wore as jewellery were priceless. After Scarron's death she had had to sell her portrait by Mignard and Poussin's *Ecstasy of Saint Paul*, and survived on the pension given to her by Anne of Austria.

She despised the vanities of court life, and the vices it bred. Louis spent a great deal of time in her apartment, where he received both his children and his ministers. Her acceptance of orthodox Catholic theology did not remove her largely Huguenot spirituality, her suspicion of the mass and of devotion to the Virgin Mary. Her personal religion was as far from dependence on credal orthodoxy and devout practices as she could take it and remain Catholic, which is no doubt what would attract her, later on, to the teaching of Mme Guyon, dismissive of both rites and credal propositions.

Although Louis was disappointed in the incompetence and cowardliness of his favourite son, the duc du Maine, in his army command, he continued to treat him as a favourite. He still found him amusing, and bought the château of Sceaux from the Colbert family for him when he married the grand-daughter of the grand Condé. He was also jealous on his behalf of the much superior gifts of the younger of the Conti brothers, who had little money and was shown no favour at all between the mailbag incident and Condé's death.

Louis was also hostile to the gifted duc de Chartres, son of Philippe and Liselotte, born in 1674, and bullied by Louis into marrying

Louis's own youngest daughter by Athénaïs, born in 1677. Philippe had to be bribed by a huge dowry and the coveted Ordre du Saint-Esprit for his long-term lover, the chevalier de Lorraine. Liselotte was horrified that her son should marry a bastard, however legitimized. Under Mme de Maintenon's influence, Louis himself started to enforce an almost Puritan strictness at Versailles. Lent was kept more strictly. Behaviour was monitored; people absent from mass, or those who failed to make their Easter duties were now actually summoned and admonished. Père de la Chaise was sent to reprimand Liselotte for being rude to the dauphin.

Meanwhile Mme de Maintenon took charge of her brother's child, eventually marrying her to the heir of the duc de Noailles, sent her brother to a home at Saint-Sulpice to be cared for, and his wife to a convent. Saint-Aignan, the son of the trusted friend of Louis's youth, had married one of Colbert's daughters, Henriette, in 1671, when he was twenty-three and she fourteen, and in 1679 became the duc de Beauvillier. Neglected as a child, he had turned to a disordered life with a military command, but was reformed by his wife, and became in 1691 the only member of the old nobility to be made a member of Louis's council.

He also became not so much devout as dottily pious, obsessively reproaching himself for what sanity demands should be regarded as quite normal behaviour. Colbert's eldest daughter, Jeanne-Marie-Thérèse, had already married the duc de Chevreuse, and the two couples became very close to Mme de Maintenon. The quartet, Beauvillier, Chevreuse and their wives, both Colbert's daughters, in loose association with Fénelon and Mme de Maintenon formed a link between a passive spirituality in devotional matters and a firm anti-war pressure group acting on Louis. By 1687 Madame de Beauvillier had seven daughters, and it was for her that Fénelon wrote his *Traité de l'éducation des filles*, warmly welcomed by Pierre Bayle and the Amsterdam Huguenots for its reliance on religious experience over dogmatic commitment. It was the Beauvilliers who introduced Fénelon to Mme de Maintenon.

Mme de Maintenon and her friends were gradually impinging on Louis's attitudes, although they never brought them into conformity with their own. Madame de Maintenon had also become friendly with an Ursuline nun, Mme de Brinon, whose convent had had to close and who had started a residential school at Rueil intended chiefly for the daughters of the minor nobility, often military, who were otherwise frequently obliged to enter unsuitable marriages or religious orders, or otherwise to become virtually servants. The school was moved to Noisy, and Mme de Maintenon interested the king in it.

They decided to bring it to Versailles, where at the other end of the park there was a hamlet, Saint-Cyr, with a convent of Benedictine nuns. Louis tried to persuade the nuns to move to Paris, but they preferred to stay where they were. In 1685 Mansart was instructed to put up a large, plain house, using soldiers as builders as was normal in times of peace. The interior decoration and the fittings were determined down to the last detail by Mme de Maintenon herself and were plain, but of the highest quality, as in the more fashionable Paris convents. The *Mercure galant* of September 1686 congratulated Louis on ensuring that there would always be pure souls to pray for his armies.

The school was to be staffed by thirty-six 'dames' and twenty-four lay sisters, who were to take only 'simple' or temporary vows to avoid creating another religious congregation, which would have been subject to strict papal regulation, and was to take in and educate 250 young ladies from the ages of seven to twenty. Dames and pupils came from the same social milieu, requiring four degrees of nobility on the father's side. Louis himself determined the contents of the foundation deed, and Mme de Maintenon drew up the constitution which gave her complete authority and a flat for herself and her household. Mme de Brinon was to be superior for life. The whole institution, known as the Maison Saint-Louis, bears the stamp of Mme de Maintenon, a simple, relaxed piety, eyes cast down, praying not for victory in wartime, but for peace. The philosophy of education was largely taken from Fénelon. Intended for life in the world, which meant marriage, pupils were encouraged to take care of their appearance, and they wore the same uniform as the dames.

Saint-Cyr opened its doors in 1686. One of the first pupils to be welcomed by Mme de Maintenon was Mme de Montespan's ten-year-old daughter, Françoise-Marie. Mme de Brinon wrote an anthem mixing piety with military ambition to greet the king, which Lulli set to music.[24] Louis used to visit, and apparently felt at ease with his wife's pretty pupils, getting to know them well, and knowing their individual circumstances. Mme de Maintenon was there from six a.m. for ten or twelve hours two days out of three, supervising everything in the smallest detail.

Mostly verse drama in Latin or French had been introduced and heavily promoted as an educational tool by the Jesuits a century earlier. It was a way of teaching rhetoric, how to move the 'passions', and of course, how to construct rhythmic, grammatically and syntactically accurate sentences. It was normally also didactic in a moral sense, full of elevated sentiments and morally appropriate reactions. Mme de Brinon's dramaturgical efforts were found insipid, and the girls were allowed to act the *Andromaque* of the converted Racine, now a courtier and royal historian, reconciled with his old schoolmasters at Port-Royal, and not yet disgraced. It had been his first play to centre on the intense emotion of a strong female character, and was written for Thérèse du Parc, who was, or who became, his mistress. The first night was in November 1667.[25]

Mme de Maintenon, perceiving that the enthusiasm with which the young ladies played *Andromaque* was unlikely to provide the required moral uplift ('Ah! je l'ai trop aimé, pour ne le point haïr!'), wrote to Racine asking him whether he would not write a biblical play for Saint-Cyr. He wrote *Esther*, a biblical heroine triumphing over a rival easily identifiable with Athénaïs, as a compliment to Mme de Maintenon. Louis and the court attended the première on 26 January 1689, the guest list drawn up by Louis himself. There were four performances in all, the fourth attended by Louis again, with James II and his queen. Mme de Sévigné was there, transported with delight at exchanging a couple of half sentences with Louis.

Racine did on request go on to write another play for Saint-Cyr, *Athalie*, of which Louis attended a rehearsal with James II on 5 January 1691. It was never given a performance in Racine's lifetime because Mme de Maintenon had abruptly revised her ideas. She had been wrong to envisage a type of finishing school for polished young ladies. Literature lessons were stopped, and then all lessons were dropped in favour of housework. Two girls were expelled for trying to poison a dame who had thrown make-up away. It was Louis who insisted that the girls be allowed to continue with music, and that *Athalie* at least be rehearsed, even though without scenery, costumes, or make-up.

Mme de Brinon began to overestimate her own importance, as was perhaps inevitable, and had to be removed by Louis, who issued a *lettre de cachet* ordering her to a convent. Relations with Mme de Maintenon were not entirely broken, and Mme de Brinon went on to play a part as an intermediary in the ecumenical efforts of Bossuet and Leibniz. Meanwhile Mme de Maintenon had taken as her chief *confidant* the recently appointed tutor to the duc de Bourgone and his two brothers, Fénelon, but neither he nor Bourdaloue was willing to accept the task of directing her. She eventually chose Godet des Marais, the bishop of Chartres, as her new confessor.

He turned Saint-Cyr into a contemplative convent, installing six priests from the order founded by Vincent de Paul as confessors and offering the dames and the sisters the chance to go back to the world, to join other convents, or to stay as religious at Saint-Cyr. Most of them had little other alternative than to stay. One of those, especially valued as intelligent, popular and devout, who had doubts about taking the permanent vows of religious profession, was Elise de la Maisonfort, whose cousin was Mme Guyon. Mme Guyon came to help resolve her cousin's doubts. She quickly did so, ingratiating herself with Madame de Maintenon, Fénelon and the group constituted by the Beauvilliers and the Chevreuses. The author of *A Short Method of Prayer* and *Explanation of the Song of Songs*, she preached that perfection consisted in a continuous act of contemplation, with no obligation to defined acts, and that prayer required the elimination of distinct ideas.[26]

She split the Saint-Cyr community into her own circle of adepts and those who opposed her, and when Godet des Marais told her to get rid of Mme Guyon, Mme de Maintenon immediately sent her away. Louis appears to have been unaware of the storm at Saint-Cyr and, on Mme de Maintenon's suggestion, appointed Fénelon to Cambrai, the richest see in France.

Mme de Maintenon was displeased with Fénelon, but tried in vain to disgrace Beauvillier, who remained a minister and governor to the dauphin's eldest son, the duc de Bourgogne. When Louis was finally made aware of the antagonism of Bossuet and Fénelon and the train of events leading up to it, he was of course annoyed. He considered Mme Guyon to be mad, and even for a very brief period seems to have been on the verge of abandoning Mme de Maintenon.

Her influence on his behaviour and attitudes, while very strong, was also limited in its range. It was most striking in the matter of sexual morality and public propriety, but remained a matter of style more than content. It may have awakened a genuinely discerning appreciation of court preaching, and the religious style of the court became governed by stricter devotional norms, but neither in belief nor in practice, other than in matters of sexual morality, did Mme de Maintenon bring about any very striking change in Louis's religious behaviour, and it brought about none at all in his counter-reformation Catholic beliefs. She had understood, like Fénelon, that Louis's religion was driven by a fear of hell but, in this also like Fénelon, had signally failed to alter his beliefs on the morality of war.

10

The Royal Religion and Christian Beliefs

Louis's upbringing, for whatever reason, had left him vulnerably insecure. His anxieties cannot have been assuaged by his vicissitudinous relationship with his mother, the only human creature on whose love he could absolutely depend; by the need to conceal his mother's relationship with Mazarin and probably his own paternity; and by the clash between his very strong amorous inclinations and the religious obligations imposed by his conscience. By 1668, Louis at thirty had been led from the premature boyish enjoyment of great power to the need to steel himself to assert his authority; and the discovery that its exercise could disguise and compensate for the deficient self-confidence. The *Mémoires* are patently sincere. What they chiefly show is Louis's need to justify himself to himself, and the extent of his self-deception.

The insecurity was to go on to lead him to the profligate dissipation of the resources of a country in which the population suffered sometimes extreme hardship, to ferocious acts of gratuitous cruelty in his wars, to petty bullying and to a narcissism carefully disguised by the intricate complexity of court ritual. It made him erratic, too. He was capable of acts of consideration and kindness, particularly to favourite family members, but also to members of court, which their recipients had no real right to expect.

Profoundly affecting Louis's insecurity was his religion: not his beliefs, on which he simply accepted without reflection the conservative orthodoxy he had been taught, but his conscience and the moral imperatives it imposed. His relations with the Protestants and the popes, which briefly involved his excommunication, were political matters, not regarded by him as directly affecting his personal salvation, and therefore best treated outside the present context.

Within French Catholicism during Louis's reign, it is normal to count two major heterodox movements – Jansenism and quietism – both of which caused Louis agonies of conscience, and both of which drew on theological assumptions which continue to be seriously misunderstood. Louis's attitude to each of them as religious movements was rooted not in theological, but in political considerations. Jansenism as a theology of grace scarcely concerns us directly, but as a spirituality it was regarded by Mazarin and then by Louis as politically subversive. It was only equivocally related to the Gallicanism which Louis was determined to defend, and detrimental to the deferential attitude which Louis thought appropriate to the clergy.

Both as a theology and a spirituality, 'Jansenism' claimed uniquely to embody the inheritance of Augustine, and the views on grace which it promoted, however doctrinally different, gave it a natural affinity with the passive spiritualities generally lumped together as 'quietist' and associated with Fénelon, Mme de Maintenon and the Beauvillier circle. If God had preselected those whom he would save by the bestowal of irresistible grace, as the self-proclaimed upholders of Augustine held, Christian spirituality had no logical alternative but to base itself on the passive acceptance by the individual of the decision of the divine will with regard to salvation or damnation.

The religious groupings close to the theological heterodoxies were not unreasonably seen by Louis as political dangers. 'Jansenism', associated with Augustine and Port-Royal, had dangerous implications because, even when its overstated relationship with Gallicanism led it to support Louis's policy, it rated the role of the clergy in the regulation of French society too highly. The Beauvillier circle was for its part forthrightly opposed to Louis's willingness to subject his citizens to intense hardships to further the glory and political hegemony of France. While the rigours of Augustinian spirituality went hand in hand with the severity of the moral values explored by even secular authors, the Beauvillier circle with Fénelon and Mme de Maintenon were in the forefront of the critics of Louis's pursuit of France's glory at the expense of the welfare of its citizens. Jansenism and quietism have a spiritual affinity. That both had a political importance is confirmed by the way in which their values are reflected in secular art and literature, most notably in the *Querelle des anciens et des modernes.*

Louis inherited a country different in two particularly important respects from other western European countries. Its culture had firstly been immensely affected by its religious wars, conventionally dated 1562–98. The historical reality cannot be so neatly schematized, since the wars were not in the end predominantly religious, and smouldered on even after the 1598 edict of Nantes gave the Huguenots a measure of recognition. The result was the only western European country where a second religion was given a form of official acknowledgement. A single state religion was the European norm, and continued to be demanded by constitutional theoreticians from Thomas More in his early sixteenth-century *Utopia* to Rousseau and Montesquieu in the mid-eighteenth century.

The reaction to the religious wars among France's intellectual elite had been an overwhelmingly defensive neostoic relativism. Then, in roughly the first third of the seventeenth century, their relativist and neostoic attitudes gave way to an extraordinarily euphoric imaginative exploration of confidence in human potential. A radical new sexual morality, upgrading the morally enriching power of physical sexual relationships, derived from *quattrocento* Italy, swept right through western Europe. Both Honoré d'Urfé's *Epistres morales* (1598–1608) and his pastoral novel *L'Astrée* (1607–1628), like Gomberville's 1629 *L'Exil de Polexandre,* probe the compatibility of physically consummated love with moral perfection and end with a triumphant affirmation of its attainability.

François de Sales promoted a daring new lay spirituality which, allowing make-up and dancing, relies on a natural desire to love God which appears to go well beyond the strict dogmatic orthodoxy laid down by the sixteenth-century council of Trent and the church's discipline on sexual matters. Even his asceticism is subordinate to peace of soul, while a chapter from his 1609 *Introduction à la vie dévote* 'De l'honnêteté du lit nuptial' is radical enough to have been omitted as disedifying from most nineteenth-century editions.

[225]

Descartes rehabilitates the 'passions' as morally indifferent, backed by a strength of will which his contemporaries could regard as heroic, even if directed towards evil, like the jealousy of Cléopâtre in Pierre Corneille's *Rodogune,* presented in the 1644–5 season.[1] Descartes believed that there was a mathematically demonstrable path to the maxima of happiness and virtue of which human beings are capable. Pierre Corneille examines in the 1637 *Le Cid* whether the heroic merit of Rodrigue does not excuse Chimène's acceptance of him in marriage although he has just killed her father in a duel.[2]

The similar focus of imaginative interest in devotional literature, philosophy, drama and fiction, to which might also be added painting, as for instance represented by the great landscapes of Claude and the canvases of Poussin, both religious and secular, means that we are dealing with a phenomenon which covers the whole cultural spectrum of cultivated France. Rubens and van Dyck amply show that it was not limited to France, although it is there that it was at its most intense. The change, when it came, is generally associated with 'Jansenism', although it owes more to Bérulle than to Jansen.[3] Outside a technical context concerning the theology of grace, what we call Jansenism is a spiritual movement associated with an abrupt change in the early 1630s in the spiritual teaching of Jean Duvergier de Hauranne, from 1620 abbé de Saint-Cyran, the name by which he is generally known. Essentially it was an overwhelming loss of confidence in the moral powers of human nature, a consciousness of guilt and a sense of sin which permeated much of literate society and many of the clergy, even when Jansen's theology was itself rejected.

The theology faculty of Louvain university had in the sixteenth century taken the view, controversially fathered on Augustine, that after original sin, fallen human beings could do nothing at all to affect or contribute towards their own salvation. Neither behaviour nor belief made any difference at all to the final destiny, heaven or hell, unchanging through unending time, of any human being. This view, as so stated, belongs to the realm of theology, not religion. There never was a major Christian spirituality strictly consonant with such a religiously devastating theology. All forms of Christianity continued to make the soul's eternal destiny to some extent depend on adherence to specified norms of belief and behaviour.

In the 1560s a Louvain professor, Michel du Bay (Baius), had attempted to restate the relationship between nature and grace in fifth-century Augustinian terms, before the high middle ages had invented the distinction between 'nature' and 'supernature'. He was condemned because, without such a distinction, he had to hold that nothing at all that was upright remained in human nature after the fall, whereas the Jesuits, who had established their own university in Louvain in 1542, and tended to exaggerate the dichotomy between nature and supernature, could hold that Adam's sin destroyed only that which was supernatural, leaving nature as it had been created. The theological dispute is important on account of the public repercussions in France among authors like Pascal, and of the formal condemnation of Jansenist propositions. What affected Louis personally was the general tightening of moral imperatives, both ecclesiastical and secular, contemporaneous with the rise of 'Jansenist' spirituality.

Cornelius Jansen, born in 1585 and from 1636 bishop of Ypres, was a professor of scripture at the older university of Louvain. His three-volume posthumous folio of 1640, *Augustinus,* is a technical theological defence of du Bay in 1,300 double-column folio pages against the attack on him by the Jesuit Luis Molina in a work reconciling human liberty with the gratuity of grace, the *Concordia liberi arbitrii cum gratiæ donis* (1588). Jansen concerns the reign of Louis XIV firstly because propositions from *Augustinus* were condemned in 1653, causing severe turbulence in the French church, but also because what purported to be Jansen's teaching was defended by Antoine Arnauld, lawyer, theologian and un-disputed leader of the Jansenist group who brought together the theology and the spirituality in his *De la fréquente communion* of 1643. He was thought by Mazarin, and later by Louis, personally to be a focus of civil dissension. Under the leadership of Quesnel a re-birth of Jansenism early in the eighteenth century certainly promoted a political conspiracy hostile to Louis's rule in France.

Arnauld was to take the papal side against Louis in the important quarrel over the *régale* or right to the income from vacant benefices, including bishoprics, which would lead to Louis's excommunication. Arnauld had picked out for strong attack in *De la fréquente communion* the practice of frequent communion energetically promoted by the pastoral forces of the Catholic revival. The spiritual attitudes of Saint-

Cyran being defended by Arnauld had turned hostile to the eucharistic piety and the adoration of the Blessed Sacrament which were central to the devotional practice of French baroque. Jansen, who had also from 1611 for some years intermittently lived and worked with Saint-Cyran, had died in 1638 and Saint-Cyran in 1643.[4] Arnauld organized his campaign for their joint defence round the monastery of Port-Royal to which he was linked by the presence in the community at various times of his widowed mother, at least four of his sisters and five nieces, together with five male great-nephews who became known as 'solitaires', loosely attached to the monastery.

Saint-Cyran had started his ecclesiatical career as a fairly typical intellectually and pastorally inclined priest of the explosion of Catholic missionary activity and devotional intensity known as the Catholic revival, and certainly not untouched by the heroic values of his generation.[5] The change in Saint-Cyran's spiritual teaching was no doubt ultimately due to the long-term effects of his intimacy with Bérulle, whose controversial spiritual teaching he discussed with him for an hour a day during most of 1622.[6] The change did not however become clear until 1634, when Saint-Cyran was called to Port-Royal, in the process of an attempted merger with a new Institut du Saint-Sacrement, to help defend a eucharistic devotional writing by a sister of Antoine Arnauld, Mère Agnès. Dating from some years previously, it is known as the *Chapelet secret du Saint-Sacrement*, of which only a revised version has come down to us.

Saint-Cyran gradually took spiritual charge at Port-Royal and at the new Institut du Saint-Sacrement, which accepted from him what by this time was an aggressively ascetic spiritual teaching, based on feelings of unworthiness and guilt. Saint-Cyran was by now exalting in the eternal damnation of most of the human race, including the virtuous pagans of antiquity. His association with Bérulle, who had died in 1629, together with his writings, indiscretions and considerable spiritual influence led to his imprisonment at Vincennes by Richelieu in 1638.[7]

Richelieu had objected strongly to Jansen's publication of a work, the 1635 *Mars Gallicus*, criticizing his policy in the Low Countries and his alliance with Protestant powers. Shortly before he died, he had charged the senior theologian attached to Notre-Dame, the *théologal* Isaac Habert, to preach against *Augustinus*, which he did on the first and last Sundays of Advent in 1642, and on Septuagesima

Sunday 1643. Further sermons on grace were prohibited, but there was a flurry of pamphlets. Arnauld, a protégé of Saint-Cyran under whose guidance he had taken his doctorate in 1641, contended that Jansen's doctrine was only that of Augustine, while Habert and the Jesuits accused it of Calvinism. The dispute appeared to die down.

In 1639 the princesse de Guémené had moved from a Jesuit confessor to Saint-Cyran. The rich, neurotically hypochondriac and witty hostess, Mme de Sablé, friend of La Rochefoucauld and later halfway to being a Jansenist sympathizer, had told Mme de Guémené that she thought it legitimate to take communion in the morning and dance in the evening. Mme de Guémené passed to her in reply a rule of life given to her by her own confessor which Mme de Sablé passed on to her Jesuit confessor. He undertook with two colleagues to refute it.[8] It was that refutation which provoked from Antoine Arnauld the *De la fréquente communion,* started late in 1640, finished in September 1641, and left fallow until Arnauld obtained a *privilège* in May 1643 and published it that August. The preface, which was to cause the chief trouble, was by Saint-Cyran's nephew, Martin de Barcos.

Baroque optimism never died out. The defenders of the *modernes* in the *Querelle* continued optimistically to believe in the autonomous human power of moral self-determination, in cultural progress, and in the superiority of modern civilization, as epitomized in the person and environment created to glorify Louis XIV. In secular life it was vigorously defended by popular authors like Thomas Corneille, Donneau de Visé, Charles Perrault and the directors of the *Mercure galant*. It was in the end victorious, but it was opposed by religious thinkers in the ambit of Bossuet, 'Augustinian' without being theologically Jansenist, and by literary authors who believed in unchanging aesthetic values, like Boileau and Racine. The clash is summed up in Pascal's *Lettres provinciales* of 1656–7, where the immutability of Christian moral teaching is firmly defended, and the Jesuits are mocked as much for the *extravagance* of their baroque values as for the laxity of their norms for allowing sacramental absolution.

Mazarin suspected what was not so much a movement as a group consisting of friends, families, salons and sympathizers associated with Port-Royal of being a focus for civil unrest and of complicity with Retz, openly Mazarin's enemy from 1651.[9] Five propositions alleged to be in *Augustinus* were finally condemned in the bull *Cum occasione* signed by Innocent X on 31 May.[10] By the mid 1640s, all sides had wanted peace, but Barcos's preface to the *De la fréquente communion* had compared saints Peter and Paul in such a way as to compromise the jurisdictional and teaching primacies of the Roman see. Barcos defended himself in two works which were themselves condemned, as *De la fréquente communion* had not been, in January 1647.

That had re-ignited the dogmatic flames, and eighty-five bishops wrote to Innocent X asking for the condemnation of the five propositions, drawn from an original list of seven. Innocent X made clear that he condemned the five propositions 'cum occasione', that is 'on the occasion' of a publication, but he had not condemned a book in which it was alleged they could be found. Mazarin was certainly going to do nothing to prevent the registration of *Cum occasione* by the Paris *parlement*, if only because, however little interested in the theology of the confrontation, Mazarin needed Rome's coopera-tion to achieve its acquiescence in Retz's resignation from the see of Paris, to which even in prison he retained the reversion. The proximate occasion for Louis's distrust of Jansenism was his fear of Retz as a potentially disruptive force.

Retz in prison had empowered a priest to act on his behalf when-ever his incumbent uncle died. To Mazarin's fury, the imprisoned Retz was in titular possession of the diocese of Paris within an hour of the death of his uncle at four-thirty a.m. on 21 March 1654. The chapter had met at five a.m. Retz did a pseudo-deal, resigning the archdiocese a week later in return for freedom to live under the sympathetic supervision of Hortense Mancini's future father-in-law at Nantes, which he did with some style while, as he had foreseen and probably arranged, Innocent X refused to accept his resignation.

On 8 August, he made a dashing escape from Nantes, but fell and broke his shoulder while climbing down to a waiting horse. He had none the less crossed the Loire within two hours, arrived to stay with a cousin the next day, revoked his resignation and arrived by barge at Belle-Ile on 17 August. He left for San Sebastián on 9 September, was allowed to cross Spain, and arrived at Rome on 28 November. When Innocent X died on 7 January 1655, Louis forbade French delegates to the ensuing conclave to have anything to do with Retz, and to press for the election of Giulio Saccheti. It was however the candidate favoured by Retz, Fabio Chigi, who became Alexander VII.

The Jansenist faction, seen by Mazarin as a reflection of the Fronde, had nothing to do with either Retz's escape, or the papal election. But the exile of Retz from 1654 until 1662, after Mazarin's death, when Louis allowed Retz to return to France, but not to Paris, meant an effective vacancy in the Paris see, which increased the armoury of weapons in the hands of both the king and the new pope, each of whom could block any appointment made by the other. The pope was personally aggravated by the vengeful support of Mazarin, hostile to his own election, for the claims to papal lands being pressed by the Este and Farnese families.

Mazarin had lost no time in having the bull *Cum occasione* registered by letters patent of 4 July 1653 for promulgation throughout France. For good measure he had inserted the words 'extracted from Jansen's book' into his accompanying *mandement* or order, although Rome had carefully avoided putting them into the bull. He was being pressed by Anne of Austria, whose fear of a new Fronde was even greater than his own, and by Père Annat, Jesuit confessor of Louis, appointed by Mazarin at the beginning of 1653.[11] The French bishops were assembled in Paris, and Mazarin called them together, six archbishops and twenty-two bishops, on 11 July to deliver his instructions. At first the episcopate made no difficulty, agreeing that the propositions were heterodox (the matter of *droit* or law) but saying nothing about whether they were in *Augustinus* (the matter of *fait* or fact).

Four of the bishops, however, promulgated the bull in the last half of 1654 in various ways offensive to Mazarin, and on 23 April Innocent X condemned the diocesan *mandement* of Henri Arnauld, bishop of Angers. Père Annat had held in a tract of January 1654 that the five propositions were word for word in *Augustinus,* and Mazarin, anxious for a reconciliation with the pope, called together on 9 March 1654 the thirty-eight archbishops and bishops still in Paris after their meeting there. They now agreed by a majority to condemn the five propositions 'in the sense in which Jansen presented them'. On 2 June 1655 Louis, aged seventeen, would send instructions to all French dioceses demanding the signature of an anti-Jansenist formulary by all clergy, members of religious orders and members of universities, along with a papal brief of 29 September 1654, conciliatory in tone, but affirming that in condemning the five propositions, the pope had condemned the doctrine of Jansen.

The ordinary meeting of the Assemblée du clergé opened in October 1655. It was to last twenty instead of the usual six months, and in 1656 accepted the terms of the formulary. But on 16 October 1656 Alexander VII, no doubt unaware of the consequences, confirmed *Cum occasione* with a new document *Ad sacram beati Petri sedem,* which meant that a reference to it had to be added to the formulary. The assembly passed the revision in 1657, but the *parlement* refused to register it. Mazarin thought the whole matter was becoming too time-consuming. Formulary and signature, both voted, were left on the shelf. They would be dusted off again in 1660.

Meanwhile the duc de Liancourt was refused communion at Saint-Sulpice for Jansenist sympathies and Antoine Arnauld wrote his *Lettre à un duc et pair,* dated 10 July but published in September.[12] In it Arnauld maintained that the believer was not obliged to find propositions in a book if they were not there, even if the pope had authoritatively stated that they were, which was true but provocative, but also that Peter denied Christ because he was denied the grace not to sin, which was now heretical. A Sorbonne commission was set up to examine the second letter and in due course Arnauld was stripped of his doctorate. Séguier himself 'on the king's command' came to supervise the commission's hearings, surrounded by his usual entourage of bailiffs and sheriffs, and the voting was rigged, although we do not know to what extent.[13] Arnauld went into what was scarcely more than mock hiding. In the meanwhile Pascal attempted to rally support for him in the brilliant *Lettres provinciales,* called by Voltaire 'the first work of genius in prose to be seen in France'.[14]

When Arnauld was stripped of his doctorate, Louis was seventeen, and certainly unable to judge the theological issues, or even to appreciate the political ones, for himself. His training none the less shows itself certainly by 1660 when, just twenty-two, and still no doubt executing Mazarin's policy, he called the presiding council of the assembly of the clergy to the Louvre on 13 December, telling them that Mazarin was too unwell to come to them. Its members were astonished that Louis had meant what he said when he instructed them to come early. They found themselves most unusually in the presence alone of Louis and Mazarin, without officials. It was Louis himself who spoke to say that he had decided to eliminate all traces of Jansenism from France, and Mazarin who then took an hour and a quarter to spell out in detail what that meant.

Louis never became a theologian, any more than Mazarin, and both were frightened of the sort of factional formations represented by the anti-Huguenot Compagnie du Saint-Sacrement as well as by Arnauld's supporters. But both were vulnerable to the lobbying of the religiously confident and devout Anne of Austria, mother of the one and lover of the other, and both sufficiently devout to know that any state religion on which, rather less than most of the rest of Europe, they counted to help keep social order, would crumble before a doctrine which deprived human beings of any chance of salvation and which so totally divorced religion from morality as Saint-Cyran's spirituality did not, but Jansen's theology certainly did.

An immutable set of moral rules, such as those defended by Pascal as being revealed and unchangeable, was implicit in the moral teaching of Saint-Cyran.[15] This alone was sufficient to make Louis and his succession of Jesuit confessors unsympathetic to the spirituality which derived from him and was affecting segments of the higher echelons of Paris society. By the date of Mazarin's death, however, Louis was clear that there was a link between Saint-Cyran's spirituality, Arnauld's challenge to his ecclesiastical policy, the condemned propositions from *Augustinus,* the danger represented by Retz, and the view that the culture over which he presided was beginning to disintegrate, and that all five represented a challenge to his authority, which is what he had been trained above all to impose.

It is unlikely that Louis ever made the mental association, but the religious alignments come sufficiently close to congruence with those of the theoreticians of painting, architecture and literature to make it certain that the defenders of immutability in the church's moral teaching tended to defend rigid aesthetic norms, and that both were opposed to the advocates of progress.[16] Boileau changed sides. His appointment as royal *historiographe* appears to have been arranged by Mme de Montespan and was announced in the *Mercure galant* for October 1677. Paris gossip, as relayed by Mme de Sévigné to her cousin Bussy-Rabutin on 17 October, suggests that the joint appointments of Racine and Boileau as *historiographes* at a salary of 6,000 livres each were in return for an end to Boileau's *satires* and Racine's tragedies, which were causing real bitterness between *anciens* and *modernes*. The two authors shared a grant of 12,000 livres to equip themselves to follow, record and praise Louis's campaigns.

The religion of Saint-Cyran was grounded in a belief in the profound sinfulness of the human race, on account of which most humans were destined to damnation, and the only appropriate devotions were founded on feelings of guilt, and consequent unworthiness to receive the sacrament. This was what had affected Louis in 1664. Pascal had suggested in the fifth of the *Lettres provinciales* that the casuist laxity of Jesuit practice in granting absolution was the cause of their doctrine of grace, which he regarded as heretical because it allowed to human nature the autonomous power to accept or to reject grace. The canonization in 1665 of François de Sales, who had adopted the Jesuit doctrine of grace, was intended by Alexander VII as a specifically anti-Jansenist gesture.

Anne of Austria's devotions were flamboyant and, despite her liaison with Mazarin, quite sincere. Louis attended mass daily, but lived a life of constant and sinful sexual liaisons. What Saint-Cyran's spirituality did for Louis, however anti-Jansenist Louis's policies, was to enhance his sense of guilt and play on his insecurity. It is doubtful whether Louis understood the supreme importance of the mass as in some way identical with the sacrifice on Calvary in which the faithful participated. During mass, Louis said his rosary, a common enough practice among the devout even to the present day, but one which denotes a failure fully to participate in the liturgical action, the re-enactment of Calvary, regarded as constitutive of Christ's redemptive sacrifice. One did not need a priest, a liturgy, or a religious ceremony to say the rosary, essentially a means of linking multiple identical repetitions of a prayer formula by means of a series of imaginative meditative considerations. Yet, like his mother, Louis knew that, by his presence at mass, he was nonetheless undertaking a meaningful religious act, and not merely performing an empty rite, whether for the sake of propriety or simply to give example.

The only possible conclusion with regard to the sexual morality of Louis, as well as of Anne and Mazarin, is that none of the three really experienced their behaviour as so seriously sinful as to be likely to lead to damnation, whatever the official teaching of the church on the matter. Louis, youngest of the three and subject to the strongest cultural reaction against devotional baroque, sporadically experienced the greatest sense of sin of the three, finally resolved through his marriage to Mme de Maintenon, whom he genuinely loved.

There is a baroque and period-specific casuist case to be made for the permissibility of Mazarin's relationship with Anne even when, before the death of Louis XIII, it was adulterous, on grounds of the overriding importance for Europe of ensuring dynastic succession in the direct line. Louis, urged by Bourdaloue, who was a Jesuit, Bossuet and above all Mme de Maintenon, whom Louis was clandestinely to marry almost indecently soon after Maria-Teresa's death, was going to take a stricter view of the need for conjugal fidelity from the early 1680s, when he was just over forty.

Louis's change in behaviour was not just a matter of diminished libido, because Mme de Maintenon complained to her confessor twenty years later, when she was over seventy, that Louis was insisting on his conjugal rights every day, and sometimes twice. She asked whether she might legitimately refuse him. Nor was it a religious 'conversion' in any sense other than a tightening of values in the direction of the stricter sexual ethic to which Catholic teaching after Pascal was still moving. It has to do with the quite general distrust in France of the exuberant, ebullient values which had characterized the earlier part of the century and which were being strongly challenged in the second half.

Louis was seriously devout. The church taught unequivocally that even fornication was a mortal sin which, once committed, meant damnation unless repented. Did he disbelieve the church's teaching on sexual morality? Or did he accept it, but risk dying before he could be absolved? The probability is that Louis would never have denied the church's teaching, but simply did not before the death of Maria-Teresa more than sporadically feel in his own conscience that his behaviour was such as might lead to damnation, at least until Mme de Maintenon replaced Mme de Montespan in Louis's affection, and brought him to think differently.[17]

Mme de Maintenon was to succeed in persuading Louis of the sinfulness of his sexual behaviour, but she did not change his view that the cruelty of his military exploits was incompatible with Christian morality, or redeemed by token acts of compassion towards a peasantry on which, assisted by atrocious harvests, he was imposing starvation. Louis resisted pressure to moderate what came increasingly to be regarded as an unchristian attitude towards war and the often intense deprivations inflicted on the people. Occasional bouts of serious concern for the alleviation of starvation, such as are recorded the *Mémoires,* seemed to Louis in the circumstances to justify the prosecution of policies which bred the suffering imposed on the French people.

Fénelon was ahead of his generation in his sensitivity to the malice of war-mongering. He was however probably not far out of line with discerning contemporary opinion when, in December 1693 or in the spring of 1694, he wrote his long letter of sustained invective to Louis, the *Rémonstrances.*[18] He is coruscating in the blame he puts on those responsible for teaching Louis an art of governing 'made up of nothing but mistrust, jealousy, distaste for virtue, fear of outstanding merit, a liking for men who were compliant and servile, aloofness, and concern only for your own interest'. Unsurprisingly, Fénelon blames those responsible for Louis's formation for failures in the result of their efforts. He had written a series of *Dialogues des morts* for the duc de Bourgogne, the grand Dauphin's son born in 1682 of whom he was tutor, and in the 74th of them, between Richelieu and Mazarin, written some time between 1692 and 1695, he light-heartedly blames them.

The *Rémonstrances* letter returns to the theme of the impoverishment of France 'to introduce at court a monstrous and incorrigible luxury', a theme frequent in Fénelon's other works, but to be found also even in Saint-Simon.[19] In *Les Aventures de Télémaque,* a fable invented for the instruction of Louis's grandson, the duc de Bourgogne, around 1694, but published anonymously and without Fénelon's knowledge by the widow Barbin in 1699, the political morality held up for admiration is that he shared with Mme de Maintenon. Fénelon is sometimes thought to have intended to send her his *Rémonstrances* in the hope that she would act on the king. It is full of the ordinary advice found in treatises on the education of princes since Erasmus: avoid flatterers, be just, be a true father to your subjects, regard war as a last resort. The kingly ideal is remarkably close to that sketched in his *Mémoires* by Louis for the dauphin, and from which he himself strikingly departed.

Popular songs, minor uprisings, court gossip and the comments of the gazettes from abroad made it impossible for Louis to be unaware of the swell of criticism, and of the feelings among his literate subjects. It is not easy to estimate the audacity of Fénelon's text, even if it was not sent. Louis was well aware of popular sentiment, whatever Fénelon says about his susceptibility to flattery. A number of such letters were sent and read to Louis, who would listen unenthusiastically but, if he respected their authors, without resentment. He was fifty-five years old, unsure of himself, but shored up by obsolescent values, and he scarcely dared to think clearly about the consequences of his whims, desires and rages. It is difficult to suppose that Louis had not received, or heard in detail about the *Rémonstrances* of 1693/4, when he gave Fénelon in December 1694 the lucrative abbey of Saint-Valéry-sur-Somme, producing 14,000 livres a year, and then, on 4 February 1695 the archbishopric of Cambrai, the richest in France, with an annual income of 100,000 livres. Fénelon was consecrated at Saint-Cyr by Bossuet, assisted by Noailles, and in the presence of Mme de Maintenon. Louis said he hoped Fénelon would continue his preceptorate of the duc de Bourgogne.

To accept Fénelon's invitation to admit that the whole basis of his policies was politically inept and morally indefensible would have destroyed Louis's belief in his own authority and shattered his still vulnerable personality. But he was neither stupid, nor ignorant, nor entirely insensitive to the political as well as the personal need to have a conscience he could hear. In spite of his general policy, it is not impossible that he had some covert respect for Fénelon's opinion. Perhaps it helped that Fénelon expressed himself intemperately, and that parts of what he said could therefore decently be disregarded.

The text turns into a passionate appeal, quivering with emotion:

> [His Majesty's ministers][20] have made his name hated and the whole French nation intolerable to all our neighbours . . . Meanwhile, your peoples whom you should love as your children, and who until now have committed themselves to you with such passion, are starving. The cultivation of the land has nearly been abandoned, the towns and the countryside are being depopulated'.

The wars have been motivated by a misplaced desire for *gloire* and vengeance; and predatory aggression to possess the territory of others is not justified by the desire to establish secure frontiers.

> This *gloire*, which hardens your heart[21] is dearer to you than justice, than your own peace of soul, than the preservation of your peoples

who are dying every day of sicknesses caused by the famine, and even than your eternal salvation, incompatible with the idol of *gloire.*

Fénelon knows that Louis's religion is essentially not the love of God, but the fear of hell, and goes on in the *Rémonstrances* to threaten him:

> You do not love God; your fear of him is only that of a slave; it is hell and not God that you fear. Your religion consists only of superstitions, in superficial little practices . . . you are scrupulous in small details, and hardened to horrible evils.

Catholic usage demands that God should be at once the object of fear and of love. Fénelon is reflecting his religious position by restricting the virtuous 'fear' of God to reverence for the omnipotent but benevolent deity. For Fénelon, the fear of hell is inadequate as a worthy religious motive.

The distinction raises the whole question of 'quietism', more a dangerous spiritual aberration than a propositional heresy. Among the reasons why quietism requires consideration here are two of particular importance. Firstly, both Mme de Maintenon and Fénelon, who were wrongly accused of it, were tarnished with its brush through their association with Mme Guyon,[22] who, although mentally unstable, was also innocent although suspect of it. Secondly, the religious attitudes of Mme de Maintenon and Fénelon, although not 'quietist', are distinctive and are associated with opposition to Louis's wars. Any examination of what happened also reveals the unamiable nature of Bossuet's character as well as the unsubtle nature of his religious thought, and the relationship between Mme Guyon, Mme de Maintenon and Louis in matters of spirituality.

It is necessary to distinguish three different spiritual doctrines, no one of which implies any of the others. First, quietism[23] consisted in the belief that spiritual fulfilment, indifferent to the morality of bodily actions, regarded as mere distractions to the life of the spirit, demanded complete mental inertness. Secondly, passivity in prayer which differed from inertness in demanding behaviour in accordance with the church's teaching, neither disregarded ecclesiastical legislation nor discouraged ordinary devotional practices. Passivity in prayer, which was defended by Mme Guyon, could look back to a long mystical tradition, including all the Rhineland mystics,[24] Teresa of Avila and John of the Cross. Thirdly, there was Fénelon's own doctrine that the love of God ideally could and should be 'pure' in the sense of disinterested. The highest forms of virtue demanded that God should loved 'for his own sake'.

If, as Fénelon claimed, Louis feared hell, he was not alone. François de Sales was psychologically unhinged for six weeks with a paranoid conviction that he was to be damned. It is due to the dossier of his canonization process that we know in such great detail about his life and in particular about the spiritual crisis of December 1586 and January 1587 in which sexual repression may have played some element, but which manifested itself in the conviction that he belonged not to the predestined, but to the reprobate. His crisis exhibits in peculiarly acute form the spiritual panic caused by Jansenist spirituality, which emphasizes the human inability to alter by any moral choice the predestinatory decree about the soul's eternal fate already decided by God.

François de Sales tried to cultivate an attitude towards God so purely motivated as to be independent of any hope of eternal reward. He lost all appetite, could not sleep and became pale, thin and physically ill for six weeks. The crisis was resolved when Sales went to pray at the chapel of the Blessed Virgin at the Dominican church of Saint-Etienne-des-Grès in Paris, ending his prayer with the petition:

> Let me love you in this life, if I cannot love you in eternity ...
> Allow me at least not to be among those who curse your name
> even if because of my faults I am to be cursed among the number
> of the accursed.

The anguish suddenly subsided and the intellectual problem stimulated him to accept the view that his eternal fate did depend no doubt on grace, but also on his own moral choices. Bossuet was to think the doctrine expounded by Sales on the natural desire to love God heretical, and to repudiate his authority in matters of dogma, although Sales was later to be a doctor of the church, guaranteeing the orthodoxy of his teaching.

Sales's devotional desire to love God even if he were destined for damnation opened up the question of disinterestedness. It was complicated by the centuries-old scholastic anthropology which insisted that all acts of the will, being necessarily directed to a perceived good, necessarily also sought gratification. Transposed from abstract scholastic anthropological categories, that seemed to mean that, psychologically, all acts of will were interested. The thirteenth-century psychology of the faculties lasted to the end of the seventeenth century and created dilemmas for both Descartes and Pascal,[25] clashing with mystical tradition, which insisted that the highest forms of the love of God had to be psychologically disinterested.

The whole subject of self-interest took on a renewed importance with Jansen's recourse to Augustine, who used self-love as opposite to and exclusive of the love of God. The two cities, those of God and Satan, were founded on the two loves in Augustine's *City of God*, the love of God taken as far as the contempt of self and the love of self taken as far as contempt for God.[26] Augustine used the words 'amor sui' for self-love. It was easily translatable into French as 'amour-propre'.

The difficulty was that Jansen, and the body of French moralists, both religious and secular, who took over the usage of Saint-Cyran, sometimes, like Augustine, write as if 'amor sui' or amour-propre entails the absence of justifying grace, a state of sin whose presence or absence in the soul automatically results in salvation or damnation, and is not empirically verifiable. On the other hand, sometimes both Augustine and Jansen as well as the moralists, write as if self-love were an ordinary psychological motivation, often empirically discoverable, compatible with virtue and excluded by only the very highest mystical states from the love of God. Purely disinterested love of God was possible, if rare.

The mystical theologians were in danger of abolishing the cardinal virtue of hope, as in 'faith, hope and charity'. La Rochefoucauld and others notoriously secularized the distinction, although La Rochefoucauld, who daily visited the Jansenistically inclined but moderate Mme de Sablé, while allowing that authentic virtue can be psychologically motivated by self-interest (intérêt), never uses the term 'amour-propre' of any true virtue. Its theological overtones had carried into the domain of secular writing.[27]

The first major clash on pure love occurred outside any context of Jansenist debate. The close friend of François de Sales, Jean-Pierre

Camus, bishop of Belley, preacher, novelist and devotional writer, wrote a defence of his sermons, the 1640 *La Défense du pur amour,* elaborating his views in the longer *Caritée,* and was attacked by the Jesuit Antoine Sirmond in the 1641 *La Défense de la vertu.*[28] Sirmond uses another traditional distinction to distinguish between the affective and effective love of God, which furnished Pascal with some ammunition for the *Lettres provinciales.*

During Fénelon's years of study in Paris, his spiritual director Louis Tronson, who was superior of the Congregation of Saint-Sulpice, made him confront the possibility that he was among the reprobate, doomed to eternal hell. The effect on Fénelon was analogous to that which the same experience had had on François de Sales. From 1685 Fénelon took a Jesuit confessor. He became part of Bossuet's circle and was also tutor to Colbert's son, Seignelay, whose brother-in-law, Paul de Beauvillier, was governor to the dauphin's eldest son, the duc de Bourgogne. In 1689 Beauvillier, close to Tronson and head of the *conseil de finances,* had Fénelon made tutor to the young duke, who had been born in 1682.[29]

It was in 1688 that Fénelon met Mme Guyon, and it was to her that he wrote in particular the letters of 28 March and 11 August 1689 outlining his response to the need to confront the possibility that he was damned, which was disinterested abandonment to the divine will.[30] Mme de Maintenon was impressed by Mme Guyon, whom, as we have seen, she invited to stay at the establishment which she had founded at Saint-Cyr. Fénelon appears at first to have put himself under the direction of Mme Guyon, and wrote letters of spiritual advice to Mme de Maintenon, which she treasured. He was therefore close to Louis's wife, as Mme de Maintenon had become, and tutor to his eldest grandchild, expected in due course to become king of France.

Mme Guyon's influence on the community at Saint-Cyr was denounced, and trouble was further stirred by Harlay de Champvallon, archbishop of Paris from 1671 to 1695, who disliked Mme de Maintenon. Mme Guyon had to withdraw from Saint-Cyr while Bossuet studied her works during the winter of 1693–4. From September 1693, when Mme Guyon left Paris, Fénelon ceased to correspond with her, and did not even know where she was. In June 1694 she asked for a commission to examine her behaviour, but instead Bossuet, Tronson and Noailles, to become archbishop of

Paris on the death of Harlay de Champvallon in 1695, were appointed to examine her writings at what became known as the Conférences d'Issy, held from July 1694.

Fénelon showered the commission with advice about the church's mystical tradition, in which he had only very recently begun to take any interest. Bossuet had by now turned against not only Mme Guyon but against the whole mystical tradition of interior prayer. Fénelon nearly became a member of the commission and, even though he did not, altered four and added four propositions to the draft of its conclusions. It was his redaction which was actually signed.

What followed, although it reads like high comedy, did raise serious considerations. In December 1695, Fénelon thought Bossuet had invited him to colloborate on a devotional work, but it became clear by February 1696 that Bossuet intended a book on spiritual matters in which he contemplated attacking Fénelon and Mme Guyon, who had been arrested in the previous December and imprisoned at Vincennes. On 24 July 1696, Fénelon refused to sign an *approbation* for Bossuet's *Instruction sur les états d'oraison* and read to a group including Tronson, Beauvillier and Noailles a memoir giving his reasons. A copy reached Mme de Maintenon on 16 August. Fénelon now elaborated it into a reply to Bossuet's *Instruction,* of which the *privilège* is dated 21 October, in the work commonly known as the *Maximes des saints.* Bossuet, furious that Fénelon had not only attacked his book, but also that he had got in first, denounced the *Maximes* as subversive of all true religion, before ever he had seen the book. In fact Fénelon's book was on sale on 29 January 1697, and Bossuet's *Instruction* did not leave the printers until 25 February.[31]

Mme de Maintenon understood exactly how damaging the situation would turn out to be for Fénelon. Bossuet recruited as an ally the archbishop of Reims, whose historic distinction relies largely on having his niece as his mistress, and on his knees begged Louis's pardon for not having denounced Fénelon earlier. He was to get only what had the outward form of a censure against Fénelon who, on 27 April 1697, wrote to Rome asking not to be condemned without a hearing. It was left to Louis himself to send to Rome on 26 July a letter drafted by Bossuet to ask Innocent XII to have the doctrinal issue decided. The Paris Jesuits had stirred the pot by defending the proposition that the disinterested love of God was not only possible, but of obligation.

The commission split five-five towards the end of 1698. A new commission of cardinals met an extraordinary fifty-seven times between September 1698 and March 1699. Bossuet, represented in Rome by his scandalous nephew, a priest twice in trouble on account of his love life and now about to become his sister-in-law's lover at Bossuet's episcopal palace, decided that a sexual scandal involving Mme Guyon was the surest way to win. He could not find evidence of any, but fabricated some innuendoes for his *Relation sur le quiétisme* of 26 June 1698, and had Mme Guyon in and out of confinement until 1703. Fénelon's allies had to retire from court, and his brother from the army. Fénelon, however, was made in France to appear disgraced.[32] He himself wrote with insolent hauteur, asking the pope to have pointed out to him exactly which passages of the *Maximes* were being condemned, and in what sense.

Bossuet pressed Louis hard to obtain a condemnation from an unhurried Rome. Fénelon lost his tutorship in January 1699, and also the biggest sign of favour at court which Louis bestowed, his apartment at Versailles. Rome did finally issue a 'condemnation' of twenty-three propositions, but turned it into an exoneration by issuing a brief, *Cum alias,* and not a bull, by condemning the propositions globally and not individually, which meant that the status of the document became a mere admonition with nothing precise condemned at all, and by using the mildest possible theological qualifications, coming nowhere near heresy, blasphemy, impiety, or even 'offensive'.

The propositions 'in their obvious sense' were 'dangerous' or even 'respectively' erroneous, which removed any specificity from the condemnation. 'Respectively erroneous' means no more than that there was a misleading imprudence of language somewhere, without pinpointing a place. The brief, drawing on the whole repertoire of refined curial drafting techniques, was in fact exculpatory, and for those capable of decoding the further ambiguities and omissions built into the curial Latin, a veiled rebuke to Louis, whose request it ostensibly granted. What it did achieve with absolute certainty was the removal of any possibility that Bossuet would ever get the red hat he had confidently expected, or either of the major sees of Paris or Lyon.

11

War and Foreign Affairs

Louis, still anxious for military glory, clearly desired to establish France as the most powerful as well as the most cultivated nation of western Europe. His temperamental tendency to bully worked at all levels, from inside relationships with the individuals close to him to his execution of grand strategy. The reason why the skirmishes of the 1667–8 'war of devolution', ending in the peace of Aix-la-Chapelle, had such disastrous consequences for France, was that it alerted all the European powers to the dangers of predatory French military ambition in Europe. There was no real need for France to expand eastwards to ensure the security of her frontiers. The fortresses linked by waterways which Vauban wished to erect into a *barrière de fer* to defend the routes to Paris from the Low Countries and prevent the invasion of France proper did not need to be placed exactly where they were.

Eventually Louis's aggressiveness, partly masquerading as France's 'need' to make the Rhine its only defensible eastern frontier, became self-defeating. The rest of Europe may have over-reacted, but in order to prevent the emergence of a Franco-Spanish bloc capable of dominating Europe, which it perhaps unnecessarily feared, it roused itself into imposing on France the crushing reversals of the War of Spanish Succession. Louis's early educational experiences, whatever they were devised to achieve, made him capable of the harsh and unnecessary cruelties later inflicted by his armies, about which he knew and for which he became responsible.

At the date of Louis's marriage to Maria-Teresa, it did not seem important that the claim to the succession to the throne of Spain would extend to any offspring of the sickly three-year-old son of Philip IV by his second wife, Maria-Teresa's half-brother Carlos II, if, as seemed likely, he were to die without offspring. The admittedly complicated arguments for and against the legality of Maria-Teresa's claim to the Spanish Netherlands after the death of her father Philip IV on 17 September 1665 can be taken too seriously.

The customary pamphlet literature was commissioned by each side upholding or repudiating Louis's claims, but the legal arguments on the French side, while plausible although actually not cogent, amounted anyway only to routine face-saving.[1] The claim of Maria-Teresa to the throne of Spain had not yet arisen. What had been at stake in 1666 was a claim to territorial compensation for the unpaid dowry, in place of which Louis had demanded absurd amounts of territorial compensation.[2] Although it fooled no one, Louis could enforce his claim by military seizure while pretending not to be the aggressor, but merely the vindicator of his wife's inheritance.

From the peace of Aix-la-Chapelle in 1668, France had formally been at uneasy peace, but Louis and his advisors had been concerned that France's former allies, the Dutch, had been the prime movers against France's attempts to claim parts of the Spanish Low Countries. France therefore entered into another secret treaty, this time with the English in the 1670 treaty of Dover, that England would support France in any future war against the Dutch in return for a cash subsidy from France.

It is still clearly necessary to separate the war of devolution, scarcely more than menacing armed manoeuvres, the Dutch war of 1672–8, the war of the League of Augsburg of 1688–97, and the war of the Spanish succession of 1701–13 into discrete 'wars', but the shifting political tensions and alliances which occupied the intervening years cannot properly be described as peace.[3] France would quickly recover from its ruinous state at the end of Louis's reign, but in the meanwhile western Europe was suffering from a sense of unfinished business in which sectarian as well as territorial interests played their part. There was a gradation between peace and war, passing through situations of hostile diplomatic activity without either armed combat or the strain on the exchequer that field armies imposed. Although the heavy contribution of French aggression cannot be justified,

Louis's upbringing and his obsolescent attachment to personal glory earned on battlefields as the principal means of acquiring entitlement to rank and honour cannot reasonably be accounted alone responsible for the fighting.

When on his death-bed Louis admitted that he had 'often gone to war too lightly', the Dutch war was the one he ought primarily to have had in mind. It lasted from 1672 to the peace of Nijmegen signed in 1679, and was at least partly the result of Louis's desire to engage in a military campaign which would result in a speedy and glorious victory with worthwhile spoils. Speed was important because the French treasury could not withstand a lengthy struggle, and the war against Spain likely to result from the death without issue of Carlos II risked reuniting all Europe against France. Carlos married again after the death of his first queen, Marie-Louise, daughter of Louis's brother, Philippe, but Louis and his advisers rightly supposed that he was incapable of generating issue.

The United Provinces and France had been confronting one another in a trade war since 1667. The religious difference counted for little or nothing, but the United Provinces were undoubtedly a focus for French dissidents, and in particular for the Huguenots. Louis was reverting to the sentiment which prevailed in the rest of Europe, but which Richelieu, in advance of his time, had tried to change, that religious dissidence entailed civic disloyalty. Aid to French Huguenots began to look in Louis's eyes like hostility to France. In addition, anti-French propaganda was being disseminated from Amsterdam, although not everything with Amsterdam on the title page was actually printed there.

If the Spanish came to the aid of the Dutch, Louis would have a pretext for attacking the Spanish Netherlands without alarming the rest of Europe by his predatory intentions. Dutch maritime commerce, colonies and banking arrangements made the United Provinces a desirable trophy as well as a suitable background for the remaining members of the French aristocracy forced by Louis to seek promotion, rank and therefore wealth in the glory earned in battle.

Louis wanted war, but a war he could win quickly. The French had been actively preparing for it for some years. The raising of tariffs by Colbert in 1667 had been an irritant, and at first Colbert and Lionne had tried to ward off war by diplomacy, while Louvois and

Turenne had been in favour from the beginning of urging Louis towards the military solution he wanted. Unfortunately France's most skilful diplomat, Lionne, who might have diminished or avoided some of the disaster which befell France, died in 1671. He was replaced by the young and comparatively inexperienced marquis de Pomponne. Colbert supported a military solution from 1678, when his tariffs failed to produce their desired effect. The treaty of Dover had weaned England from its triple alliance with Sweden and the United Provinces. Sweden, whose armies were virtually for sale to the highest bidder, was prepared to renew its alignment with France. Louvois visited both the elector of Cologne and the Bishop of Münster and persuaded them to ally themselves with France.

Meanwhile, Vauban was strengthening the fortifications at Ath, Oudenaarde, Charleroi, and using 9,000 men on a shift system at Dunkirk. The elector of Brandenburg had promised neutrality. The French army would have a safe passage to the territory of its prey. Louvois, raised to ministerial rank in February 1672, had built up its strength to 120,000, and equipped it well. The Dutch had only 27,000 troops, although they quickly increased the number to 80,000 when war began. Louvois had stocked all the arsenals for six months, was getting the army accustomed to wearing uniforms and persuaded Louis to take responsibility for strategy away from the commanders in the field, compelling them to take orders from Paris.

Condé, pardoned in 1659 for his services to Spain and now fully rehabilitated, gave a magnificent three-day celebration for the king at Chantilly in April 1671. He had failed to have himself elected king of Poland in 1669, but his grandson was eventually to be married to the king's eldest daughter by Athénaïs. He was given charge of the company of the *gendarmes*. With him were Turenne, Luxembourg and the king's brother, Philippe, who, given his temperament, was surprisingly good at war. The Dutch, feeling threatened, sent an ambassador with whom Louis made an appointment which he broke, and to whom, when he was eventually received, Louis was arrogantly unpleasant. The ambassador was told that France would increase its armament and, when he was ready, make such use of it as he saw fit.

The 'Dutch war' began when Louis declared war on the United Provinces in April 1672 and opened a two-pronged attack, using his English allies' naval forces and his own troops, who marched through the Rhineland. The naval battle of Sole Bay on 7 June was a farce.

The Anglo-French force of 108 ships were caught revictualling. The English had fifty-two ships under the future James II and the Earl of Sandwich, but were undisciplined, and had difficulty in using their flags for communication. The French had thirty ships under d'Estrées, who misinterpreted the signals. Together they had 1,664 guns. The Dutch under van Ruyter had about seventy-five Dutch ships of the line, and although the action was indecisive, the Dutch were strategically victorious, preventing the Anglo-French fleet from approaching the Dutch coast 'for some time'. Lord Sandwich was killed, and the French lost an admiral.

Condé famously led his troops across the Rhine at Tolhuis on 12 June 1672, an event instantly mythologized for home consumption, but in fact devoid of drama. Two regiments of Dutch infantry with no artillery fled, as did 500 cavalry, when confronted by Condé's army of 20,000, which knew from earlier reconnaissance of a spot where the Rhine could be forded without danger, except for some eighteen metres in the middle, across which the army had to swim. In fact, no shot need have been fired if Condé's nephew had not shot into the surrendering Dutch, killing an officer. The Dutch in despair took up their arms again and Condé's nephew was killed. Condé himself was wounded in the hand.

The Dutch abandoned their fortresses, and in twenty-two days the French had taken forty towns along the IJssel, one of the rivers of the Rhine delta. The French could have taken Amsterdam, as Condé wanted, but Turenne's caution won the day. In July the Dutch sued for peace. Characteristically, Louis, following the advice of Louvois, demanded terms so pointlessly humiliating that the Dutch had no option but to fight on.[4] They were given five days and played for time while Spain, the elector of Brandenburg, whose Rhine fortresses the French had occupied, and the emperor all pledged support.

Louis gradually increased his demands, and then the Dutch played their trump card. They opened the sluice gates at Muiden, turning Amsterdam into an island in the IJsselmeer, separating the French troops from the rest of the country, and uniting the Dutch into solid resistance against their invaders. They appointed the twenty-two-year-old fanatical Calvinist William of Orange their military leader and Stadtholder on 8 July, bringing to an end the burgher republic dominated by the bourgeois merchants of Amsterdam and led by Jan de Witt, known as the Grand Pensionary. De Witt and his brother

Cornelis were massacred by the anti-pacifist Amsterdam mob on 20 August.

Louis, accompanied by his wife, Louise de la Vallière and Mme de Montespan, left Saint-Germain on 1 May 1673. With Vauban, who designed the trenches through which the town might be approached and used 20,000 peasants to dig them, Louis went on to capture Maastricht with an army of 25,000 in 1673. The victory was entirely due to Vauban, to whom Louis gave a gratification, but whom he did not mention in his account of his glorious victory, in which French losses were in fact quite high. Vauban bought a château in Burgundy with his reward.

The French now pursued a policy initiated by Louvois, in which Louis certainly acquiesced, of the utmost rigour in conquered territory, which meant savagely pillaging or sometimes burning whole villages. Louis had in any case set Europe's alarm bells ringing. He could not be allowed to bully his way into European hegemony. Spain, Austria, Brandenburg, Denmark, Saxony and several small German principalities stepped in to aid the Dutch against him. Turenne forced the Brandenburgers to withdraw, but in 1673 Münster and Cologne, which had lost its capital, Bonn, to the Austrians, took away their support from France, and in 1674 so did England.

By the end of 1673 Louis had withdrawn his troops from the United Provinces to concentrate on the Spanish Netherlands and the Rhineland. He was fighting a pan-European war he had not started, did not want and certainly could not afford. He had not even achieved the sought-for glory, although he disposed of an army which was five times as big as that of his intended victim. He had attempted to shore up his self-confidence, and bungled.

Louis had returned to Saint-Germain on 1 August 1672. By the end of that year he had had to split his forces between the north and the Rhineland, where Turenne stopped the imperial forces from joining up with the Dutch army. By 1674, with the withdrawal of England, France had lost its numerical superiority, while Condé, Turenne and Luxembourg were finding it hard to accept Louvois's overall direction. As France's allies fell away, leaving Louis in alliance only with Sweden and the elector of Bavaria, Louis could rely only on the talent of his generals. It was thanks not to a general but to to Vauban, the engineer, that Louis could personally lead a successful twenty-seven-day siege of Besançon in May 1974, and to squabbles among the coalition partners that Condé and Turenne were enabled to score important victories. Turenne, however, was killed by a stray cannon-ball in July 1675, and in September Condé, having successfully defended Alsace, retired from the war.

On 8 June 1674 Louis took the queen and Gaston's daughter, la grande Mademoiselle, to see Dôle in Burgundy just after it had been taken. They did not enter the town 'because of the bad air', a phrase used to designate the germ-laden air of putrefying bodies and rotting sewage. Many of the survivors were badly wounded and there was blood on the walls. Louis and his party were lodged in the houses of peasants, whose windows were at this date still unglazed. Mademoiselle's cottage had been prettified with tapestries and a carpet: 'I slept as well as if I had been in the Luxembourg.' They ate in tents made to look as like Versailles as possible, 'There were always violins and oboes at the King's dinner and supper. We had the idea of playing cards after dinner when the King was with his Council and the Queen at her prayers.[5]

By the summer of 1674, however, Louis was looking for peace. There were uprisings and savage reprisals in Roussillon, Guyenne and Brittany in 1674 and 1675 at the poverty imposed on the peasantry to finance the war. In Brittany there were 15,000 rioters, and the chevalier de Rohan conspired to bring about an armed invasion of Brittany by William of Orange. The plot was betrayed, and he was executed.

Senior figures, like the *intendants,* were advising Colbert that the peasants could not believe that Louis was aware of their distress. Others, including ecclesiastics, were warning Louis that the country would be ruined if, simply to sustain the possibility of achieving greater *gloire,* Louis kept the war going. That policy was self-defeating, as the king's desire for military glory depended on a country prosperous enough to fight wars.

Louis had managed to secure his own frontiers by reoccupying Franche-Comté and established control over Alsace. A costly victory by Condé at Seneffe, near Charleroi, over William of Orange prevented invasion from the north. Condé with 45,000 men attacked the rearguard of the Dutch army of 60,000. There were 20,000 deaths. But the war dragged on, and Louis, in 1675 and 1676 on the defensive, was saved from humiliation by outstanding naval victories against the Spanish in the Mediterranean. Colbert's maritime policy paid a massive dividend, and the French navy destroyed the Spanish fleet in two sea battles in 1676. That year, after careful soundings in 1675, peace negotiations opened at Nijmegen.

Louis left Saint-Germain on 7 February 1678 disseminating by the route he took the disinformation that he was headed for Nancy. The strategy was devised by Louvois. In fact his destination was Metz, where he arrived on 22nd. After several more diversions which further confused the Spaniards, Louis left the queen at Stenay to lead his troops already investing Ghent. Louis arrived on 4 March, the hardship of riding eighty kilometres a day for three days, drinking the 'vilest wine in the world' and sleeping in farmhouses being both much quoted and much exaggerated. The city surrendered on the 9th and its citadel on the 12th. The king and Luxembourg went on to take Ypres, which surrendered on the 25th.

Complex negotiations resulted in a number of peace treaties signed in 1678 and 1679, to be known collectively as the peace of Nijmegen. With the Dutch, Louis restored Maastricht and ended the tariff war. With the Spanish, Louis retained Franche-Comté, Artois, and a number of towns which formed the foundation of the *pré carré* (duelling area) for which Vauban had been pressing since 1675, and which allowed him to fortify the north-eastern frontier. Effectively this involved partitioning the Low Countries. In a treaty with the emperor, France retained Freiburg, but gave up Philippsburg, abandoning parts of Alsace in return for bridgeheads across the Rhine.

This result, and the ramifications it had for relations between Sweden, Prussia, Spain, Denmark, the empire, the Low Countries, the United Provinces and England, was represented in France as a great victory, and is still seen in that light by some French historians. The myth was swallowed. Louis le Grand, wrote Choisy 'reached the pinnacle of human glory. After myriad demonstrations of his military leadership and his personal valour, he lay [sic] down his arms amidst his victories and, contenting himself with his conquests, gave peace to Europe.'[6] Louis did indeed show personal courage in leading as many of the 1672 sieges as he could. The myth worked. Where he personally led, the discipline and courage of the troops was enhanced.

In the short term, France did strengthen its position. The cost, however, had been incalculably greater than Louis had anticipated and, given France's initial superiority in military strength and organization, the gains were paltry. Worse, France's reputation emerged thoroughly tarnished. Louis was the bully endangering the stability of western Europe, the creator, especially by his cruelty to civilian populations, of a Francophobia which would still ensure that what Napoleon was to create over a century later would again be demolished by the rest of Europe. France had emerged politically the preponderant power in Europe, but Louis had given Spain, the empire, the Dutch Republic and England lasting cause to resent it.

New military technology had made Richelieu's fear of 'gates' in frontiers obsolete. Vauban could make linear frontiers punctuated by fortified towns impregnable. To strengthen weak points in a line which Louis hoped would reach from the North Sea to the Mediterranean, Louis now appointed four *chambres de réunion* at Tournai, Metz, Breisach and Besançon to search out 'dependencies' of territories awarded to France under the peace treaties of Westphalia, the Pyrénées and Nijmegen in order to identify further territories to which France might lay claim. As a result of the work of the *chambres,* Louis now also forcibly acquired between 1680 and 1684 much of the region between the Moselle and the Rhine, parts of Alsace and Luxembourg and in 1681 Strasbourg. The emperor Leopold negotiated a peace of Ratisbon by which the affected countries would leave the seized 'réunions' in French hands for twenty years.

Just as Louis appears not to have felt more than ineffective stirrings of guilt at his extra-marital sexual liaisons, although they were unequivocally condemned by the church, so he does not appear to have felt more than ineffectual twinges of concern for the peasantry he was starving. In his eyes the all-important task, to which he was fitted by upbringing and driven by psychological need, was to prove to himself that he possessed the courage and skills which entitled him to the reality and not just the pretence of the superhuman authority and respect accorded to him as Sun King in establishing the grandeur of France.

Destiny was to take a hand as if in punishing him for his hubris, but the years between 1679 and 1684 saw the turning point, the apogee of his career. He had luckily escaped having to pay for the arrogant intransigence of the Dutch war, largely because the capture of Ghent had put a powerful bargaining tool into his hand with which to pay Carlos II for peace. But the bill for antagonizing the whole of western Europe and uniting its constituent elements against France was still sure to be presented. It was to be steeper because Austria succeeded in repressing the Hungarian uprising and in repulsing the Turks, freeing her forces for action in the west, and because, once James II was overthrown, William and Mary succeeded to the English throne and resolutely put England in the anti-French camp.

The German principalities had been afraid of Louis's need to assert himself by aggressive warfare. None of the smaller European states could have withstood French military might at the onset of the Dutch war. However, with the Austrian suppression of the Hungarian rising and the repulse of the Turkish onslaught, helped by a fire in Belgrade which in 1686 destroyed the Turkish grain store, imperial troops might now well be able to halt French aggression. The whole Danube basin was open to attack from the west and the *réunions* ratified at Ratisbon were menacing as well as insulting. Protestant Europe was incensed at Louvois's *dragonnades* – the billeting of cavalry officers – on Huguenot families, obliging them to supply them with food and lodging. In July 1686 the princes of south Germany met representatives of Sweden and Spain to form the League of Augsburg for the defence against the French of the upper Rhine. For the moment it intended to do nothing, but its ambition was to push the French frontiers back to where they had been before the war of devolution.

The immediate causes of the war of the League of Augsburg, also known as the Nine Years' war, started in 1688, were two successions, to the Palatine electorate and to the archbishopric of Cologne. The Golden Bull of 1356 had made the count Palatine one of the seven electors of the Holy Roman Emperor. Although the power had evaporated, the position remained immensely lucrative. The elector, brother of Liselotte, died childless in 1685. Liselotte, married to Louis's brother, was the elector's sister but not, according to imperial law and the will of the late elector, his heir. The heir was the emperor's father-in-law, Philip William of Neuburg. Louis had no rights in the matter at all, and neither did his sister-in-law, but Louis saw a pretext and demanded a share in the succession.

When the pro-French archbishop of Cologne died on 3 June 1688, Louis wanted him replaced by the bishop of Strasbourg, William

Egon von Fürstenberg. However, a slumbering conflict with Innocent XI had recently come to a climax with Louis's excommunication, and it is not at all astonishing that the pope chose a rival, the seventeen-year-old Joseph Clement of Bavaria, bishop of Freising and Regensburg, nephew of the deceased archbishop, and the imperial candidate.[7] Louis, as might by now be expected, issued an aggressive declaration. Dated 24 September 1688, it demanded that the Ratisbon twenty-year arrangement be made permanent for the defence of the French frontiers; Liselotte had to be indemnified for renouncing any claim to the Palatinate succession; Fürstenberg had to have the archbishopric. As the rest of Europe realized, there was no justification for any of the three demands. Louis was making himself tyrant of Europe. With Colbert now dead and Louvois his principal adviser, he was also badly misjudging the situation.

By the end of August 1688 it was already clear that no such ultimatum would be met, so Louis launched what he was sure would be a short victorious war. Each side now had about 400,000 men at its disposal, although the imperial forces would swell as they were freed from Turkish pressure. Louis had already ordered 6,000 troops into Bonn on 10 September. On the 15th Cardinal d'Estrées read out to the pope why it was he who was to blame for all the disorder, and French troops entered the papal enclave at Avignon and took over the surrounding comtat Venaissin. Louis's forces also entered into part of the Palatinate, capturing in October 1688 the fortress of Phillipsburg, strategically important not only for its position, but because, surrounded by marshes, it was easily defensible. Louvois thought that raids into the Danube basin would weaken the imperial will to resist, debilitate and frighten the enemy, and lessen the cost to France of the war, whose army would live off the fertile region's produce. In November, Louis ordered the bombardment of Koblenz to 'punish' the elector of Trier for refusing to surrender the city.

Louis explicitly ordered the creation of a *cordon sanitaire* to protect the new French borders. Among the towns ordered to be burnt to ruins on the direct orders of Louis were Heidelberg, Worms, Mannheim, Tübingen, Bingen and Speier. Louvois wanted stones from Mannheim, whose destruction was ordered by Louis on 26 November 1688, shipped up the Rhine for the reconstruction of Philippsburg. The list was drawn up by Louvois and shown to Louis, who showed reservations about completely destroying the palace at

Heidelberg and a few churches, but not about human habitations which might be used to harbour an enemy.

Happily, his orders were not totally obeyed.[8] The insistence on a *cordon sanitaire* was founded on the medieval custom of clearing the ground in front of a fortress to force any assailants to attack across open land. Louis was extending this practice to France itself, as if it were a fortress. His willingness, indeed insistence, on destroying so much of medieval Europe is important in any attempt to assess his artistic taste and patronage. He was not interested in the historic. Indeed, when he called on his countrymen to surrender their silver objects to the mint, he put forward as a positive advantage that, when one day they were returned, they could be made up to suit fashionable modern taste.

The dauphin was in supreme command, but Louis was insistent that any advice given by Vauban was to be implemented, however difficult it might be for marshals of France and princes of the blood to allow strategy to be determined by an engineer. As the German cavalry began to appear, and to occupy what Louvois had intended to be winter quarters for the French army, demolition became more urgent, but there was clear reluctance from the French generals to destroy towns which had surrendered and to leave German peasants without shelter.

The tone of the letters from Versailles became more insistent and angry all through the winter as the reluctance of the commanders in the field became ever clearer. None the less, in spite of a spate of demolitions half done, and difficulties which prevented others from being undertaken at all, Mannheim was destroyed, as eventually was Heidelberg, with its palace, for the second time, on 26 May 1693, although there the inhabitants were at first allowed to put out the fires. In Paris there was naturally a *Te Deum*. From 31 May to 3 June 1689, Speier, Worms, Bingen and Oppenheim were all fired. Saint-Simon's story that Louis threatened Louvois with fire tongs when Louvois told him he had ordered the destruction of Trier is unfortunately not true.[9]

Meanwhile, on 10 June 1688, Mary of Modena, wife of the Catholic James II, king of England since 1685, had given birth to a male Catholic heir to the English throne.[10] It was James's second marriage. His elder daughter by his first marriage had in 1677 married William of Orange, and was, like her younger sister, Anne, a member of the

English church. Mary of Modena had lost five daughters and a son in infancy, and was sickly. It was thought that she was unable to bear children, so that an Anglican succession seemed secure, but the survival of the new infant changed everything, and William of Orange was encouraged to invade and take the throne from James.

William landed at Torbay on 15 November 1688, and James fled to France, where the château of Saint-Germain was put at his disposal. Louis hoped that William and England would be so occupied with civil war as to be useless to the imperial alliance. When no civil war broke out, Louis backed the attempt by James to regain his kingdom by way of Ireland. He set out on 12 May 1690 and was landed by the French fleet under its admiral, Tourville. The French sent reinforcements of disciplined troops and supplies, but James was relying on untrained Irish peasants, and was defeated by William at the battle of the Boyne on 1 July, another disaster for late seventeenth-century French interests whose reverberations have extended to the present. The French evacuated James from Dublin, and on 10 July Tourville, with seventy-eight ships, confronted a force of fifty-eight English and Dutch ships, and sank seventeen of them, establishing a supremacy in the English Channel which greatly pleased Louis, although it lasted only two years.

In 1689, England, now in the hands of William and Mary, Austria, Spain, Savoy and the Dutch republic joined with the German states of the League of Augsburg. Louis, prompted by his brilliant but destructive genius, Louvois, had now united the rest of Europe against France. Its only remaining alliance was with the retreating Ottoman empire. In France, Louvois began to see his influence diluted. The fiscal implications of the war were horrific. Yet the *Te Deums* rang out, in November 1688 for the capture of Philippsburg, in June 1690 for Ath, in July 1690 for victories at Fleurus and off Beachy Head.

Fighting now extended from the Low Countries to north Italy, in the colonies, in India and on the sea, but no side could convincingly defeat the other. Victories were countered with subsequent defeats, or with defeats elsewhere. The currency dropped by a third in value. Samuel Bernard, the great financier, was bankrupted. France had no parliament that could create debt or incur debt. Only the king could raise the money to finance expenditure. On 3 December 1689 Louis ordered nearly 1,200 pieces of solid silver furniture and his gold dinner service to be melted down to raise 2.5 million livres, about a third of what he might have got before the war. Henceforward he ate off silver-gilt. It was only a gesture. Louis ordered that the balls and parties continue. It was Marie-Adélaïde of Savoy, duchesse de Bourgogne, who would later have them stopped. Comparatively few of the affluent handed in their silver services, many of which were heirlooms, stipulated in marriage contracts dating back a century or so.

Louis had led his troops at Mons in the spring of 1691, taking with him only the male members of the court. He rightly wanted Vauban to conduct the operation, but that meant re-assuming command himself, since none of his generals would easily take orders from an engineer. The genius of Vauban made certain that the French were bound to take the fortress. Louis, however, was plainly losing some of his vigour and, above all, his decisiveness. He upset Louvois's logistics by having more cavalry near Mons than the situation warranted, and it consumed food and forage required for the rest of the army.

There were apparently other serious moments of disagreement between Louis and Louvois before Mons capitulated. Louis was depressed when he returned to Versailles, refusing any compliments offered to him on his victory. He was working quietly with Louvois on Monday, 16 July 1691 when Louvois suddenly felt unwell. He died within hours of what was referred to as a 'pulmonary apoplexy'.

Louis made several visits to war zones, including the siege of Namur in 1692. After his return to Versailles in June 1693 he never again led his armies in person.

Louis wanted peace from 1693, but serious talks did not begin until 1696, when Louis signed a separate peace with Savoy on 10 September 1696, leaving Savoy in possession of Casale and Pinerolo, where Fouquet had died in 1680. The agreement with Savoy was to be sealed by the marriage of the eldest son of the grand Dauphin, Louis, duc de Bourgogne, who was fourteen, and the eleven-year-old Marie-Adélaïde, daughter of Victor-Amadeus II of Savoy and his wife, Anne-Marie, who was the daughter of Louis's brother Philippe d'Orléans and his wife, Henriette d'Angleterre. The marriage appears to have been consummated late in 1699.[11] That agreement freed French troops to move north, at which prospect the other powers agreed to negotiate and Sweden accepted the role of mediator.

A settlement was negotiated at a villa owned by William of Orange in a village near the Hague called Ryswick. William's wife Mary, joint sovereign of England with him, had died in 1694, but Louis recognized William as king of England. Adjustments were made in colonial territories. Louis agreed to a commercial treaty favourable to the Dutch and to Dutch occupation of eleven fortified towns on the border between France and the Spanish Low Countries, including Courtrai, Mons and Charleroi. Louis withdrew from Catalonia, returned all the *réunions* on the frontier with the Low Countries and Luxembourg. In the Rhineland, Louis gave way on the two successions, to the Palatine electorship and the Cologne archbishopric, and returned the *réunions*, but kept Alsace and Strasbourg. The final agreement was signed on 30 October 1697.

Since the emperor Leopold now had children, he was no longer likely to honour the partition resolution of the Spanish succession which he had signed with Louis in 1668. Louis had therefore been cultivating pro-French sentiment in Spain, where Carlos II still tenuously held on to life. Feeling in Spain radically opposed to partition was growing stronger, and there were three claims to the succession, all flawed. The first claim was French, deriving from Maria-Teresa's status as the daughter of Philip IV, who had died in 1665. Her eldest grandson, the duc de Bourgogne, would presumably succeed his father the grand Dauphin as king of France, but her claim might be transmitted to her second grandson, Philippe d'Anjou. The abdication of her rights on marrying Louis had never been acknowledged in France because the dowry had not been paid.

The second and third claims were Austrian. The emperor had married three times, having by his first marriage a daughter, Maria Antonia, great grand-daughter of Philip III and grand-daughter of the infanta, Maria-Anna. Maria-Antonia had died in 1692, after renouncing her claims to the Spanish throne and marrying Maximilian Emmanuel of Bavaria. By his third marriage, Leopold had two sons. The elder, Joseph, was being reserved for the imperial throne, which he would occupy in 1705, but Leopold's younger son, the archduke Charles, was being groomed for Spain. His rights, however, were dependent on the recognition of the renunciation by his half-sister, Maria-Antonia. If that renunciation proved invalid, then Maria-Antonia's rights could be claimed by her son, Joseph Ferdinand. The situation basically resolved into a straight clash between a French and an Austrian succession, with two possible Austrian candidates.

To avoid a war that they did not want, the French signed a partition treaty with the English and the Dutch in 1698. The Spanish throne would go to Joseph Ferdinand. France would receive Naples and Sicily, and Milan would go to Austria, which had not been consulted. Louis was by now at last showing genuine concern about the sufferings war would inflict on his subjects, although the mellowing of his attitude may also partly have been inspired by a fear of insurrection. It was no doubt also due to the influence of Mme de Maintenon whose concern for the poverty of the country was partly the cause of her bitter opposition to the erection of the grand chapel at Versailles.

However, Joseph Ferdinand died on 6 February 1699, and a new partition treaty was signed in 1700, giving the Spanish throne to Leopold's son Charles; France would acquire Milan as well as Naples and Sicily. Louis issued widespread warnings that he was prepared to defend the implementation of the 1700 treaty by force if necessary. When word of the provisions spread, Spain rejected it because it opposed partition, and Austria rejected it because it would mean allowing French dominance on the Italian peninsula. Carlos II of Spain died on 1 November 1700, naming in his will as his successor Philippe d'Anjou, Louis's grandson, because he thought France alone had the power to keep the Spanish inheritance intact. He had written to the pope, Innocent XII, to obtain his confirmation that Philippe d'Anjou was the rightful heir to the Spanish throne. The affirmative reply may not have been as disinterested as it sounded, since Innocent XII, as Voltaire points out, was not anxious to strengthen the influence of the house of Austria on the Italian peninsula.

The *conseil d'en-haut*, meeting at Fontainebleau where the king was shooting in the mornings and hunting with hounds in the afternoons, had misgivings, because acceptance of the will would entail resentment in England, the Dutch republic and even Austria, since Leopold's son would not occupy the Spanish throne. Rejection in favour of the 1700 partition might have been preferable. The dauphin and Mme de Maintenon favoured acceptance of the will. Louis did accept the will, and made his decision known to the Spanish ambassador, who knelt before his new king, and to the rest of the court at Versailles on 16 November. Louis brandished the nobility of his sacrifice of the advantages in Italy that would have been conferred by the 1700 treaty. Philippe d'Anjou went to Spain as Philip V in January 1701.

It was not long before the Spaniards were clamouring for the stronger hand of Louis himself to take charge, which he did, more and more imperiously giving his grandson instructions to which he demanded obedience, whatever the Spanish council might say. Philippe was seventeen, and had not yet matured into the more conscientious king he was to become. He would rise two hours later than he said, keep the council waiting, leave letters unopened for days and sometimes turn up three hours late for supper. On 5 September 1701 he married the twelve-year-old Marie-Louise of Savoy, younger sister of the wife, Marie-Adélaïde of Savoy, of his own elder brother, the duc de Bourgogne. Marie-Louise came completely to rely on Anne-Marie de la Trémoïlle, the princesse des Ursins, who was to be the recipient of a hoard of important letters from Mme de Maintenon during the war of the Spanish Succession.

Louis's intentions might have been, and indeed probably were benign, but his actions were certainly insensitive in so tense a diplomatic atmosphere, and they were interpreted as provocative. He rather inadvisedly proclaimed in February French succession rights for Philippe d'Anjou, now Philip V, in such a way as to raise suspicions that he wanted to create a massive Franco-Spanish bloc which would crush the rest of Europe, when he wanted merely to preserve his grandson's right to abdicate the Spanish throne and accept that of France should he ever, against all probability, inherit it. Louis secondly, at the 'invitation' of his grandson, allowed French troops to occupy the forts protecting the Spanish Low Countries from French invasion, so alarming the inhabitants of the Low Countries. Thirdly, Louis acquired a monopoly for a French company of the provision of slaves to South America, creating fears that he wanted in the New World the same sort of hegemony that he was suspected of trying to acquire in the old.

To prevent the establishment of a Franco-Spanish bloc, in 1701 the emperor Leopold sent troops into the Italian peninsula, where they captured Spanish territories. This was a challenge to Louis which seemed bound to lead to war. The emperor also reanimated the Grand Alliance of Brandenburg, Hanover, the Palatinate, the

Dutch republic and England, which Spain had joined in 1690. It was reformed into a treaty between England, Austria and the Dutch republic, signed on 7 September 1701.

When James II died in France at Saint-Germain, Louis picked up the challenge by immediately and unnecessarily recognizing James's thirteen-year-old son as James III, going back on his recognition of William as English king at Ryswick. He was trying to re-establish himself as leader of Catholic Europe, now that the emperor had Protestant allies. In defending the claims of his grandson to the throne of France and of 'James III' to the English throne he was also, however factitiously, defending the genealogical derivation of the divine right of kings.

William III, as the king of England had become, died in March 1702 and was succeeded by Mary's younger sister, Anne. On 15 May 1702 the Grand Alliance declared war on France. The participants had mixed aims. Austria wanted a Habsburg on the Spanish throne and the annexation of Milan, and they wanted to protect the Rhineland. The Dutch and English wanted primarily to preserve the autonomy of the Spanish Netherlands and to prevent any Franco-Spanish colonial integration. Both sides still had armies of between 300,000 and 400,000, but the allies had the better generals in Marlborough and Eugene of Savoy.[12] Armies of this size imposed new and very tight logistical conditions limiting the length of daily marches and of campaign seasons, and requiring the most careful placing and guarding of supplies of food, fuel and munitions along routes which had to be pre-ordained, or in unwieldy convoys with yet more men and horses to feed.[13] Armies normally marched between fifteen and twenty kilometres a day, mostly between about three a.m. and nine a.m., resting one day in five, more on account of food preparation and distribution and other organizational matters than on account of human fatigue.

In 1703 Louis thought of ending the war with despatch by taking Vienna. A French army under the maréchal de Villars would join with the forces of the Bavarian elector and with an army under Vendôme, the illegitimate grandson of Henri IV, to be brought over the Brenner pass from Lombardy. Marlborough and Eugene of Savoy determined to intercept the French and Bavarians and marched 400 kilometres. At Blenheim they saw the French on 12 August in a position which could quickly be rendered impregnable, determined immediately to attack next morning, and routed the French and Bavarians. That summer English forces also took Gibraltar. Marlborough retreated to the Rhine and made his winter quarters at Trier, so that everything he needed could be brought safely and cheaply from the Dutch republic by water.

In 1705, the emperor Leopold died. Marlborough suffered a minor reversal near Trier, but the next large-scale battle did not occur until the French and Bavarian armies were defeated at Ramillies on 23 May 1706. Against the reiterated advice of his officers, the French general, Villeroy, decided on battle, and again on the positioning of his forces. Marlborough took advantage of all the mistakes, and the French lost 20,000 men and control of the Spanish Low Countries. From 31 May we have the letters of Mme de Maintenon to the princesse des Ursins commenting on affairs. Louis tried to shield Villeroy from widespread criticism, but yielded to general opinion by giving the Flanders command to Vendôme.

Victor-Amadeus of Savoy turned against both France and Spain, thereby pitting himself against the husbands of both his daughters, the queen of Spain and the duchesse de Bourgogne. Louis decided to besiege Turin, putting La Feuillade in charge. Vauban proferred advice on the conduct of the siege, La Feuillade rejected it on the grounds that some were born to command and others, like engineers, to obey. Vauban had on 2 February 1708 been appointed a member of the order of the Saint-Esprit, the highest at Louis's disposal, having been dispensed from the ordinary need for generations of nobility in the ascendancy of members. Saint-Simon was contemptuous. Philippe d'Orléans, son of the king's brother of the same name, was to take command in Lombardy. His advice, too, was neglected by La Feuillade, who was defeated at the gates of Turin.

It is noteworthy that, in spite of the loss to the English of the Spanish Netherlands, the line of fortifications prepared by Vauban was only once breached, in 1712, when Eugène's advance towards Paris was halted by the French commander, Villars. Vauban was now elderly. In 1706 he had submitted to the king a pamphlet arguing that the greatness of a monarch is to be measured by the prosperity and contentment of his subjects. He included ideas for the reform of military recruitment and advancement.

Nothing was done, so Vauban, neglecting the prescribed censorship, had a small edition printed. It was a plea to consider the welfare of the lower classes and to reform the tax system in their favour. The *Projet d'une dîme royale* was eagerly welcomed by the duc de Bourgogne, as might after all be expected from Fénelon's former pupil, but Louis issued a decree ordering the seizure and destruction of all copies. Vauban was still honoured by the king and invited to Marly, although he was too ill to accept his last invitation. Not only Europe's leading siege engineer and a brilliant military tactician, he was also Louis's most reliable statistical adviser on the demography of France. He died at the end of March in 1706.

Marlborough now planned his final strategy: a strong attack in the fortified regions of the Low Countries accompanied by an invasion of France from the south by Eugène of Savoy through Toulon, which the English navy was to seize. Mme de Maintenon's foreboding became worse and worse through 1707, but the Toulon enterprise failed. After James II's son failed to land with French backing in Scotland, peace talks began during 1708 with both the Dutch and British.

That year the grand Dauphin's two sons remaining in France, the ducs de Bourgogne and Berri, were sent by their grandfather, Louis, to Flanders. Vendôme was to serve under Bourgogne; so, too, was Berwick, a marshal of France, a Catholic and the illegitimate son of James II and Marlborough's sister, Arabella Churchill. He was reluctant to take orders from anyone less than Bourgogne, the senior prince of the blood present.

Most sources, except formal ones, such as letters from Louis, write as if Vendôme were in effective command. Several letters from Fontainebleau make clear that Bourgogne had the better strategy, but was under instructions from his grandfather to take orders from Vendôme. In one of his more perceptive remarks, Saint-Simon says that he foresaw that Vendôme, the stronger of the two, would destroy Bourgogne 'in the eyes of the court, of France, of the whole of Europe'. The lack of sympathy between him and Bourgogne was partly temperamental. Vendôme was *libertin*, homosexual and possibly atheist, while Bourgogne was pious, thanking God in a letter to Beauvillier for the humiliations he was suffering to keep him from pride. While Vendôme and Bourgogne indulged their dislike of one another, appeals to Louis took nearly a week to get to Versailles and back. The French successfully took Ghent and Bruges, but Eugène arrived on 6 July. The allied victory at Oudenaarde was the result of

French hesitations, slowness and lack of a proper command structure. France lost both Lille on 23 October and, with it, Flanders.

At court, gambling and theatricals were suspended after Oudenaarde. Bored normality had given way to clear anxiety. The worst was yet to come. On top of the starvation imposed by the fiscal regime, the exceptionally severe winter of 1708–9 produced unanticipated natural hardships and military hazards. Not only did people freeze to death, but rivers, like the Rhine and the Loire, froze over, so that wagons could cross them. In the autumn of 1708 prices started to rise. Harvests of arable crops and grapes were late and poor.

In Toulouse the cost of corn rose 75 per cent in the year, while wine doubled in price. In Paris there was frost in October, and ten consecutive days of it in December. Most communities did whatever was possible, but it was seldom of much help. Hoarding became seriously anti-social. Bonfires were lit everywhere against the cold. Louis cancelled visits to Marly and Trianon out of consideration for the officers who would have had to accompany him. It even became impossible to dig graves. The winter corn crop failed. Levies were decreed to assist the poor. In spite of genuine and energetic official efforts, there were uprisings and lampoons.

By the early spring the allies realized that France was defeated, and that they could demand what they wanted. Louis was reaping what he had sown, and fresh claims were coming in on all sides. Ignoring ultimatums ending on 4 June and 1 August, Louis went as far on 12 August as to make an ultimate appeal to his countrymen to support his rejection of the humiliating terms offered to him, which included the removal of Anjou from the kingship of Spain, 'setting grandfather against grandson'.

The war was to continue and, incredibly, morale in the army was high. Everyone had trust in Villars, Louis's new general, encamped in a favourable position, and both sides wanted a pitched battle which would deliver control of Mons. It took place near Malplaquet on 11 September 1709. Those who were wounded were not taken prisoner, but were all killed. The losses were horrendous, and more British than French, although it was the French who retired, defeated. Letters reaching the court surprisingly give the sense that the battle raised rather than lowered French spirits. It was not until 26 June 1710 that Douai, with a garrison of 8,000 French soldiers, finally capitulated after a British siege.

Louis was calm, and continued to write careful letters explaining his wishes, but now leaving as much strategic responsibility as was possible to his generals on the ground. He continued to build his magnificent chapel at Versailles, designed by Mansart with its vault painted by Coypel, although the old chapel in use since 1682 was still serviceable enough and, like the new one, had a tribune which dispensed Louis and his guests from having to use the nave. Mme de Maintenon opposed the project not only on account of the unseemliness of so much unnecessary expenditure against a back-ground of so much national poverty, but also because she did not believe that Versailles would remain the permanent residence of the French monarchy.

The foundations had been laid in 1689, and the height of the projected building was subsequently increased above the rest of the Versailles roofline. Saint-Simon famously described it as having 'the mournful appearance of an immense catafalque'. Everything was carefully tested. The statues were modelled in wax and submitted to Louis, then plaster models were tried in position. The chapel, for which Lulli and Lalande were to write music, was completed in the spring of 1710 and finally consecrated on 5 June. The château was now complete, and much admired and imitated throughout western Europe, as were French style, taste, food, clothes, music and manners. French became the court language east of the Rhine. Peter the Great took a French architect back with him to Peterhof. Robert de Cotte, who became Louis's first architect, produced designs for Brühl, Bonn and Poppelsdorf.[14]

The war continued unresolved, but the deaths in 1711 and 1712 of the grand Dauphin and the duc de Bourgogne completely and suddenly changed the situation, creating a crisis which was to leave as heir to the French throne Louis's great grandson, the third son of the duc de Bougogne born in 1710, also called Louis. Bourgogne's father, the dauphin, was not yet fifty, and was well. On Maundy Thursday, 9 April 1711, however, he felt unwell in the morning. By the evening he had a high fever and was lapsing into coma, and by the next morning it was clear that it was smallpox. Louis went immediately to be with him at Meudon, stopping the dauphin's eldest son, the duc de Bourgogne and his wife, who had not had the disease, from following him. Bourgogne wrote to Mme de Maintenon expressing concern more for Louis, his grandfather, than for his own father. Marie-Adélaïde also wrote to Mme de Maintenon, insisting that she had to see the king, without whom Versailles was intolerable to her.

Saint-Simon, who did not at all relish the dauphin's succession, was informed that the dauphin was out of danger, but returned from his château near Chartres, where he had intended to spend Holy Week and Easter. At Meudon, deputations from the people of Paris, with whom the dauphin was always popular, arrived to offer their good wishes. The dauphin ordered that they should be shown round, dined and given presents of money.

News then came to Versailles that the dauphin was holding his own, and was now out of danger. Saint-Simon and his wife had an apartment near that of the duc de Berri, the dauphin's son, and his wife, who were entertaining Liselotte. The Saint-Simons joined them, and Saint-Simon dutifully, if guiltily, reports that the whole company, including the duc de Berri, the dauphin's third son, were disappointed at news of the dauphin's recovery.

There is a letter from Mme de Maintenon of 16 April, Thursday of Easter week, describing to the princesse des Ursins what happened next. On Tuesday Louis had come into her room with the news that the dauphin's head had swollen so that his eyes were scarcely visible. Fagon, the doctor, was still reassuring, and Louis supped. The dauphin's state was meanwhile deteriorating, and panic was breaking out among those who were with him. Fagon arrived just as Louis rose from table, to announce that all was lost. Mme de Maintenon tells us that, when they went down to his room he was in convulsions but unconscious. The curé of Meudon arrived before Louis's own confessor and appeared to extract from the dauphin a sign of sorrow for his sins sufficient to warrant giving him absolution. Louis was trembling; others were silent or sobbing. The grand Dauphin was anointed before he died on 14 April 1711.

Saint-Simon is much more interested in the reactions of the individual members of court than in the event itself. He found members of the court everywhere betraying themselves, revealing ambition, hope, spite, dislike, plans, plots, connivances. Attention switched from the death at Meudon to the apartment of the duc de Bourgogne at Versailles, where members of the court were now crowding to make their condolences or pay their respects to the new dauphin and heir to the throne, some in night clothes, doors open, turmoil everywhere.

Saint-Simon's own close relationship with Bourgogne came through his intimacy with the Beauvilliers and the Chevreuses, and he was excited at the prospect of advancement now held out to him by the new dauphin. Chevreuse and he worked at plans for reform, partly at a modest Chevreuse establishment at Chaulnes, which Fénelon could visit without endangering himself by breaching the terms of his exile. Saint-Simon, Fénelon and Chevreuse all expected to be counsellors to the new dauphin when he became king after Louis's death, which could not be very far off.

It was during his visit to Chaulnes in November 1711 and his conversations principally with Chevreuse that Fénelon, following his political *Mémoire sur la situation déplorable de la France en 1710* and his *Lettre à Chevreuse* of 4 August 1710, wrote the *Table de Chaulnes*, a third practical plan outlining principles for reform. Together, they advocated above all an end to the war, even if it meant sacrificing Arras and Cambrai. After the establishment of peace, they called for a reduction in the size of the army, a reform of taxation, a decentralized judiciary and administration, the clearer separation of church and state, and a revamped function for the aristocracy, from among whose members the senior ecclesiastics should be chosen, and who would be allowed to hold offices in the magistracy and take part in commercial activity.

Bourgogne's spirituality differed little from that of his erstwhile preceptor. Bourgogne believed, like his grandfather, in the sealed, non-evolutionary nature of revelation, in the independence of the state and in the divine right of kings. Unlike his grandfather he was sensitive to the welfare of the subjects of a monarch, not to glory, except that founded on virtue and humility, and was driven by his sense of the need for divine help. The grandeur of his position as monarch should be used to acquire greater virtue 'by humiliating myself beneath the almighty hand of God'. On one evening described by Saint-Simon at Marly on 3 September 1712, some months after Bourgogne's death, Bourgogne had enlarged on his view that the glory of kingship lay in the execution of duty.

Within a week of his wife's death, he was himself dead. Unfortunately, almost all his own writings were destroyed after his death by his grandfather Louis. Early in 1712, within four weeks, Louis lost Marie-Adélaïde, her husband the new dauphin, still known as the duc de Bourgogne, and the elder of their two surviving sons,

Louis.[15] On Sunday, 7 February Marie-Adélaïde had a very bad headache. It was the onset of measles. Seven of the most distinguished doctors in the country held a consultation. They prescribed yet another phlebotomy, an opening of a vein to let blood flow out. She died on the Friday, 12th February.

Louis went immediately to Marly. Bourgogne tried to follow but felt so ill he had to return. He accepted the will of God in the matter of the death of Marie-Adélaïde, his wife, whom he adored. On Saturday 13th he did get to Marly, but had to be carried to his coach and taken in to Marly through a window. Philip V of Spain, Bourgogne's brother and formerly Philippe duc d'Anjou, wrote letters of condolence to his grandfather and to Bourgogne on the death of the grand Dauphin. When the letter to his brother was written, Bourgogne had already been dead for ten days. He had spent his final days passively resigned to accepting the will of God, whatever it should be. He made gifts to his household, set aside money for the poor of the parish and for masses to be said for the salvation of those who had died while serving under him in Flanders. He did not leave anything for masses to be said for his own salvation.

He was preparing for death and wished to take communion. The church would waive its ordinary rule, that communion may be taken only after fasting from midnight, only in the case of viaticum, which could be given whenever danger of death was imminent. Bourgogne's doctors were adamant that he would recover. Viaticum could therefore not be administered. The expedient was found of saying mass and giving Bourgogne communion at midnight in his room. No fasting was involved, and doctors were not being provoked by being told against their own judgement by a miscellany of priests and royalty that the danger of death was imminent, although it was.

But if the doctors were not made to feel that their ministrations were publicly regarded as useless, they were, in fact, positively worse than useless. Calm induced by the reception of communion was used by the doctors to inflict more remedies. Bourgogne offered up to God his own sufferings as a sacrifice for the salvation of his wife's soul. He was anointed when he entered into his death agony in the early morning of Thursday 18 February, and died that day. Almost surprisingly, in view of Louis's remarkable ability to suppress his emotions, the news made Louis ill enough to force him to have himself put to bed.

Both Bourgogne's surviving sons caught the disease, in spite of being kept away from their dying but infectious father. The elder, the duc de Bretagne, dauphin and heir to the throne of France for just over a fortnight from 18 February 1712, died on Sunday 7 March. The only survivor of the Bourgogne family was the heir to the Anjou title who also became dauphin on his brother's death, who had also gone down with the measles which had killed his mother, father and brother. He survived, heir to the throne of France, because his governess, the duchesse de Ventadour, simply refused to let a doctor come near him.

The death of the grand Dauphin had radically altered the political situation in Europe. After Bourgogne's death the succession moved to Bretagne too briefly to be of consequence, and then to Anjou, the remaining Bourgogne son born in 1710 and still an infant. While the rest of Europe no doubt now considered that, when Louis came to die, a regency would be possible until Anjou's majority, speculation was inevitably renewed about the likelihood of Anjou's early death. Philip V of Spain, Bourgogne's brother, had come that much nearer the French succession.

All Europe realized that the death of the frail two-year-old Anjou would make Philip V of Spain king of France by divine right, however much he wanted to stay in Spain, and would almost certainly entail another decade of ferment and, probably, war. If the infant Louis failed to survive, and, as seemed not improbable, Philip were to succeed to the French throne, would he abdicate the Spanish one?

Whether he did or did not, the chances of a new war seemed high, although for different reasons. If he did abdicate, who would take over the Spanish empire, with its immense sources of New World wealth? And how would that affect the balance of power in Europe? If he did not, how could Europe avoid a Franco-Spanish bloc? The Tory government elected in England in 1710 wanted to make peace. The Austrians and the Dutch called a conference which met in Utrecht in January 1712.

Meanwhile, it looked as if Eugène might make good his threat to make peace from Versailles when he had taken it. Louis was advised to abandon Versailles and re-establish his headquarters on the Loire, although he resolutely rejected the advice. He would rather rejoin the army and die in battle at the age of seventy-four. His whole personality was supported by the creation of what had become his life's achievement.

The English then came up with a proposal for Philip to cede Spain and the Indies to the duke of Savoy, in return for which Philip would take over Savoy, Piedmont, Montferrat and Nice, and might retain his rights to the throne of France, should the infant great-grandson of the king not survive.[16] Louis was much attracted to this solution, but it became unnecessary when his general, Villars, succeeded in stopping prince Eugène from progressing towards Paris by over-running Denain, on the north-east border, cutting Eugene's communications with his supply base, and enabling Villars to raise the siege of nearby Landrécies, a victory for France which removed the final objections to a peace conference.

A series of treaties signed in 1713 and 1714 are collectively known at the Peace of Utrecht, to which has to be added the Peace of Rastadt between France and Austria in 1714. Most importantly, Philip V renounced any claim to the throne of France in return for recognition as king of Spain. Louis withdrew support for the Stuarts and renounced Nova Scotia and Newfoundland to Britain. The French monopoly on supplying slaves to South America was transferred to Britain and Austria acquired the Spanish Low Countries, Milan, Naples and Sardinia.

The Dutch acquired only the right to occupy the barrier forts in what had been the Spanish Low Countries, and in effect the Spanish empire was partitioned, losing the erstwhile Spanish Netherlands and Milan. Louis was lucky; his grandson remained king of Spain; the north-eastern frontier was upheld; France retained Alsace and Strasbourg, losing only its conquests east of the Rhine; he was even allowed to retain the fishing rights at the mouth of the St Lawrence river.

It seems clear that Louis had had enough of war after Ryswick, and had blundered into the war of the Spanish Succession through a mixture of tactlessness and insensitivity, although on political issues he did not generally lack the required antennae. It is sometimes asserted, and remains just possible, that there was some sort of latent conspiracy to drag Louis into a war which, after the war of the League of Augsburg, might finish France altogether as a major European power. In fact, the strength and riches of the country allowed its remarkable regeneration within a score of years after Louis's death.

Broken by Ryswick, and further humiliated at Utrecht, Louis's feelings in 1714 are difficult to gauge. In 1708, at the age of seventy, Louis was still in reasonably robust health. His emotional resilience appears to have been as great as his physical prowess. The court life had virtually come to a halt, in spite of momentary revivification on the advent of Marie-Adélaïde. According to Saint-Simon, the year of Oudenaarde, 1708, began with 'thanksgivings, fêtes and pleasures'. One is reminded of Voltaire's quip that 'they died of hunger to the sound of Te Deums'. That was the April when Louis sent the ducs de Bourgogne and de Berri to the front. A little later, on 11 July, Louis had ordered a court picnic, an occasion, reports the diarist Philippe Dangeau, celebrated with much joyousness.[17] That was the day the battle began at Oudenaarde.

The court, however, was no longer the festive scene of entertainments, amusements, scandal, gossip and complaints it had once been, partly because of the war, its sadnesses, absences and privations, and partly because the younger members of Louis's extended family found Paris more amusing. Rifts developed at Versailles with the formation of a coterie round the grand Dauphin known as the *cabale de Meudon*. which disliked the duc de Bourgogne, his exaggeratedly ostentatious piety and his moral severity. Vendôme belonged to the dauphin's coterie, while Mme de Maintenon was close to Marie-Adélaïde and her husband, the duc de Bourgogne. The tension between the two parties became very strong when it came to apportioning at court the blame for the disaster of Oudenaarde in 1708.

Marlborough had been dismissed on allegations of peculation, and the English were interested in making peace. This was the point at which Eugène laid siege to Landrécies prior to an attempt to march on Paris. The French general Villars pushed the British back over the Scheldt, where the bridge broke under their weight. About 1,000 men were killed and 1,500 drowned. The death of three successive heirs to the French throne, the joint claims of the Bourbons to France and Spain taken together with the impossibility of uniting the countries under one king, Louis's age and Eugène's defeat at Landécies constituted the most important parameters inside which the Utrecht treaties had to be designed. Matters were not helped by the theology of the Bourbon succession. The death of Anjou would make Philip king of France by divine right, but Philip wanted to stay in Spain. And in the eyes of Louis, the death of Queen Anne would restore the divine right of the house of Stuart to govern England, Scotland and Ireland.

On 3 May 1714 the duc de Berri, youngest brother of the duc de Bourgogne and Philip V, had a hunting accident at Marly. He ruptured a blood vessel in his stomach trying to hold up his horse, which had slipped. He vomited a great deal, was in agonizing pain, and died in the early hours of the following day, 4 May. That left only Anjou of the senior Bourbon line to succeed Louis, aged seventy-five. The senior member of the junior branch was the Philippe, duc d'Orléans, who was the son by Liselotte of Louis's brother, also Philippe, duc d'Orléans, who had died in 1701.

Louis suspected his nephew of libertinism, atheism and poisoning, and in an attempt to keep him away from the throne should Anjou not survive childhood, he had legitimized his two illegitimate sons by Mme de Montespan, his favourite, the duc du Maine and the comte de Toulouse. The necessary measures were ratified by the *parlement* in July 1714. Even at the age of seventy-six, Louis was energetic and forceful. By 1714, it is true, his intellectual powers and grasp of political situations were beginning to dwindle. Louis also established by will a regency council which would fetter the power of his nephew Philippe as regent, making him only *chef de conseil*, bound by a majority vote, although he knew that his wishes were unlikely to be respected. His mother, after all, had thwarted Louis XIII's exactly similar attempt to avoid allowing her to become regent.

It was left to Villars to point out that, after a war which he put at fourteen years, during which the emperor and the king of France had nearly been forced from their capitals and so much of Europe had seen such devastation and death, peace was concluded on much the same terms as could have been negotiated at the outbreak of hostilities.

12

Protestants and Popes

In spite of the suffering, death, economic catastrophe and international demonization which they caused, Louis's military campaigns achieved little for France that could not have been achieved without them. While, in the second half of the seventeenth century, the papacy no longer commanded a military force to be reckoned with, it had not yet abandoned the use of spiritual weapons for political ends. In its generally hostile relations with the papacy, as in its military campaigns, France under Louis XIV achieved nothing that diplomatic negotiations could not have obtained more easily. In other areas of religious policy, European countries, from the 1685 revocation of the 1598 edict of toleration ('edict of Nantes') including France, were still steadily enforcing uniformity of religion as integral to full citizenship.

Yet Louis's dealings with the papacy and with the Huguenots, or what was bitterly but routinely styled by the Catholics in power the 'RPR' (*Religion prétendue réformée*), do significantly illuminate his character. His dealings with both help us understand his attitude to the burgeoning 'enlightenment', heralded by the victory of the *modernes* in the *Querelle des anciens et des modernes* at the end of his reign.

Louis's attitudes towards the Huguenots had very little to do with his attitude towards the papacy.[1] His relations with the Huguenots were the legacy of a complex situation deriving from the need to put an end to the French religious wars of the late sixteenth century.

Louis XIII's father, Henri IV, became a Catholic, but won for the Huguenot colleagues with whom he had fought in battle certain rights to worship publicly, to hold public offices and to educate their children as Huguenots. They were enshrined in the 1598 edict of Nantes. At the time, when the whole of the rest of the Europe looked on unity of religion as essential to social and political unity, and all subscribed to the dictum, *cujus regio, ejus religio,* (whose the region, his the religion)this could not have been envisaged as more than a stop-gap solution.

However, it worked well enough, in spite of the separatist Huguenot uprising of 1617 and the need to crush Huguenot political resistance in La Rochelle and Languedoc which had seemed to Richelieu to threaten the creation of the unified, independent France he wanted. In all matters not threatening the political unity of France, Richelieu's attitude towards the Huguenots had been liberal. The political threat ended with the pacification of 1629, and by the date of the Fronde the Huguenots were on the whole royalist.

At their peak, after counting those in the territory of Béarn conquered in 1620, Huguenots numbered about 1 million, but they were concentrated in the south and south-west where they were sometimes locally in a majority. There was a seepage of converts to Catholicism, like Turenne, and increasing numbers of Huguenots went into exile, so that numbers were declining, to the point at which the revocation of the edict was even at the time widely regarded as pointless. From 1676 a cash incentive was provided to converts. It was as superior of a house run by nuns for 'nouvelles catholiques', little better than a women's prison, that Fénelon first came into prominence.

Louis's hardening attitude to the Huguenots was undoubtedly to some extent a reflection of popular and ecclesiastical pressure. Huguenot places of worship had begun to be closed down since 1659 and a more rigid interpretation of the edict of Nantes had gradually been enforced. Huguenot emigration had been forbidden, and the financial inducements for conversion introduced, but Louis's determination to speed up the suppression of French Protestantism rather than to allow it to erode with time seems to have dated from about 1679, when severe penalties were introduced against relapsed heretics. The special courts to ensure equity in civil disputes between Catholics and Huguenots were closed by the *parlements* of Toulouse and Grenoble, and conversion from Catholicism to Protestantism was made illegal in June 1680.[2]

Politically the Huguenots were no longer a danger when Mazarin died. Why then did Louis gradually increase the pressure on them from the beginning of his personal rule, to start with mostly in petty and often localized regional measures? At first this was often achieved merely by insisting on strict adherence to the terms of the 1598 edict. It is true that there was increasing pressure on him from the provinces, partly on account of Huguenot commercial success. Huguenot communities were tightly organized, supportive of their members, industrious and often contained a high proportion of successful merchants or skilled artisans. Their schools were good, and their literacy rate presumably high.

It is also true that, theologically, they did not believe in that essential tenet of Louis's world view, monarchical succession by divine right. In fact, their most important constitutional theoretician, Althusius, formulated in his 1603 *Politica* the theory of the inalienability of the sovereignty of the people, later to be adopted by Rousseau in the *Social Contract*. Some allowance can perhaps be made for the fact that, even if the Huguenots made no move to interfere with the French state, Louis could not rid his imagination of the spectre of Charles I, whose execution he blamed on the Puritans.

As the pressure increased, in 1681 the Huguenots were forbidden to leave the country, although many still did, and Louvois began his *dragonnades*. The number of soldiers per billeted Huguenot household was entirely at the discretion of the commander of the dragoon company. In practice this came near to being a licence to pillage and rape with impunity. Some stories of the atrocities were no doubt exaggerated, but this was a culture which in the name of law could inflict the most horrific of cruelties as a matter of course. But terrifying atrocities specifically associated with the elimination of Protestantism in France and involving no crime other than that of the exercise of the Huguenot religion are widely attested.

Protests about the *dragonnades* and other cruelties came from countries which accepted Huguenot refugees, and profited by them. There is evidence that Louis was personally aware of and approved of the actual nature of Louvois's *dragonnades*, and there are documented accounts of reports of atrocities being read by him.

[277]

Released from the restraining advice of Colbert, he must be accounted to have been simply indulging his determination to create the most powerful independent nation in Europe, in which everything was unified by being under his control and contributing to his grandeur. His own responsibility was not in the context of specific instances of religious repression, but for the degree of force used in its general enforcement. Europe was in some way being prepared for what was to happen in the Palatinate in 1688–9.

The number of Huguenot temples, as they were called, was reduced by two thirds between Mazarin's death and the revocation, and it has been estimated that the pressures of the *dragonnades,* backed up by two-year *taille* exemptions, produced between a quarter and half a million converts. Over a quarter of the Huguenot population left the country in spite of the orders of the crown. The tax exemptions offered to converts intensified popular hostility to the Huguenots on the eve of the revocation, because they proportionately increased the burden on everyone else, but there was no valid religious reason for the revocation. Bossuet, although he had started his career heavily involved in ecumenical discussions, none the less later regarded the revocation as 'the great work of religion' and 'this triumph of the faith and fine monument to the king's piety'.[3]

Louis had wrongly hoped that the revocation of the edict of toleration would ingratiate him with the papacy, while Clement X wrongly supposed that religious reasons might persuade Louis to join in a common front against the Turks. Louis no doubt also hoped to repay his silent contract with the clergy which, in return for tax exemption, made over to him a *don gratuit,* but called for the total Catholicization of France. He hoped to lessen the hostility of Innocent XI, and he may have hoped to atone for his refusal to help out the Austrians when Vienna was being besieged by the Turks in 1683. He can scarcely have been hoping to achieve the salvation of the Huguenots by their conversion, because the devout who were concerned with founding or promoting the new religious orders and congregations of the 'Catholic revival' earlier in the century had been less concerned with missions to the unconverted, as in the New World or the far east, as with the spiritual reforms required within the church and the succour of the poor, the sick and the suffering.[4] This seems to have been true even of the Compagnie du Saint-Sacrement, much as it worked for the conversion of the Huguenots.

Louis's alliances with Protestant powers like Sweden show that he cannot have been primarily concerned in the revocation with the establishment of a Catholic Europe for the glory of God, as Gregory XV had been. Perhaps he deluded himself by thinking that he was. 'I am persuaded,' he wrote on 7 November 1685, 'that God will consummate in his glory the work which he has inspired in me'.[5] Not only, as his quoted utterance makes clear, might God well be grateful for what Louis had done for him, but God would achieve his purposes by consummating what he inspired Louis to commence. Such a view both justified to Louis whatever he believed right in the matter of religious policy, and elevated its status to the supernatural, even if he was deceiving himself. He was in the 1680s still trapped in the role in which the painters and sculptors of the baroque had cast him, exaggerated, magnified, distorted to maximum tension in the interests of inspiring awe, status and grandeur, in as strongly lit an unachievable and certainly as unsustainable a pose as any to be found in a van Dyck painting.

The revocation of the edict of Nantes took place on 15 October 1685 and was replaced by an 'edict of Fontainebleau' of the same month. There would no more special status for Huguenots, but the anti-Huguenot legislation prohibiting their assemblies, disadvantaging them in the courts and hindering their access to the liberal professions would continue, as did the *dragonnades*, although Innocent XI, Fénelon and Mme de Maintenon all condemned them. Mme de Sévigné, on the other hand, shared the emphatic general enthusiasm in a letter to Bussy of 28 October 1685:

> The dragoons have been excellent missionaries so far; the preachers being sent at the moment will finish off their work. You will no doubt have seen the edict by which the king revokes the edict of Nantes. Nothing is better than all it contains, and no king ever has done or ever will do anything better.

Whether fired by loyalty or devotion, that sentiment was intensified as one descended the social scale.

Paradoxically, Louis's relations with the papacy were less complicated by religious issues than by his relations with the Huguenots, where the core issues concerned belief and the practice of Huguenot forms of worship. There had necessarily always been tension between the holders of temporal and the holders of spiritual power in Christendom wherever sacred and secular functions were separated. In the west the tension waxed and waned for a millennium before it became monodirectional with the emergence of the very large nation states in the late fifteenth century.

The detailed compromises were chiefly dictated by financial considerations as the sacred and secular powers moved apart. The concordat of Bologna concluded in 1516 between Leo X and François I of France had theoretically regulated the relationship in France, but its enforcement had become sporadic, and the seventeenth century had seen a growing 'Gallican' pressure for more autonomy for the French church. It is against the background of the need in changing circumstances to arrive at a reasonable division of income and authority that the relationships between Louis and a succession of popes must be understood. Bishops and other ecclesiastical dignitaries needed to be appointed by both ecclesiastical and by civil authorities because they had both ecclesiastical and civil functions. Church and state in seventeenth-century France each had a stranglehold on senior ecclesiastical appointments.

The concordat had largely fallen into abeyance. Gallican ecclesiastics sought to promote the autonomy of the French church by using delegated ecclesiastical jurisdicticiton and the apostolic succession of its own bishops to confer on priests and bishops the ordination without which there could be no mass, no power of transubstantiation, no sacraments. The opposite 'ultramontane' tendency inclined to leave all matters involving ecclesiastical juris-diction to Rome and to regard all ecclesiastical jurisdiction, even episcopal, as delegated, and therefore subject to revocation, by the pope. Louis's relationships with the papacy were entirely governed by clashes often of the minutiae of dual authority, and conducted through the interplay of Gallican and 'ultramontane' pressures, or other power plays involving, in Louis's view, the grandeur of France.

Papal relations had not been good under Mazarin, who took his revenge on Alexander VII for harbouring cardinal de Retz after his escape from France by supporting the Farnese and the Este familes in their claims to papal territories, and by excluding the pope from any participation in the peace of the Pyrénées of 7 November 1659. Already shut out from the treaties of Westphalia, the new exclusion meant that the papacy had finally been forced back into its spiritual and diplomatic role in European affairs. It was no longer considered the territorial power of political consequence that it had been as recently as thirty years previously. The Roman curia retaliated by refusing to extend the right of the French king to nominate to benefices outside the territories which François I had controlled when the Concordat of Bologna was drawn up in 1516. This meant also that he was not entitled to the income from those benefices whenever they were vacant.

In 1662 Louis had surprised everyone by sending Charles de Créqui as ambassador to the papal curia.[6] Créqui's real task, in which he was successful, was to prepare for the next conclave and the election of a pope favourable to France. He arrived at the French embassy, then as now the Palazzo Farnese, very near the barracks of the pope's Corsican guard. By the end of July cardinal Chigi, the pope's nephew with whom Créqui's mother is improbably rumoured to have had an affair, was predicting trouble between Créqui's household and the Corsicans.

Three Corsican guards and three Frenchmen met in the street in front of the embassy, at least one group having had too much to drink. There was a quarrel. Swords were drawn, shots were fired and reinforcements arrived from both sides, with a crowd hostile to the French. Créqui returned in the middle of the uproar, and shortly afterwards came out on to the central balcony, where he was shot at. His wife said it was by five pistols. There were several deaths, and Créqui's diplomatic immunity had no doubt been infringed. The Holy See's responsibility for the behaviour of its guards is less certain.

Louis demanded an immediate apology, and Chigi offered to call on Créqui provided he could be assured that he would not be subject to discourtesy, thereby further insulting Créqui. Five days later he did call to apologize on behalf of Alexander VII, arguing that the Corsican guards were not under papal control. They were, however, in papal employ, and Créqui's demand for reparations was met by the assurance that a committee was considering the matter. The Corsican command knew who was guilty, but any Corsicans who wished to were allowed to leave Rome. Louis wrote an exceedingly intemperate letter, saying that no one who represented his dignity should be exposed to such outrages, unequalled even by 'the barbarians themselves'. There was, however, nothing much he could do about it, 'we think it best to leave to your own discretion those decisions in accordance with which ours will be guided.'[7] Letters with endings as weak as that are better not sent, especially not from a twenty-three-year-old king to a sixty-three-year-old pontiff.

Louis withdrew Créqui, and told the papal nuncio to leave Paris. He also occupied the ancient papal enclave of Avignon and the surrounding comtat Venaissin. Alexander then yielded, and agreement was reached in a treaty of 12 February 1664. A monument in the shape of a pyramid with an inscription injurious to Corsicans was put up opposite the Corsican barracks. Chigi was sent to Paris as a special nuncio, arriving with a splendid household and was as splendidly greeted, but by this date Colbert was in overall charge and foreign affairs were entrusted to Hugues de Lionne.

Louis insisted on receiving the legate at Fontainebleau rather than pay him the formal compliment of returning to Paris. It was as far as he was allowed to go in offensiveness. The *Gazette* crowed in appropriate fashion, 'satisfaction proportionate to the insult . . . full atonement'. The monument was quietly taken down in 1669, when the Gobelins began weaving a tapestry of the apology at Fontainebleau. It says something about Louis that he had two tapestries woven depicting foreign potentates making formal apologies. More significantly, the restraints put on Louis's behaviour were sufficient to allow the Holy See to play one of its key cards by refusing to provide new bishops with jurisdiction.

It had been in December 1660 that Louis, at Mazarin's request, had called the council of the assembly of the clergy to the Louvre, where Mazarin informed them that it had been decided to eliminate all traces of Jansenism from the kingdom. On 1 February 1661 the assembly decided to impose signature of the formulary agreed in 1657 and police action was taken during the summer ordering that the Paris house of the convent of Port-Royal should send its boarders home. Some, to the annoyance of the court and the amusement of everyone else, were hurriedly given the veil. The male *solitaires* had to disperse, and various doors were bricked up, but the formulary still admitted condemnation of the five propositions without any admission that they were in *Augustinus*. There were pamphlets, and disappearances to avoid the serving of a *lettre de cachet*.

However, the formulary was attacked as inadequate, since it allowed the crucial reservation that the propositions were not in

Augustinus. It was quashed by the council of state on 14 July, and condemned in Rome on 1 August 1662, less than three weeks before the Créqui incident. A new formulary was prepared and signed by the grand vicars of Paris on 31 October, but it needed registration and approval by ecclesiastical authority. Harassment of the nuns continued sporadically, but the Paris theology faculty was supporting strongly Gallican theses which alienated Rome, Louis was pressing for heavy reparations for the Créqui incident, and the archbishop of Paris was still Retz in Rome.

Orthodoxy had been made safe by the condemnation of the five propositions, which the nuns, Pascal and Arnauld all accepted, and Rome was not going to help Louis out with the suppression of a convent of perfectly harmless nuns who did not understand the theology, but merely irritated Louis's desire for control of the ecclesiastical sector in his kingdom, in addition to all the others. Retz finally resigned his archbishopric on 14 February 1662. His successor was Pierre de Marca, who had drawn up the original, inadequate formulary, but who died on 29 June 1662, three days after receiving his bulls of appointment, and two months before the Créqui incident. His successor, Hardouin de Beaumont de Péréfixe, was later to become a laughing stock in his efforts to close Port-Royal. For over six months the nuns ran circles round him, so much so that he lost the archiepiscopal temper, resorted to crass abuse, and was forced to change carriages in the street to avoid being publicly laughed at as he arrived yet again with paper and ink to cajole or bully a few more nuns to sign the formulary.[8]

In the meanwhile, however, Rome was not going to surrender any aces. Péréfixe was validly nominated to his see by Louis, but he had no jurisdiction to act as archbishop until it was conferred by his Roman bulls, and Alexander VII simply did not issue them. There was no ordinary or delegated ecclesiastical jurisdiction in the archiepiscopal see of Paris between the death of Marca on 29 June 1662 and the agreement between Louis and Alexander VII of 12 February 1664. Péréfixe's bulls arrived on 10 April 1664.

On 19 April, Louis made the signature of the revised formulary mandatory for everyone in university or ecclesiastical life or in receipt of a benefice. In the end the nuns were dispersed to other convents, with other nuns brought in to Port-Royal. Those nuns from Port-Royal who still resolutely refused to sign, even if they had been dispersed to other convents, were finally sent to Port-Royal-des-Champs in the Chevreuse valley to the south-west of Paris, where they were kept under guard and without the sacraments from July 1665 to February 1669.

There had not been any serious theological debate since January 1656 when Arnauld was stripped of his doctorate for denying that Saint Peter sinned because the grace not to was not available to him. Arnauld, a skilful and courageous lawyer, had successfully turned a serious theological debate into an absurd dispute about whether or not there were five sentences in a book. Louis had used his own Gallican authority to impose the formulary, for which, even after Péréfixe had received his bulls, Roman authority was required.

A pamphlet of Arnauld and Nicole questioning his authority to impose the formulary finally forced him to write to Alexander VII, who congratulated him on his zeal, sent yet another formulary, but rebuked the king by informing him that he would henceforward act directly on his own papal authority when it came to formularies of orthodoxy. Alexander sent this brief dated 16 December 1664, knowing perfectly well that it was insufficient authority and would make Louis formally recognize he had no authority in spiritual matters. Louis needed more than a brief, and was made to ask formally for a bull. Alexander recognized the capitulation by issuing the bull *Regiminis apostolici* on 25 February 1665.

Most of the clergy found ways of eluding the direct and un-modified signature, but four bishops issued pastoral guidance allowing reservation on the question of whether the propositions were or were not in *Augustinus*. Implicitly, they were asserting that the pope was wrong, and that therefore in this matter the Gallican church could make its own decision. Louis, naturally, was strongly on the Gallican side, but the pastoral instructions of the four bishops were condemned by the Holy Office in January 1667, and a commission of nine bishops was appointed on 22 April to bring the four into line or to face degradation.

Alexander then died on 22 May, and his successor, Clement IX, and Louis XIV both sought peace. In 1668, after negotiations between Lionne and the nuncio, the pope tacitly conceded the question of fact: he did not have the right to impose assent to the proposition that the five propositions were in *Augustinus*. Signatures with reservation on the point of fact were now acceptable. The *conseil d'en-haut* accepted this position on 23 October 1668, and the next day Louis received Arnauld, who had been in semi-hiding for four years. 'Semi-hiding' was a device to which recourse was quite often had. It meant that the fugitive's whereabouts were easily discoverable but that the police would not look too hard, for instance to deliver a *lettre de cachet*. However, any public activity by the fugitive would attract arrest. Clement IX's brief to the four bishops was signed on 19 January 1669, and on 13 February the nuns submitted in a form accepted as satisfactory. Five days later the interdict and corporate excommunication were lifted, and the two communities, Port-Royal and Port-Royal-des-champs, were permitted to return to normal activities and given subsidies denoting discriminatory degrees of pardon.

Trouble, however, broke out again. Louis managed to mislead the curia that his Dutch war was for the restoration of Catholicism, and at first attracted papal support. By the summer of 1674, however, Clement X, who had immediately followed Clement IX, realized that he had been deceived. Louis XIV, engaged in the Dutch war, was not remotely interested in Clement's organization of an anti-Turkish front. The Spanish ambassador noted in 1681 that Louis treated the pope as if he were merely his 'first chaplain'.[9] Louis also squeezed the church for revenue to support the war by a series of requisitions and confiscations.

Louis had inherited the right known as the *régale*, conceived feudally but ratified by the 1516 concordat, to the income from vacant benefices (*régale temporelle*) and to nominate to non-parochial, non-exempt benefices (*régale spirituelle*). On 10 April 1673 and 2 April 1675 Louis issued edicts extending this lucrative right from the feudal territories which had been fiefs of the fifteenth-century kings to all territories subsequently incorporated into France, which included Brittany, Provence and Béarn. Clement X did nothing, but two bishops of Augustinian views, Nicolas Pavillon of Alet and François-Etienne de Caulet of Pamiers, alone among the French episcopy, opposed this Gallican move, which enhanced the autonomy of the French church.

Pavillon died in 1677, after appealing to the new pope, Innocent XI, elected in 1676. The Roman curia, hitherto ill-informed about the affair, decided to oppose Louis's pretensions. Pavillon died within days of receiving the reply, but Caulet had also written to the pope on 26 October, and Innocent wrote letters of increasing firmness to Louis on 12 March 1678, 19 July, and 29 December 1679 demanding the annulment of the extension of the *régale* proclaimed in 1673 and 1675. Then from the consistory of 17 January 1681, Innocent issued a formal condemnation of Louis.

Tension had been building up outside the matter of the *régale*.[10] Arnauld de Pomponne, regarded as too conciliatory on a number of issues, had been replaced at foreign affairs by Colbert de Croissy in November 1679. Louis attempted to remove the exemption from episcopal jurisdiction from which the major religious orders benefited. If they had been founded before the approval of the Jesuit Institutes in 1540, they were responsible directly to the pope. The French episcopate, with the exception of Caulet, condemned by his own metropolitan at Toulouse, was solidly behind Louis, who summoned an extraordinary assembly of the clergy on 31 October 1681, which on 3 February 1682 accepted Louis's original edict of 1673.

On 19 March 1682 the assembly, whose rhetorical heat appears to have disturbed Louis himself, promulgated its celebrated *Declaratio* containing the famous four Gallican articles. They were drawn up by Bossuet, and represented a less anti-papal view than that of the chancellor, Le Tellier, and his son, now secretary of state for war, Louvois. The first stated that the pope had no authority to interfere in any way with the temporal sovereign's exercise of temporal power; the second recognized the pope's spiritual powers, subject to the superior authority of a general council; the third affirmed that even papal spiritual authority was limited by custom, tradition and consent; and the fourth reiterated that, even in matters of faith, papal decrees are irreformable only if they have the consent of the church.[11]

Innocent XI rejected the declaration of the clergy of 3 February 1682 accepting Louis's original edict of 1673 (but not at this stage the articles themselves) and refused to provide those appointed to bishoprics with the necessary jurisdiction if they had subscribed to them. That led to thirty-three vacant sees in France by January 1688. Innocent XI was aggravated by the actual reduction of Gallican feeling to a formal statement of principles, and was not mollified by the revocation of the edict of Nantes in 1685. He approved of it while deploring the measures which accompanied it.

Innocent XI's own rigorous reform programme had included a purge to elevate the appalling standards of public decency into which the city of Rome had lapsed. This had led to the removal of the right of embassies to grant asylum to law-breakers. The French alone refused to accept the new ruling, although the pope had declared that he would refuse to receive any new ambassador who did not explicitly accept the suppression of the right to grant asylum.

When the French ambassador to Rome, the duc d'Estrées, brother of the cardinal, died there on 30 January 1687, the pope suppressed the French diplomatic immunity in a bull dated 12 May under the sanction of excommunication. Louis appointed Henri-Charles Beaumanoir, marquis de Lavardin his new ambassador, and instructed him to behave as if the French exemption still existed. He arrived in Rome on 16 November at the head of a hundred troops. The pope forbade any priest to say mass if Lavardin was present, and when Lavardin received communion that Christmas at the French church, which was therefore put under interdict, the pope had little choice but to excommunicate Lavardin. Lavardin protested that he had only been following Louis's orders. What made matters worse was that Louis was privately told in January 1688 that the excommunication extended to himself and his ministers.

Innocent XI followed up the excommunication, which was never made public, with the affair of the archbishopric of Cologne.[12] Louis's candidate was Cardinal William Egon von Fürstenberg, bishop of Strasbourg, who had long been acting as assistant to the now elderly archbishop of Cologne, but in French pay. The emperor's candidate was Joseph-Clement of Bavaria. Neither candidate had the majority he needed when the canons voted for a successor in chapter on 19 July 1688.[13]

Innocent XI, to whom the choice was therefore left, decided in favour of seventeen-year-old Joseph Clement of Bavaria, bishop of Freising and Regensburg although not yet a priest, but the nephew of the deceased archbishop, Maximilian Henry of Bavaria, who had died on 3 June.[14] He was also the brother of Maximilian-Emanuel, who was besieging Belgrade in an attempt heavily supported by the pope to push the Turks back still further to the east. Louis regarded the nomination of Joseph Clement as a hostile act, and broke off relations with Rome. They would not be restored until 1693. Meanwhile Louis retaliated by again seizing Avignon and the comtat, which the *parlement* of Provence declared reintegrated into the kingdom of France, and Louis sent his troops to occupy Cologne, while the grand Dauphin besieged Philippsburg.

Neither Louis nor the pope wanted to take matters to war between them or to a French schism.[15] Rome put out feelers for a deal involving the appointment of Egon von Fürstenberg in return for abandonment of the right to give asylum in Rome and the replacement of Lavardin, but Louis turned it down. Louis then sent to Rome the marquis de Chamlay, a close personal friend on whom Louis had come to rely for political advice, with instructions from Louvois to exaggerate the dangers of non-compliance with French demands, but Innocent would not receive him, just as Louis would not himself receive the nuncio sent to Paris. The situation was dangerous, since the imminent fall of Belgrade would release the emperor's troops for action in the Rhineland.

There were parties giving counsel in both Verssailles and Rome which saw the pressing need for reconciliation between Louis and the Holy See. The grand Dauphin, his wife and, even more, Mme de Maintenon were pressing for a resolution of the hostility but, on the other hand, Louis's *conseil de conscience*, meeting on Fridays to discuss ecclesiastical affairs and appointments, consisted of the hawkish François de Harlay de Champvallon, successor to Péréfixe as archbishop of Paris in 1671, and Louis's only slightly milder Jesuit confessor, Père de la Chaise.

When Innocent XI died on 12 August 1689, he was succeeded by Alexander VIII, who made partially successful efforts to break the deadlock. Louis's position had weakened since James II late in 1688 abandoned the English throne and William and Mary were established sovereigns in 1689. Louis handed back Avignon and the comtat Venaissin and abandoned extravagant claims to grant asylum in Rome, while the pope received the French ambassador and created another French cardinal against the emperor's wishes and despite his participation in the 1682 clergy assembly. He stood firm, however, against providing with their bulls bishops appointed by Louis unless they repudiated the four Gallican articles.[16]

The quarrel then broke out again. The moves towards reconciliation had proved inadequate in France, but sufficient to aggravate the emperor. Alexander's failure to elevate Leopold's candidates to the cardinalate and diminution of subsidies for the Turkish war caused Leopold to withdraw his ambassador to the Holy See. Meanwhile, in a constitution drafted on 4 August 1690, but published only on 31 January 1691 after mediation by Mme de Maintenon had failed, Alexander repudiated the four articles and annulled the concession by which the *régale* was extended to territories currently French but which had not been part of France in 1516.

Alexander VIII died on 1 February 1691 and was succeeded in July by Innocent XII, under whom matters were finally resolved and the French hierarchy legitimized. Seignelay, Colbert's son and from 1689 himself a minister, had in 1688 suggested calling in Fénelon, then simply a fast rising young ecclesiastic about to be appointed tutor to the children of the grand Dauphin. Fénelon wrote a skilfully judged memoir, probably in October 1688, starting with a list of historical papal usurpations, from personal infallibility to interference in the temporal domain of princes and accepting the official French view that Innocent XI was responsible for the League of Augsburg.

He then moved on to counsel calm and moderation, suggesting harmless concessions and criticizing the erection of Paris into its own archdiocese in 1622 as necessarily conducive to schism. He pointed out that some of the more aggressive positions taken in French official pronouncements were undoubtedly heretical. He was particularly contemptuous of ill-tempered attacks on the papal ownership of Avignon and the comtat Venaissin. It was Fénelon's memoir, joined to the more persuasive argument that Protestant victory in England raised dangers of a mass relapse of French 'new converts' into Calvinism, which persuaded Louis to settle.

The pope ratified the French bishops appointed by Louis since 1682 who had not taken part in the assembly of 1682. Louis then revoked the declaration that obliged the bishops to subscribe to the four articles, and the bishops wrote to retract their signatures, at which Innocent XII formalized their canonical institution. He also accepted the extension of the *régale* to the whole of current French territory. The final solution satisfied Louis's demand for an extension of the *régale* which had been the initial issue in 1673 and would have been reached then, had it not been called into question by the two prelates of strongly Augustinian views, Pavillon and Caulet, who wished to influence Louis's ecclesiastical policy with regard to Jansenism.

It was intellectually if not politically easy enough to condemn Jansenism as a doctrine. It was almost impossible to condemn Jansenism as a pure spirituality unless it found expression in books, rites, or civically unacceptable activities. For Saint-Cyran the link between the devotional attitudes he adopted in the 1630s and the propositions included or implied in the 1640 posthumous *Augustinus* had been factitious and tenuous, but there were personal friendships and loyalties to link the spirituality to the book. Indeed, it is curious how strong a role personal loyalties rather than credal commitments played in the whole history of Jansenism. It seems very unlikely that Pascal or Racine ever read the book, although they both elected to be buried at Port-Royal-des-Champs, and it is next to certain that none of the Port-Royal nuns had read the book or understood the doctrinal niceties of the disputes it caused.

What happened was that Louis quite defensibly felt that the spiritual and devotional attitudes were forming round a hard core of theologians and directors who, whether or not they totally followed the theological arguments, were at the centre of a largely aristocratic, religiously deviant, and socially disruptive movement which menaced the religious and social cohesion of the kingdom, and needed therefore to be suppressed. The 'peace of the church' lasted from 1668, when the remnant of nuns who refused to sign the formulary was removed to Port-Royal-des-Champs, to 1679, when Louis decided that the monastery was still a hotbed of dissidence, and was attracting too many pilgrims. Arnauld, tipped off in time, joined Nicole in Brussels on his way to the Dutch Republic, leaving Paris on 18 June 1679. It is possible that, had he chosen to go to Rome, he would have been given a cardinal's hat.

The community at Port-Royal-des-Champs was slowly suppressed. More signatures to protestations of orthodoxy were exacted. Barcos's posthumous *Exposition de la foi* was condemned in 1696; the community was forbidden to elect an abbess in 1706; its possessions were removed to Port-Royal in Paris in February 1707; the community was dispersed. In June, the buildings were razed to prevent pilgrimages.

However, both as a theology and as a spirituality Jansenism was to know a renaissance before the end of Louis's reign. The Oratorians had developed Bérulle's spirituality not only in the direction of optimistic neoplatonism represented by Descartes and Malebranche, but also on the basis of the view of Condren, second general of the Oratory, that spirituaal progress consisted of nature's annihilation and replacement by a life of grace. Bérulle's disciple, Gibieuf, had produced the matching theology, although *Augustinus* formally repudiated his terminology, and some Oratorians adopted a spirituality very near to that of Saint-Cyran. Among them was Pasquier Quesnel, who published in 1692 the revision of a much-praised 1671 *L'Abrégé de la morale de l'Evangile* now known as the *Réflexions morales,* which the new archbishop of Paris from 1695, Louise-Antoine, cardinal de Noailles, had formally approved before his elevation. It was to be condemned as Jansenist by Clement XI on 13 July 1708.

Quesnel had gone into exile in the Spanish Low Countries in 1684. The Jesuits denounced Quesnel's work as Jansenist, and he was arrested in the Low Countries and imprisoned in 1703, when his papers showed that he was undoubtedly at the centre of a Jansenist network which, because it was also largely Gallican, put Louis in something of a dilemma. However, the network also showed that the 'Jansenism' at the centre of which was Quesnel did regard itself as above pope, king and law, and was triply subversive of social order.

Louis persuaded Clement XI to issue on 15 July 1705 the bull *Vineam Domini* condemning the view that, while condemning the five propositions allegedly taken from *Augustinus,* it was legitimate to maintain a 'respectful silence' about their actual presence in the book. Louis instructed the assembly of the clergy of 1705 to adopt it immediately and had it registered with the Paris *parlement.* He could have let the matter rest there, having after all a major war on his hands, but he pressed for a further condemnation of 101 propositions from Quesnel's book, which Clement XI duly supplied in the constitution *Unigenitus Dei Filius* of 8 September 1713.[17] That document changed the meaning of the word 'constitution' in French. Historians faced with it in the context of eighteenth-century political theory have sometimes failed to realize that the French word belongs not to the realms of political theory, but refers to a single papal condemnation.

13

Character, Health and Death

Was Louis cruel? Cruel is not quite the right word, although the answer is nearer yes than no. Surrounded by court and family, he would bully. In spite of the ease Louis felt with the young pupils at Saint-Cyr, and the charm he lavished on them, the bullying tendency manifested itself elsewhere in all sorts of ways, from apparently arbitrary decrees of exile, to a refusal to entertain military promotion for those whom 'he did not know', including those members of the court who did not attend it, or of whose behaviour he did not approve.

He bullied the dauphin, abandoned his son by Louise, the comte de Vermandois, who as a boy was mixed up in a 'homosexual' scandal. He bullied in quite trivial matters, from keeping his discarded mistress, Mlle de la Vallière, at court when his new love, Mme de Montespan, was already installed, to failing to re-arrange the accommodation, so that he had to walk through the apartments of the abandoned Louise to visit Mme de Montespan. The pattern repeats itself from flinging open windows while Mme de Maintenon stayed huddled in blankets, and even to subjecting his wife and mistress not only to travelling together in his coach, but to refusing them any chance to relieve themselves on long journeys. They did not dare betray weakness by asking. Women, too, were expected to be up and about within forty-eight hours of giving birth.

The way in which requests for invitations to Marly were processed and a hundred other details reinforce the impression that it was the inner uncertainty within the outer shell of the glorious Louis le Grand which bred a deeply corrosive need to demonstrate power over others by enforcing excessively complex indications of social rank in all its minute gradations, dependent on caste and precise positioning on the ladder of royal favour. Less trivial as a means of building self-confidence of course is the whipping of the woman who shouted abuse after her son had died helping to build Versailles, or the execution of the old *frondeur* who had offered food and shelter to a lost court hunting party.

For the sake of France, its unity, its power and its standing among nations, he would murder, starve, raze and destroy, but think himself right, generally even obliged to act as he did in defence of the divine authority he had been brought up to believe it was was his duty to exercise. He believed his authority in France superior to that of the pope in all but uniquely spiritual matters. He cannot be excused on grounds of insensitivity or stupidity, because he was neither insensitive nor stupid. He was assiduous in the performance of his monarchical duties as ruler of France and, in spite of the lapses, generally possessed the enviable self-control required for the dissimulation demanded by his circumstances.

Louis's brother, Philippe, father of the duc de Chartres, had been furious with Louis over Louis's refusal to recognize his son's merits, and to give him military honours. Chartres, too, was clearly more gifted and more intelligent than du Maine but, bored and frustrated at court, was beginning to team up with Conti and to behave in scandal-generating ways the family could ill afford. The duchesse de Chartres complained to her father, the king, about her husband's behaviour, and in 1701 Louis upbraided his brother who spiritedly answered back that Louis was not in any position to complain if others flaunted their mistresses at court. He mentioned the occasion on which Louis had taken two mistresses, Louise and Athénaïs to Flanders in the same coach as the queen. This can be added to the other occasions on which Louis lost his temper, showing extreme anger. There was shouting. A servant came in to point out that people were listening outside. Philippe lowered his tone but heightened his attack. Had not Louis lured Chartres into a ghastly marriage with his own daughter? Louis said he would cut off Philippe's allowance.

Dinner was served, with Philippe red in the face. Louis said he ought to be bled and threatened to have it done there and then, if necessary by force, but they calmed down and ate a huge meal. Philippe went back to Saint-Cloud, but later that night a messenger arrived from the duc de Chartres that his father was ill. Louis, still annoyed with Philippe, took no notice and went to bed after supper. At three in the morning another messenger arrived. Louis and Mme de Maintenon hurried to Saint-Cloud. Philippe was unconscious, having collapsed at supper. Liselotte had been in bed with a cold and Philippe had just had time to call her. There was nothing Louis could do, so he returned home. Philippe died that night, and Louis, guilt-ridden, told Chartres henceforward to regard him as his father and showered him with gifts.

Liselotte was upset at her husband's death, although she had never been in love with him, and had the presence of mind to go through his papers, burning everything with gay associations. She detested the prospect of relegation to a convent, being barely a convert to Catholicism, and faced up to the need to make her peace with Mme de Maintenon, knowing that Mme de Maintenon had been informed of the disparaging material about her contained in Liselotte's German letters, including speculation about whether Mme de Maintenon was the king's wife or his mistress. Mme de Maintenon actually showed Liselotte one of the more imprudent letters she had written, particularly in what concerned the misery of the people of France. Mme de Maintenon did, however, as Liselotte requested, arrange for her to stay on at Versailles.

1661 had been the year of Mazarin's death, the carrousel, the conception and birth of the dauphin and Louis's twenty-third birthday. He was presiding over his council with no first minister, and was sufficiently insecure to be exceedingly touchy about having his dignity acknowledged as Europe's most important king. In London, his ambassador, the comte Godefroy d'Estrades, to no one's great surprise, found relations with the Spanish ambassador difficult.

That July, a special ambassador arrived in London from Venice. Both French and Spanish ambassadors accepted the suggestion from Charles II that, in order to avoid conflicting claims to precedence, neither should send their coaches to accompany the procession. Louis was furious, writing a curt reprimand to d'Estrades from Fontainebleau on 13 August to complain at the parity accorded by Charles II to the Spanish ambassador, and at the acceptance of that parity by d'Estrades. In September, Sweden sent a new ambassador.

Samuel Pepys had heard on 30 September that there was going to be 'a fray' that day between French and Spanish ambassadors, with which the English should have nothing to do.

The Spanish won. Their coach was guarded by fifty drawn swords, their harnesses lined with chains to stop them being cut, and it occupied the most advantageous position. Every horse, the coach and the coachman was guarded. Three French coach horses were killed. Choisy says that six Frenchmen were killed and twenty-three wounded, and Pepys says 'one or two of the Spaniards and one Englishman were also killed 'by a bullet' .

Louis received the news at Fontainebleau after returning from Fouquet's arrest. Brienne received it and went straight to the king who had just begun his supper at eleven p.m. Louis, furious, marched Brienne to the queen's apartment to have the despatch read, and then made injurious remarks to her about her father, whose ambassador the Spaniard was. The normally meek queen herself rose in anger at her husband, who would not return to his supper. Brienne remarks that he had hardly even seen Louis angry except for this occasion. Louis swore on the spot that he would enforce his ambassador's title to precedence in every court in Europe, told the Spanish ambassador to leave France and withdrew his own from Madrid. He even threatened to renew the war with Spain. Philip IV of Spain sent Fuentes as special ambassador to make an apology formally accepted on 24 March 1662 in the newly decorated Louvre. Henceforward Spanish ambassadors would yield precedence to French ones. A dozen years later Louis had the apology commemorated in a tapestry.

The London fracas had nothing to do with the pope, but showed how hard Louis's lack of self-confidence was driving him. He desperately needed to satisfy the aspiration implanted in him to be acknowledged as Europe's grandest monarch, which naturally made him sensitive to the dignity of his ambassadors to a degree even in 1661 regarded as risible.

But by a training, whose consequences were not foreseen by those responsible for it, Louis united Europe against France as Mazarin or Colbert would never have done, and inaugurated with his policies in the Palatinate a hatred of France east of the Rhine whose final ripples, now happily dying away, are still in certain lights discernible. He picked his own evil genius, Louvois, but had ample opportunity to rein in the excessive aggressivity with which Louvois implemented his policies.

As Louis grew older, he mellowed, and the image-making mechanisms set up by Colbert began to creak with the military reversals. On his devoutly Christian deathbed, the feelings of insecurity removed by the lack of any further need to sustain an impossible role, Louis virtually recanted. He recommended to his child successor policies which were the antithesis of those he himself had followed.

Before that, however, Louis had become worse tempered, and even more authoritarian, tyrannically imposing fierce discipline, even if he was less aggressive than during the Dutch war. He needed to impose discipline on his troops, but he had had burnt those caught looting what they had been told to destroy,[1] and in 1683 imposed a horrendous degree of censorship on printed material. It was measures such as these and the razing of the Palatinate towns that made inevitable the eighteenth-century invention of international law.[2]

Psychologically speaking, Louis's remarkable character developed under the twin constraints of pervading emotional insecurity, which he notably attempted to assuage whether in womanizing, or warfare, or petty domestic bullying, and the tyrannical powers thrust on him by Mazarin and Anne of Austria, and intended to protect him from undergoing, as they had undergone, the horrors of the Fronde. All his attitudes and activities derived from the grafting of immense personal power on to a deep-seated failure of self-confidence. This remains true whether the environment was his intimate family, his wider court, or the vast theatre of Europe's power plays. The insecurity was the natural result of the devoted affections of an over-protective mother, a need for guilt-provoking secrecy and dis-simulation about his relationship with Mazarin, and a feeling of inadequacy at the role of Sun King which Colbert needed him to play.

His ability to conceal both physical and emotional pain suggest that he took a necessarily cultivated discretion to the lengths of almost uncanny impassivity, as does his apparent insensitivity to the discomfort, or much worse, which he inflicted on others. There is very little evidence of what, except for anger and contempt, he ever actually felt, although there are occasional accounts of tears, as of joy on the revelation to the court that Carlos II had nominated

Philippe d'Anjou as his heir to the Spanish throne, or at grief when he received the procession bringing viaticum to the dying Marie-Adélaïde, or of strong emotion, as when he stayed up all night to help the dauphine through her labour at the birth of the duc de Bourgogne. He was saddened by the family deaths that occurred towards the end of his life, as he was by military reversals, but did not show signs of emotional upset. Mme de Maintenon says he told her that he was near to tears on seeing the physical change that preceded the death of the grand Dauphin in 1711.

When on 30 July 1683 Maria-Teresa died, in the arms of Mme de Maintenon, did Louis really say, 'Poor woman, it's the only time she has ever given me any trouble'? Can even his disastrous upbringing have made him as self-obsessed as that? And what are we to make of his reaction to Ramillies, 'God seems to have forgotten all I have done for him', a sentiment which could never have crossed Fénelon's mind.[3]

Louis's health was robust.[4] Antoine Vallot, premier royal physician from 1652, initiated a medical journal of Louis's illnesses and treatments which was kept from 1652 to 1711. We therefore know in some detail about all the aches and pains he suffered and the treatments to which he was subjected – although since Louis himself had, and used, access to this medical diary, dry narrative is mixed with flattery and prudence. The diary incidentally expresses the hope that Louis had inherited the vigour of his mother, rather than the sickliness of Louis XIII, his presumed father.

Vallot was from the Montpellier school which had adopted Islamic elements into its pharmacopoeia, and relied on chemical drugs and antimony for purgative medicinal purposes. Purges, enemas, emetics and bleeding were the major remedies available in different proportions for every ailment, while the Paris school stuck to mainly herbal purges, often prescribing something no stronger than rhubarb or a herbal infusion. Guy Patin, who made himself spokesman for the Paris faculty of medicine, believed in the strictest Galenic orthodoxy and, like Descartes, simply refused to accept Harvey's discovery of the circulation of the blood.

Almost everything conspired to breed germs, and would arouse horror in the least hygiene-conscious of recent generations. The heating of water was costly and cumbersome, so there was little bathing. Glazing was not yet universal, or even in ordinary dwellings common, and wherever rooms were glazed, it was primarily to keep the warmth from the huge stoves from getting out since it was unnecessary for allowing the light to come in. Architects were only just beginning to consider the effects of light when the Hall of Mirrors was built. As a result high-ceilinged palace rooms, warmed by their enormous stoves, were carefully sealed, used heavy curtains, and were often over-heated. Clothes worn by courtiers were heavy and undergarments in general infrequently changed, although some members of the royal family changed their linen more often than once a day.

Formal eating still relied heavily on napkins for frequent finger-wiping, for forks were only beginning to be used. Dog-generated dirt was everywhere and the dogs were not infrequently taken to bed with their owners, between blankets which were not washed. Foul smells were not themselves dangerous, and could be disguised with pungent, but expensive perfumery, but there was much health-risk in the sources from which they derived. Bodily functions, however, were not a matter for shame, and were discussed in public. Marie-Adélaïde is recorded as having been given an enema while chatting to Louis in his apartment. A standing quip about the inconvenience of kingship was that it imposed the obligation of eating in private and using the *chaise percée* in public. At least Louis could wipe his hands on rising with a cloth soaked in brandy. He was occasionally prescribed a bath for medicinal reasons.

Clean water was becoming a concern. Louis himself drank water only from a spring uncontaminated with sewage. His frequent gastric upsets were due to unrestricted gluttony. He was also the subject of the determination of his physicians to demonstrate by the frequency of their ministrations their superiority over the old wives' remedies, superstitious practices involving exotic ingredients, and reliance on astrologers and horoscopes still to be found among the apparently sophisticated members of the court.

Most intelligent people at court knew that physicians were little better, and often less good than charlatans, but few, like Mme de Ventadour, dared simply to send them away, so great was the stronghold of established practice. Mme de Ventadour only saved the life of the duc d'Anjou, only surviving son of the Bourgognes and the future Louis XV, by refusing access to doctors, and putting the child back to breast-feeding at two. She herself was able to dance when over ninety years old.

Louis's first serious illness was smallpox, later to kill the grand Dauphin, in 1647. The symptoms were fever, pain in the kidneys and lower back, pustules and delirium, but after four bleedings and a fortnight, Louis recovered. This already suggested a relative robustness, since his offspring proved less resistant to the disease. By 1652 Louis was having frequent bouts of diarrhoea, caused by over-eating. The source of the vertigo from which he also suffered was constipation. Of strange importance turns out to be his vulnerability to catching cold, as he was to become virtually insensitive to even abnormal degrees of frost.

Later in life, when he threw open windows as soon as he entered a room, and left Mme de Maintenon huddled, shivering and covered in rugs, Louis slept with open windows throughout winter, or opened coach windows to the acute discomfort of his wife and mistresses. In the terrible winter of 1708–9 he refrained from intended expeditions because his guards would suffer too much from the cold. He showed an unusual insensitivity to discomfort. That might help to explain his much admired heroic fortitude during the operation to remove his anal fistula.

Louis's second serious illness was the almost inevitable gonorrhoea, contracted at the age of sixteen in 1655 from Mme de Beauvais, first lady to his mother's bedchamber. The *Journal* entry is extremely circumspect about this 'inexplicable' ailment, and the prescribed remedy was to ride his horse a little less. In everybody's mind was the need to leave his power to generate children unimpeded, and treatment, including the consumption of huge quantities of mineral water, continued for seven months. Happily for the succession, it worked. We cannot be quite certain how many pregnancies Maria-Teresa had, but it was at least six, and only one child survived. Happily again, it was a male, the grand Dauphin. Louis did find out what his ailment had been, and enjoined silence on the doctors who had access to the diary over a matter considered so delicate.

The third illness was typhoid, then common on battlefields littered with rotting corpses. Louis, not yet twenty, was taken from Mardyck to Calais, where Vallot gave him an enema and took three basinfuls of blood. The symptoms were dreadful, high fever, delirium, red, violet and blackish spots, inflamed throat, thick and black tongue, total incontinence. It says a great deal for his constitution that he recovered, surviving not only the disease, but between 29 June and 22 July 1658 eight bleedings, four purgings and three ounces of emetic wine on 8 July.

The final disease of Louis's youth was measles, often fatal, as for the duc and duchesse de Bourgogne and their elder surviving son, caught by Louis from his recently married queen, whose bed he had continued to share. He fell ill on 28 May, but by 5 June was convalescent. A young poet, by inclination always more a courtier than a dramatist, wrote an ingratiating ode to congratulate Louis on his recovery. His name was Jean Racine. Thereafter Louis's ailments were for a long period merely trivial, but do attest to a certain robustness of digestion.

His appetite was colossal, generally thought to be due to intestinal worms. There is one attested meal of four bowls of different soups, a pheasant, a partridge, a large bowl of salad, two slices of ham, a slice of mutton and a dish of pastries, finished with fruit and boiled eggs.[5] The noise of chewing was audible in the next room. He drank very little wine, much diluted, but coffee kept him awake.

Louis had poor teeth, as did most people of the period, but Louis's may have been bad enough to contribute to his gastro-intestinal troubles. He soothed toothache with essence of clove or thyme. In September 1678 he caught a cold while out hunting, and developed a dental abscess. In 1685 all the teeth had to be extracted from his upper left jaw. The operation was clumsily performed and took out some of his palate, so that whatever he drank risked passing through the mouth into the nose, from which it flowed. When dental problems put an end to chewing, the solution was wolfing, for instance, globe artichokes and peas in their pods, with disastrous results for sometimes uncontrollable bowel movements.

Vallot was succeeded by Antoine d'Aquin, physician to the queen in 1667 and to the king in 1672. From this time Louis began to be ill more frequently, with some chronic complaints. From 1662 there was diet-induced gout, and in 1679 a cold caught hunting which developed into a cough lasting several months. In 1683 exposure during a hunt brought on middle ear infection and a fall from his horse dislocated an elbow. The same month saw the onset of an inflammation of the left armpit. From this time on Louis hunted in a small horse-drawn barouche or calèche from which with great skill he controlled the horses.

The early medical history leads to an account of Louis's conduct over the excision of his anal fistula (a pus-filled cavity near the anus), and that in turn to major questions about his emotional and physiological make-up. Accounts of a clearly unpleasant surgical intervention appear to have been subjected to propagandist spin before they reached posterity through the memorialists.

It was 15 January 1686 when Louis complained of a small tumour two finger-widths from the anus. It produced no pain, even on horseback, and did not pulsate. It was insensible to the touch. It did however grow and harden, and on 5 February a poultice was applied to which the tumour did not respond. By 11 February Louis stayed away from the opera because he could not bear to remain seated for three hours.[6] A lady of the court was allowed to prepare and apply a plaster, but that did not help either, and Louis, in pain and hardly able to walk, took to his bed.

The physicians now decided to drain the tumour with a lancet cut and cauterizing stones, but the caustic they applied made an opening insufficient for complete drainage and, after a second attempt at draining, a fistula developed which penetrated into the rectum. By the end of March Louis could walk a little, to Mme de Maintenon's room, and by 9 April he could mount his carriage. Further cauterization was needed, which cost him three days in bed, but Louis recovered sufficiently to ride again on 22 May.

By mid summer everyone knew of the complaint, and many had remedies to propose. Surgery was thought to be a last resort. Four volunteers with similar complaints were sent at royal expense to try the waters at Barèges, but the surgeon who accompanied them found that daily injection of the waters produced no improvement. Other volunteers were sent to Bourbon, but to no avail. Louvois set up a marshalling point in Paris for sufferers with the complaint to try the various remedies vouched for, but none proved effective.

Finally Louis agreed to surgery. Surgeons still ranked lower than physicians, although they had emerged from the association with barbers, and now rated more highly than apothecaries, dentists and oculists.[7] The royal surgeon gained practice at an operation he had never performed, and perfected the instruments he needed to minimize pain, on 'volunteers', some of whom are said to have died. He contrived to introduce the scalpel in a sheath, so that it cut only as it was withdrawn. On 17 November Louis had been in great pain walking in the park at Versailles. The received account is that he slept well and, on 18 November 1686 a preparatory enema was administered at five o'clock. At seven Louis was placed on the edge of the bed with a pillow under his belly and his thighs held wide apart by two apothecaries. Louvois and Mme de Maintenon were present. One source says that Louvois held Louis's hand throughout. Louis was cut eight times with scissors and twice with a lancet. He is said neither to have flinched nor groaned, and his breathing did not alter its rhythm. The operation was a complete success, and an hour later Louis held his usual *lever,* with a meeting of the *conseil d'en-haut* that afternoon. D'Aquin was given 100,000 livres and the surgeon 300,000 livres and an estate.

By 2 December Louis was eating more or less normally, but the sources now diverge. According to one court chronicler,[8] calluses had formed by 7 December which prevented a cure and required removal by new incisions, causing the king 'great pain' and even giving him a touch of fever. However, he continued to see people two or three times a day. Another diarist[9] says on the 9th that there was to be further cutting, but Mme de Maintenon on the 11th wrote that the king suffered for seven hours 'as if he had been on the wheel' and 'I am afraid that this pain may recur tomorrow'. There were masses, *Te Deums,* and expositions of the Blessed Sacrament. The *Mercure galant* reported the whole operation in detail, with strong emphasis on the king's apparently heroic courage.

Thereafter Louis's medical history is the story of slow ageing, with gout chronic and sometimes incapacitating with pain from 1686, with all the earlier intemperances duly presenting bills to be paid. From 1688 Louis needed to be carried about the château at Versailles, or use a wheelchair fitted with a device by which he could steer, but which had to be pushed. The doctors switched his modest drinking from the wines of Champagne, not yet fizzy, to those of Burgundy. On 6 August 1686 Louis had a first bout of malaria, caught from the rustic surroundings of Marly, an ideal breeding ground for the Anopheles mosquito which carried the malaria then endemic in northern Europe. Marly brought on attacks every summer, but quinine, a cure prepared from the cinchona bark discovered by Jesuits in the Far East, had happily been introduced to France by an English pharmacist. In 1693 d'Aquin was replaced as the result of a palace intrigue by Guy-Crescent Fagon, previously physician to the dauphine, then the queen, thereafter to Louis's grandchildren, and finally to the king.

Two carbuncles developed on Louis's neck. They had to be drained in 1696; the long and heavy colds gave way to heavy nasal discharge and prolonged coughing; gravel and renal colic appeared in 1709; then bouts of constipation and flatulence. Only the appetite remained unchanged, with a light supper consisting of bread and soup, followed by three roast chickens. The diary stops in 1711, but there was no further dramatic illness until the final weeks.

The questions opened up by the medical history concern the universal emphasis on the king's fortitude in great pain. We do not even know with certainty what procedures were undertaken after the operation on 18 November 1686, and there are inconsistencies even in the accounts we have of that, none of which is by anyone who was present. Whatever happened must have been undignified, unpleasant and certainly painful. Within an hour or so Louis certainly held his routine *lever*. But the whole episode is smothered in the adulation of the *Mercure* for the Sun King, depicted as endowed with superhuman qualities whether of fortitude or impassivity. The important question is which Louis really showed.[10]

It is tempting to wonder about the physiology of the Louis who did not feel the cold, who could go shooting at the age of seventy-five and return with thirty-two pheasants brought down with thirty-four shots, who could go hunting at the same age and control a team (pair?) of runaway horses which threatened to take him over a cliff, and who caused his wife to write to her confessor in her seventies to ask whether she was still obliged to go to bed with him twice a day. Could this Louis not have been partially exempt from a normal degree of sensitivity to pain?[11]

If that were the case, then we should better understand his contempt for the discomfort of others. In 1711 he was preparing to go to Fontainebleau. The duchesse de Berri was expecting her first child and was unwell, and the doctors ordered her to stay at home and rest. Those who dared plead for her to be allowed to stay at Versailles simply goaded Louis to an anger he was at no pains to conceal. The duchess was simply ordered to come to Fontainebleau, but was at least sent by boat to avoid the jolting of the coach.

The boat hit a bridge, broke in two, and the duchess immediately gave birth to a dead daughter. She never gave birth after that to a child who survived infancy, and most of her babies were still-born. Was that a case simply of crass emotional insensitivity possibly mitigated by a failure to register the physical pain likely to be felt by the sick duchess, because Louis did not himself feel pain as much as do most people? Was it a bullying need to reassure himself by exercising absolute control over his immediate entourage? The king merely said that since the dead infant was female, it did not much matter. By 1711 such a remark was recognizably offensive.

The comte de Toulouse was similarly forced to go to Fontainebleau, although in severe pain from the stone. The journey caused him much pain and served no purpose, since he was too physically ill to leave his room for most of the visit. Much earlier had occurred the 1673 journey to the front with Mme de Montespan heavily pregnant, Louise de la Vallière and the queen all in the same coach, a physically dangerous journey for a pregnant woman, and an emotionally brutal imposition on each of the three.

Colbert's daughter, the duchesse de Chevreuse, travelled alone with Louis from Versailles to Fontainebleau, a journey of some six hours. Although the coach stopped and a meal was served, she was given no opportunity to relieve herself, nor did she dare ask for one, preferring to travel on in agony, such was the terror struck by this awe-inspiring tyrant. Yet his charm could inspire popularity among his people in the midst of the anguish his policies were inflicting on them, and he could when he wished charm the ladies of his court. It is difficult to suppose that Louis was unaware of the pain he expected members of his entourage to endure or was insensitive to their distress. The paradox is the product of the upbringing, responsible for the cruelty, and the public relations skills learned from Mazarin and then Colbert, which stopped most even of those at whom it was directed from perceiving it as outrageous.

Yet we know from his reactions to the gout as well as the tumour, that he felt pain to much the same degree as anyone else, and we know that he could be, and normally was, courteous, and even considerate. We also know that he was brave enough to have put up with the considerable pain of the fistula operation with unusual steadfastness. Was Louis merely subject to bouts of sulky bad temper? It insults his undoubted intelligence to presume that he was unaware of the feelings he aroused. There must have been more than an incidental element of bullying, causing distress because it amused him. It could have been a way of proving to himself that he really was whom he had been taught to pretend to be.

Louis's fondest affections for the younger generation had gone to the duc du Maine, his eldest son by Athénaïs, and to Marie-Adélaïde of Savoy, duchesse de Bourgogne, who died in 1712. Unfortunately the duc du Maine disappointed him by his cowardice when serving under Luxembourg in 1691, but he was amused by his gossip and his mimicry, bought Sceaux for him from Colbert's children when he married, and gave him the governorship of Languedoc. He was reinstated as favourite soon before Louis's death, and had always been the favourite of Mme de Maintenon among Louis's children since, as Mme Scarron, she had first looked after him.

A ray of light had entered the court in 1696 when the twelve-year-old Marie-Adélaïde of Savoy came to marry the duc de Bourgogne and enchanted everyone, but in particular the king and Mme de Maintenon, whom she addressed as 'ma tante' and by whom she was called 'mignonne'. Mme de Maintenon saw to her education, her diet and every detail of her upbringing, and Louis himself learnt for the first time when he was nearly sixty how to handle children gently. Marie-Adélaïde went to school at Saint-Cyr and the king took her for a walk every day. Eventually the duc de Bourgogne fell furiously in love with her, but at first they met coolly, daily, but never alone until the marriage was consummated.

She had her adolescent rebellion, being unkind to her elders, safe in the presumption that, married to Louis's eldest grandson, she would one day be their queen. She spent much of the time in fancy dress, bathed in the river, slept in a tent and would spend all night dancing before supping in Paris, going to mass and returning to kiss Louis good morning. She would prance round the park with her ladies, and fell in love, she thought privately, with two or three young men who were then successively removed from the court. Eventually Mme de Maintenon allowed her to see a report on her conduct, compiled virtually hour by hour, and let her know that she had kept nothing secret, and that such reports regularly arrived from several quarters.

In 1708 her husband was sent to the front, where he performed lamentably. Then, after the death of the grand Dauphin in 1711 Marie-Adélaïde became the dauphine and, like her husband, took her new status seriously. She had had her first baby in 1704, but lost him at the age of one. Then came the duc de Bretagne, born in 1707, to die of measles in 1712 and the duc d'Anjou in 1710, who would live on to become Louis XV. The three live births had been interspersed with six miscarriages. She herself died of measles in 1712, followed within hours by her husband and her elder surviving son, the duc de Bretagne. Liselotte, seeing the emetics and bleedings to which Marie-Adélaïde was being subjected, had tried to intervene, but was told by Madame de Maintenon to be quiet and leave matters to the nine doctors in attendance. They killed her.

The leading figures among the younger members of the court, however, were the duc de Chartres, son of Louis's brother Philippe by Liselotte, and regent of France after Louis's death, and the younger prince de Conti who, having gone off to fight the Turks with his brother, and inherited the title on his brother's death, finally married the grand-daughter of the grand Condé.

The duc de Chartres, although Louis's nephew, married the youngest daughter of Athénaïs and Louis, and was known for his scandalous behaviour, which included a flaunted public affair with one of his mother's attendants, and another with an actress by whom he had a son at the same time that he had a daughter by his wife. He was falsely suspected of poisoning the Bourgognes, a possibility correctly discounted by Louis, and was the last to be called in to Louis's deathbed in 1715, when his uncle assumed that he would be made sole regent until the five-year-old Anjou, son of the Bourgognes and hence great-grandson of Louis, was of age to succeed.

Between 1701 and the end of Louis's life there was more bereavement than pleasure and more defeat than victory. To some extent Mme de Maintenon dictated the tone. She had once been pretty but became dowdy, genuinely if a little ostentatiously virtuous, anxious to do good, almost tiresomely concerned to be kind, willing to listen to stories of the day's hunt provided that details of the kill were omitted, but totally uninterested in presiding over a court sufficiently lively and entertaining to amuse the young. The dauphine had died in 1690 and Louvois in 1691, the year Mme de Montespan finally left Versailles, with both Clagny and her flat taken over by her son, du Maine. Her other children were taken away, the comte de Toulouse to the army at the age of thirteen, Françoise-Marie, a year younger still to be cared for by a governess until she married the future regent, her uncle Philippe's son. Her husband, too, died in 1701.

As news from the front got worse, Louis became more ill-tempered, but now hunted all day, having post from the front to all the Versailles residents opened only on his return, another unhappily authoritarian touch, given the anxiety with which most of the court waited for news. The year 1709 followed the terrible frost which caused the spring harvest to fail. The condition of rural France became even more pitiable. Père Le Tellier, naturally also a Jesuit, replaced la Chaise as the king's confessor. Louis, forced to sue for peace, found the terms on offer so humiliating that he preferred to carry on in spite of a country starving to death.

The awful loss in such quick succession of the grand Dauphin, the two Bourgognes and their elder son practically broke him. No further effort was made to amuse the court. The entertainments and receptions ebbed away, and Versailles, as if it felt its function exhausted, slowly began to empty as the remaining courtiers drifted off. In his final years Louis's preoccupation was first the promulgation of the anti-Jansenist constitution *Unigenitus* now that Jansenism was showing signs of making a come-back, and then rejoicing at the victory of Denain, opening the way to the peace treaties of Utrecht.

There was to be one more bereavement. In 1714 the duc de Berri had an accident while hunting. But the day following the accident he went out hunting again, and on his return brought up blood. He was given the usual emetic, and died. Louis went himself to fetch the priest. After his death, his wife had another still birth. This meant that Anjou, now the dauphin and duc de Bourgogne, was the only remaining descendant in the direct line. Louis had had his illegitimate children legitimized and made eligible to succeed, but it is difficult to imagine that the cadet line, now headed by his brother's son, Philippe II d'Orléans, a prince of the blood, would not have challenged the Montespan sons for the monarchy, had the young Anjou, Louis's great grandson, not survived to become Louis XV.

In 1714 Beauvillier and his two sons died of smallpox, and Fénelon died on 7 January 1715. In July 1715 Louis went to Marly where he enjoyed parties and a concert early in August, and made arrangements to hunt at Fontainebleau at the end of the month. But on

9 August he felt unwell and came back to Versailles after hunting. He looked very ill indeed, and had lost both weight and appetite. He still worked with ministers and officials, discussed buildings with Athénaïs's son by her husband, the marquis d'Antin, *surintendant des bâtiments* from 1708, visited his family in their apartments, and called for music and singers. The doctors, led by Guy-Crescent Fagon, prescribed sweating at night. He began to feel pain in his left leg on 11 August, and from the 15th was bed-ridden. He was carried to the chapel to attend a service in memory of Louis XIII on the 20th, and for the Fête Saint-Louis on the 25th. During the last week of his life, from 24 August, senile gangrene developed and spread from foot to thigh. It was too late for amputation, but the leg was kept in a bath of wine from Burgundy and soothed with ass's milk. The end was relatively gentle.[12]

On 24 August Louis, about to dine in public, felt such pain that he asked everyone except Villeroy to withdraw. That is the day on which he wrote a final memoir to the duc d'Anjou, his young great grandson and successor, commending to his care the duc du Maine, and urging him to be a true Christian father to his people, virtually repudiated his own past, counselling the need for peace and for a diminution of the tax burden.

On Sunday 25 August, Louis dined as usual in public, talked to courtiers, and called for musicians, although he fell asleep while they were playing. That night the sacrament was brought to him, and he received viaticum. Louis knew by now that he was dying and asked to be spared the incisions the surgeons were futilely but painfully making in his leg. On the Monday Louis asked how much longer he had. They hoped until Wednesday, was the answer. In fact he lasted until the following Sunday, but had made himself ready by the Wednesday. By Monday night the gangrene had reached the bone, and the chancellor reported that sensation in the leg had ceased. On the Tuesday Louis spent time with Mme de Maintenon and the chancellor sorting and burning papers. He gave instructions, cancelling the Fontainebleau hunt, and making arrangements for the Vincennes château to be prepared to receive Anjou as soon as he himself should die.

Mme de Maintenon and du Maine persuaded Louis to put du Maine in charge of the education of his successor, the young Anjou, displacing Louis's nephew, the still scandalous Orléans. Louis knew that this codicil to his will, like the 1714 will itself stipulating a regency council, would be overturned, but signed what Mme de Maintenon and du Maine put before him to buy himself peace. He knew that Orléans would be in a position to take sole charge. He wanted a reconciliation with the Jansenist archbishop of Paris, Noailles, but Mme de Maintenon and Le Tellier prevented it by insisting that Noailles should first accept the anti-Jansenist constitution *Unigenitus*. He was given the last sacraments by the cardinal de Rohan, generally thought to be his own son. The ladies close to him, Liselotte, the princesse de Conti and the others were briefly admitted to his room, but tired him.

He gave sage and pious advice to his five-year-old successor, asked forgiveness of the male courtiers who had the right of admittance, saw du Maine and Toulouse together, and then his nephew, Orléans, alone, and gave him detailed instructions about what to do on his death. On the Thursday he rallied, took a little nourishment, but he relapsed in the early hours of the Friday. His farewells to du Maine and to Madame de Maintenon brought tears to his eyes. He commended Mme de Maintenon to Orléans. He was then alone with her, the priests and the doctors, lucid until he started drifting in and out of consciousness. He finally lost consciousness for the last time on the Friday, and died at about quarter past eight, on the morning of Sunday 1 September. Dangeau remarked how effortlessly Louis died, 'like a candle going out'.

Notes

1   Louis's Inheritance

1   This was pointed out by Georges Mongrédien, *Présentation de Louis XIV,* Paris 1963, pp. 62–5. Mongrédien rightly acknowledges that elements of a psychological portrait can be found in both Saint-Simon's eighteenth-century *Mémoires,* written between 1739 and 1751, and in Ernest Lavisse, *Louis XIV,* 2 vols, Paris 1906–8, although both works suffer from what have become other disqualifying inadequacies.

   Much excellent work has been published since Mongrédien's 1963 book, but nothing which attempts an adequate psychological portrait. Even the best of recent biographers have lacked the theological expertise necessary to understand the nature and genesis of 'Jansenism' or the ostensibly theological issues which arose between Fénelon and Bossuet, but masked the difference of political attitudes which they reflected.

2   One recent exception which does take the clash of value systems into account is Mark Bannister's perceptive *Condé in Context. Ideological Change in Seventeenth-Century France,* Oxford 2000. Like the present work, Bannister's takes into account the elevated status of the quality which the seventeenth century knew as *gloire.*

   The term 'éthique de la gloire' had been coined by Octave Nadal, who used it in his *Le sentiment de l'amour dans l'œuvre de Pierre Corneille,* 1948, and defined it in 'L'Ethique de la Gloire au XVIIe siècle,' *Mercure de France,* vol. 308, 1950, pp. 22–34. The cultural reverbations of *gloire* are also analysed in F.E. Sutcliffe, *Guez de Balzac et son temps. Littérature et politique,* Paris 1959. As a quality *gloire* appeared in the 1950s to offer a key to an understanding of the ethic of mid seventeenth-century French society. It has subsequently been tested on too many locks which it does not open.

3 The neoplatonist mystical theology of the influential cardinal Pierre de Bérulle lent itself to support both the strongly optimistic views of Descartes and the pessimism about the moral incapacity of human nature associated with the devotional Jansenism of Saint-Cyran.

4 The figure of 20 million inhabitants for seventeenth-century France became quasi-canonical with the publication in 1966 of *Louis XIV et vingt millions de Français* by Pierre Goubert. It is very widely accepted, but the 5 per cent margin of error, particularly upwards, may well prove ungenerous. For the figures, see Fernand Braudel, *Civilization and Capitalism, 15th-18th Century*, revised English translation by Siân Reynolds, 3 vols., London 1985, vol.1, pp. 54–6.

5 It is known that the number of schools fell far short of what was legislated for, but for an estimate of the size of the literate population in whose hands was all French administration, it is possible to rely on little but the schools that are known about. All we have as a starting-point for any assessment of the level of literacy is the knowledge that the percentage of males able to sign their names on rural marriage registers in the period 1686–90 reached as high as 40–50 per cent in only about half of the extreme north-east region of the country.

There was a scattering of well-run secondary schools in the hands of the Jesuits, the Oratorians and the Dominicans. Their number rose to 200 by 1715, and education, at least to the level of basic literacy, was also provided chiefly by city schools, and for apprentices who were trained by the manufactories being established by Colbert half a century earlier. Sons of the nobility were often trained while serving as pages in other grand households, where they might be attached to the stables and form their own educational units, generally with a military bias. A royal edict of 1695, backed by a declaration of 13 December 1698, ordered the creation of an elementary school in every parish. It was dictated by the need to see that those converted to Catholicism on the 1685 revocation of the edict of toleration (the edict of Nantes) learned and practised their new religion, but it was only sporadically put into effect.

6 See on the matter of literacy F. Furet and J. Ozouf, *Lire et écrire*, Paris 1977 (translated as *Reading and Writing: Literacy in France from Calvin to Jules Ferry*, Cambridge 1982). The distribution map of percentages of signatures by males on marriage certificates for 1686–90 is reproduced by Braudel in the third volume of the work referred to in note 3, p. 340 (English translation, p. 49). Ozouf and Furet based their distribution maps on the astonishing freelance, unremunerated work of a retired French nineteenth-century civil servant, Louis Maggiolo, who enlisted the help of all the village schoolteachers in France to record all marriage signatures in their village for four five-year periods, of which the earliest was 1686–90. The distribution map for that period, inevitably reflecting primarily the situation in rural areas with single village schools, shows the proportion of men able to sign their names nowhere touching 70 per cent, and reaching 60 per cent only in the

Lyonnais and Normandy. In only about half the north-eastern quarter of France do the figures for males reach the 40–60 per cent band. In only one small area are the figures for women as high as 30 per cent. In her introduction to Jacques Prévot's *La première institutrice de France. Madame de Maintenon*, Paris 1981, Dominique Desanti says that by the end of the seventeenth century 14 per cent of women could sign their name. She gives no source, but must be relying on the Maggiolo statistics, with which her figure is consistent.

7 There is a whole correspondence on the subject in Jules Guiffrey (ed.), *Comptes des Bâtiments du Roi sous Louis XIV,* 5 vols, Paris 1881–1901

2   The *Dieudonné*

1 Pierre de Bérulle (1575–1629), on whom see Henri Bremond, *Histoire littéraire du sentiment religieux en France depuis la fin des guerres de religion jusqu'à nos jours,* 12 vols, Paris 1921–36, Jean Dagens, *Bérulle et les origines de la restauration catholique, 1575–1611,* Paris 1952, and Yves Krumenacker, *L'Ecole française de spiritualité,* Paris 1999, established the Oratorian congregation and brought the discalced Carmelites to France. He based his strongly christocentric spirituality on a form of neoplatonist mysticism which demanded the renunciation of natural human powers and came to rely heavily on baroque eucharistic piety. He allied a firm credal Catholicism with a strongly pro-Spanish political orientation. Richelieu, once an admirer, became hostile to his pessimistic views about human nature. See the author's *Cardinal Richelieu and the Making of France,* London 2000.

2 See Pierre Chevallier, *Louis XIII, roi cornélien,* Paris 1979; François Bluche, *Louis XIV,* Paris 1984, tr. Mark Greengrass, Oxford 1990, pp. 9–11; and Ian Dunlop, *Louis XIV,* London 1999, p.2. Pregnancies after those of 1622 and 1626 had not infrequently been rumoured, and Claude Dulong, Anne's biographer, speaks of two earlier miscarriages, in 1619 and 1621, see *Anne d'Autriche,* Paris 1980, p. 40.

3 Gaston d'Orléans came to Saint-Germain a fortnight before the birth, but left abruptly for his estates, where Goulas, his *intendant,* tells us in his memoirs that he complained 'with thousands of tears'. See John B. Wolf, *Louis XIV,* London 1668, p.4. Louis XIII gave his brother 6,000 crowns to soften the blow.

4 Given the horrendous infant and maternal peri-natal death rates, which seem actually to have been worse among those for whom medical provision was available, it was according to standard practice that the infant was immediately *ondoyé,* conferring sacramental baptism on him. That meant that, were the newly born dauphin to die before reaching the 'age of reason', he would immediately be admitted to heaven, and therefore that the grand ritual baptism could be deferred, with plenty of time to make suitable arrangements.

[313]

5 The *Gazette* had a stormy beginning caused largely by the efforts of the printers'guild, still dependent on the university, to safeguard its monopoly rights. Its stable foundation is normally dated back to 1631, the date of the *privilège* accorded to its founder, Théophraste Renaudot. Always subject to unofficial censorship under Richelieu and Mazarin, it soon became a forum for government-spun announcements and court news, although also carrying other material, including news of events from all over Europe, and comments from abroad on French affairs. After the draconian censorship law of 1683, it shrivelled into a forum for government news hand-outs, but continued to sell profitably until the revolution

6 For a résumé of the history of the marital relations of Louis XIII and Anne of Austria, see the author's *Cardinal Richelieu and the Making of France*, London 2000, and the sources there referred to, as also Pierre Chevallier, *Louis XIII, roi cornélien*, Paris 1979.

7 A translation of the name given by Saint Augustine to his son Adeodatus.

8 See René Taveneaux, *Le catholicisme dans la France classique, 1610–1715*, Paris 1980, second edition Paris 1994.

9 Tallemant des Réaux, relying on a roughly contemporary document (now in the Bibliothèque Nationale, fonds français 10210), gives a partial list of Louis XIII's male lovers in the 'historiette' he devoted to the king, (*Historiettes,* ed. Antoine Adam, 2 vols, Paris 1960–61, vol. 1, p. 334) adding more detailed notes on the relationships with Barradas, Saint-Simon, father of the memorialist, and Cinq-Mars, said by Tallemant to have been loved by Louis XIII '*éperdument*', a judgement which Tallemant amply justifies in his account of the history of the relationship. Tallement's text was complete by 1659, although the attested intention to publish the *Historiettes* was abandoned in the early 1660s.

10 In canon law the partners conferred the sacrament of matrimony on one another not, as had once been argued, by consent, but only by due consummation. The marriage was merely witnessed on behalf of the church by the officiating clergyman with appropriately delegated jurisdiction. Since Anne's father was the king of Spain, there were important dynastic consequences at stake, involving rights of succession to the Spanish throne, and the Spanish court needed absolute reassurance that the sacrament had indeed been bestowed, or in other words that consummation had taken place.

11 François de Paule de Clermont, marquis de Montglat (1620–75) whose *Mémoires* were published in Amsterdam in 1727.

12 Claude Dulong, *Mazarin*, Paris 1999, p.65, remarking on the diminution in the number of executions and exiles after Richelieu's death in December 1642, none the less notes the burning of a 'sodomist', whose accomplice was a lawyer, in 1644.

13 Mme de Motteville, born in 1621, married at eighteen and widowed at

twenty, had been close to Henriette de France, widow of Charles I, was loyal to Anne, and left four volumes of *Mémoires*.

14 Strictly speaking Mazarini until his adoption of French nationality late in 1639. The relationship between Mazarin and Anne of Austria is discussed by all historians and biographers concerned with the France of the 1640s and with the civil war known as the Fronde (after the adolescent slang for fights with slings and stones). See especially the two important works of Claude Dulong, *Anne d'Autriche*, Paris 1980, and *Mazarin*, Paris 1999, and also Auguste Bailly, *Mazarin*, Paris 1935, and Georges Dethan, *Mazarin et ses amis*, Paris 1968.

15 Mazarin had gone to Spain in 1622 when he was twenty to study at Alcalà de Henares as a companion to a member of the Colonna family. In October 1630 he had dramatically procured the armistice at Casale, and thereafter in the papal service negotiated the peace treaties between France, the pope, the emperor and the duke of Savoy in 1631 and 1632.

16 For instance, A. Lloyd Moote, *Louis XIII, the Just*, Berkeley and Los Angeles 1989.

17 For instance, Claude Dulong, *Anne d'Autriche*, Paris 1980.

18 Montagu was well known to both Anne of Austria and Mazarin. He was in the entourage of Buckingham when Buckingham first met Anne during his brief 1625 visit to France, and was with Buckingham when he died, assassinated, in 1628. Montagu had been imprisoned by Richelieu in the context of affording assistance to the Huguenots of La Rochelle, but protected Anne of Austria by refusing to mention her name, although she, too, knew of the European conspiracy to thwart Richelieu's attempt to reduce La Rochelle. On his release Montagu remained attached to the English embassy to the French court, and was converted to Catholicism on being taken to see the exorcism of Jeanne des Anges at Loudun. In 1635 during Mazarin's Paris nunciature, Montagu became close to Mazarin, who called him to Avignon for two months in the autumn of 1636. From 1641 the converted Montagu found it more prudent to live in France, where he received the abbey of Saint-Martin at Pontoise and became Anne's frequent and perhaps closest, if informal, adviser, fostering her friendship for Mazarin, whose Spanish origins and connections he no doubt glorified. Mazarin was to use him as an intermediary with Mme de Chevreuse, and the ascendancy of Pierre Séguier as chancellor is due to Montagu's friendship with Séguier's sister, prioress of the Pontoise Carmelites.

19 There had been a time in 1626 when Anne might have found an escape route by marrying Gaston if the coup to remove Louis XIII had succeeded, but Gaston, widowed, married Marguerite de Vaudémont, sister of the duke of Lorraine, in January 1632. If Louis XIII had died leaving her childless at thirty-six, Anne would instantly have become superfluous to Europe's political requirements.

20 It is known that in 1713 Mme de Maintenon burnt many of the king's letters to her, and that in the following year he burnt hers to him. Unfortunately the critical edition of her letters (ed. Marcel Langlois, *Madame de Maintenon, Lettres,* vols. 2–5, Paris 1935–9) stops in 1701. A few later letters are dispersed in archives and no doubt elsewhere, but are unlikely to be brought together for scholarly analysis. For years after the death of the king, Anne was able to carry on her liaison with Mazarin known only to less than a handful of people. When he was away and was reduced to writing to her, she retired to her private chapel to make her devotions and read his letters in privacy.

21 'Il m'ennuie bien que la reine ne soit accouchée pour m'en retourner en Picardie, si vous le jugez à propos, ou ailleurs: pourvu que je sois hors d'avec toutes ces femmes, il ne m'importe où.' Louis made a similar complaint on 24 August.

22 See Claude Dulong, *Anne d'Autriche,* Paris 1980, pp. 181–2 for a commentary on the king's brutality towards his wife, whose life seemed momentarily at risk during the delivery.

23 On the assassination of Henri IV in 1610, the eight-year-old Louis XIII had immediately become king, and the regency of his mother, Marie de' Medici proclaimed the same afternoon, its consitutional validity confirmed in a *lit de justice* held formally by the boy king on the following day. A *lit de justice* was essentially a special royal court at which the monarch re-assumed the totality of jurisdiction over the territory over which he was sovereign. It had been part of the fundamental law of France that the princes of the blood had by reason of their birth the right to participate in the government of the kingdom. That is why, for instance, Gaston was always treated so leniently after his part in conspiracies to overthrow his brother.

24 See for instance Nancy Mitford, *The Sun King,* London 1966 (of which the more widely available Penguin Harmondsworth edition is used here, 1994, pp. 23–4), who speaks also of a nose 'rather pinched above the nostrils' and refers to 'the Jewish and Moorish blood' in his ancestry. John B. Wolf notes that Louis XIV did not have the looks of his 'father, uncle, and brother'. Later on Louis was almost never to mention Louis XIII, presumed by outsiders to be his father, although he took his presumed grandfather, Henri IV, as one of his role models.

25 'Anne d'Autriche' in *Divers portraits,* Caen 1659, p. 247. This was the sumptuously bound collection of 59 portraits which Mme de Montpensier herself, Gaston's daughter by his first wife, known as 'la grande Mademoiselle', edited and partly composed in 1659. It was published in an edition of about thirty copies, probably as the result of a famous house party held at Saint-Fargeau shortly after the emergence of the group of half a dozen aristocratic young women known as *précieuses*. The collection inaugurated a commercial vogue for the portrait genre, already initiated by Madeleine de Scudéry's ten-volume novel *Clélie*, of which the first volume was published in

1654. See the author's *French Literature: Beginnings to 1789,* Andover and Detroit 1994.

26 Unpublished letter of Mlle Andriéa to Mme de Sencé of 9 April 1639, quoted by John B. Wolf, *Louis XIV,* p.7.

27 La Valette was the son and heir of the duc d'Epernon, and elder brother of the cardinal. He fled to England and was executed in effigy after condemnation by Louis XIII at a *lit de justice.*

28 Anne's second son, Philippe, was born Philippe d'Anjou and known as 'le petit Monsieur' until the death of Louis XIII's brother, Gaston d'Orléans, known as 'Monsieur'. Gaston died on 2 February 1660, after which Philippe was elevated to the duchy of Orléans, the traditional fief of the dauphin's next youngest brother, and in turn became known as 'Monsieur'.

29 The two dukes were Bouillon, elder brother of Turenne, and Guise, born in 1614. Guise was formally archbishop of Reims at the age of fifteen, married Anne de Gonzague on 4 May 1638, inherited the Guise title in 1640, and hoped to keep his benefices within the family while making his marriage public. As a result of his uprising with Bouillon and Soissons, he was condemned to death in his absence and excuted in effigy on 11 September, a solution which achieved Richelieu's aim of confiscating his vast possessions. Guise, whose grandmother was a Clèves, was to have his marriage annulled on grounds of undispensed consanguinity, and to remarry a nineteen-year-old widow. On Richelieu's death, Anne allowed Guise back to France, where he regained his wealth and became an important literary patron.

30 François de la Mothe le Vayer (1588–1672) does not deserve his reputation for religious cynicism on account of the pseudonymous *Quatre dialogues* of 1630, and the further five of the following year. For the next ten years he was employed by Richelieu and produced works of impeccable orthodoxy, including an anti-Jansenist tract on the authenticity of pagan virtue (1642). Given charge first of the education of Philippe, Louis XIV was entrusted to his care from 1652 to 1660.

31 See Claude Dulong, *Anne d'Autriche,* Paris 1980, pp. 224–27.

32 Michel le Tellier was the father of Louvois, Louis XIV's war minister, but was no relation to the Jesuit Père le Tellier who was the confessor of Louis XIV from 1709 to 1715.

33 Louis XIII had had himself moved to the château neuf, which he now preferred and where he thought the air was better, some weeks before the onset of his last illness.

3 The Boy King

1 That the sovereignty into which Louis was born was sacerdotal as well as secular was made clear by the coronation ceremony, or *sacre,* which included an anointing, and was in part indistinguishable in nature from

a ceremony of episcopal ordination. That royal infants were more highly endowed from birth than ordinary children was not publicly challenged in the ongoing debate about the relationship between rank and the underlying qualities which justified it among the *moralistes* of the seventeenth century. Louis XIV himself, in the *Mémoires* which he later wrote for the instruction of his son, the new dauphin, is everywhere insistent on the prince's duty to justify the rank into which he is born by the exercise of the superior qualities with which princes were endowed by nature. Louis's son is known here as the 'grand Dauphin' to distinguish him from Louis himself prior to 1643 and from Louis's grandson, 'grand' being a reference to height and not, as in 'le grand Condé', to greatness. Psychologically, Louis XIV could not be inclined to forget his moral superiority as well as his political sovereignty over those of lesser condition. The *Métier du Roi* is a short document containing notes compiled in 1679 for an addition to the *Mémoires* in which Louis justifies himself for the dismissal in that year of Arnauld de Pomponne from the position of minister and ambassador to Sweden.

2 The *parlements* were by now devoid of any executive power, vested in the king alone and exercised through the various royal councils. The councils could revise or revoke any decision of a *parlement*, although only the *conseil d'en-haut*, into which the king's *conseil privé* was to develop, could annul the decrees of the Paris *parlement*. When Mazarin invited the Paris *parlement* to alter the will of Louis XIII, the annulment of the registered will should probably be construed as having taken place as an exceptional invitation, which could only validly be issued by the sovereign, to interfere in the affairs of state by ratifying a constitutional decision negotiated by an *ad hoc* body consisting of the senior prince of the blood, who was Gaston d'Orléans, Mazarin as chief minister, Anne, Pierre Séguier as chancellor and the other principal secretaries of state who belonged to the *conseil privé*. Since the king was an infant and there was not yet a regent, there was no royal authority which could simply impose registration on the *parlement*. The office-holders of the *parlement* apparently interpreted their convocation as a general invitation to participate in executive decisions, which would have entailed constitutional change and which the council of state was in 1648 to declare had not been the intention of Anne and Mazarin. It certainly never became that of Louis, who on 8 July 1661 confirmed 'la suprême autorité du Conseil' over the sovereign courts of the *parlement*, whose sphere of authority was limited to private rather than public law.

3 Since the kingdom was not a possession, to be treated as a legacy and not necessarily left to the next in line, the French constitution regarded it as essential for the continuity of the monarchy's commitments and obligations that the monarchy should be inherited by right of succession in the male line, as originally defined in the canon law rules for the orders of consanguinuity. This rule could not be altered by the testamentary dispositions of Louis XIII, but the arrangements for the

regency needed to be activated in a *lit de justice* held nominally by the child monarch and registered by the *parlement* of Paris, which the provincial *parlements* would in this case have to follow.

Cardinal Le Bret, in his *Traité de la souveraineté du Roi* of 1632, had held that the exclusion of the female line was 'in conformity with natural law, which, having made woman imperfect and weak in both body and mind, has subjected her to the power of man', see Roland E. Mousnier, *The Institutions of France under the Absolute Monarchy 1598–1789*, tr. Brian Pearce, Chicago and London 1979, p. 650.

The other fundamental laws were constituted by the oaths sworn at the *sacre* by the king on attaining his majority at the age of thirteen to the French bishops and the French people, by the continuity of monarchy according to the rules of succession from the moment of the death of a monarch, by the inalienability of crown domain without consent of the Estates General, and by the restriction of the crown to a Catholic monarch.

4 The best account of the proceedings is to be found in the *Journal* of Olivier Lefèvre d'Ormesson, 2 vols, ed. Adolphe Chéruel, Paris 1860–61.

5 By the middle of the seventeenth century there were several estates of *noblesse,* from the simplest *écuyer,* raised above the *bourgeois,* to the *gentilhomme,* denoting nobility of four generations of lineage, and not including nobility of more recent origin acquired by office or elevation. The *nobles de race* counted only the paternal line in the ascendancy of four generations, disregarding non-noble blood in the maternal line. The privileges of *gentilshommes,* apparently ritual and ceremonial, actually included important tax exemptions. Through prestige, wealth and their technical role as representatives of the king in the administration of justice, the *nobles de race* gradually came to equal or to regard themselves as superior to all but the grandest members of the old military aristocracy, the *noblesse d'épée,* some of whom by now also held offices, but who continued to regard the marriage of a daughter to a member of the *noblesse de robe,* or magistracy, even if also *noble de race,* as a *mésalliance.* Later in the reign of Louis XIV social distinctions, marked by who, when and in the presence of whom, which members of court might cover their heads or be seated (and whether on *tabouret* or *fauteuil*) came to play a prominent part in court etiquette and consequential political intrigue.

Within the *gentilhommerie* of the court, the men might be invited to ride in the king's carriages or to go hunting with him, and ride his horses when they did. The women might be invited to offer their cheeks to be kissed by the royal family and princes of the blood, and to enter the royal carriages. Above and beyond was admission to the *cercles de la cour* with invitations to balls and receptions. Some social privileges were temporary, or at the king's immediate discretion, in a court immensely sensitive to the slightest gradations of favour or disfavour, or the degree to which the king raised his hat.

Socially, the most important distinction, decided on criteria of class (social function) as well as of caste (birth), was between those who had been presented at court and those who had not. Only those presented, and therefore 'known' to the king, could hope to be given the highest military ranks and non-military offices, ambassadorships, and royal pensions. Meticulous protocol, although observed and backed by legislation, was increasingly to depend on the king's personal decisions. The regulation of detail is well exemplified by the fact that from 1643 the *premier président* of the Paris *parlement* was allowed to keep his hat on when asking the opinion of a peer only if the peer was not a prince of the blood.

The intricacy of such arrangements raised the king to an apex of authority which suited those whose desire to exercise the king's theoretically absolute political power required them to keep the king himself largely occupied in presiding over the complex trivia of decorum. However, the trivia were used as signs of favour or disfavour, and favour meant an increased royal readiness to grant favours requested by third parties, from whom courtiers received an ample commission. The smallest signs of Louis's favour became a serious source of income for members of the court.

6 Mazarin continued to sign himself 'Mazarini', although he was known as Mazarin. Lavisse, in his great, if out-dated two-volume biography of Louis XIV (1906–8), part of his 1900–11 *Histoire de France depuis les origines jusqu'à la Révolution,* suggests that Mazarin kept the Italian form of his name because it might prove useful 'pour devenir pape, par exemple'. Much of this chapter depends on the important published research of Claude Dulong, *Anne d'Autriche,* Paris 1980, and *Mazarin,* Paris 1999.

7 Turenne was born into the dissident Protestant aristocracy, trained in the bodyguard of his uncle, Maurice of Nassau, and entered French service in 1630. He was made a maréchal in 1643 and converted to Catholicism by Bossuet in 1668. He formed a strong attachment to Mme de Longueville.

8 See Henri d'Orléans, duc d'Aumale, *Histoire des princes de Condé pendant les xvie et xviie siècles,* 7 vols, Paris 1863–96, vol. 5, p. 395.

9 On Rocroi and Thionville, see Adolphe Chéruel, *Histoire de France pendant la minorité de Louis XIV,* 4 vols, Paris 1879–80.

10 Quoted by Mathieu Molé, président of the Paris *parlement,* and keeper of the seals, in his *Mémoires,* ed. Champollion-Figeac, 4 vols, Paris 1855–7.

11 See Claude Dulong, 'Du nouveau sur le palais Mazarin: l'achat de hôtel Tubeuf par le cardinal' in *Bibliothèque de l'Ecole des chartes,* CLIII, 1995, pp. 131–55.

12 'Italy' is used throughout the text to avoid repeating the cumbersome 'the Italian peninsula'. It was not of course a single country in the seventeenth century.

13 See also Ian Dunlop, *Louis XIV,* London 2001, pp. 3–7.

14 Louis's tutors included Jean Le Bé for writing, Le Camus for arithmetic, Antoine Oudin for Italian and Spanish, H. Davire for drawing, Bernard for reading. See Henri Carré, *L'Enfance et la première jeunesse de Louis XIV, 1638–1661,* Paris 1944.

15 Paris, Ecole des Chartes, 1847–8.

16 Similar views, imputing to Mazarin motives of varying nefariousness, were commonplace even during the king's childhood. Choisy suggests that Mazarin wanted to turn Louis only into a soldier and a lover who would leave to himself the running of the state. Saint-Simon, who thought so little of Louis's intelligence, is at his most bitter, 'Le Cardinal avait tenu le roi dans la plus entière ignorance et la plus honteuse dépendence.' Giovanni Batista Nani, Venetian ambassador from 1644 to 1648 and again from 1659 to1660, left an invaluable portrait of the king in 1660, emphasizing Louis's deference to his mother's authority and the extraordinary sympathy which existed between himself and Mazarin. But in 1648, Nani had seen Mazarin's principal intention as the cultivation in the young king of a devotion to himself. Ian Dunlop, (*Louis XIV,* London 1999, p. 39) expresses the view that 'The affection between the Cardinal and the King was almost like that of father and son,' which is exactly what it is most likely to have been. A later Venetian ambassador, Giovanni Sagredo (1653–5), was to repeat in 1654 the allegation that Mazarin deliberately deflected the king's attention to his amusements, in order that Mazarin should himself have the power to run the state. Nani later states how successful he was in acquiring it.

17 The *Histoire de France* of François Eudes de Mézeray (1610–83), brother of the future saint, Jean Eudes, began to appear in 1643. Mézeray was royal historian from 1662, but was hostile to Mazarin and Colbert, who first cut his pension in half (1671) and then abolished it. He became perpetual secretary of the Académie française.

18 Notably by John B. Wolf, *Louis XIV,* London 1968, p.24. Within a page or so of the beginning of his *Mémoires* for 1661, Louis XIV recounts how from his childhood he had been turned against his unmilitary predecessors, 'Dès l'enfance même, le seul nom des rois fainéants et de maires de palais me faisait peine quand on le prononçait en ma présence' (ed. Jean Longnon, Paris 2001, pp.32–33). Pellisson, who actually wrote this passage, wrote in the margin that he had heard Louis's view expressed here from Louis's tutor, Hardouin de Péréfixe.

19 During the reign of Louis XIV the king's council grew and split into four. The *conseil d'en-haut,* which usually met on the first floor at Versailles,was the highest and most private council, also known as the *conseil étroit* or *conseil privé.* The *conseil des dépêches,*or *conseil de l'intérieur,* dealt with despatches to and from the provinces. The *conseil des finances* or *conseil de direction* assessed and levied taxes, serving also as a court of appeal in matters of taxation. The *conseil des parties* or *conseil d'Etat privé* was the supreme royal court of appeal, which was trying to wrest the

final appellate function away from the *parlement*. The councils at first generally met daily for two or three hours.

20 La Porte speaks of the personal search of Anne by Séguier, and Montglat reports that 'il visita dans ses poches et sous son mouchoir de cou, la traitant comme une criminelle'. The search took place at Chantilly some days after Séguier and the archbishop of Paris had dismissed the abbess of Val-de-Grâce where they had searched, naturally in vain, for incriminating material, which must certainly once have existed and will as certainly have been destroyed. Tallemant says of the search of Anne's person that Séguier 'ne l'interrogea pas seulement, mais il la fouilla en quelque sorte; car il luy mit la main dans son corps, pour voir s'il n'y avoit point de lettres; au moins y regarda-t-il, et approcha sa main de ses tetons' (*Historiettes,* ed. Antoine Adam, vol. 1, Paris 1967, pp. 237 and 906–07).

21 Mazarin's notebooks contain a self-congratulatory reference at having made Mme de Chevreuse believe that he was impotent. Marie de Chevreuse, born Rohan-Montbazon (1600–79), was the widow of Luynes, the older companion through whom Louis XIII ruled France from the death of Concini to Luynes's own death in 1621. Marie then married her lover, Claude de Lorraine, third son of the duc de Guise, later duc de Chevreuse. Mme de Chevreuse became, with Mlle de Verneuil, illegitimate daughter of Henri IV, a close companion of Anne of Austria, whose more frivolous side she encouraged. Among the lovers of Mme de Chevreuse were Anne's brother, Philip IV of Spain, Buckingham, by whom she had a child, and cardinal de Retz. She took part in several anti-Richelieu intrigues, was banished in 1626 and 1633, and was helped by La Rochefoucauld to flee to Spain in 1637. She returned to France after Richelieu's death but in 1643 quarrelled with Anne. The princesse de Guémené, later a strong supporter of Port-Royal and the Jansenist movement, also had Retz as a lover.

22 See Claude Dulong, *Mazarin,* Paris 1999, p.71.

23 Mme de Rambouillet is credited with inventing the system of reception rooms opening off one another in series instead of the usual system of a central grand staircase and reception rooms opening on to corridors. She also favoured blue and gold over the usual brown. She received the Condés and nourished the talent of many of the great literary stars of the second and third quarters of the century. Her eldest daughter, Julie d'Angennes, married Charles de Saint-Maure, duc de Montauzier, governor of Louis XIV's son. Mme de Sablé was part of the circle which included La Rochefoucauld, who at one time called on her daily. Its principal pastime was the confection of moral observations or 'maxims'.

24 The letters were in fact from a Mme de Fouquerolles to the marquis de Maulévrier.

25 In a newly planted and ultra-fashionable 'casino' garden where today the Tuileries give way to the Place de la Concorde. It was run chiefly for the relaxation of young bloods, who notoriously drank too much there.

26 Mme de Chevreuse, born in 1600, was the daughter of Hercule de Rohan (1568–1654), duc de Montbazon, generally regarded as so dull-witted as to be a laughing-stock. Hercule remarried in 1628 at the age of sixty the daughter of the comte de Vertus. His daughter by his second marriage married the son by his first marriage, brother of the duchesse de Chevreuse, who was herself at least ten years older than her mother-in-law. The husband of the duchesse de Chevreuse had a well-known liaison with his step-mother, Mme de Montbazon. The reader is invited to be aware only that everyone present knew all this, and much else besides.

27 See H. Chérot S.J., *La première jeunesse de Louis XIV 1643–53,* Paris 1892.

28 Godeau was the bishop of Grasse, and, like Bensserade, an habitué of the salon of Mme de Rambouillet.

29 The constitution of the German diet finally acknowledged that the empire was not a unitary state, and the diet became a congress of envoys representing the emperor, the seven electors, the princes and the towns. The decrees of a diet were known as its 'recess' (from the Latin 'recessus imperii'), and the last diet to issue one was that of Regensburg in 1654. The next diet, Regensburg 1663, was never formally dissolved, but continued inactively until the dissolution of the empire in 1806.

30 On the equivalent in specie of French income, expenditure and debt, see Pierre Goubert, *Mazarin,* Paris 1990, and on the actual figures and dates for the borrowing, on Mazarin's willingness to gamble by borrowing ahead in anticipation of further military victories, an end to the war and a satisfactory peace treaty before actually bankrupting France, see Richard Bonney, *Political Change in France under Richelieu and Mazarin,* Oxford 1978, pp. 50–6.

4   The King Comes of Age

1 See Orest Ranum, *The Fronde: A French Revolution,* New York/London 1993. Professor Ranum's essay, published separately without notes, was written as a pendant to his *Paris in the Age of Absolutism,* New York 1968. See on the Fronde also Adolphe Chéruel, *Histoire de France pendant la Minorité de Louis XIV,* 4 vols, Paris 1879 and, especially, Françoise Bayard, *Le Monde des Financiers au XVIIe siècle,* Paris 1988.

2 On these uprisings and their context in French social history see, for instance, the author's *Cardinal Richelieu and the Making of France,* London and New York 2000, pp. 201–10.

3 The Grand' Chambre was the most important chamber of the Paris *parlement,* hearing appeals from lower courts and cases involving either royal rights or holders of high legal office. It must be distinguished from the Grand Conseil, which was not part of the *parlement,* but the most important of the special courts, judging cases referred by the king or cases referred by the Conseil des parties, a section of the King's council

which under Louis XIV became the ultimate interpreter of law and took over the appellate function to which the *parlement* aspired. See on these bodies Roland E. Mousnier, *The Institutions of France under the Absolute Monarchy 1598–1789,* tr. Brian Pearce, Chicago/London 1979.

4 See Régine Astier, 'Louis XIV, "Premier Danseur",' in *Sun King. The Ascendancy of French Culture under Louis XIV,* ed. David Lee Rubin, Washington/London/Toronto 1992, pp. 73–102.

5 Rossi, by birth a Neapolitan, had become attached to the Barberini family while retaining his post as organist of the French church in Rome. Cardinal Antonio Barberini commissioned his first opera *Il palazzo incantato,* and it was the success of this work which led Mazarin to invite Rossi to Paris.

6 The king's dancing lessons were aimed at developing coordination, agility, and balance, especially on account of the vestigial unevenness in the length of his legs left over from infancy. The *courante,* which became Louis's favourite dance, was danced by one couple at a time, normally after a *branle* involving all the assembled couples, and was notoriously difficult to bring off with grace. See Régine Astier's essay indicated in note 4. Monsieur Vincent (Saint Vincent de Paul) persuaded the regent to postpone commissioning the structure for an *Andromède* for the following season. See Claude Dulong, *Mazarin,* Paris 1999, p.340.

7 Henriette de France, daughter of Henri IV and Marie de' Medici, who had married Charles I of England, must be distinguished from her daughter, Henriette d'Angleterre, sister of Charles II, who was to marry her own first cousin, Philippe d'Orléans, Anne of Austria's second child and therefore brother of Louis XIV.

8 The interpretation of the royal decrees and the reaction of the office-holders given by Orest Ranum, *The Fronde,* NewYork/London 1993, has been significantly modified by that of Claude Dulong, *Mazarin,* Paris 1999.

9 Charles de la Porte, duc de la Meilleraye, was a distant relative of Richelieu, much advanced by the cardinal partly for his reliable support, and partly in gratitude for the support given by the La Porte family when Richelieu's mother was impoverished on the unexpected death of his father. La Meilleraye was made captain of the artillery, *lieutenant-général* of Normandy, governor of Rouen and of Nantes, and a *maréchal de France.* He was a crassly incompetent general. Tallemant's portrait is unusually hostile (*Historiettes,* ed. Adam, vol. 1, Paris 1967, pp. 324–333).

10 For a detailed discussion of these matters, see Hubert Méthivier, *La Fronde,* Paris 1984, and for the various organs of government and legal administration, Bernard Barbiche, *Les Institutions de la monarchie française à l'époque moderne,* Paris 1999.

11 The tension between court and *parlement* was not made easier by the ambiguous political position of the coadjutor bishop of Paris, Jean-

François-Paul de Gondi, from 1652 Cardinal de Retz, and from 21 March 1654 archbishop of Paris. Retz (who pronounced and from 1671 spelt his name 'Rais'), was the famous author of what he never called *Mémoires*, which he also did not publish, had the right of reversion of the Paris see on the death of his uncle, had been involved with Beaufort, whom however he despised, and at least affected to be strongly populist. He presided over the *Te Deum* celebrating Condé's victory at Lens on 26 August 1648. He had not decided which side to join, court or crowd, and thereby lost the initiative to Condé. Gondi and his friends began to accept the name *frondeurs.*

12 On the wider European perspectives, see G. Parker and L.M. Smith (eds.), *The General Crisis of the Seventeenth Century,* London 1978.

13 See chapter 2, note 14.

14 On Gondi, see note 11 above. His hostility to Mazarin developed only slowly between 1645 and 1648, although he was still working for Mazarin in 1651, when the final break came. For some account of the gossip generated by his scandalous youth, see Tallement's *Historiettes* (ed. Adam, vol. 2, Paris 1961, pp. 303–12). Retz wrote the posthumously published '*Mémoires*'between 1675 and 1677. Addressed to a 'Madame' who can only have been Mme de Sévigné, a major portion of the first of three parts has been destroyed, and the self-justificatory text has been generally misinterpreted by later generations. For details of the life and a guide to the contents and interpretation of the *Mémoires,* see the author's, *Guide to French Literature: Beginnings to 1789,* Andover/Detroit 1994, pp. 705 –17.

15 The modern reader, confronted by the sexual liaisons of high-placed clerics like Gondi, bound by vow to chastity, may be too easily tempted to think instantly in terms of cynicism and hypocrisy. Such categories may scarcely be out of place according to the values of today, but are not appropriate to the same degree when applied to baroque culture. Liaisons of this sort even in the seventeenth century certainly infringed the vow of chastity taken with the conferring of the sub-diaconate, and were mortally sinful, as were the adulterous or merely extra-marital sexual liaisons even of the laity, a matter which requires confronting when considering Louis's own liaisons. But Mazarin, although a cardinal, was not in holy orders, and was at least not bound by a solemn vow of chastity. However, the occasions on which the sexual liaisons of the great were considered to be in the public forum, and on which abstention from the eucharist was and was not imposed, still constitute a difficulty encountered by modern readers concerned with the religious history of seventeenth-century France. This was the apex to the baroque, and then the strong moral reaction to it, rather than a matter of merely corrupt or simply lax confessors.

    Confessors may have felt it possible to condone frequentation of the sacrament in spite of seriously sinful liaisons if it could be expected that scandal imperilling the eternal salvation of others might thereby be avoided or diminished. To have refused Louis XIII, head of the French church, access to the eucharist on account of his well-known homosexual liaisons might well have caused public scandal, even schism, whereas the tightened moral norms of Saint-Cyran had become widespread by the time Pascal wrote the *Lettres provinciales* in 1656–7 and Louis XIV exchanged Mme de Montespan for Mme de Maintenon. The casuist literature of the reign affords ample opportunity to look at the different and changing moral principles which the church sought to enforce, including the moral preferability of the choice of the lesser evil and the relative malice of different forms of transgression of the moral law.

16 Among other important sources for this incident are the memoirs of some of the participants and the works of the literary memorialists. There is an eye-witness account of events in the strongly monarchist *Journal* of the royal *maître d'hôtel,* Jean Vallier (ed. H. Courteault and P. de Vaissière, Paris 1902).

17 On this incident, see Orest Ranum, *The Fronde,* New York/London 1993, pp. 159–160.

18 Peace with the emperor was signed on 24 October.

19 The *parlement* condemned Mazarin on 9 January, giving him eight days to leave the kingdom, and on 13 February ordered the confiscation of the contents of the 'palais Mazarin' (the former hôtel Tubeuf). The furniture and collections Mazarin had left behind were sold for 160,000 livres, although they are said to have been worth 800,000 See Claude Dulong, *Mazarin,* Paris 1999, pp. 124–5.

20 This may have been mere bravado on his part, but it is more likely that he wanted to know what was being alleged, and in what tone. One of Mazarin's mistakes was to have failed to cultivate a team of writers of his own, and to have failed to pay generously and soon enough the few writers, like Jean Silhon, Jacques Esprit and even his librarian, the learned Gabriel Naudé, who did publicly support him. On the Mazarinades, see Hubert Carrier, *La Presse de la Fronde (1648–1653): Les Mazarinades,* 2 vols, Geneva 1989–91.

21 The matter remains delicate. When François Bluche published his *Louis XIV* in France in 1984, it won the Grand Prix de l'Histoire Moët-Henessy, was for many weeks France's number one best-seller, and was extravagantly and often deservedly praised. Yet it dismisses the fact that Mazarin and Anne of Austria were lovers as 'an old libel' (tr. Mark Greengrass, Oxford 1990, p. 40) although the truth of that allegation was simply incontrovertible, certainly since Claude Dulong, a professional archival historian, published *Anne d'Autriche* in 1980. Mme Dulong, who admits that the couple were lovers, but, to save the paternity of Louis XIV, only from a date as late as she can possibly hope to retain credibility for, nevertheless maintains that Mazarin was not in France at the moment of the conception of Anne's elder son, although Georges Dethan had published Mazarin's letter headed 'Paris

16 September 1637' in 1968. Apparently Mazarin, based in Rome, did visit Paris that autumn, although it is not surprising that traces of any such visit have vanished. Bluche surmises that Louis must have known about the allegations from La Porte, who was still his valet, and still intensely hostile to Mazarin.

22 Both here and later it is essential to bear in mind that a chancellor could not be dismissed but that custody of the seal of France might be removed from him and bestowed elsewhere. With the custody of the seals went the chancellor's principal power.

23 According to Mathieu de Molé, *Mémoires* (ed. A. Champollion-Figeac, 4 vols, Paris 1855–57, vol. 4, p. 359) Mazarin wrote with apparent seriousness to this effect to Le Tellier, the minister for the army: 'Mme de Longueville songe et travaille à me faire tuer.'

24 The two frondes were considered to be that of the *parlement* and that of the nobles. But the isolation of two different *frondes* in this way is historically misleading and has here been abandoned. Various members of the higher aristocracy at different times allied with or separated from the Paris *parlement*. What has as far as possible to be respected in this complex narrative are the chronological developments in the relationships between *parlement* and different members of the aristocracy, much complicated by the way in which and the frequency with which Gondi and Turenne changed sides. The relationships between Gaston and the other main players were seldom quite clear.

25 According to an ordinance of 1374, kings of France attained their majority on their thirteenth birthdays, 'for it has often been observed that these persons anointed by heaven's special favour are commonly enriched while still young with many virtues and fine qualities which are not to be found in others of baser condition.' See Roland E. Mousnier, *The Institutions of France under the Absolute Monarchy 1598–1789,* tr. Brian Pearce, Chicago and London 1979, pp. 651–52.

26 On the correspondence, see Claude Dulong, 'Les signes cryptiques dans la correspondance d'Anne d'Autriche avec Mazarin. Contribution à l'emblématique du XVIIe siècle' in the *Bibliothèque de l'école des chartes,* vol. CXL, 198, pp. 61–83 and 'L'S fermé et les signes d'amour dans la correspondance Anne d'Autriche–Mazarin' in *Revue française d'héraldique et sigillographie,* 50, 1980, pp. 31–8. In addition to the letters of Mazarin to the regent during the Fronde published by J. Ravenel, Paris 1836, and to the nine volumes of letters published by A. Chéruel and G. d'Avenel, Paris 1872–1906, the partial publication of Mazarin's *Carnets* by Victor Cousin, *Journal des savants,* Paris 1854–6 and 'Les Carnets de Mazarin pendant la Fronde, sept–oct. 1648,' ed. A. Chéruel, *Revue historique,* May–August 1877, pp. 103–8, there are still unpublished letters in the Archives du ministère des Affaires étrangères, série Mémoires et documents, France 268.

27 Mlle de Chevreuse was still Gondi's mistress, earning her the sobriquet of 'la coadjutrice' because Gondi was still coadjutor bishop of Paris.

Since the duc de Longueville was not a prince of the blood, the young and pretty Mlle de Chevreuse, by marrying Conti, who was, would also become Mme de Longueville's superior in the social hierarchy, which was altogether unacceptable to Condé's sister. A formidable woman, Geneviève de Longueville is known for her statement that she did not enjoy 'les plaisirs innocents'. After being the mistress of La Rochefoucauld and almost certainly of Turenne, she was at this period about to launch into a liaison with the duc de Nemours.

28 The surviving series of letters from Anne to Mazarin dates only from 1653.

29 Millet de Jeure, in particular, went out of his way to reassure Mazarin how constantly he was in Anne's mind.

30 On this incident, see Claude Dulong, *Anne d'Autriche,* Paris 1980, pp. 369–73, and *Mazarin,* Paris 1999, pp. 140–3.

31 Condé hoped to find support in Périgord and Poitou, largely controlled by his allies, as well as the west coast through which he might have received help from Cromwell. His brother-in-law, Longueville, was governor of Normandy, and both Bouillon and Turenne had followings and lands in Auvergne. While Turenne and Bouillon were on his side, and with Spanish support assured, Condé represented a real threat.

32 Known as the princess Palatine on account of her marriage to the duke of Bavaria, Anne de Gonzague de Clèves, daughter of the duc de Nevers and sister of the queen of Poland, had secretly married Henri de Guise, cardinal archbishop of Reims, probably in 1639. She followed her husband in male attire to the Low Countries, but was discovered and stopped at the border. She then learned that her husband had married elsewhere, and she herself married the duke of Bavaria in 1645. She had developed what may well have been an inherited gift and taste for intrigue, and felt at home with Gondi's chameleon tactics. She must of course be distinguished from the Wittelsbach 'princess Palatine', generally known as 'Liselotte', who became the second wife of Louis's younger brother, Philippe.

33 Anne-Marie-Louise d'Orléans, duchesse de Montpensier (1627–93), it is to be remembered, was Gaston's daughter by his first wife, who died in giving her birth. Until the events here related, she much hoped to marry her cousin, the king. In 1662 she was exiled to Saint-Fargeau for a year and a half for refusing to marry the king of Portugal, but did almost certainly finally marry in secret the comte de Lauzun, six years her junior, at the age of forty-two. Lauzun had been sent to prison at Pinerolo for insultingly taunting Louis, who had withdrawn his consent to the marriage.

34 In French at this date 'arrêter' means both 'arrest' and '(cause to) wait'. It is possible that Retz thought that he had been told to wait when Louis, who had gone to hear mass, had in fact given orders for his arrest.

5   The *Sacre*, Marie Mancini and Marriage

1   In 1653 Louis was with the army for the capture of Mouzon and Sainte-Menehoulde, in 1657 for the fall of Montmédy, and in 1658 he joined it after the taking of Dunkirk on 25 June.

2   The evidence is further conveniently analysed in considerable detail by John B. Wolf in his *Louis XIV,* London 1968, pp. 67–81.

3   Most recently John B. Wolf (see previously note). Earlier generations of historians sometimes simply assumed that Louis must have agreed with their own widespread hatred of Mazarin, but since that assumption has been shown to be wrong, the strong influence of Mazarin on Louis has not been contested.

4   The view that Mazarin and Anne actually married one another, as they might have done without canonical or constitutional impediment, derives from a direct assertion to that effect by Philippe's second wife, Elisabeth-Charlotte von Wittelsbach ('Madame Palatine' or 'Liselotte'), and has been investigated by Victor Molinier in *Notice sur cette question historique: Anne d'Autriche et Mazarin étaient-ils secrètement mariés?* Paris 1887. Molinier accepted the marriage, as more recently and tentatively does Professor Wolf, in *Louis XIV,* London 1968, p. 626: ' . . . circumstantial evidence points to marriage. My own studies support this thesis', although most subsequent historians who have not ignored the question have rejected the marriage hypothesis. Although such a marriage might validly and licitly have taken place, custom (rather than law) would certainly have been strong enough to entail the resignation of the cardinalate if knowledge of any marriage had become public. Those who do support a marriage tend to put it in 1647.

For a printed version of some of Anne's letters to Mazarin, see Victor Cousin, *Madame de Hautefort et Madame de Chevreuse,* Paris 1856, pp. 469–83, and for an (incomplete) edition of the letters of Mazarin, *Lettres du cardinal Mazarin pendant son ministère,* ed. A. Chéruel and G. Avenel, 9 vols, Paris 1872–1906. The possibility of a clandestine marriage between Mazarin and Anne seems in fact remote, although the reasons for rejecting it do not seem to be those advanced by Claude Dulong *Anne d'Autriche,* Paris 1980, and *Mazarin,* Paris 1990, which hinge on difficulties of privacy before a somewhat arbitrarily chosen 1653, a date which for Mme Dulong has the advantage of excluding Mazarin's legitimate genetic paternity of Louis.

5   The *Mémoires de Louis XIV,* edited and annotated by Jean Longnon, Paris 1978, were originally intended to become and to be entitled *Instructions.* They were a series of comments, reflections, excuses, explanations, and pieces of both self-delusion and advice written by Louis to be worked up into guidance for his son, the grand Dauphin. They were first shown to him between 1674 and 1677, soon after he reached his royal majority at thirteen. The dauphin died in 1711, before his father, and Louis tried to burn the unfinished *Mémoires* in 1714, but yielded to the pleas

of the maréchal de Noailles to hand them to him for safe-keeping. Noailles deposited them in the Bibliothèque du Roi in 1749. Their final version was based on a draft by Paül Pellisson.

Begun as a series of diary-like short reflections, dictated to a secretary called Rose, and drawing with Colbert's help on Colbert's account of the council's activities immediately after Mazarin's death, Louis continued to dictate notes, headings and short passages. From 1666 he left a higher proportion of the draft material in his own hand. Work forced Colbert to resign from his cooperation, and his place was taken by the président de Périgny, tutor to the grand Dauphin, who reworked the earlier material drafted probably by Rose. When Périgny died in 1670, his place was taken by Pellisson. What we now have is the portion of the text based on the years 1666 to 1668, written contemporaneously, and that for 1661 and 1662, written ten years after the years to which they are devoted. The manuscripts contain modifications in the text made by Louis as well as marks of his to denote passages which required adjustment. In a panegyric read to the Académie on 3 February 1671, Pellisson describes the *Mémoires* as containing 'Les secrets de la royauté et les leçons éternelles de ce qu'il faut éviter ou suivre'.

6 See Mme Dulong's *Anne d'Autriche*, Paris 1980, pp. 416–24, and the appendix, pp. 477–82, which traces the recent history of the emblem, and gives bibliographical indications of other treatments of it.

7 The singular is worth noting.

8 On Mazarin's position as 'the king's surrogate father' see, besides Claude Dulong, *Anne d'Autriche*, Paris 1980, especially chapters xiv and xv, John B. Wolf, *Louis XIV*, London 1968, pp. 68–9 and 84–8, 'One thing that we can sure of is that Louis was privy to the relationship between his mother and Mazarin' (p.86). Professor Wolf is inclined to support the theory of a marriage primarily to avoid imputing to the flamboyantly pious Anne, much given to the rites, ceremonies and trappings of the Catholicism of the Spanish baroque, the sinfulness of an extra-marital union.

9 Choisy's titillating and gossip-ridden, entertaining, unreliable and occasionally salacious memoirs have been edited and annotated by Georges Mongrédien, *Mémoires de l'abbé de Choisy: Mémoires pour servir à l'histoire de Louis XIV; Mémoires de l'abbé Choisy habillé en femme*, Paris 1966.

10 *The Sun King*, Harmondsworth 1994, pp. 54–5. Philippe's two wives were Henriette d'Angleterre, daughter of Charles I of England and Henriette-Marie, the daughter of Henri IV, who died in 1670, and Elizabeth-Charlotte von Wittelsbach ('Liselotte'), princess Palatine (the Palatinate being the province east of the Rhine to the south and west of Heidelberg) whom Philippe married on 21 November 1671. To marry Philippe, she had to become a Catholic, thereby forfeiting a claim to succession to the English throne stronger than that of George I. Philippe is described as 'a caricature of his brother, three-quarters

his height and more oriental-looking, swarthy', interested chiefly in 'clothes and jewels, parties, etiquette (on which he was sound), objects of art and boys'. The identity of his father is as doubtful as that of the father of Louis. If Louis XIV was Mazarin's son, the identity of Philippe's father need not necessarily have been the same. Philippe's mistress was Hortense Mancini, daughter of Geronima, Mazarin's sister.

11 The volume of eighteen pages with four engravings was published by the Imprimerie royale, entitled *La Guerre des Suisses, traduite du premier livre des 'Commentaires' de Jules César, par Louis XIV Dieudonné, roi de France et de Navarre.*

12 Both Richelieu and Mazarin would have felt some self-satisfaction had they lived to read Louis's *Mémoires,* to be written later for the dauphin. The sentiments expressed by the king are those Mazarin had striven to cultivate in him, not excluding the insistence on caution when dealing with the clergy, rather apt to exaggerate its importance in the governance of the realm. The sentiments Louis expressed in the *Mémoires* do not, however, correspond to the values he actually embraced.

13 See on this matter Georges Lacour-Gayet, *L'Education politique de Louis XIV,* Paris 1923, p.170.

14 *Mémoires,* ed Longnon, Paris 1978, p. 90. It does not seem likely that Louis is consciously comparing his role to that of Christ (Ephesians, I, 23). The comparison is more likely to be one of those revealing linguistic lapses which unconsciously reveal patterns of thought which are scattered throughout the *Mémoires.*

15 *Mémoires,* ed. Longnon, p. 133.

16 La Mothe le Vayer's essays for the king on geography, rhetoric, and morals date from 1651, on finance from 1653, on politics from 1654, on logic 1655, and on physics from 1658 and reflect the conservative orthodoxies of their dates of composition.

17 See Ian Dunlop, *Louis XIV,* London 2001, p. 23.

18 The tonsure was still important in civil society as it conferred clerical status, with the right to be tried in ecclesiastical courts and to be exempt from certain taxes. The four 'minor orders', not part of the sacrament, but deriving from functions in the liturgy of the early church and in recent centuries usually conferred together as a stepping stone to the major orders are ostiarius, lector, exorcist and acolyte.

19 On Bensserade, see Chares Silin, *Benserade and his Ballets de cour,* Baltimore 1940.

20 Published as *Mascarade en forme de Ballet, dansé par le Roi au Palais-Cardinal.* The ballet, although performed only privately, was noticed in the *Gazette,* in Loret's *La Muse historique,* and in a letter of Mme de Sévigné of 2 March 1651 to Antoine Godeau.

21 Sagredo, Venetian ambassador from 1653 to 1655, called it a 'very rich and costly ballet'. Giacomo Torelli was the Italian stage designer who introduced fabricated rather than merely painted décors and invented the machinery for moving wings about the stage, so facilitating the

creation of French opera. He used fireworks, fountains and often more spectacular contrivances on stage, is said to have flooded a theatre's pit to stage a naval battle, and was in Paris at Mazarin's invitation from 1645 until 1662. The *Ballet de la nuit* was staged on 23 February 1653, but Torelli had already been at work on the scenery for four months before Christmas.

22 On the symbolism of the roles danced by the young king, see the essay by Jean-Pierre Néraudau, 'Du Christ à Apollon' in *La Tragédie lyrique*, Les carnets du théâtre des Champs-Elysées, Paris 1991, pp. 4–21, and the same author's *L'Olympe du Roi-Soleil. Mythologie et idéologie royale au Grand Siècle*, Paris 1986. The Venetian Cavalli was invited to Paris in 1660 by Mazarin to write a prodigiously lavish opera for Louis's wedding to Maria-Teresa, but his opera *L'Ercole amante*, written to a libretto by the Venetian Francesco Buti with long ballet interludes by Lulli, was not a success in Paris, where taste in the 1660s was already moving towards the simpler *comédie-ballet* of the Molière–Lulli collaboration, and away from the imaginative, artistic and technical prodigality that Cavalli had conjured up for the wedding. In 1670, Louis was finally to dance for the last time. He had had himself replaced for the second performance in the roles of Neptune and the sun-Apollo for which he had carefully rehearsed in the ballets of the prologue and finale of *Les Amants magnifiques*. This was a 'divertissement' for which Louis had commissioned the libretto from Molière, a genre which in France was to develop swiftly through the *tragédie-ballet* to the *tragédie lyrique* of the Quinault–Lulli cooperation.

23 It seems certain that Mme de Sévigné's daughter Françoise-Marguerite (later the comtesse de Grignan) was among them, and that the king's interest might have proved very damaging to her future. Loret's *Muse historique*, reporting on Bensserade's 1664 *Ballet des Amours déguisés*, alludes to her worthiness to become the king's mistress. See Roger Duchêne, *Mme de Sévigné ou la chance d'être femme*, Paris 1982, pp. 189–202.

24 Ian Dunlop, *Louis XIV*, London 2001, p. 39.

25 Geronima's remaining child, Philippe, later to become duc de Nevers and to marry a niece of Mme de Montespan, did not seem to Mazarin adequate to carry on the succession to the position and wealth which Mazarin had amassed. Mazarin made the husband of Hortense, La Meilleraye, his principal heir, providing he changed his name to become in his turn the duc de Mazarin. Hortense was to leave him, and live with her brother Philippe, the duc de Nevers, in an apparently incestuous relationship. She died an alcoholic. Marie-Anne later protected La Fontaine and was an important advocate of the party of *modernes* in the famous *Querelle des anciens et des modernes*. She married the son of the duc de Bouillon who had been implicated in the 1643 conspiracy against Richelieu. Like Hortense, she was also to be compromised in what is known as the poisons affair, of which some account must come later.

26 The most important source for Louis's medical history is Vallot's *Journal de la santé du Roi Louis XIV de l'année 1647 à l'année 1711*, ed. J.-A. Le Roi, Paris 1862. Drawing on this, together with letters, memoirs and other sources, C.D. O'Malley has compiled a succinct account in 'The Medical History of Louis XIV: Intimations of Mortality' in *Louis XIV and the Craft of Kingship*, ed. John C. Rule, pp.133–54. As a boy, Louis's health had been in the care of Jacques Cousinot, a graduate of the Paris school which, led by Gui Patin, adhered to the orthodoxy of Galen's herbal remedies, and was rigidly hostile to the Islamic influences which had permeated the Montpellier school, relied on antinomy, and been supported by Richelieu. Cousinot was succeeded by François Vaultier, also of the Paris school, although in fact a Montpellier graduate, and criticized by Patin for ignorance of Galen and Hippocrates and for reliance on astrology and alchemy. Vallot was an alumnus of Montpellier and a friend of Vaultier, to whom he gives much retrospective credit for the cure of Louis from smallpox in 1647. The reliability of the *Journal* is less than total, since Vallot knew it would be read by the king, whose faults of character, gluttony and sexual indulgence were on that account systematically glossed over.

27 Bussy-Rabutin remarks on her beauty, but says that it was the perfection of her dancing that first attracted the king's attention. She went to a convent.

28 There is what purports to be an autobiographical memoir of challenged authenticity by Marie Mancini which is well informed and the ultimate source for much that has been written about her, the *Apologie, ou les véritables mémoires de Marie Mancini, connétable de Colonna écrites par elle-même*.

29 On Marie Mancini, see Claude Dulong, *Marie Mancini*, Paris 1993.

30 The agreement at Westphalia between France, Sweden and the empire had ceded Alsace to France, but the cession was not water-tight, as it excluded Strasbourg itself and its bishopric, and included widely dispersed free imperial towns (Landau, Wissembourg, Haguenau, Rosheim, Obernai, Sélestat, Colmar, Münster, Turckheim and Kaysersberg) where overlordship was virtually unenforceable.

31 Mazarin signed a commercial treaty with England on 28 November 1655, and, on 23 March 1657 the military and political Treaty of Paris, to be renewed on 28 March 1658

32 The first wife of Gaston d'Orléans, Marie de Bourbon-Montpensier, had died giving birth to Anne-Marie de Montpensier, known as 'La grande Mademoiselle'. By his second wife, Marguerite, sister of duke Charles III of Lorraine, he had three daughters, Marguerite, who married the duke of Tuscany, Elizabeth, who married the duke of Guise, and Françoise-Madeleine, who married Charles-Emmanuel II, duke of Savoy, but died before she was seventeen.

33 Mme Dulong, in *Mazarin*, Paris 1999, pp. 268–9 points out that there are two versions of what Marie said: 'Ah, sire, vous êtes roi et je pars!'

(abbé de Choisy), and 'Vous pleurez! et vous êtes le maître!' (Mme de Motteville).

34 Claude Dulong, *Mazarin,* Paris 1999, p. 278.

35 Ian Dunlop, in his *Louis XIV,* London 2001, p.52, quotes an old Spanish colonial saying on Spanish procrastination: 'If death came from Spain, we should be immortal.'

36 France further received, as well as Roussillon and most of Artois, Gravelines, Bourbourg, Bergues and Saint-Venant in Flanders, and in Hainault the fortifications of Landrécies, Quesnoy, Thionville and Damvillers.

37 There are at least half a dozen surviving anonymous contemporary pamphlets giving reasonably full details of the ceremony of the signing of the peace, and of both the wedding ceremonies.

6 Mazarin's Death and the Fall of Fouquet

1 The original has disappeared, but is quoted from a nineteenth-century transcription by Ch.-A. Walckenaer in *Mémoires touchant la vie et les écrits de Marie de Rabutin-Chantal . . . marquise de Sévigné,* vol.3, Paris 1845, by Claude Dulong in both *Anne d'Autriche,* Paris 1990, p. 450, and *Mazarin,* Paris 1999, p. 365.

2 The entry is the scene of a number of surviving engravings, while the generally classical symbolism used in the procession and the street decorations is explained and the spectacle described in a dozen or so contemporary pamphlets.

3 See Ian Dunlop, *Louis XIV,* London 2001, p.65.

4 On the editing of the *Mémoires,* see chapter 5, note 5. They were begun in 1661, and taken up again in 1666. The last revisions in the hand of Louis XIV were made in 1668.

5 Callot's famous engravings are almost more striking for the resigned expectation of death by starvation, or by physical assault, and by the general cheapness in which life was held which they communicate, than for the hideous suffering they depict.

6 See Nancy Mitford, *The Sun King,* London 1966. Ms Mitford offers these episodes as examples of Louis's ruthlessness stemming partly from lack of imagination and 'partly because he thought it was his duty to uphold the dignity of God's representative on earth.' Louis wanted the dauphin to think of himself as by divine right ruler of France, which is not the same thing. It is also bizarre to accuse the creator of Versailles and Marly of a lack of imagination, even if admiration for his personal taste has never been strong.

7 It says much about the evolution of French culture that ordinary people were clumsily introduced as vehicles for tragedy on the stage only in the *drames bourgeois* of the second half of the eighteenth century, and that, after the renaissance, love was never explored for its own intrinsically tragic potential until Racine took up the theme from

Thomas Corneille after the middle of the seventeenth century. After euphoric rehabilitation in the first half of the century, love, like the other 'passions', began to be explored again by Racine, Port-Royal and the secular moralists later in the century for its destructive potential. The eighteenth century examines passionate love for its innocence or its life-enhancing properties again in Fragonard and Boucher, Rousseau and Diderot. The exploration of love for its capacity to provoke tragedy was to be reinstated by the romantic generation of the second quarter of the nineteenth century.

8 'Mais Dieu même dont la bonté n'a point de bornes ne trouve pas toujours à récompenser, et est quelquefois contraint de punir. Quelque douleur que nous ayons de faire du mal, nous devons en être consolés, quand nous sentons en nous-même que nous le faisons comme lui, par la seule vue juste et légitime d'un bien mille fois plus considérable' see *Mémoires*, ed. Jean Longnon, Paris 1978, p. 146.

9 *Mémoires*, op. cit., p. 256. Few even of Louis's court preachers would have endorsed this interpretation of the Christian ethic.

10 The word 'généreux' has an almost technical meaning in the middle third of the seventeenth century, where in Descartes it formally denotes the principal virtue, and includes courage, determination, strength of purpose and something of the Roman *virtus*. It is the basis of the merit which itself in the literature of the period is the foundation of the worthiness which justified becoming the object of even passionate love. It is, however, not necessarily either ethically good or bad. From very early in the seventeenth century major French authors were aware that heroic grandeur, strength of purpose and determination of will were moral but not ethical qualities. They could underpin evil actions as well as good ones, as in Pierre Corneille's Cléopâtre from *Rodogune,* and for La Rochefoucauld, 'Il y a des héros en mal comme en bien.'

11 On the motivation and causes of the Dutch wars, see Paul Sonnino, *Louis XIV and the Origins of the Dutch War,* Cambridge 1988.

12 The unreliable Choisy relates that Mazarin's Theatine confessor told him on his deathbed that he would be damned if he did not make restitution of all his illegitimately gained wealth, whereat Colbert suggested giving everything to the king, who could be relied on to return to Mazarin his enormous wealth. This means of obtaining absolution without making restitution sounds only too plausible, and Choisy's dates, like his list of executors, are correct. Colbert, still unknown, was in complete charge of Mazarin's affairs, and is alleged by Choisy to have had a private, and secret, entry into Mazarin's room, and to have known the whereabouts of 15 million livres in cash belonging to the cardinal, of which 1.2 million livres was to go towards the marriage of each niece, and the rest to the state: 'Ce fut là le commencement de la fortune de Colbert.' See Jean Meyer, *Colbert,* Paris 1981, pp. 164–5.

13 Giuseppe Dongo Ondedei was called to France by Mazarin in 1646. He was made bishop of Fréjus in 1654.

14 Mazarin had became almost obsessed by the need to prevent the compilation of an inventory. The king none the less ordered on 18 March an inventory of Mazarin's possessions and papers to be made. The papers, including Mazarin's private accounts, were divided into three, with one part to go to the new duke and duchess, one part to Colbert, and a third part, not subject to inventory, also to Colbert.

15 Colbert's biographer, Jean Meyer, in *Colbert,* Paris 1981, p. 141, points out that it is not entirely clear how Colbert came to pass from Le Tellier's service into that of Mazarin, since both claimed to have initiated the transfer after a serious dispute in 1650. It is clear that Colbert took on Mazarin's *intendance* only after being guaranteed full authority over the totality of his private business. See Colbert's letter to Mazarin of 17 February 1651.

16 Anne of Austria had begun the building of the new church at Val-de-Grâce in 1645 on plans by François Mansart. Work had been interrupted by the Fronde, but Anne was still to ask Bernini for plans for a new altar when he came to France in June 1664. Her piety, which included washing the feet of the poor on Maundy Thursday, was undoubtedly genuine, if a little self-conscious, even ostentatious. It was given to posing, posturing, exaggerated expression and elaborate decoration, no doubt tinged with superstition, but was none the less authentic. Exactly how her confessors reconciled her devotion with her taking Mazarin as a lover is a question which defeats her biographer, Claude Dulong, but it would not have been difficult for one the more euphoric casuists not yet under attack from Pascal's *Lettres provinciales* to construct a defence of her conduct according to the religious values of the 1630s, which would no longer obtain for her son half a century later. Especially if the marriage to Louis XIII was not consummated, and therefore void, it may well still have been argued in 1638 that the damage that would be done to religion and the state, whose authority was ultimately also religious, by the scandal of a revelation of Mazarin's paternity of at least her eldest son, and a break-up of the relationship, which was not adulterous and involved the breaking of no vow, would have outweighed the evil of Anne's failure strictly to adhere to the prohibition of what would have remained fornication between two unmarried persons.

17 The authority on Mazarin's finances is, apart from the biography, Claude Dulong's *La Fortune de Mazarin*, Paris 1990, and two articles in particular by the same scholar: 'Le processus d'enrichissement du Cardinal Mazarin d'après l'inventaire de l'abbé Mondin,' in the *Bibliothèque de l'Ecole des chartes*, vol. 148, 1990, pp. 355–425, and 'Les comptes bleus du Cardinal Mazarin,' in *Revue d'histoire moderne et contemporaine*, vol. 36, 1989, pp. 537–58.

18 *Mazarin,* Paris 1999, pp. 308–10. This is now the usually quoted figure

and as far as we know is easily the biggest sum left by anyone in France before the revolution. See also Daniel Dessert, 'Pouvoir et fortune au XVIIe siècle: la fortune de Mazarin', in *Revue d'Histoire Moderne et Contemporaine* (23) 1976, pp. 161–81. Other estimates put Mazarin's wealth at death nearer 40 million livres. Richelieu may not have left more than about half that amount, (see Joseph Bergin, in *Power and the Pursuit of Wealth*, New Haven and London 1985, pp. 243–56, who makes a conservative estimate of 20 million livres), and the figure given for Condé, father of the 'grand' Condé, is 14.6 million, followed by roughly 4 million amassed by the chancellor Séguier. Colbert's attack on Fouquet may well have been partly inspired by the need to deflect attention from the means by which Mazarin acquired so vast a sum, and particularly the speed with which Mazarin's wealth appears to have gone from 8 million livres in June 1658 to 35 million plus jewellery and silver at the date of death less than three years later, see Dessert, *Fouquet*, Paris 1987, pp. 236–7).

19 By no means all the relevant material has been published, and, just as we have to discount the erroneous assumptions of the authors of memoirs, so we cannot trust seventeenth-century inventories and other lists of revenue or possessions which are frequently, even generally, understated to avoid taxation, the damage done by law suits and individual bequests in the interests of residual legatees. There were also different legitimate ways of assessing wealth. Other sources include the subsequent letters of Colbert, together with the two volumes of registers of Mazarin's 'conseil d'affaires' kept by Colbert and now in the British Library. See also Daniel Dessert, 'Pouvoir et fortune au XVIIe siècle: la fortune du cardinal Mazarin', in *Revue d'histoire moderne et contemporaine*, vol. 23, 1976, pp. 161–81.

20 The term 'banker' must be used with care. There were no state banks, and in France no large and stable private houses, like the Medici in fifteenth-century Florence or the Fuggers in sixteenth-century Augsburg. The most important bank in Europe at this date was that of Amsterdam, which was taking over from the banks of Venice and Genoa. Bankers were simply merchants who dealt in foreign exchange, large loans and complex deals. The most important of France's bankers during Louis's reign was Samuel Bernard, on whom see Jacques Saint-Germain, *Samuel Bernard: le banquier des rois*, Paris 1960. Bernard was not born until 1651 and died in 1739.

21 Claude Dulong, *Anne d'Autriche*, Paris 1999, p. 313, referring to a document in the Archives étrangères (France 876, f.459 verso).

22 Le Tellier, it should be remembered, was to be first assisted and then succeeded by his son Louvois. Lionne was the nephew of Abel Servien, who had shared the *surintendance* of finance with Fouquet from 1653 until Servien's death in 1659.

23 Saint-Simon, the diarist son of the favourite of Louis XIII, is well known for his view that 'L'esprit du Roi était au-dessous de médiocre, mais

très capable de se former.' Saint-Simon's eye was as sharp as his tongue, and on many matters pertaining to Versailles and the court of the 1680s he is shrewd as well as accurate.

24 The *conseil d'en-haut* was so called because it always met on the first floor, which normally had the grandest rooms. Louis's *Mémoires* for 1661, composed some time later, speak of the circumstances, including Mazarin's death, which obliged him no longer to postpone what he had wanted, and at the same time feared, for so long. He found that in the government of the country 'disorder reigned everywhere' and that 'the finances which power the movement and functioning of this whole great monarchical body were entirely exhausted . . . Payments were unacceptably delayed, or supported only by credit, while the men of business lived in abundance, on the one hand using every kind of artifice to disguise their malpractice, and on the other hand revealing it by the insolence and effrontery of their luxury'. After a brief survey of the state of other countries, the *Mémoires* give Louis's account of the orders issued on 10 March 1661, 'I ordered the four secretaries of state to sign nothing at all without speaking to me; and the same for the *surintendant,* and that nothing should happen in the department of finance without being registered in a book I kept, with a much abbreviated synopsis where I could always see at a glance the state of funding and of the expenditure made or needing to be made.'

25 On Fouquet, see chiefly Daniel Dessert, *Fouquet,* Paris 1987.

26 The Compagnie du Saint-Sacrement, so called from 1631, was a highly secret society of influential Catholics founded in March 1630 at the Capuchin convent in the Faubourg Saint-Honoré. It was at once a pious confraternity, an important charitable organization as well as a militant promoter of religious reform and of Catholic norms of belief and behaviour. It never wanted the letters patent which would have given it legal legitimacy, although it did obtain a papal brief in 1633. There were about fifty branches outside Paris, and its members included the nuncio, Guido Bagni, the prince de Conti, the Jesuit confessor of Louis XIII, Père Suffren, the general of the Oratorians, Charles de Condren, many senior lawyers and military figures and, among the ecclesiastics, Vincent de Paul, Olier and Bossuet. It was active in enforcing the interdicts against duelling, in promoting missions to country parishes and abroad, in bringing alms to the poor and aid to the sick, in improving the conditions in hospitals, galleys and prisons, and in ensuring pastoral help where it was needed. Its charitable activity was massive, but it was resolutely anti-Huguenot, urgently sought conversions, gave inducements to the converted, and is said by contemporaries to have contributed to the build-up of the anti-Huguenot hostility which resulted in the 1685 revocation of the edict of Nantes under which the Huguenots had been given a measure of religious freedom. The power and intense secrecy of the Compagnie made it suspect to some of the higher clergy, and it eventually dissolved itself under pressure at the

end of 1660, leaving a small group which hoped to revive it, but which became extinct in about 1665.

27 Fouquet paid an annual 6,000 livres calculated on a capital value of 120,000 livres. He then paid 10,000 livres on repairs before, four months later, buying for 40,000 livres half of the *vicomté* of Melun on which Vaux depended.

28 The post was worth 450,000 livres, but Fouquet was required to find only 250,000 in cash.

29 The word 'creature' is not here pejorative, and meant little more in contemporary usage than 'favoured' or 'protected' by, 'protégé'.

30 As published by Longnon (Paris 1978), this section is based on a draft edited by Pellisson which contains numerous suggestions or questions to be put to the king before the text was finalized.

31 Ed. Longnon, pp. 11–12.

32 The language is strong, ' . . . quelque artifice qui'il pût pratiquer, je ne fus pas longtemps sans reconnaître sa mauvaise foi; car il ne pouvait s'empêcher de continuer ses dépenses excessives, de fortifier des places, d'orner des palais, de former des cabales, et de mettre sous le nom de ses amis des charges importantes qu'il leur achetait à mes dépens, dans l'espoir de se rendre bientôt l'arbitre souverain de l'Etat.' Of Fouquet's arrest on 5 September 1661, Louis dictates, 'Toute la France, persuadée aussi bien que moi de la mauvaise conduite du surintendant, applaudit à cette action, et loua particulièrement le secret dans lequel j'avais tenu, durant trois oui quatre mois, une résolution de cette nature.'

Dessert meticulously analyses the entrepreneurial activities, especially the important sea-going commercial ventures, as well as the malicious exaggerations and outright calumnies lying behind Louis's self-congratulatory account of his reaction to Fouquet's alleged misdeeds. Louis is writing for the dauphin, 'Vous serez un jour étonné, comme l'a été toute la France, de ce que je me suis engagé à cette fatigue dans un âge où l'on n'aime ordinairement que le plaisir . . . J'eus à ce travail, quoique fâcheux, moins de répugnance qu'un autre, parce que j'ai toujours considéré comme le plus doux plaisir du monde la satisfaction qu'on trouve à faire son devoir'. See *Mémoires,* ed. Longnon, pp. 81–3). That surely goes beyond mere priggishness into the realms of self-delusion.

33 Notes which had been assigned to revenues already spent were rendered next to worthless by the bankruptcy, and were readily available at some 5–10 per cent of their face value. The larger financiers were buying them up for re-assignation and redemption at par whenever better days came.

34 On Fouquet's fiscal policies and principles, see Dessert, *Fouquet,* Paris 1987, *passim.* Direct taxation passed from 12,680,000 livres in 1637 to 37,244,000 in 1645, and from 29,362,000 in 1654 to 38,103,000 in 1655. The rise in the farmed taxes was from 11,239,000 livres in 1634 to 23,959,000 in 1644 and from 16,880,000 livres in 1653 to 20,252,000

in 1659 (pp. 99 and 105–6). By 1660 Fouquet had instituted reforms which raised the farmed revenue to 32,020,000 livres (p.115), reduced direct taxes, and had begun to reduce government expenditure by reducing annual payments to individuals. Colbert, committed to increasing Mazarin's personal wealth, strongly calumniated Fouquet for his lenience, subtlety and moderation, although the importance attached by Fouquet to restoring or retaining the confidence which had to underlie the granting of credit was undoubtedly in the national interest.

35 Saint-Mandé was a property bought by Fouquet at the extreme north-west corner of the present Bois de Vincennes, on the south-east of Paris.

36 This is not the place to understake the detailed defence of Fouquet (for which see Dessert's biography). It should, however, be remarked that Fouquet's inheritance and first marriage alone had brought him some 400,000 or 500,000 livres by 1641, to which must be added the fruit of his own activities. By 1653, he was worth more than 4 million livres, and none of this sum had been acquired illegitimately. Given the date and the values of French society early in the second half of the seventeenth century, there is some merit in Fouquet's contention that his luxurious lifestyle and vast expenditure, like the purchases of royal debt, in which he was joined by friends, family and business associates, was a useful, if not necessary means of assuring the availability of credit from the banking community. The strong association of his family with the charitable works of the Catholic revival also helped his standing. He certainly had at the beginning of his career an ample basis from which anyone as intelligent, ambitious, and socially and commercially well situated as Fouquet could launch a soaring career. The early wealth holes Colbert's hostile argument below its waterline.

The eight heads of accusation against which Fouquet defended himself were:

(i)   to have made false loans on which interest was payable to him
(ii) to have made personal loans to the king in spite of being in charge of crown borrowing
(iii) to have mixed crown funds with his own
(iv) to have himself taken part in tax farms through nominees and to have sold crown debt cheaply
(v)   to have accepted bribes for allocating tax farms on favourable terms
(vi) to have traded in old debt, bought cheaply but due for rehabilitation
(vii) to have rehabilitated worthless old debt to his own profit, and
(viii) to have concluded contracts prejudicial to the crown and negligently managed crown expenditure

See Dessert, *Fouquet,* Paris 1987, p. 246.

37 Louis was also to have eight children by Mme de Montespan as well as five infants in addition to the dauphin with the queen. It is unlikely

that we shall ever know the exact number of live-born infants of whom Louis was the father.

38 This is the classic perspective adopted by the two volumes of Ernest Lavisse's *Louis XIV,* Paris 1906–8, a work which still however remains of fundamental importance for subsequent historians.

39 Louise fled the court on 24 February 1662, two days before the anticipated denunciation of her liaison with Louis in Bossuet's first Lenten sermon. Louis continued to attend some of the sermons, and invited Bossuet back in 1665. Later, in the convent, Louise knowingly did penance for her liaison, adulterous because Louis was married, and it may only have been in the convent that she came actually to experience her former relationship with Louis as having been seriously sinful, as distinct from publicly scandalous. Louis knew at least that the liaison was regarded by the devout as guilty and, probably under pressure from his mother, abstained from 1664 from causing the scandal that would have been occasioned if he had added blasphemy to adultery by receiving communion, as he was annually around Easter obliged to do. The church's rule was to refuse communion to those who approached the altar in a public state of sin.

40 The music was composed by Beauchamp and played by his musicians; the naiad was Madeleine Béjart, co-founder with Molière of L'Illustre Théâtre; the scenery was by Le Brun; and the production was by the brilliant Italian machinist Torelli, already known as Le Grand Sorcier after his production of Pierre Corneille's *Andromède.* Possibly on account of Fouquet's disgrace, *Les Fâcheux* did not receive its Paris premiere until 4 November 1661, during the celebrations following the birth of the grand Dauphin. We know from the inventory of his wardrobe which of the various 'fâcheux' were played by Molière himself.

41 A few years later in 1668, Louis's liaison with Mme de Montespan was to be behind the subject, and was also to be behind a famous couplet of Molière's *Amphitryon,* in which Jupiter, chief of the gods, takes the place of the general Amphitryon in his wife's bed: 'Un partage avec Jupiter N'a rien du tout qui déshonore.'

42 For details of Fouquet's wealth on arrest, and a comparison with that of Mazarin and of Servien on their deaths, see Daniel Dessert, *Fouquet,* Paris 1987, pp. 348–53.

7 The Young Ruler

1 *Mémoires,* ed. Longnon, Paris 1978, p. 83.

2 On this celebrated letter, see, for instance, John B. Wolf, *Louis XIV,* London 1968, pp. 152–3, Georges Mongrédien, *Colbert,* Paris 1962, pp.151–2, and John C. Rule's essay on the 'Roi bureaucrate' in the collection which he edited, *Louis XIV and the Craft of Kingship,* Columbus

1970, p. 32. The abrupt refusal of argument is a further sign of insecurity.

3 In 'Roi bureaucrate', p.48.

4 The standard modern biography is by Jean Meyer, *Colbert,* Paris 1981, but see also Inès Murat, *Colbert,* Paris 1980 and Georges Mongrédien, *Colbert 1619–1683,* Paris 1963. For his role in establishing the super-terrestrial image of the king, see Peter Burke, *The Fabrication of Louis XIV,* New Haven and London 1992.

5 There were three daughters, all of whom became duchesses. In 1667 Marie-Thérèse married the duc de Chevreuse, grandson of the duchesse prominent in the Fronde; in 1671, Henriette married Saint-Aignan, later duc de Beauvillier, later an important ally of Fénelon; and in 1679, Marie-Anne married the duc de Mortemart, nephew of Mme de Montespan.

6 See Ian Dunlop, *Louis XIV,* London 2001, pp.125–6.

7 The full theoretical exposition of this doctrine, to be found for instance in a memorandum of Colbert to the king of 1670 or in Jacques Savary's 1675 *Le parfait négotiant,* is really a product of the 1670s, but the economic theory is foreshadowed in other realms by activity undertaken by Colbert almost immediately after the confirmation of his ascendancy by the arrest of Fouquet. His economic views are consistent with his attempts to increase France's population, to improve its roads, rebuild the maritime ports and the fleet, diminish the very high number of religious holidays, well over 100, or nearly one in three working days, and construct the 279-kilometre Languedoc canal, or 'Canal des deux mers', which linked the Garonne to the Golfe de Lion, giving direct access from the Atlantic to the Mediterranean. It was inaugurated in 1681. François Bluche gives a good synoptic account of the trading intiatives inaugurated by Louis under Colbert's impulsion, with some reason for the partial or total failure of his manufacturing and other enterprises. See *Louis XIV,* Oxford 1990, pp. 144–52.

8 The visit of Louis to the Académie des Sciences by Le Clerc engraved for the frontispiece of the *Mémoire pour l'histoire naturelle des animaux* by Claude Perrault did not actually take place. It was merely a product of Colbert's superb public relations team. One supposes that Louis XIV knew about it and gladly played his part by acquiescing in its creation.

9 Thomas Corneille was born in 1625, nineteen years after his brother, Pierre, author of *Le Cid,* and fourteen years before Racine, born in 1639. The complex relationship between the texts of all three, which both challenged and borrowed from one another, has still not been the subject of proper critical attention, no doubt largely because Thomas Corneille, a co-director of the fashionable gazette, *Mercure galant,* was still interested in spectacle at a date when Racine was writing powerful and impassioned psychological tragedy.

10 The date normally given, 1635, is actually wrong. Richelieu failed to engineer the registration by the *parlement* which brought the Académie

into being until he was able to exploit Pierre Corneille's quarrel with Jean de Mairet in 1637, as a result of which the Académie group was reluctantly forced to act as censor and coordinator of dramatic and literary activity in France, and initially kept busy by the task laid on it of producing a French dictionary and grammar. On the manipulations to which Richelieu resorted to found the Académie, see the author's *Richelieu and the Making of France*, London and New York 2000.

11 See for these and further detailed examples, Peter Burke. *The Fabrication of Louis XIV*, New Haven and London 1992, pp. 51–4 and Georges Mongrédien, *Colbert*, Paris 1963, pp. 92–6. The number of non-French literary benefactions was quickly reduced, sometimes on account of ambassadorial wariness of praise for the French king.

12 See Antoine Adam, *Histoire de la littérature française au XVIIe siècle*, vol.3, Paris 1962, pp. 10ff. Mézeray was paid more than any other French national. Pierre Corneille steadily received 2,000 livres until he was dropped in 1674, Molière received 1,000 livres and Fléchier 800, while Quinault's payment rose from 800 to 1,200 livres in 1672 and 1,500 in 1674, no doubt on account of his association with Lulli. Bensserade, Perrot d'Ablancourt and Conrart, centre of the group round which the Académie was formed, all received 1,500 livres. Charles Perrault was increased from 1,500 to 2,000 livres in 1667. Racine received 600 livres in 1664 and 1665, and then steadily increasing sums. After the fracas following *Phèdre et Hippolyte*, as *Phèdre* was originally called, his silence, like that of Boileau, was bought by nomination as royal historian and a payment of 2,000 livres a year. Ménage was dropped for refusing to write encomiastic verse for money.

13 La Croix blanche was an inn frequented by a youthful group of literary figures, generally irreverent, and including Boileau-Despréaux, Molière, Furetière, Racine and La Fontaine. Racine's ode did earn him a 'gratification' in July 1663, but therefore also an unpleasant reference in Boileau's first satire. The two later became close allies. Molière became a favourite of Louis until displaced by Lulli in 1672, and La Fontaine remained faithful to Fouquet.

14 See Peter Burke, *The Fabrication of Louis XIV*, New Haven and London 1992, p. 51.

15 See Antoine Adam, *Histoire littéraire de la littérature française au XVIIe siècle*, vol.3, Paris 1962, pp. 12–13.

16 John C. Rule, 'Roi-bureaucrate', in *Louis XIV and the Craft of Kingship*, Columbus 1970, p. 32, estimates 100,000,000 livres.

17 The 'Spanish letter' was anonymous and in Spanish. François-René Crespin du Bec, marquis de Vardes, a military captain, was sent to the Bastille, then to the citadel of Montpellier, and finally exiled to his command at Aigues-Mortes. He was allowed to come back to Paris only in 1683, the year of the queen's death.

18 John B. Wolf, *Louis XIV*, London 1968, p. 289.

19 Georges Mongrédien points out that the court had grown by 1664,

when 600 invitations were issued to the festivities at Versailles known as the *Plaisirs de l'Ile enchantée* from 7 to 13 May. By the time the court and the seat of government moved to Versailles in 1682, the palace and its suroundings had to accommodate some 10,000 persons.

20 See Jacques Néraudau, *L'Olympe du Roi-soleil*, Paris 1986, pp. 47–55.

21 By Inès Murat in her *Colbert*, Paris 1980.

22 In his *Mémoires* (ed. Longnon, pp. 132–3), Louis justifies the holding of this 'premier divertissement de quelque éclat', and instances it as an example of how monarchy was conducted in France through 'l'accès libre et facile des sujets au prince. C'est une égalité de justice entre lui et eux, qui les tient pour ainsi dire dans une société douce et honnête, nonobstant la différence presque infinie de la naissance, du rang et du pouvoir.' This is another flagrant example of meretricious self-justification inadequately covering insecurity. That Louis should have wished to impress these principles on his dauphin is comprehensible, but is it to be supposed that Louis, while preserving the rigid hierarchies of birth, rank and power, had genuinely been led to believe that his 'personal rule' had brought him closer to his people in some meta-physical 'égalité de justice'? What is true is that it was with courtiers that he tended to stand on ceremony, rather than the ordinary people with whom he came into contact only when attempting to impress them by his own paternalistic magnificence.

23 It remains true, as is pointed out in the 1970 second edition of Anthony Blunt's *Art and Architecture in France:1500–1700*, 1953, that the dependence of French artistic taste on Italy was largely reversed during the latter part of the seventeenth century, precisely under the impact of what had been achieved at Paris and Versailles under the organization of the arts by Colbert.

24 Anyone interested in any physical resemblance between Louis and Mazarin might well compare this bust of Louis XIV, which has a promi-nent, straight nose pinched at the top, with Philippe de Champaigne's sitting portrait of Mazarin at Chantilly (Musée Condé). Mazarin's right hand in the Champaigne portrait has the long slender fingers depicted on Louis's right hand in both Nicolas de Largillière's portrait of Louis with the dauphin, his sons, and the duchesse de Ventadour now in the Wallace Collection in London, and in Henri Testelin's 1667 painting at Versailles of Louis at the establishment of the Academy of Science and the foundation of the Observatory.

25 See Jean-Marie Apostolides, *Le Roi-machine: Spectacle et politique au temps de Louis XIV*, Paris 1981. It is a mistake to regard the house and gardens at Versailles as merely elegant, even grandiose, creations to please the eye, refresh the senses and provide fresh country air for the lungs. Almost everywhere were signs, allusions, coded identifications and complex insinuations, as of course also in the paintings of Poussin and Claude.

26 Nancy Mitford states, no doubt correctly, that eight of the original Louis

XIV orange trees were still alive in the Versailles orangery when she wrote for publication in 1966, see *The Sun King*, Harmondsworth 1994, p. 20. One of the last surviving oaks planted at Versailles by Le Nôtre in 1680/1 and known as the Marie-Antoinette oak was killed off by the heat in the summer of 2003.

27 It is often asserted that Louis used to import 4 million tulip bulbs a year from Dutch nurseries when France was not at war in the Low Countries, which means no later than the 1680s. But Clusius (Charles de l'Ecluse) had introduced the tulip to the Low Countries when appointed professor of botany at Leiden only in 1593. Even if he brought cultivars with him rather than just seeds from his previous gardens in Vienna and Frankfurt, he was almost certainly at first cultivating from seed. It was the apparently outrageous prices he charged for bulbs which led to their theft from the garden behind the recently founded academy, and it was from the bulbs stolen from his garden that the Dutch tulip industry developed. In spite of the tulipo-mania of 1634–7, when only continuing rarity can explain the astonish-ing prices, it seems unlikely that there were 4 million bulbs a year available for sale even to the king of France within thirty or forty years of the bursting of the bubble. The statement that two of La Quintinie's pear trees lasted until 1963 seems much more likely to be true (see Nancy Mitford, *The Sun King*, Harmandsworth 1994, pp. 41–2).

Little of what was created by Le Nôtre at Versailles still exists, chiefly the two rectangular bosquets, crossed with *allées* on either side of the central axis, flanking the Allée Royale broadened in 1667 to lead west from the Latona fountain basin, completed in 1666 although not raised until after 1680, and using as a model the Venus discovered at Arles in 1663. The Petit Parc was originally three times as extensive as it is now (1,738 hectares against today's 684). Its 'great canal', 1,500 metres long, extended the axis westward from the Bassin d'Apollon. The Ménagerie stood at the southern end of the cross canal. At the northern end, the hamlet of Trianon was pulled down to create the Trianon de Porcelaine for Mme de Montespan, a miniature palace with Chinese architectural features. It was later transformed into the Grand Trianon.

28 Figures quoted by François Bluche, in *Louis XIV,* tr. Greengrass, Oxford 1990, pp. 171–2 and 193–7, from the five-volume *Comptes des bâtiments du Roi sous le règne de Louis XIV,* ed. Jules Guiffrey, Paris 1881–1901.

29 See Ian Dunlop, *Louis XIV,* London 2001, p. 110.

30 Saint-Aignan was among those who encouraged Louis in his amorous as well as his poetic enterprises. Mme de Sévigné wrote on 1 December 1664 that Saint-Aignan had been teaching the king to write verse. The king had shown to the maréchal de Gramont a madrigal he had himself written, seeking his agreement that it was the most paltry thing he had ever seen before revealing, to Gramont's consternation, his own author-ship, and no doubt half-seeking reassurance about his own abilities. The incident is trivial but of interest for two reasons. It shows Louis

with an infrequently indulged sense of fun, able to risk having to laugh at himself, but conceivably hoping for reassurance, and it enables Mme de Sévigné to wish that it might have taught the king the lesson that he could expect always to be flattered and never to be told unflattering truths about himself or his actions. It is true, as Mme de Sévigné's editor remarks, that Louis's attitude towards Fouquet had been warped by the flattery that he alone was worthy of the house and lifestyle epitomized at Vaux-le-Vicomte. See Mme de Sévigné, *Correspondance*, ed. Roger Duchêne, 3 vols, Paris 1972–8, vol.1, pp. 67 and 903.

31 The vicious in-fighting of the commercial Paris theatre yields nothing to more modern times. Molière's theatre, the Petit-Bourbon, admittedly scheduled for demolition in the distant future, was knocked down overnight in mid-season. Torelli's sets and machines were salvaged and transported to the Palais-Royal where the queen mother still lived, and where Molière's troupe was offered free accommodation in the larger of the two theatres which Richelieu had had built. Carlo Vagarani came to Paris when his father, Gaspare, was called from Italy by Mazarin. Carlo certainly lived for a while in a grace-and-favour apartment in the Louvre and was still alive in 1693. He was a friend and employee of Molière, and simply had Torelli's sets burnt.

32 It cannot be too greatly stressed that the 'casuists', anxious for pastoral reasons to remove obstacles from salvation and not at all confined to the Jesuit order, were uniquely concerned with minimizing the conditions required for sacramental absolution with all the baroque confidence which the age allowed, not with laying down the moral norms of the church's teaching. In the meanwhile Rome reacted to Pascal's brilliantly successful *Lettres provinciales* of 1656–7 with two sets of *Errores* against the casuists concerning moral matters, forty-five under Alexander VII in 1665 and 1666, and sixty-five more under Innocent XI in 1679. It is not totally surprising to find Primi Visconti declaring that there is no lady of quality who would not like to be the king's mistress, and that there are many who believe that it would offend 'neither their husbands nor their fathers nor even God himself if they were to succeed in winning the love of the king'.

33 The relentless multiplication of masses for the 'repose of a soul' reflect a distortion of devotional practice bred not merely of baroque exaggeration but also of late medieval theological confusion. The theologians could not explain how the mass was at the same time identical with the sacrificial death of Jesus on the cross and yet not a repetition of it. The doctrine also took root in the thirteenth century that there was a *thesaurus ecclesiæ*, or treasury of grace which could be applied by the church not only as a corporate pleading, *per modum suffragii*, but as a jurisdictional act by which the merit of Christ's sacrifice was applied for the salvation of souls. The result on the popular devotional level was the assumption that the repetition of masses applied for the repose of an individual soul enhanced that soul's

chances of salvation, although the theologians doctrinally still held that salvation or damnation depended on the soul's state of grace or sin at the moment of death. From the fourteenth century greater emphasis was put on God's decree of predestination or reprobation at the moment of the soul's creation, sometimes considered to be three or six months after conception, dependent on gender.

34 See Bluche, *Louis XIV,* Oxford 1990, p. 239. The provinces were Antwerp, imperial Flanders, Malines, Limburg, Upper Gelderland, Brabant, the remainder of Artois, the Cambrésis, Hainaut, the Namurois, Roche-en-Ardenne, Arlon, with parts of Luxembourg and Burgundy.

35 The rewards bestowed on Athénaïs and her family were huge. Her father was made governer of Paris and her brother, the duc de Vivonne, was made captain-general of the galleys and governor of Champagne. One sister was a nun who never came to court, but the other two, the Marquise de Thianges and Mme de Fontevrault, were prominent and popular members of the court. Mme de Thianges was one of Louis's many occasional lovers, and acquired with Athénaïs a share in the income from all meat and tobacco sales in Paris.

36 A *legatus a latere* received full delegated papal jurisdiction in the legatine territory for the period of the legation. He was generally a cardinal. The function of the post was changing. A century earlier lords chancellor, like Wolsey in England and Du Prat in France, were made *legati a latere* to combine the supremacy of civil with the supremacy of sacerdotal jurisdiction, so that one could not be played off against the other.

8 Public Policies, Private Pleasures, Poisons and Punishments

1 On Colbert's policy in general and, in particular, on his relations with Brittany, see François Lebrun, 'Colbert et les provinces', in *De la mort de Colbert à la Révocation de l'Edit de Nantes: Un Monde Nouveau?* ed. Louise Godard de Donville, Marseilles 1984, pp. 315–25. The first *intendant* in Brittany, Auguste-Robert de Pomereu, was appointed only in 1689, six years after Colbert's death.

2 Of the 692 sentences at the Clermont assize court, 87 were against members of the nobility, of whom 23 were physically executed, see François Bluche, *Louis XIV,* Oxford 1990, p. 113. Others, with or without connivance, no doubt removed themselves and were executed only in effigy, which meant that they escaped with their lives but that their property was confiscated to the crown, a solution to which recourse in France was frequent right up to the revolution.

3 Jean Meyer, *Colbert,* Paris 1981, pp.272–95, relying on statistics from the end of Colbert's life and just after his death in 1683, shows the reason for the apparently puzzling increase in France's Mediterranean

galley fleet, when Lepanto, in 1571, had shown how vulnerable to broadships their inability to fire broadsides had made them. In 1661 in the western Mediterranean the Christian powers, including more than half a dozen Italian states, but excluding France, had scarcely more than forty-five galleys between them, and there was a scarcely higher total operating from Islamic north Africa. Richelieu had realized the usefulness of cheap, elegant, easily built galleys for intercepting Spanish silver being transported from Catalonia to Genoa, and then to Franche-Comté or the Low Countries, even if their expected life did not exceed ten years. By 1688 the French galley fleet had grown from fifteen to forty, its further enlargement constricted by public sympathy for the oarsmen, made to work in the relatively frequent periods of windless calm in the western Mediterranean. A galley required only 30 or so seamen, of which there were relatively few, and 50 or so soldiers, to 300 or 400 convicts or captives.

In 1683 Louis spent 7.74 million livres on the navy, and in addition 3.2 million on the galley fleet, some 9.5 per cent of a total expenditure of over 115 million livres. The army took 54 million (47 per cent) and in 1683, the year the court moved to Versailles, Louis spent 7.22 million on his palace (6.27 per cent of the national expenditure), to which must be added 9.78 million (8.5 per cent) for the cost of the court. The figures well illustrate the contrast between Colbert's leaning towards economy measured against Louis's towards prodigality.

Under Colbert, the tonnage of the French navy exceeded 100,000, exclusive of galleys, only one of the vessels operative in 1661 surviving until 1677. The average survival of a warship was twenty-one years. By 1677 the navy possessed 209 ships, of which 116 were line warships.

The body of galley oarsmen consisted of between 10–15 per cent of Turkish slaves, bought in the market, with the rest convicts, some of whom had served their sentences but, although treated better, were not released. Colbert pressed for sentences to the galleys and received a mixture of deserters, violent and non-violent criminals, and 15 per cent of those convicted of domestic offences, blasphemy, or disturbing the peace. In the Huguenot persecution following the revocation of the edict of Nantes, the percentage of Huguenots rose to nearly 12.

4 The classic work on seventeenth-century Paris, Louis Bernard's *The Emerging City: Paris in the Age of Louis XIV,* London 1970, tells of 372 murders in one year.

5 Mazarin had left 2 million livres for the building, and an annual income of 45,000 livres. The college was intended for young nobles from the four provinces annexed by France in the Peace of the Pyrénées (Artois, Alsace, Roussillon and Pinerolo), and Colbert was one his executors. The architects were Le Vau, Lambert and Orbay.

6 La Reynie installed some 6,500 lanterns about seven metres above street level at intervals of twenty metres. Together they burned annually 200,000 candles of tallow weighing over half a kilogram. At Louis's

death in 1715, one report asserts that the capital had 22,000 houses and 5,522 street lamps.

7 Louis is known to have had a child by Mlle des Œeillets, Athénaïs's maid. Among Louis's fleeting liaisons were those with Marie-Elizabeth de Ludres, who retired to a convent in 1677, and Marie-Angélique de Scorailles de Roussille, duchesse de Fontanges, as empty-headed as she was beautiful. She came to court before she was twenty, very possibly with the idea of seducing Louis, and almost immediately became the king's mistress in the winter of 1678–9. She became pregnant, lost her vivacity and high spirits, miscarried and died in 1681, basically of loss of blood following the miscarriage, after retiring to Port-Royal in 1681. Mme de Montespan is known to have helped her dress for a masked ball, but became jealous when she was made a duchess and insisted on eight horses for her carriage, as against Mme de Montespan's six. She also omitted to curtsey to the queen. Like Louise and Athénaïs, Mme de Ludres and the duchesse de Fontanges finished their lives in convents. Mme de Sévigné makes clear that Mme de Soubise was among Louis's lovers, and with her husband's permission. When her husband was in Paris, her appearance was much less lavishly prepared than when he was absent. Mme de Sévigné regards the behaviour of Mme de Soubise as stupid.

8 *Mémoires et Réflexions*, ed. Michaud et Poujoulat, series 3, vol. 8, 1850.

9 Nancy Mitford goes as far as to suggest that Athenaïs sought help, whether pharmaceutical or supernatural, in preventing the queen from conceiving. Since the dauphin was born on 1 November 1661, this seems unlikely. See Nancy Mitford, *The Sun King*, Harmondsworth 1994, pp.46–7.

10 One of the eight was still-born, so the number is often given as seven.

11 The paragraph on Le Nôtre's garden at Clagny is one of Mme de Sévigné's set pieces of polished prose, breaking the overall chattiness of the letter. It starts 'C'est le palais d'Armide', the seductress from Tasso's *Gerusalemme Liberata*, who lures men into her garden where they are held captive by its marvels. The famous letters to her daughter were designed to be read by a small but influential circle of her daughter's friends, so that, while they bubble over with affection and gossip, they are circumspect about such matters as Louis's lovers, often using pseudonyms.

12 Tallemant tells us in the *Historiettes* that the deformity originated in treatment for a venereal infection. Another account has it that Scarron, disguised during the carnival of 1638 with feathers attached with honey to his skin, had to dive into the Sarthe to avoid being mobbed by girls intent on ripping the feathers off the naked canon. The story is improbable, but says something about the lifestyle which gave rise to this sort of anecdote.

13 The earliest and most probable date proposed is the night of 9–10 October, 1683. See Langlois, 'Madame de Maintenon et le Saint Siège'

in *Revue d'Histoire Ecclésiastique* XXV, 1929, pp. 33–72 and the same scholar's Paris 1932 biography.

14 It is probable that a physical liaison with him started before 1683, perhaps as early as 1674, although more likely a year or two later, between 1676 and 1680.

15 Mme Scarron is said to have bought Maintenon. In fact it must have been found for her and bought on her behalf with the 200,000 livres she had been given. The second 100,000 livres must have been added either because the first property thought to be desirable could not be acquired, or because Maintenon cost more than anticipated.

16 There is a portrait by an unknown artist in the Uffizi showing a slim and extremely elegant Mme de Montespan at Clagny which cannot be earlier than 1675 and another stylized baroque full-length portrait of her of the late 1670s in the Musée de Versailles with four of her children after Mignard, showing enhanced height and an almost grotesquely pinched waist. By the end of 1676, she was thirty-five and had had six children.

17 The first major infidelity, with Louise de la Vallière, dated from July 1661, when the the queen was five months pregnant; the liaison with Athénaïs started in 1667 when Louise, heavily pregnant, was sent home from Flanders; the liaison with Mlle de Fontanges took place at a time when Athénaïs was losing her figure and was having her last children in 1676, 1677 and 1678. Louis's period of sustained promiscuity dated from 1676, the date of the relationship with Mme de Ludres. Des Noyers, writing to the queen of Poland in 1677 says it involved in addition to names already mentioned Mme de Roure, Mme de Heudicourt and Mlle de Fiennes. There was also a Mlle Doré in 1680–1. The definitive break with Athénaïs took place during the pregnancy of 1678, at a time when Louis's liaison with Mlle de Fontanges was taking over his private life and Mme de Maintenon, whether or not she was yielding to any advances from Louis, was urging the king, for the sake of his immortal soul, to remain faithful to the queen. Whatever the precise state of their relationship, Louis and Mme de Maintenon can scarcely have envisaged the final solution of marriage until after the queen's unexpected death in 1683 at the age of forty-four.

18 There were different rules for Catholics, where the *congrès* was witnessed by clergy, and for Huguenots, for whom the arrangements were made by the civil authorities and where the jury was carefully composed according to quite elaborate rules. There are a number of well-attested incidents of a *congrès*, often financially important to one of the partners, and often ending in a declaration of nullity.

19 Henriette, born in 1644, died in 1670 and was the subject of a spectacular funeral at which Bossuet preached one of his greatest funeral orations. She was widely thought to have been poisoned, but a post-mortem revealed that she had not been. Six of her children were either still-born or died at birth.

20 *The Sun King*, Harmondsworth 1994, p. 56.
21 There is no full and satisfactory edition of the letters, but the Paris 1961 *Lettres de Madame Palatine* (ed. Hubert Juin) is helpful. The three children were born in 1673 (duc de Valois, died in infancy), 1674 (Philippe, duc de Chartres, to become regent of France), and 1676 (Elisabeth-Charlotte).
22 See on this episode Ian Dunlop, *Louis XIV*, London 2001, pp. 183–7 and John Wolf, *Louis XIV*, London 1968, pp. 309–13.
23 On La grande Mademoiselle see André Ducasse, *La grande Mademoiselle 1627–1693*, Paris 1963.
24 See François Bluche, *Louis XIV*, tr. Mark Greengrass, Oxford 1990, p. 487, and Nancy Mitford, *The Sun King*, Harmondsworth 1994, p. 63.
25 See on Mlle de Fontanges note 7 above.
26 The superstitious practices most concerned were derived from the transubstantiation of the wine at mass into the blood of Christ, apparently by the simple pronouncing of a verbal formula by a priest.
27 Mme de Sévigné writes: 'Mme de Fontanges est duchesse avec vingt mille écus [60,000 livres] de pension; elle en recevait aujourd'hui les compliments dans son lit. Le Roi y a été publiquement . . . Voici une manière de séparation qui fera bien de l'honneur à la sévérité du confesseur . . . Il y a des gens qui disent que cet établissement sent le congé . . . Mme de M[ontespan] est enragée. Elle pleura beaucoup hier. Vous pouvez juger du martyre que souffre son orgueil. Il est encore plus outragé par la haute faveur de Mme de Maintenon. Sa Majesté va passer très souvent deux heures de l'après-dîner dans sa chambre à causer avec une amitié et un air libre et naturel . . . '
28 This book was already in proof when Anne Somerset published *The Affair of the Poisons* (London 2003).

9 'Sans vue, sans bois, sans eau': Versailles

1 Unfortunately the cost figures for Versailles given by Jules Guiffrey in the five-volume *Comptes des bâtiments du Roi sous le règne de Louis XIV*, Paris 1881–1901, do not tally with those given in 1691 by Marinier, clerk to the architect Hardouin-Mansart, and printed by Pierre Clément in the fifth volume of his edition of Colbert's *Lettres, Instructions et Mémoires*, Paris 1868. Guiffrey's figures have generally been followed, and are used here, but not without misgivings. Overall, however, and including the cost of failed projects, of pulling down and starting again, and of providing water, it would not be unreasonable to say that Versailles, in round figures, cost 100 million livres. For a pictorial account of plans and phases in the construction, taken largely from prints and plans, see Guy Walton, *Louis XIV's Versailles*, Harmondsworth 1986.
2 *Louis XIV*, London 2001, pp. 106–7.

3 Other than garden estates, like Catherine the Great's Oranienbaum, once having access to the Gulf of Finland, it is worth remarking how, in the mid-eighteenth century, Balthasar Neumann's great interior staircases created works of architectural art whose appreciation required the viewer to move. Neumann's vision, and immense architectural daring, came together with Giambattista Tiepolo's spectacular gift for pictorial irony in the magnificent Treppenhaus of the Würzburg Residenz, in which the ceiling can be seen from no single spot. You have to look at the ceiling while climbing the stairs. And, since changing light is built into the architectural effects planned by German rococo architects, you need to do it several times a day. On the Treppenhaus, see above all Svetlana Alpers and Michael Baxandall, *Tiepolo and the Pictorial Intelligence,* New Haven and London 1994.

4 Jules Hardouin, born in 1646 was the great-nephew of François Mansart, became known as Hardouin-Mansart, and is now usually in non-technical books referred to as Mansart.

5 Guy Walton, *Louis XIV's Versailles,* Harmondsworth 1986, p. 79, surmises that there must from the plans have been problems of alignment and light, and speaks of the 'hit-and-miss character' of this phase of the planning, and the 'chaotic early history of the building of the Enveloppe'.

6 On the aesthetic effects, interior and exterior, contributed by the changes after Nijmegen, see Anthony Blunt, *Art and Architecture in France 1500 to 1700,* Harmondsworth 1953.

7 The decision of the secret meeting of the council is reported by Claude Nivelon in the manscript fonds fr. 12987 of the Bibliothèque Nationale, *Vie de Charles Le Brun,* of which Pierre de Nolhac publishes extracts in *La Création de Versailles,* Paris 1901. Guy Walton, *Louis XIV's Versailles,* p. 100, finds in the painting of Louis as Minerva 'a grand architectural setting reminiscent of a corner of the Versailles park', but it may have too many ruins. At the opposite end of the painting France's enemies are depicted by three women.

8 Le Brun may have used as a model the ceiling planned but never executed by Giovanni Lanfranco for the benediction loggia in Saint Peter's, drawings for which had been published in 1663. See Guy Walton, *Louis XIV's Versailles,* pp. 102–3.

9 The whole staircase, with its paintings, had to be destroyed in the eighteenth century when a structure made to support a glass skylight to let in more light failed.

10 The hounds were divided into five packs, each owned by a different member of the royal family. They hunted, mostly stag, boar and wolf. Louis kept a few hounds in his own apartment and fed them himself, so that they would recognize him as their owner. He derived great enjoyment from working his hounds himself.

11 Guy Walton, *Louis XIV's Versailles,* p. 167.

12 On the water problem, see P. de Nolhac, *Versailles Résidence de Louis XIV,* Paris 1925.

13 The figure comes from the clearly over-awed abbé de Bourdelot, physician to the Condé family, invited to a *Jour d'appartement* during the carnival of 1683. There were no doubt a large number of candles, but it is not to be supposed that the abbé counted the chandeliers, and the figure should not be taken literally.

14 In a letter of 2 May 1681 even Mme de Maintenon could write of the 'astonishing beauty' of Versailles, mentioning some of the pleasures to be experienced there, 'a ball in the king's suite', 'a play at Monsieur's', walks, and often a midnight collation.

15 On Louis's relationship with Colbert at the end, see in particular Ian Dunlop, *Louis XIV*, London 2001, pp. 138–9. There is no foundation for the view of the Venetian ambasador, Sebastiano Foscarini, in his sensitive and sympathetic 1683 report on Louis, that Colbert was on the brink of disgrace.

16 See for instance *Les Souvenirs de Madame de Caylus*, ed. Bernard Noël, Paris 1965. Mme Caylus (1673–1729) was the daughter of a first cousin of Mme de Maintenon. Her *Souvenirs* are delightfully written and a precious source of information. Married at thirteen, she had 'several' children, and her *Souvenirs* reveal a liveliness of spirit which twice got her exiled from Louis's court.

17 The accounts of the *bâtiments* show an expenditure on Versailles, not counting the water works, of 4.6 million livres for 1684, 6.1 million for 1685, 2.5 in 1686, and 2.9 in 1687. War preparations cut the total back to just under 2.0 million in 1688. Marinier's table from Mansart's office shows 5.7 million livres for 1684, 11.3 million for 1685, 6.5 for 1686, 5.4 for 1687, and 4.5. in 1688. The big drop in Marinier's figures comes in 1689, with expenditure of 1.7 million livres, down to under 400,000 in 1689. François Bluche puts the total cost from 1661 to 1715 including water works at 82 million livres, which sounds like an underestimate. Marinier's accounts stretch only from 1664 to 1690 and total 81.1 million livres. The water works cost, according to the *bâtiments*, 9 million for the work on the Eure and the abandoned aqueduct.

18 See Ian Dunlop, *Louis XIV*, pp. 300–2.

19 There is however a magnificent set of coloured drawings of Marly dating from 1714 by Pierre Denis Martin in the Archives Nationales.

20 For details of the etiquette enforced for the indication of rank and status, see Henri Brochet, *Le Rang et l'étiquette sous l'ancien régime*, Paris 1955.

21 Racine himself was to die in disgrace in 1699. Mme de Maintenon had asked him to write down his thoughts on the state and treatment of the peasantry, and had then shown them to the king, who was furious. Racine kept his post, and was therefore frequently at Versailles and Marly, but the king appeared never to notice his presence. Racine himself thought that it was because he had an aunt at Port-Royal, and was himself suspected of Jansenism. He had had a bitter quarrel with Pierre Nicole, collaborator with Antoine Arnauld who inspired Pascal,

about the morality of the theatre, which Racine defended. However, he was later fully reconciled with Port-Royal, and in 1697 wrote his *Abrégé de l'histoire de Port-Royal*, unpublished until 1742 (full version 1767).

22 Nancy Mitford points out that this was just as well, as the Spanish Habsburg line was ruined by in-breeding, Maria-Teresa and her sister having been its last viable heirs. See *The Sun King*, Harmondsworth 1994, p.110.

23 Mme de Ludres had been a canoness, and was therefore entitled to be addressed as Madame.

24 Nancy Mitford prints it in *Louis XIV*, Harmondsworth 1994, p.160:
'Grand Dieu sauvez le roi/Grand Dieu vengez le roi/Vive le roi/ Qu'à jamais glorieux/Louis victorieux/Voie ses ennemis toujours soumis/Vive le roi.'

25 Racine had jettisoned Molière's company by having his *Alexandre* played by the stronger *comédiens du roi* while custom demanded that Molière still held the copyright. Thérèse followed him and was to die, almost certainly of poison, in December 1668.

26 Mme Guyon's ascetic practices were exaggerated, but no worse, for instance, than those of Angélique Arnauld, Saint-Cyran's disciple in the reform of Port-Royal, and the conventual regime instituted at Saint-Cyr was no harsher than that of other contemplative communities. However, there can be little doubt that Mme Guyon, for all that she briefly captivated Fénelon and introduced him to the mystical tradition, was mentally unstable. Born in 1648, she was unhappily married. Her husband died in 1676; her spiritual director went mad and died in an asylum; and she appears to have had a homosexual relationship with a young girl. The story is much complicated by the widening of the dispute about Quietism into a debate in which Bossuet and Nicole attacked the church's whole orthodox mystical tradition, which Fénelon and the Jesuits defended.

10 The Royal Religion and Christian Beliefs

1 Corneille wrote in 1660 of *Rodogune's* Cléopâtre 'tous ses crimes sont accompagnés d'une grandeur d'âme qui a quelque chose de si haut, qu'en même temps qu'on déteste ses actions, on admire la source dont elles partent.' The concept of moral heroism divorced from ethical quality was quite widely diffused. La Rochefoucauld borrowed and made famous the aphorism: 'Il y a des héros en mal comme en bien.'

2 For a detailed analysis of the movement of cultural optimism from the beginning of the century to the mid 1630s and beyond, see Mark Bannister, *Privileged Mortals. The French Heroic Novel 1630–1660*, Oxford 1983, and the analyses of the works of the authors mentioned, and many others of the same period, in the author's *Guide to French Literature. Beginnings to 1789*, Andover and Detroit 1994. It is a sign of the

hardening of moral atttitudes that Corneille removed from his text in 1660 the couplet which made the marriage of Rodrigue and Chimène certainly admissible in 1637.

3 The second strand of thinking which can be traced to Bérulle's neoplatonism is the highly optimistic philosophical endeavour of Descartes, whose fundamental inspiration comes, according to his early biography by Adrien Baillet, *La Vie de M. Descartes*, Paris 1691, from long conversations with Bérulle. Pierre de Bérulle was the founder of the French missionary congregation of the Oratory based on the model of the Oratory of saint Philip Neri in Rome. His neoplatonist spirituality came to emphasize the nothingness of the human creature, and the need to annihilate the life of nature and replace it by the life of grace. His language and doctrine were inspired by the Rhineland mystics, and his spirituality came to centre on the 'vows of servitude' to Jesus and Mary, taken by the members of the Oratory in 1614 to Mary and in 1615 to Jesus, which he also attempted to impose on the French Carmelites, to whose own spirituality they were quite alien. Following the *Hierarchies* thought to be by Denis, the first convert of saint Paul, Bérulle intended to elevate the status of the priesthood in the church, and regarded the church's renewal as dependent on the reform of the priesthood. His most important work was the 1623 *Discours de l'estat et des grandeurs de Jésus,* a long defence of the vows of servitude. His political and mystical views alienated Richelieu, but he was made a cardinal in 1627.

4 Although the theologian, Jansen, and the spiritual director, Saint-Cyran, have very different starting points, they did collaborate again when in 1623 Jansen sent Saint-Cyran a score of copies of the Louvain 1555 edition of Augustine's work on grace, and Saint-Cyran sent Jansen the panegyric on Augustine from which Jansen elaborated the preface to the second volume of *Augustinus.* The theology of Jansen and the later spirituality of Saint-Cyran are nevertheless not intrinsically connected and have different spiritual and theological origins.

5 Saint-Cyran's first work, the 1609 *Question royale,* on a moral problem put by Henri IV, glorifies acts of patriotic suicide, combining stoic values with the cult of heroic *gloire,* while his second, the 1615 *Apologie pour M. de Poitiers,* argues the rights of ecclesiastics to take up arms and defends the development of the church's moral values to accord with changes in society shortly to be attacked by Pascal.

6 On the complex relationships between Jansen, Saint-Cyran, Port-Royal and other closely connected persons and institutions, the classic works by Sainte-Beuve (*Port-Royal,* 6 vols, Paris 1840–59) and Bremond (*Histoire littéraire du sentiment religieux en France,* 12 vols, Paris 1921–36) need now to be supplemented by the five volumes of *Les Origines du jansénisme,* Paris/Louvain 1947–62, by Jean Orcibal and Annie Barnes.

7 Quite apart from ecclesiastical politics, his spirituality and the general disruption of which he was the centre, Saint-Cyran disturbed Richelieu

on two counts. He took Bérulle's side against the religious orders exempt from episcopal jurisdiction, and the links with Bérulle and Jansen suggested a pro-Spanish political Catholicism hostile to Richelieu's policy of allying with the Protestant countries of northern Europe against the Habsburgs.

8   There are several versions of this incident, on which see Antoine Adam, *Du Mysticisme à la révolte*, Paris 1968, pp.164–7.

9   See P. Jansen, *Le Cardinal Mazarin et le mouvement janséniste en France 1653–1659*, Paris 1967.

10 Of the five propositions only the first is textually in *Augustinus*, but the other four are logically entailed by the text, and the fifth is verbally there in the sense condemned as heretical. Only the fifth is not unequivocally and individually condemned as heretical. They are

(i) There are some commandments of God which, even for those in a state of grace who have the will and make the effort, are impossible with their present forces. They lack the grace which would make observance possible.

(ii) In the state of fallen nature, interior grace can never be resisted.

(iii) In the state of fallen nature, in order to merit, and incur guilt, it is not necessary to be free from all interior necessity, but it sufficient to be free from external constraint.

(iv) The Semi-Pelagians admitted the necessity of foregoing interior grace for each act, even for the beginning of faith; they were heretical in that they wanted that grace to be such that the human will could either resist it or yield to it.

(v) It is Semi-Pelagian to say that Christ died or shed his blood generally for all human beings.

The word 'Semi-Pelagian' is first attested in the late sixteenth century and, although not precisely defined, is generally used of views which affirm that pure or fallen nature can in some way initiate, persevere in and autonomously either accept or cooperate with proffered justifying grace.

11 Antoine Adam thinks that Annat's appointment as confessor to Louis may well have been at Rome's instigation. See *Du Mysticisme à la révolte*, Paris 1968, pp. 205–6.

12 This was a second 'letter' addressed to the duc de Luynes, a well-known supporter of Port-Royal, in fact a quarto volume of 250 pages and a Jansenist manifesto. The first had been the *Lettre d'un Docteur de Sorbonne à une personne de condition* of 24 February 1655. Charles Picoté, a priest at Saint-Sulpice, had gone too far in refusing to accept Liancourt's declarations that he was not a Jansenist and that he accepted the pope's latest decree. Picoté demanded a public abjuration. Three editions of Arnauld's first letter were sold out in ten days. Picoté's provocatively confrontational attitude must have had firm backing from ecclesiastical superiors higher than Olier, founder and first superior of Saint-Sulpice, from the acting archbishop if not from Mazarin himself.

13 Each of the four older mendicant orders, Dominicans, Carmelites, Franciscans and Augustinians, was limited to two votes in order that the votes of members of religious orders should not swamp those of the hierarchical clergy, but many more of them were teaching members of the faculty, and probably on that account entitled to separate votes. The restriction of two per order was anyway of doubtful validity. It is therefore impossible to know how many of the votes cast were technically valid. Sainte-Beuve says in *Port-Royal* that he found in 'le plumitif' that forty regulars were allowed to vote. On the most favourable count Arnauld lost the first vote, on whether the pope could compel assent to the statement that the propositions were in *Augustinus,* by 124 votes to 71. There are no meaningful figures for a vote on Arnauld's assertion that Saint Peter was denied grace not to sin, because the proceedings were too disturbed.

14 *Le Siècle de Louis XIV,* ch. 32.

15 If most human beings belonged to the *massa damnata* and grace, if bestowed, was irresistible and unrelated to meritorious behaviour, as Jansen held, it is difficult to speak of the consequences of Jansen's theory of grace for human conduct. It was logically destructive of any ethic. Pierre Nicole, the cooperator with Arnauld and Pascal on whom Pascal was dependent in the *Pensées,* can offer no solution in his *Essais de morale* (in 'De la charité et de l'amour-propre', first published in 1671) better than to suggest behaviour in accordance with the law, which is at least compatible with pre-ordained salvation, which behaviour not in accordance with the law was not.

16 That some alignment was popularly noticed is clear from the quip attributed to Ninon de Lenclos, but in fact by Paul Scarron in a letter of 8 May 1659, that the *précieuses,* a handful of well-bred young ladies who reacted against the baroque treatment of women, were the 'Jansenists of love'. See Roger Duchêne, *Les Précieuses ou comment l'esprit vint aux femmes,* Paris 2001, p.175. See also, by the same author, *Ninon de Lenclos, ou la manière jolie de faire l'amour,* 2nd edition, Paris 2000.

17 That the devout could without any feelings of guilt flout the church's teaching on sexual morality is clear from Marguerite de Navarre's *L'Heptaméron* (day three, conte 25), written in the late 1540s, when France's culture was at its Renaissance peak. Marguerite de Navarre, the undoubtedly devout sister of the devout François I, puts into the mouth of one of her fictional story-tellers as an example of her brother's virtue his habit of passing through a monastery to visit his mistress and of spending a long time in prayer in the monastery church on his way back, to the vast edification of the monks on their arrival for matins. Montaigne, writing in the defensive culture of the religious wars in 1580 (*Les Essais,* ch.lvi, 'Des prieres'), draws the conclusion that women should not discuss theology, 'Je vous laisse à juger, l'ame pleine de ce beau pensement, à quoy il employoit la faveur divine! Toutefois elle allegue cela pour un tesmoignage de singuliere devotion. Mais ce n'est

pas par cette preuve seulement qu'on pourroit verifier que les femmes ne sont guiere propores à traiter les matieres de la Theologie.'

Given the interpretation of Louis's behaviour adopted here, it seems necessary to confront the delicate issue of the evolution of the moral norms imposed by the church's teaching. Historically, that evolution has been, and still is, powered by a selective neglect of norms imposed by the church, but felt by significant numbers of devout members of the faithful to be simply irrelevant to their moral welfare. In that way, official moral norms, especially since the mid-seventeenth century and Pascal's attack on laxity, have lagged behind and eventually been modified by the ultimate theological authority, which is the *sensus fidelium.*

18 The letter may very well not in the end have been sent at all, and it is possible that it was sent to Mme de Maintenon, although addressed to the king. Professor Bluche thinks that if the letter had 'leaked', Fénelon would have been sent to the Bastille, but that is clearly not the case. See *Louis XIV,* Oxford 1990, p. 453.

19 Saint-Simon, we may recall, was son of the favourite whom Louis XIII had raised to become a duke and peer. He inherited his father's diaries and notes, himself became a noted defender of the established order and traditional privilege, an assiduous attender at court and a meticulous observer of the minute signs of favour and disfavour meted out there by the king. The *Mémoires,* written between 1739 and 1751, were probably not intended for publication, are shot through with prejudices of which Saint-Simon was aware, and contain viciously malevolent personal remarks and brilliantly descriptive set pieces.

20 Fénelon has been attacked for the *Rémonstrances,* regarded as 'of no importance' by François Bluche, 'Not even Saint-Simon reached such heights of bad faith.' Bad faith is not the right reproach for Saint-Simon, and is patently wrong for Fénelon. In fact, Fénelon's view was becoming widespread. Even La Bruyère, placed by Bossuet to serve in the Condé household, is moved to indignation and compassion. Fénelon repeats the core elements of his view in a letter to the duc de Chevreuse of 14 August 1710, quoted in a balanced account of the situation in Ian Dunlop, *Louis XIV,* London 2001, 'It is not only a question of putting an end to the war in Europe; it is a question of providing bread to people who are at death's door; of reestablishing agriculture and commerce ... of tempering the despotism which is the source of all our ills.' Louis's most ardent defenders can point to no more than his 'constant preoccupation with the suffering of his people' and his mobilization of the 'entire administration ... in the struggle against food shortages'. Neutral ships carrying grain were indeed allowed to reach French ports, but the prosecution of the war remained paramount and its cruelties obscene. Louis's strongest defenders are not to be found among the specialists in literary or religious history.

21 Fénelon uses the word 'endurcit', thereby alluding to the scriptural 'I shall harden (indurabo) the heart of Pharaoh' (Exodus, vii, 3). Bayle

had famously argued in the 1680 *Pensées diverses sur la comète* that the verb cannot be taken literally in the case of God and Pharaoh.

22 Married at sixteen and widowed at twenty-eight Mme Guyon wished to devote herself to the welfare of the poor and the sick. Drawn by genuinely quietist spirituality she was imprisoned in 1688, but had attracted the attention of Mme de Maintenon, who obtained her release. She was again imprisoned in 1695.

23 The term was first used of the teaching of Miguel de Molinos in 1682, and the doctrine was condemned as heretical by Innocent XI in the apostolic constitution *Cœlestis Pastor* of 19 November 1687. See Yves de Montcheuil, *Malebranche et le quiétisme,* Paris 1946.

24 The main Rhineland mystics include Ruusbroek, Eckhardt, Harphius and Suso.

25 On the attempts of Descartes and Pascal to grapple with the problem, see the author's *French Moralists: the Theory of the Passions: 1585–1649,* Oxford 1964.

26 Augustine was a rhetorician. There are half a dozen definitions of the two cities in the *City of God,* and they are not co-terminous. The crucial reference is at XIV, 28 of the *City of God,* and in Jansen, *Augustinus,* 'de statu naturae lapsae 25'.

27 Self-love had been a vice conferring blindness both in antiquity, notably in Plutarch, and in the renaissance, when it is used by Rabelais, borrowing it from Erasmus's Folly, who is blinded by it in the *Praise of Folly.*

28 On this dispute, see Gabriel Joppin, *Une Querelle autour de l'amour pur,* Paris 1938, and his *Fénelon et la mystique de l'amour pur,* Paris 1938, which corrects some of Bremond's views on the debate in the eleventh volume of his *Histoire littéraire du sentiment religieux.* Camus wrote about 200 books, a third each of fictional, devotional and controversy.

29 The authoritative document on the life and views of Fénelon is the impressive edition of the *Correspondance,* Paris 1972–99, inaugurated by Jean Orcibal. The first volume contains the biography. Tronson was the superior of Saint-Sulpice and Fénelon's early spiritual director.

30 On 28 March he wrote 'The Christian, who practices an abandon without reserve, can indeed consent to be eternally punished and in suffering if that is the will of God, but it seems to me that there can never be consent to hate God in hell. Otherwise there would, in conformity with God's will, be a desire to oppose that very will, which would create a contradiction.' Fénelon's longer letter of 11 August moves towards the position he will take in the 1697 *Explication des maximes des saints.*

31 On the pure love controversy between Bossuet and Fénelon, see Stéphane Harent, 'A propos de Fénelon. La question de l'amour pur' in *Etudes,* vol. 127, Paris 1911, pp. 178–96, 349–63, 480–500, and 745–68.

32 Fénelon in his *Réponse à la relation sur le quiétisme* holds that the true cause of his disagreement with Bossuet is that Bossuet 'nie tout acte de charité qui n'a pas le motif essentiel et *inséparable* de la béatitude qui

est la seule *raison d'aimer'*. See *Œuvres*, 22 vols, Versailles, then Paris 1820–4, vol. 6, p. 502. For Fénelon, love could be pure because the will was not strictly appetitive. Bossuet, the spectrum of whose works confirms that he thought of himself as the Augustine of the seventeenth century, holds that 'on ne peut se désintéresser jusqu'au point de perdre dans un seul acte, quel qu'il soit, la volonté d'être heureux, pour laquelle on veut toutes choses.' Augustine, says Bossuet, goes further, holding that 'comme il est impossible, selon la nature, de rien vouloir sans le vouloir pour être heureux, il est autant impossible à la Charité de rien vouloir que pour jouir de Dieu.' See *Réponse de M. de Meaux à quatre lettres de M. de Cambrai*, ch.9, in *Œuvres*, vol.6, Paris 1743, pp. 552–3.

11   War and Foreign Affairs

1   The principal French document was the 1667 *Traité des Droits de la Reine Très-Chrétienne sur Divers Etats de la Monarchie d'Espagne*. The legal wrangling was fuelled not only by the non-payment of the dowry, but also because Maria-Teresa's abdication of her Spanish rights had been registered neither by the Spanish Cortes nor by the Paris *parlement*.
2   See chapter 7.
3   See in particular Paul Sonnino, *Louis XIV and the origins of the Dutch War*, Cambridge 1988.
4   Louis demanded the cession to France of all captured territory, the end of anti-French tariffs, the opening of public worship and public posts to Catholics, an annual Dutch embassy to France acknowledging submission, and 24 million livres. Pomponne more intelligently proposed a settlement that the Dutch would have accepted: the retention by France of only what it had taken outside the seven provinces, that is chiefly Maastricht, Bois-le-Duc, Breda and Bergen-op-Zoom. That would have left the Spanish Low Countries entirely at the mercy of France, to take when it wished, and left the Dutch with their dignity.
5   See Ian Dunlop, *Louis XIV*, London 2001, p.232.
6   See François Bluche, *Louis XIV*, tr. Mark Greengrass, Oxford 1990, p. 263.
7   Both candidates needed multiple papal support, requiring the normal papal bulls that the pope was quite capable of indefinitely withholding, and each also needed dispensations, Joseph Clement because he was under age as well as the incumbent of two bishoprics, and Fürstenberg, because he already had four bishoprics. The matter and manner of Louis's excommunication is treated in the next chapter.
8   See for an account of the attitudes of Louis and Louvois to the medieval towns of the Palatinate, John Wolf, *Louis XIV*, London 1968, pp. 451ff.
9   John Wolf, *Louis XIV*, p.455, is reluctantly forced to the conclusion that Louis XIV, who knew and approved the incendiaries and demolitions,

is the real founder of the German nationalism that was to cost Europe so dear until the mid twentieth century. Louvois had ordered the destruction of Heidelberg for the first time in March 1689. The French general saved some family portraits for Liselotte before blowing up the electoral residence. Lavisse talks of 'l'atroce exécution' of the laying waste of the Palatinate east of the Rhine, quoting from the anonymous *Soupirs de la France esclave*, 'Les Français passaient autrefois pour une nation honnête, humaine, civile, d'un esprit opposé aux barbaries; mais aujourd'hui un Français et un cannibale, c'est à peu près la même chose dans l'esprit des voisins.'

10 The parentage of the infant was challenged, but for political purposes it had to be assumed that England had a Catholic heir.

11 Child marriages of this sort were a form of public political commitment, but were capable of being annulled until the sacrament was conferred on each other by the spouses on consummation. Dates of consummation of marriages were therefore often of political significance.

12 Prince Eugène of Savoy was the son of Mazarin's niece, Olympe, duchesse de Soissons. When his mother went into exile and Louis refused to give him a commission, he changed sides, joined the Austrian military forces and served in the imperial army.

13 See in particular the second edition of David Chandler, *The Art of Warfare in the Age of Marlborough*, Tunbridge Wells 1990 (1st edition, London 1976). Chandler estimates that, for a six-month campaign, an army of 60,000 would require 43 million kilograms of bread, needing 240 bakers, 60 ovens of 500 bricks, 60 carts to carry them, and 1,400 wagon-loads of fuel. Such an army would need 40,000 horses, which would need 1 million kilograms of oats and straw a day in winter. In summer they might graze, but that was slow. A general who won a major victory early in the season, might still have only around thirty days to advance ten or twelve miles a day. Marlborough's exploitation of the portable flour mill was not the least of his achievements.

14 That French architecture was much studied and admired east of the Rhine is clear, but Cotte's influence at Würzburg cannot be considered altogether fortunate, and the most distinguished part of Brühl's architecture is Neumann's eighteenth-century staircase. French architectural influence does however dominate some of the great rococo masterpieces of Bavaria, largely because of the stream of German artists and architects trained in France.

15 The Bourgognes had three children, all male and all called Louis. The first had died in infancy. The second was the one to die in 1712. The third, the duc d'Anjou born in 1710, then became dauphin, heir to the throne, and, was later to be Louis XV.

16 His name was Louis d'Anjou, but it avoids confusion to refer to him as 'the future Louis XV' or the 'son of the duc and duchesse de Bourgogne'.

17 Dangeau was close to the king, a courtier who lived from what he made

at the gaming tables. Mme de Sévigné has left a portrait of him playing *reversi* with a concentration and intensity which virtually guaranteed that he was a constant winner, although he was not one of those whom Louis banned from the table for cheating, as also reported by Mme de Sévigné.

12   Protestants and Popes

1   The term Huguenot is used generically for the French who broke away from Rome as followers of Calvin, and it includes Calvinists who moved away from strict Genevan norms of belief and discipline. The word derives from the German 'Eidgenossen' of members of a confederation, and is of sixteenth-century origin. 'Protestant' is the generally preferred usage for followers of Luther in German-speaking and Scandinavian countries. It alludes to the protest made against the position taken by the majority at the reconvened Speier Reichstag on 25 April 1529 and published in a document known as the *Instrumentum appellationis.*

2   In 1682, the *dragonnades* and the destruction of places of worship much accelerated; illegitimate Huguenot children would be brought up as Catholics; Huguenot sailors and artisans were forbidden to emigrate; Huguenots were not allowed to become notaries; the property of émigrés would be confiscated; assemblies might take place outside places of worship only in the presence of a pastor. For the complete list of dates and measures taken against Huguenots, see François Bluche, *Louis XIV,* Oxford 1990, pp. 402–8.

3   On Bossuet's attitude to the revocation, see A. G. Martimort, *Le Gallicanisme de Bossuet,* Paris 1953. It is possible that, like the ex-Jesuit Père Maimbourg, Bossuet still took literally, and out of context, the biblical 'Compelle intrare (force them to enter)'. In 1682 Maimbourg had published his *Histoire du Calvinisme.* His work provoked in the same year from Pierre Bayle a *Critique générale du Calvinsme de M.Maimbourg* arguing for tolerance in the positive sense of respect for the individual conscience. Bayle elaborates his position in the 1686 *Commentaire philosophique,* showing that the 'compelle intrare'cannot possibly be used as an argument for forced conversion. Bayle published a supplementary *Nouvelles critiques* in 1685, just before the appearance of Locke's very different Latin letter on toleration of that year.

4   By 1568 Pius V had instituted a congregation of cardinals 'for the conversion of infidels' with the plain intention of saving their souls. And it is true that on 22 June 1622 Gregory XV, concerned with the evangelization of the Far East, had instituted the Sacred Congregation for the Propagation of the Faith, dividing responsibility for missionary activity into twelve regions of the globe. But even under Gregory XV the prime motive of policy was political, the restoration of Catholicism as the European religion. He therefore provided financial subsidies to the emperor Ferdinand II and to the Catholic League to exploit their

victory over the Protestant elector Frederick V, and sent Cardinal Carafa to see to the reimposition of Catholicism in Bohemia. He also re-established Catholics with a majority among the Palatine electors. Even his support for Louis XIII's anti-Calvinism in 1619 seems to have had little enough to do with the personal salvation of those for whose conversion he strove. It was only with the 1653 condemnation of the five propositions alleged to be contained in *Augustinus* that the church formally, if implicitly, abandoned the doctrine that outside the church there was no salvation.

5 François Bluche, *Louis XIV,* p.409, quotes a sermon by Bourdaloue of 1 November 1686 congratulating Louis on the edict of Fontainebleau in terms which are too fulsome not to be suspect. In spite of various 'editions', including the 4-volume *Œuvres complètes,* ed. Saint-Dizier, Agen and Bar-le-Duc 1864, the authentic texts of Bourdaloue's sermons have not survived.

6 The Créqui family confuses historians. The ambassador mentioned here is Charles III (1624–87), marquis, then duc de Créqui. He was the eldest of three sons of Charles I, who was a *maréchal, duc et pair* (1652). Charles III was briefly in the Bastille for 'disrespect'. He was publicly renowned for his mental incapacity, was said by Racine, in return for a quip at *Andromaque,* to be homosexual, became governor of Paris and ambassador extraordinary to London, and died in disgrace. Saint-Simon is harsh and Bensserade alludes to his stupidity. Charles III is often confused with his youngest brother, François de Blanchfort de Créqui (1629–87), whose military career was distinguished. He died a *maréchal* on 3 February, ten days before his brother, the ambassador. When Charles III inherited the duchy, his own title became marquis, and he was exiled from court for six years until recalled to command the army of the Rhine. He was in the pay of Fouquet (10,000 livres a year, plus 200,000 in July 1661 to pay for generalship of galleys).

7 The fullest account of the Créqui affair, but not of its consequences, is in Ian Dunlop, *Louis XIV,* pp. 99–103.

8 Historians have rarely, if ever, noticed how the dates of Retz's resignation and Marca's death played into Roman hands. The definitive history of Jansenism is still to be written, but Sainte-Beuve's *Port-Royal,* if rather weak on the theology, is historically accurate.

9 There is extensive published research on the history of the relationship between France and the papacy, but much of it available only in the learned reviews of the late nineteenth century and almost all of it in French. The most useful work, which gives details of the earlier studies, is Jean Orcibal, *Louis XIV contre Innocent XI: Les appels au future concile de 1688 et l'opinion française,* Paris 1949. For the remark of the Spanish ambassador, see E.Michaud, *Innocent XI et Louis XIV,* 2 vols, Paris 1882–3, vol. 2, p.28. See also Pierre Blet, 'Louis XIV et le Saint-Siège' in *XVIIe Siècle,* (31), 1979, pp. 137–54.

10 Innocent XI was austere, rigorous and unyielding on matters of

principle, as becomes clear in the final quarrel with Louis XIV. In the meanwhile numerous small issues, only some of which are listed by Orcibal in *Louis XIV contre Innocent XI*, p.6, all had as common cause 'the belief of Louis in his absolute sovereignty over the temporalities of the French church'. Louis had stated years before in the *Mémoires* that the monarch had a 'full and free' disposition over 'all goods, whether secular or ecclesiastical' for the needs of the state. Rome condemned various pronouncements of French prelates and refused bulls to prelates nominated in those parts of France which had not been French in 1516.

11 The four articles summed up a long tradition of Gallican claims, of which the principal were enunciated by Pierre Pithou, whose *Libertés de l'Eglise Gallicane* of 1594 listed eighty-three 'liberties', and by Pierre Dupuy's 1639 *Les Preuves des Libertés de l'Eglise Gallicane,* showing the documentary support for Pithou, but reducing the number of principles to three.

12 The affair of the Cologne archbishopric has already been discussed in the context of the war of the League of Augsburg.

13 Fürstenburg needed sixteen votes (two thirds), but Joseph Clement only thirteen (a simple majority). The vote gave Fürstenberg thirteen votes and Joseph-Clement nine, with two votes going to independent candidates.

14 There were further complicating factors in the political situation. What was at stake was the long-standing friendship between France and Bavaria and the tradition that a Bavarian Wittelsbach should occupy the archbishopric of Cologne. Joseph-Clement's elder brother, Maximilian-Emanuel, was married to the emperor's daughter, Maria-Antonia. Should his brother die before he had a son, Joseph-Clement would have become heir to the Bavarian throne. Bavaria had been drifting away from the French alliance towards the coalition which would become the League of Augsburg, and the matters of Liselotte's right to some part of the Palatinate succession, the appointment of the archbishop of Cologne, and the French demand to continue to give rights of asylum in their Rome embassy all coalesced into a firm hostility between Innocent XI and Louis, whose insolent letters to the pope were almost certainly written by Louvois.

15 It should perhaps be pointed out that in the order of grace and salvation, simple schism made no difference to ordinary Christians, whose hierarchy merely ceased to be in communion with Rome. This had been the situation of the eastern-rite Christians for centuries. However, the sixteenth-century schisms in western Europe had all gone on to produce views which were in Rome's eyes heretical and, while heresy was not any longer generally thought by those accepting Roman discipline to exclude from salvation, it was still regarded as a hindrance to it. By 1688 Scandanavia and large tracts of northern Europe were in schism. They universally repudiated the Roman notion of transubstantiation of the bread and wine in the eucharistic rite. The real

problem in 1688 was the lingering existence of the Holy Roman Empire and the very close interweaving of sacred and secular jurisdictions in the countries of western Europe, which still required close relationships to be maintained between the sovereign nation states among themselves and with the papacy. One reason holding Louis back from schism was that it would have meant following the pattern of what were his enemies across the channel. Louis was being forced to understand that he was not jeopardizing his own salvation, about which he was becoming increasingly worried, by confronting the pope's insistence on Roman prerogatives which conflicted with Gallican principles. He remained deferential to the pope in purely spiritual matters such as the definition of doctrine, the absolution of sin and the determination of sacramental rites.

16 On the complex ways in which Louis bound the French hierarchy, lesser clergy and laity to support Gallican principles and the strength of the opposition, see Jean Orcibal, *Louis XIV contre Innocent XI*, Paris 1949, *passim*. The Paris theology faculty opposed the registration of the four articles of 1682, and eight of its members were exiled (p.61).

17 The remaining sympathizers with the five propositions had for political reasons changed their tactics, and concentrated now on attacking papal authority, as it had been exercised in the declaration that the five propositions were in *Augustinus*. This form of 'Gallicanism' is in fact a derivative of fifteenth-century conciliarism which held the supremacy of the general council over the pope in the exercise of all forms of ecclesiastical authority. Many members of the clergy and the *parlement* regarded the constitution as an assault on Gallican liberties, and it is probable that Louis would have held a council in France to enforce it had he not been taken ill.

13   Character, Health and Death

1 See the *Gazette* for 7 June 1673.

2 Strictly speaking theories of specifically international law can be traced back to Grotius in the seventeenth century, but they did not make any real headway until Montesquieu published *De l'Esprit des lois* in 1748.

3 See Nancy Mitford, *The Sun King*, Harmondsworth 1994, pp. 116 and 114.

4 On Louis's health and medical care, see C.D. O'Malley, 'The Medical History of Louis XIV: Intimations of Mortality' in John C.Rule, *Louis XIV and the Craft of Kingship*, Columbus Ohio, 1969.

5 O'Malley, 'The Medical History of Louis XIV', p. 146

6 This may, of course, have been just an excuse, although Louis enjoyed the Versailles musical entertainments put on by the department of *menus plaisirs*, who needed to provide distractions for the court. Louis generally preferred to spend his time at billiards, of which he was passionately fond. The opera is likely to have been the Lulli/Quinault

Roland, whose première in January 1685 had been the last Lulli/
Quinault to have its first performance at Versailles.

7   In the middle ages almost all doctoring was done by priests, who were
    forbidden by canon law to shed blood. Operations requiring the
    shedding of blood were therefore left to the surgeon-barbers. Surgeons
    only emerged from being mere craftsmen in the seventeenth century.

8   The marquis de Sourches in his *Mémoires sur le règne de Louis XIV,* ed.
    Cosnac and Pontal, 13 vols, Paris 1882–93.

9   The marquis de Dangeau in his *Journal,* eds. Soulié and Dussieux, 19
    vols, Paris 1854–60.

10 A large number of accounts of Louis's operation is available in French
    and English, all differing in detail, and all without exception enveloped
    in a mythological cloud designed to show Louis's bravery. C.D. O'Malley
    is by far the most reliable commentator on all matters pertaining to
    Louis's health, but he does not mention the subsequent surgical
    interventions of which Mme de Maintenon writes, and he does speak
    of the 'ludicrous instance' of the 'thirty gentlemen of the court who,
    in complete health, applied to the royal surgeon [Charles-François Félix
    de Tassy] to duplicate the king's operation upon them'. That may
    conceivably have been true, but it stretches credulity, and sets other
    alarm bells ringing.

    If Mme de Maintenon was in the room, why does one account tell
    us that Louvois held Louis's hand throughout, while another puts
    Louvois (more plausibly) in the antechamber? What was the light like
    in the king's bedroom at Versailles at seven a.m. in mid-November?
    Why did they choose to do the operation in what must have been partly
    artificial light, probably candle-light? If seven a.m. was the time, and
    everyone puts it in the early morning, was it because everyone was sure
    that the king would be able to demonstrate his superhuman status by
    holding his *lever* an hour or so later?

    At the end of Molière's 1673 *Le Malade imaginaire* there is a burlesque
    ballet in which a bachelor of medicine is examined for his doctorate
    before eight syringe-carriers, six apothecaries, twenty-two doctors and
    eight dancing surgeons. The symptoms of a series of illnesses are
    described and the candidate gets full marks for always replying:
    'Clysterium donare/ Postea seignare/ Ensuitta purgare'.

    When asked why opium sends to sleep, he correctly replies that it is
    because it possesses a 'dormative power'. But if syringes were in com-
    mon use, and opiates were used as analgesics, as they are known to
    have been, why was no opiate administered? We know that Louis's pain
    threshold was not abnormally high. Should Mme de Maintenon's
    unsupported account of further surgery be discounted, and could the
    apparently heroic tolerance of pain have been helped by the admin-
    istration of an opiate at the five a.m. visit?

    We know not only about La Voisin and her potions, but also that the
    archiater, the king's *premier physicien,* was in charge of the royal botanic

garden, which must therefore still have been a herb garden. Drugs were coming back from the Far East. Is it possible that some form of natural muscle relaxant was available from any of these sources? Could the pain therefore have been rendered more easily tolerable? It is known that Louis was violently homophobic, but that gay behaviour was everywhere in his court. No one was going to talk about any muscle relaxants that may have been available. La Voisin's stock list has not survived.

11 Madame de Maintenon's confessor was Godet des Marais, bishop of Chartres. She referred to Louis's occasional twice daily demands as 'these painful occasions'. The bishop replied that he would rather have seen her chaste, but that it was a work of great purity to preserve the king from the sins and scandals into which he might fall. See on this matter Nancy Mitford, *The Sun King*, Harmondsworth 1966, p. 210, and Ragnhild Hutton, *Louis XIV and his World*, London 1972, p. 117.

12 Louis's last days are recounted by Saint-Simon, and are also recorded in detail by Mlle d'Aumale, who was always at Mme de Maintenon's side, and by Dangeau, the probable source for the *Mercure galant*.

Index